Remote Viewing

REMOTE VIEWING
The Science and Theory of
Nonphysical Perception

Courtney Brown

Atlanta
FARSIGHT PRESS

FARSIGHT PRESS
First published by Farsight Press, a member of Farsight, Inc.

First Printing, April, 2005 (Revised May, 2005 and again May 2006)
10 9 8 7 6 5 4 3 2

Scientific Remote Viewing®, SRV®, and Farsight® are internationally
registered marks of Farsight, Inc.

PUBLISHER'S CATALOGING-IN-PUBLICATION DATA:
(Provided by Quality Books, Inc.)

Brown, Courtney 1952-
    Remote viewing: the science and theory of nonphysical perception /
Courtney Brown.
        p. cm.
    Includes bibliographical references and index.
    ISBN 0-9766762-0-6 (hard cover)
    ISBN 0-9766762-1-4 (soft cover)
    1.Remote viewing (Parapsychology). 2. Extrasensory perception.
    3. Parapsychology and science.   I. Title.

    BF1389.R45B76 2005   133.8
                            QBI06-600243

This book is printed on acid-free paper.

Dedicated to

Michael Raoul Duval

Contents

LIST OF TABLES

LIST OF FIGURES

Preface (Revised May 2006)

When Carl Sagan coined the phrase, "extraordinary claims require extraordinary evidence," it is doubtful that many realized how much damage was done to the scientific enterprise. This elevated-threshold demand had never before been a requirement of scientific inquiry. But unfortunately, this demand has been used in recent years to deter a willingness to examine scientific evidence with care and consideration. The reality is that extraordinary claims really require only calm consideration of evident facts, and the call for "extraordinary evidence" is typically used only to refuse to consider these evident facts. For example, Galileo's claim that the Earth revolves around the sun was extraordinary in his day. But he only requested that people calmly examine his observations to see that he was correct. Those who refused to look at his data instead demanded what amounted to "divine proof" of his claims, which was simply an intellectual filibuster intended to avoid change.

For a long while, research into psi (psychic) phenomena has been in a similar situation as compared with the problems encountered by Galileo in his day. Until recently, academia has been highly resistant to open inquiries with respect to psi phenomena. But things are changing. For example, many members of the Society for Scientific Exploration (to mention just one academic group) have a strong interest in psi phenomena. The Society currently publishes the *Journal of Scientific Exploration* which often features papers on the subject of psi phenomena generally, and remote viewing more specifically. Their 2004 membership listing contains approximately 800 members from virtually every state in the United States and most developed countries. Many of these members are academics. The institutions represented include Harvard, Yale, Stanford, most Ivy League universities, the most prestigious private and public universities, and so on. Clearly there exists a body of intelligent people today who want to openly discuss the subject of psi phenomena.

This book is about the subject of remote viewing, a specific phenomenon that falls within the more general category of psi phenomena. Remote viewers typically employ a set of clearly defined procedures to describe things that are not accessible to their normal senses of hearing, touch, sight, taste, or smell. The remote viewers always work "blind," in the sense that they are never given any information regarding what they are asked to perceive until after all of their psychic perceptions are recorded. (Indeed, remote viewing normally does not work at all if the remote viewers are given any advance information about a target.) Scientific controls require this (plus much more, as is explained elsewhere in this volume). Yet regardless of how rigorously the scientific controls have been followed in the collection and analysis of the data presented in this volume, nowhere in this book is there a demand that readers must accept the reality of remote viewing. This is simply a book of data and theory. All that is asked of the reader is that the material in the book be given calm consideration. The time seems truly ripe both inside and outside of academia for the subject of remote viewing to be examined with full seriousness. It is not difficult for any serious researcher to conduct sensible experiments with this phenomenon without soon realizing that the phenomenon itself is real, and that its reality has profound implications for all of humanity, and for science. This is the moment to engage in a serious dialogue about remote viewing and its related issues.

To clear up a common misconception right at the outset, let me state unambiguously that all remote-viewing data are always speculative until they are verified using normal physical means of obtaining information. One can never say that something is real because someone has "remote viewed it." Data collected using remote viewing always needs to be compared in detail with information obtained using physical methods before one can evaluate the accuracy of the remote-viewing data. Thus, while it may be possible for remote-viewing data to sometimes be 100% accurate, one never knows this until the data are compared with the known and verified physical characteristics of whatever the remote viewer was supposed to be perceiving. In laboratory situations, this verification process can take anywhere from a few minutes to a number of days or weeks. But in situations in which the remote viewer perceives something that cannot be verified easily, the verification process can take much longer, even many years. Until this verification process is completed (however long it takes), the remote-viewing data will remain speculative. If the data cannot be verified at all, then the data can never leave the realm of speculation, no matter how good the track record of a remote viewer's accuracy.

In this volume, many remote-viewing results are presented. The results were obtained across a variety of distinctly different projects. Each project was initiated in an attempt to learn something new about the phenomenon of remote viewing. This required laboratory conditions for the experiments, and thus exact verification of the remote-viewing results was essential. Thus, readers will learn a great deal that is very concrete about remote viewing by reading this volume. The remote-viewing data presented here have been fully verified and are not speculative any longer, even though the interpretation of these results may continue to provoke healthy debate. There are no esoteric topics discussed in this volume. If you, the reader, wish to know why remote viewing works, and how to avoid the commonly encountered pitfalls that corrupt the functionality of remote viewing, then you will find many answers among these pages. If along the way you gain further insight into humankind's spiritual nature, then you will have found an added bonus to your reading efforts.

Let me briefly turn to the issue of money. People can be so easily misled by those who argue that the only reason for one to conduct research in the area of psi phenomena is to make money, usually by appealing to the superstitions of others. Let me remove that potential impediment now. The research presented in this volume was conducted by myself and others associated with The Farsight Institute, a nonprofit research an educational organization. I am the Director of the Institute. I have never received any financial compensation for my work as Director of The Farsight Institute. Indeed, the reverse is true; I have contributed thousands of dollars to the Institute to help support research into the remote-viewing phenomenon.

The History of the Book Manuscript

The research presented in this book deals only with basic science issues relating to the remote-viewing phenomenon. That is, this book does not present an application of remote viewing, but an explanation of remote viewing itself. This does not mean that the book is boring. Indeed, I consider the research presented in this volume to be much more interesting and exciting than any application (esoteric or otherwise) could ever be.

I originally intended to publish this book in an academic press that involved a peer-review process. An editor-in-chief of a major university press was interested in the manuscript for this book, and he undertook to have the manuscript peer reviewed. Since the topic of remote viewing was (and still is) quite controversial for an academic press, the editor decided to err on the side of safety, and the peer-review process took four years and included reviews from a seemingly countless list of famous academics. This long peer-review process turned out to be a great blessing as I explain below, and the editor deserves great credit for helping to shepherd this project through so many phases. The manuscript went through numerous major revisions in which I did nearly everything that any reviewer asked me to do. The final major revision alone had six reviewers (two are normal for most manuscripts, with or without revisions). The overall peer-review process included academics who minimally spanned the disciplines of physics, psychology, sociology, statistics, and engineering. Four of the final six reviewers emphatically argued in favor of publishing the manuscript. Each of these four reviewers gave evidence of having closely read the manuscript, since their reviews engaged the manuscript at various points throughout the work. But the other two reviewers just as emphatically dismissed remote viewing as a real phenomenon and argued against publication for that reason. At first I felt that the negative reviews could be overcome since they appeared to me to have significant weaknesses. One of the negative reviewers posited that remote viewing was analogous to a "pagan religion." Other comments left me wondering how closely this reviewer read the manuscript, or even if it was read at all. The other negative reviewer gave some mention of the initial parts of the manuscript, but argued that even the claim that the remote-viewing phenomenon exists is excessive.

Given the difficulty faced by any scholar who wants to publish a book on this topic with a university press, I was quite happy with the outcome of the peer-review process on a substantive level. But for the press to publish the work, it would have required that the project be supported by the press's editorial committee, which is largely composed of faculty members, one or more of whom were quite conservative in their views with respect to controversial topics of this sort. This is a typical situation for most academic presses. Thus, despite considerable support from some of the reviewers, the management of the press ultimately felt the reviews collectively fell short of providing sufficient support to move forward toward publication. In retrospect, I now think that it is currently impossible to publish any book that supportively engages the subject of remote viewing in most (and perhaps all) academic presses, although I hope this changes one day. I know there are many academics who would like to read about this subject. Serious controversy with regard to many topics will naturally result in split reviews that are passionately argued, and academic presses will have to live with such arguments among the reviewers if the peer-review process is not to degrade into a "black-ball" situation where controversial topics are concerned.

Nonetheless, the peer-review process greatly helped me in writing this volume. Indeed, for four years some of the smartest minds on the planet gave me some of the greatest advice anyone could ask for, and I am deeply grateful to all of the reviewers, even (and often especially) the negative ones. Although this book was not ultimately published by the university press which sent it through such a long, thorough, and generally positive peer-review process, it can nonetheless be stated without ambiguity that the book gained all the benefits that are normally associated with peer-review. The primary characteristic of any working peer-review process is that the author is assisted by the reviewers in the production of a superior book, and to this end, the peer-review process worked well.

This volume is the first in a new series published by Farsight Press in the science of remote viewing. The series focuses on remote viewing as it is practiced using some of the remote-viewing styles that are derivative of those used by the U.S. military in applied espionage work. These styles normally involve having a remote viewer perceive a single target over an extended period of time (an hour or more) while using an explicit set of data-collection procedures. This series is not limited to studies which utilize data collected with only one style of such procedures (i.e., CRV, HRVG, SRV, etc.).

More generally, Farsight Press is dedicated to publishing scientific research that addresses topics related to remote viewing and consciousness. The venues available for such research are presently quite limited. On one hand, the topic of remote viewing currently appears to be too controversial to be published by an academic press. But on the other hand, serious science involving remote viewing is too complex to be supported by most commercial presses that associate the topic with a "new age" market that is primarily disposed toward subjective biographical reports and "soft science." Thus, Farsight Press offers itself as a venue for scientific work that might otherwise be ideally suited for an academic press, were it not for the controversial nature of the subject matter.

Some Special People

This brings me to the matter of who supported the research presented in this volume. All of the research presented here was supported by private contributions made to The Farsight Institute. Although I am an academic in an American university, no resources of any kind originating from my university (including time) were used to support this research or the preparation of this book. As readers will surmise once they finish this volume, I consider the results presented in this volume to be highly significant to the academy (defined as all university and other research and educational institutions). Perhaps it will one day be common for universities to support the type of research that is presented here. But until that time arrives, such research requires the assistance of private individuals who contribute their time, advice, and financial resources to the advancement of this branch of science.

I must offer special thanks to Michael R. Duval. Mike Duval was a lawyer who served in the top echelon of the White House under both the Nixon and Ford administrations. He was also a remarkably good remote-viewing student of mine, and a member of The Farsight Institute's Board of Directors for a few years. He died in 2001 (see obituary by Wolfgang Saxon, *The New York Times*, Monday, 23 April 2001, p. A19[N]). Mike Duval, more than anyone else, is the reason this volume exists. Long ago, when I was just beginning to teach remote viewing, he told me that I should separate the applications of remote viewing from research into the basic science of the phenomenon. Moreover, he told me that I should re-direct The Farsight Institute to focus only on basic science questions, while leaving individual remote viewers to pursue applied interests on their own. Finally, he told me to write a book about the basic science of remote viewing that would be directly applicable to the type and style of remote viewing that was being conducted at the Institute as well as by many of the former military remote viewers (that is, long sessions using structured protocols that result in lots of data for single targets). I generally did whatever Mike told me to do, and he was always correct. I cannot think of a single piece of advice which he ever offered to me that turned out to be wrong. If he was talented enough to be called upon to advise two presidents, I would have been the fool to ignore his advice. Years later, this manuscript was completed. Yet even now, from time to time when I close my eyes, I thank him, and miss him. I do not think I have ever missed someone so dearly, or for so long. As the reader will surmise after finishing this book, I do not doubt that I will see Mike again, somewhere in the eternity of tomorrow. I look forward to that moment of reunion.

I am very grateful for the friendship and support of Dr. John Russell. Dr. Russell is a physicist who formerly taught nuclear engineering at Georgia Institute of Technology. He is also the inventor of the first palladium SEEDS. SEEDS are those little rice-sized radioactive pellets that are used to treat various forms of cancer, including and especially prostate cancer in men (see Russell 2004). He has helped to tutor me in theories of physics, and he was instrumental in helping me work through many of the ideas that I have presented in this volume, especially with regard to chapter 8. He is also the person who urged me to consider that the phenomenon of entanglement may be at the core of the remote-viewing phenomenon.

Father John Rossner, an Anglican priest and professor at Concordia University in Montreal, has given me an enormous amount of good advice and insight over the years. He and his wife, Marilyn, are among the most spiritually gifted people I know. As directing officers of the International Institute of Integral Human Sciences, they quite often brought me to Montreal to give lectures. But when I went, I did as much listening as talking, and I undoubtedly received more wisdom than I offered with each trip. I would often ask John about complex issues that I would be dealing with in the manuscript, and I was always astounded that he inevitably had something important to say. I am grateful for his guidance.

In particular, I wish to thank Mr. Gilbert Younger, a man who is as comfortable with issues of spirituality as he is with practical business matters. This volume could not have been written without his support. I also wish to thank Mrs. Mieko Freeman and Ms. Maria M. Hallsthammar. I doubt they will ever really know the full value of their contributions. Many others contributed in non-financial ways, some by participating in remote-viewing experiments, while others in different ways. No one was ever paid anything for participating in the research presented in this volume. In this day and age in which scientific research tends to follow dollars, these investigations remind us of the value of personal commitment and volunteering. In particular, I want to thank Matthew Pfeiffer, Joey Jerome, Denise Burson, Richard Moore, Roma Zanders, all of whom contributed their time freely and without meagerness to these research efforts. I also want to thank Lynda Cowen, Diane Moore, and Dee Leslie who have worked tirelessly to support the continuing educational and research roles of The Farsight Institute, especially in recent years. Pierre Juneau also has been very helpful in a variety of informal ways, and I am grateful for his assistance and ideas.

A Note of Caution Regarding the Media

I would like to include here a note of caution that I think many of my fellow academics may value. My initial activities to investigate the remote-viewing phenomenon included a public phase, and it is toward the idea of conducting research within public view that I wish to direct my note of caution. I have always considered the subject of remote viewing an exciting area of research that would interest many people, including academics such as myself. To this end, I founded The Farsight Institute as a nonprofit research and educational organization to house the research efforts of myself and others. I did this as an act of service to both the public and the academic community.

But in early 1997, I made the decision to reduce dramatically the public presence of The Farsight Institute. I also decided to shift the focus of research done at the Institute away from all applications of remote viewing, and instead to concentrate all of our efforts on basic science issues relating to the remote-viewing phenomenon itself. We needed a long quiet period within which to conduct our experiments, and I was certain that the public would be better served by our nonprofit research and educational organization if we pursued our research program in a less visible manner. Also, by that time I had become deeply discouraged by my own experiences with the media. I realized that as an academic, I had neither the training nor the resources to manage either the media treatment of — or the public's response to — the presentation of topics about which there may be considerable controversy. Some of my own experiences with the media were searingly painful, and I share one of them below as a means of offering guidance (and a warning) to other academics or scientists who may be seeking the most productive means of exposing the public to the results of their own research. I made many mistakes. Learn from them.

In terms of background, Chuck Shramek, a now-deceased amateur astronomer photographed what appeared to be an anomaly briefly and intermittently associated with the Hale-Bopp comet in late 1996. Mr. Shramek was a respected newscaster in Houston, Texas, and his interest in astronomy was serious. As with many amateur astronomers, he was particularly fascinated with comets. He took a large number of photographs of the Hale-Bopp comet, and he posted one of these images on his web site. It is an understatement to say that it caused a significant stir at the time. He was surprised that the major observatories (including the Hubble Space Telescope) seemed to be posting few high-quality images of the Hale-Bopp comet on the Internet. It was frustration with this that led Mr. Shramek to photograph the comet himself with his 10-inch scope. In an email that he sent me two years later in April 1999, he wrote, "To this day, there never has been any clear pictures of the comet nucleus released to the public." He seemed quite concerned that some of the best photographs of the comet available to the public had been taken by a large collection of amateur astronomers using telescopes costing just a few thousand dollars, and he expressed doubts over the official position that the Hubble took only a few low-quality images of the comet. Since I am not an astronomer, I do not have the ability to verify these ideas, but it seems clear to me that Mr. Shramek's motivations were sincere.

Shortly after Shramek released his photo in late 1996 and in-between working on normal verifiable projects, at my suggestion some remote viewers at The Farsight Institute attempted to remote view a variety of celestial objects (speculatively and somewhat lightheartedly, since verification was impossible). The anomaly apparently associated with the Hale-Bopp comet was one of these unverifiable taskings. The remote viewers collected their data "blind," which means that they did not know anything about the target when they conducted their remote-viewing sessions. Also, the target tasked to the remote viewers (the identity of which was revealed to them only after they collected their data) was verbal in nature and did not reference any photograph. I talked about these speculative remote-viewing results on the program of a popular radio talk-show host who regularly invites guests on his show who present unverifiable ideas dealing with a wide range of esoteric topics.

Speculating on extraterrestrial issues is essentially a hobby of mine, and I saw no harm at the time in engaging in such speculations on a radio talk show that seemed to specialize in exactly this sort of thing. My discussion of the remote-viewing results characterized them as highly interesting and suggestive, albeit unverifiable. I never claimed that the remote-viewing perceptions were 100% accurate, and in fact did comment that some remote viewers have notably better accuracy histories than others. To this day, I still do not fully understand those remote-viewing perceptions, interesting though they may be. In retrospect, I now know that it is unwise to discuss remote-viewing results publicly before more fully understanding them. When the program ended, I naively thought that was the end of the matter.

After this radio appearance, a person whose identity I do not know with any confidence sent our Institute's web master some unsolicited astronomical images on 35 mm film of what appeared to be the same anomaly. Our web master claimed to know this person relatively well, although I cannot corroborate this. I was told that this person was an astronomer, however I now suspect that the person may have had only a tangential connection to astronomy at best. It was my fault for not demanding more information about this person at the time. I held and examined the images using a slide lupe (a magnifying glass) only once ever, and even then only for a few minutes. At the time, the pictures themselves appeared to me to be exceptionally high resolution black and white digital images that seemed to have been taken with a telescope equipped with a CCD imaging system and later transferred to the hard drive of a computer before being printed to film. This was obvious (at least to me) since razor-sharp pixel lines of a CCD system were clearly visible on the developed film when examined using a magnifying glass. These were my impressions, although I am not an authority in such matters. The 35 mm film that was sent to us had been exposed (prior to being mailed to us) using a film printer connected to a computer, which is the only way a digital image of this sort can be printed on film. The film clearly did not appear to have been originally exposed in a camera directly connected to a telescope, although subsequent rumors to this effect that spread over the Internet became virtually impossible to control.

Film printers of the sort mentioned above are similar to other computer printers except that they print on photographic negative and slide film rather than on paper. One has to develop the film after the printer exposes it in order to see the image. For those readers unfamiliar with such film printers, they have long been used by presenters to create slides for PowerPoint presentations. They are less commonly encountered nowadays since most presenters use a laptop computer connected to a data projector to show their presentations.

After receiving the film (we were actually sent three rolls), we had it processed at a local camera store. Of the three rolls we were sent, only one had any images on it. We assumed that the person who sent us the film created the exposures and printed them to the film, but we do not know if this is the case (and in retrospect, it seems doubtful). As curious as it was to receive such photos in the mail (since it was not clear why a serious astronomer would be taking us seriously at that point), the photos were of only minor interest to us since (1) they did not add to what was already apparent in Mr. Shramek's photos of the same scene, (2) they were not ours, and (3) we had no expertise in analyzing photographs (astronomical or otherwise).

I happened to mention the existence of the images in passing to the same radio talk-show host on whose program I had appeared earlier. I did not bring up the subject of the photos in the context of wanting to talk about them on his radio show. He later raised the subject of whether I could do something to help Chuck Shramek, who was being verbally attacked by others in connection with his own astronomical image. I initially hesitated to do anything, but later offered (unwisely) to talk anecdotally about the unsolicited images that were sent to our web master. I informed him clearly that the photos were not ours, and since we did not own them we could talk about them only anecdotally without releasing them to the public. The issue of not releasing something for which we did not own the copyright was (for me at least) as important as it was obvious. I naively thought that the discussion of the photos on the radio would naturally lead to a more general conversation about remote viewing, which was my primary interest. At the request of the talk-show host, we emailed the host, and one of his other guests who was to be on the show, two copies of a crude scan of one of the original film images to serve as a focus for the radio conversation. Both copies were filtered with Photoshop (color added), and one was marked-up with a circle and an arrow to identify the anomaly. We (and the Institute) thought there was a clear verbal agreement between myself and the talk-show host (later disputed) that the images were not to be released to the public. It was my understanding that the person who sent us the photos encouraged us to share them with our friends and colleagues, and so I saw no harm in sharing them with the talk-show host under the conditions that the images not be released to the public. At the Institute, we never used the photos for anything relating to our remote-viewing work or anything else, and in retrospect it was an error in judgment (actually, it was stupid) for us to discuss on air — anecdotally or otherwise — something that we did not produce ourselves or use in any way.

It is important to emphasize that I was very wrong to think that a media personality would not release the photos to the public indefinitely. At the time, I did not fully appreciate that the job of media personalities is to present news to the public, not to withhold it. Yes, I was terribly naive. I was inexperienced at dealing with the media, a condition not uncommon for most academics.

The radio appearance occurred on Thanksgiving evening in November of 1996 and began with me speaking for one hour introducing the Institute's web master and summarizing the basic points: (1) the photos appeared interesting but they were not ours, and (2) they were sent to our web master by someone whom she claimed to know personally. In general, I was mostly out of the loop since only our web master knew who sent the photos. I then talked a bit more about remote viewing, which was my real purpose for wanting to be on the radio. Then our web master got on the radio and discussed the photos and her interactions (via telephone) with the person who sent the photos. She claimed that the person who sent her the photos did not want his or her identity revealed prematurely, and that this person was to have a news conference discussing the photos in about a week or two. (Incredibly, in retrospect, we believed this.) She also vouched for the respectability of this person. As it turned out, the person who mailed our web master the photos never held the promised news conference. With each passing day following the radio appearance, it looked more and more like we had been snookered.

The talk-show host soon published the photos on his web site against our wishes and made them into a huge controversial story over which we had no control, especially since we were not on the radio with any significant frequency (and never again on his show after January 1997). Fortunately, during my final appearance on his show, the host played a recording of me asking him not to release the photos, so it was clear to everyone that it was he who was releasing the photos, not us.

Within what seemed like a blink of an eye (about one day), an astronomer from the University of Hawaii contacted the talk-show host stating that the photos were his, and that they were obtained from a publicly available university web site and altered. He even offered a brief technical analysis arguing why he thought his web photo was the same as our crude scan. The astronomer never examined the original 35 mm film from which our scan was made, nor did he contact me personally and request to see the film. I suspect that he simply assumed (understandably) that there never was any 35 mm film in the first place.

Indeed, a statement from a University of Hawaii's web site asserts, "While it cannot be proven unambiguously, the fact that the fine structure of both the fake and the original image are matching so well suggest that the whole process was digital, without any film roll and scanner involved" (http://www.ifa.hawaii.edu/images/hale-bopp/tholen-sep1/hb_ufo_tholen.html #stat).

Rumors abounded, and people even began posting on the Internet technical and logical arguments both supporting and contesting the astronomer's claims, some remarking (for example) that the stars did not seem to align perfectly when the images were carefully placed on top of one another, suggesting that they may have been taken minutes apart, perhaps by different telescopes. Some analysts even claimed to have found suggestions of residual evidence of the apparent anomaly in the official University of Hawaii photograph due to a crescent shape strangely outlined in the tail of the comet that seemed to correspond closely with the anomaly's appearance in the other image that we were sent. Not being a photographic expert, and not wanting to be drawn into trying to defend a photographic image that I had no part in producing and which I never released to the public, I simply avoided this part of the debate. The astronomer from the University of Hawaii appeared in his writings to be quite upset with me, which dismayed me deeply since it was obvious that (1) I always said the photos were not ours and that I did not know their origin, and again (2) I never released the photos to the public in the first place!

Quite frankly, I truly do not know how the person who mailed our web master the photos obtained them, and I do not know if they were legitimate or forged. I also have never suggested that anyone from the University of Hawaii was involved in this. To my eye, the originals seemed far too high resolution to have come from a web site, and I could not figure out why anyone would even want to print web photos on a 35 mm film printer. But since digital creativity can do almost anything to an image, including inserting what can pass as CCD pixel lines, I have no way of knowing if the photos were contrived or real. Again, I am not an expert in photography or astronomy. Nonetheless, from the public's perspective, it was looking more and more like we had done something wrong, and I kept repeating to myself my amazement at how we could be publicly blamed for trying to mislead the public when the photos were not ours, and we never released the photos to the public. We were stuck in the middle between someone who sent us materials with a request to remain anonymous (which we honored regardless of whether or not he was conning us) and an aggressive talk-show host who demanded details of the photos and their apparent dubious origin.

We were banished from the talk-show host's radio program following a highly confrontational appearance in January of 1997 in which I tried vainly to set the record straight (as I saw it) and place the situation in perspective. Indeed, we impotently watched over the following weeks and months as the talk-show host conducted on his radio program and his web site what seemed to us to be a very intense, long, and loud campaign against us. This continued even years later when he flew to Atlanta to appear on the Larry King Live show.

Worse still, soon after my final appearance on this talk-show host's program in January 1997, a former military remote viewer returned to this same talk-show host's radio program, claiming that our original remote-viewing data were not collected properly. He then discussed how his own group of remote viewers had collected their own data (this time done properly) involving the Hale-Bopp comet, and he made the frightening announcement that the comet was carrying a plant pathogen bomb designed by aliens that was going to drop on Africa and wipe out all plant life. He also began to market a remote-viewing instruction kit. This person also disparaged both myself and The Farsight Institute. This was particularly sad for me since I once felt I knew this former military remote viewer rather well, and when I knew him he seemed to me to have a positive and even spiritually-yearning personality. He also previously seemed to have positive working relationships with nearly all of the former military remote viewers, both while still working in the military and for a period afterwards. But things changed rather dramatically and quickly at one point after leaving the military, and it appeared that he grew publicly hostile not only toward me but also toward many of his former military colleagues. These same former colleagues then publicly distanced themselves from him.

Strangely (to me, given my past with this radio host), the talk-show host did not seem interested in forcefully challenging the predictions of planetary disaster made by this former military remote viewer. Instead, the host seemed to enthusiastically support this guest. I am not accusing the talk-show host of anything illegal or immoral. I simply did not understand why he would challenge one guest more than another. Nonetheless, it was clear that the talk-show host felt the former military remote viewer was an interesting guest to have on his show.

Thus, there were three separate themes emitting and intermixing from those confused and wild radio waves at the time: (1) a sustained campaign suggesting that I and The Farsight Institute had been involved in a photographic fraud, combined with a parallel effort (from numerous sources) that appeared aimed at disparaging our understanding of remote viewing, thereby discrediting data we collected using remote viewing (especially about the Hale-Bopp comet), (2) a general and continuing hype about a Hale-Bopp companion, eventually labeled the "Hail Mary," and (3) the airing of claims that aliens somehow related to the Hale-Bopp comet were going to drop planet-scorching, plant-pathogenic weapons of mass destruction on Africa. It is important to note that the talk-show host never publicly said he agreed with all of this (especially points 2 and 3 above). He simply reported it, or allowed others to air the reports. All of this was being witnessed in regular doses on a daily talk show by literally millions of eager radio and Internet talk-show fans worldwide. Reports also suggested that remote-viewing instruction kits were selling like hot cakes.

And if that was not enough, in late March of 1997, a group of eunuchs belonging to a fanatical cult popularly known as "Heaven's Gate" committed suicide in San Diego, declaring that they were going to be "beamed up" to the so-called UFO, illogically adding that the so-called UFO may not even exist. Like everyone else at the time, I was dumbstruck and saddened by the horrible and senseless waste of their lives. This group had existed as an organized and secretive cult exhibiting highly abnormal behaviors for many years. Without doubt they suffered from some form of collective mental illness. Clearly no one but the members of the Heaven's Gate group themselves were responsible for what they did to themselves. Neither the radio talk-show host nor anyone else outside of that group led those people to commit suicide. Indeed, their aging fanatical leader was probably on the lookout for an opportunity to wrap up his adventure into cult worship without having to tell his band of loyal castrati that it had all been a big mistake. Neither I nor anyone I knew had ever previously heard of this group, as I expect was typical for just about everyone back in those days. In general, the media acted responsibly and fairly by not associating myself or The Farsight Institute with this group or that terrible event. News reports indicated that the cult never mentioned me or The Farsight Institute in any of their internal writings, nor did they ever link to our web site from their web site. This was not surprising since the radio talk-show host's campaign regarding the photo scandal had been so publicly visible over the previous months.

Returning now to the "photo scandal," it is important to emphasize that the incident essentially resulted from opening the mail and talking anecdotally about what was in the mail. We were admittedly stupid to have talked about what arrived in the mail. But it is useful to take a lesson from how the talk-show host pushed this story. There are no guarantees when dealing with the media. Academics should never feel comforted by the knowledge that a media personality may not have challenged other guests who might have voiced controversial views.

It is important to emphasize that it is not necessary for a media personality to have malicious intent for a disagreement of the sort which I have described here to occur. For example, I am not claiming that the radio talk-show host with whom I had such an unfortunate encounter had a malevolent plan to disparage me. Perhaps he felt pressure from his listeners to get to the bottom of a mystery that seemed intriguing. He also may not have fully understood the pledge of confidentiality that our web master gave the person who sent her the photos. My refusal to force our web master to break her promise of confidentiality and reveal the identity of this person (even if I could have done this) may have led the talk-show host to distrust me. He probably felt he was doing a necessary public service by releasing the photos that we sent him, and in the end, maybe he was.

In general, media personalities simplify topics so that their audiences can perceive issues in black and white terms. They are not scientists who are willing to live with complexity. Thus, there is a fundamental difference between how media personalities and scientists tend to think, and it is inherently risky for scientists who are involved in controversial research to entrust their findings with the media. More often than not, complex issues will become distorted, and the reputation of the scientists can be damaged.

Also, I do not know the intent of the person who sent us the photos. In retrospect, I consider it highly probable that the person knew the photos would be discredited should they be released (whether or not they were legitimate astronomical images). Possibly this person was used simply as an intermediary (who conveniently knew and was trusted by our web master) for others who supplied the photos, although I have no way of determining this. Again, I have never suggested in any way that anyone at the University of Hawaii was knowingly or unknowingly involved in any act of deception related to this incident. Based on what I was told about the communications between our web master and the person who sent her the controversial images, the person encouraged us to share those photos with our friends and colleagues — without revealing the source of the images. It now seems (to me) likely that this person both wanted and expected the photos to be released eventually, leaving us "holding the bag," so to speak. Again in retrospect, had our web master relented under the pressure and publicly identified the person who mailed her the photos, it seems certain that the person would have subsequently sued our Institute for defamation of character, effectively closing down the Institute. If we are to be honest with ourselves, such traps are easy to set-up, and academics have no prior training in avoiding them. We tend to believe people at face value, just as we tend to believe our colleagues when they conduct experiments. Indeed, a dependence on intellectual honesty is a cornerstone of academic inquiry. As a result, academics in general are highly vulnerable to those who seek to entrap or deceive, and we would be foolish to think that our intelligence or academic training could fully protect us in situations such as this.

Additionally, it is a fact of life that elements of the public are prone to react wildly to the presentation of controversial information, even if that information is presented as speculative. For example and with respect to remote viewing, the reality of this phenomenon may continue to collide with misunderstandings and superstitions held by elements of the public. It is precisely because our society has so much to learn from scientific research into remote viewing that confusion can occur when new information is presented to it. There is always the risk that some people may act tragically when their unfounded beliefs interact with their misunderstandings of new ideas. There is also the near certainty that opportunists will react to exploit those misunderstandings for personal profit. There is no easy way for science to control this. Ultimately, scientists need to decide for themselves as to whether or not the long-term benefit to society gained by exposing the public to new ideas is worth the short-term risk of havoc.

The former attacks ignorance, while the latter attacks science itself.

When controversies occur, they can last a long time, regardless of the accuracy of the claims upon which they are based. They develop a "self-referral" quality due to the open-source nature of the Internet, since one posting can refer to another, which can refer to another, which can refer to the original, and so on, suggesting that a solid case has been established. This can extend the life of a controversy essentially indefinitely. Attempts to correct the inaccuracies associated with the controversies can lead to endless Internet-based attacks and counter-attacks, and ultimately it is usually not worth the effort to try to make such corrections.

Thus, my warning to my fellow academics is that if you conduct controversial research, do not seek out the media, and never modify what you do to satisfy an interview request from a media personality. The risk of long-term mayhem is just too great. Keep your head low.

Where We Are Now

By January 1997, we at the Institute decided that it was best not to interact with the public at all when we did our research. We embarked on a long-term plan to focus only on basic science issues relating to the remote-viewing phenomenon. We began to take much of our work out of public view, even taking our entire web site off-line for a number of months while we re-formulated how we wanted to proceed. Learning to manage complex interactions with the media became a moot concern, since our primary interest became how to avoid most of the media.

Fortunately, the past difficulties with the media have had little long-term impact on our institute. Indeed, the public reputation of The Farsight Institute has continued to grow since those early days, which is particularly interesting considering that we have so carefully avoided media exposure. Our web site receives tens of thousands of visitors each month, most of whom seem largely drawn by our extensive collection of free information about remote viewing, including a large quantity of free instructional material. We have conducted repeated public demonstrations of remote viewing under highly controlled conditions that were witnessed (and participated in) by literally thousands of web site visitors. We maintain full documentation about all of this plus much more on our web site. Moreover, people seem to have fully accepted the nonprofit nature of The Farsight Institute, as well as the fact that I have never profited financially in any way through my activities as Director of the Institute.

Our retreat from the media allowed us to conduct a significant amount of research over the past few years with few distractions. As a result, I believe we have resolved perhaps the most perplexing issue that has faced remote-viewing research for the past few decades: the identification of the psychic-targeting mechanism that directs a remote viewer's consciousness to perceive a given place or event. This discovery alone is enormously valuable, and it promises to make remote viewing a much more reliable phenomenon, a crucial consideration for future scientific investigation. While the topics discussed in this volume are quite diverse, a close reading will reveal that this discovery is at the core of much of the research presented here.

Due to the diversity of material presented in this volume, some readers may be tempted to jump to chapters of particular interest. However, my own suggestion is for readers to proceed systematically, chapter by chapter. The presentation of this material is organized to build sequentially on related ideas, and to jump to a middle chapter before reading the preceding information may result in the loss of the argument's logic. At the risk of sounding professorial, there is a lot of content to absorb in these pages, and patience in going through it all will likely result in the most productive reading experience.

CHAPTER 1

The Open Mind

Humanity is soon to experience one of the greatest revolutions in the realm of ideas that has ever occurred. Imagine the discovery of a phenomenon that suggests that communication across huge distances — including interstellar distances — can be done instantaneously and with little or no cost. Imagine the discovery of a phenomenon that gives evidence that time may only be an artifact of human perception. Imagine the discovery of a phenomenon that indicates that the past, present, and future exist simultaneously (that is, all at once in the here and now), and that alternate futures and even alternate pasts may also exist. Imagine the discovery of a phenomenon that suggests that we may all live multiple lives in multiple realities, all but one of which seem hidden from us. Imagine the discovery of a phenomenon that appears to offer evidence that the human soul is real. And finally, imagine that this same phenomenon can be experienced personally by normal people (albeit with significant care and effort) without the assistance of expensive machinery like a particle accelerator, space ship, or nuclear reactor. This phenomenon is remote viewing, and its discovery promises to have an impact on all of our lives.

To frame the significance of the discovery of the remote-viewing phenomenon in terms of just one of these points, consider the issue of the existence of the human soul. Whether all of us are ready for this or not, we will probably soon witness the spectacle of science seriously entertaining the idea that the human soul is real. This issue alone is a "show-stopper" of historic proportions. Nothing is more important to our existence as humans than the understanding that we are more than our physical bodies. We pray that our souls are saved. We receive counsel from ministers, rabbis, priests, and others, and many of us try to navigate our lives to a successful Heavenly ending. But Western science has never been able to place a stamp of approval on the notion that consciousness is not limited to the physical brain. It is likely that this period of scientific denial of consciousness beyond the physical may be approaching an end. Science may soon have no alternative but to grapple with the evidence that indicates that we truly are more than our physical bodies. Understanding the phenomenon of remote viewing is the key to all of this. Moreover, the science of remote viewing has matured in recent years such that virtually everyone so-interested can understand this phenomenon and its implications.

Imagine a person, say "Tom," who is told to describe a particular location or event at some point in time. Tom is not told anything about when or where this location or event happens to be. Indeed, this location or event is simply called a "target" in a generic fashion, and he is told to describe "the target," whatever it may be. He then goes into a room that is ideally designed for such purposes. The colors of the walls are bland, as is the color of the carpet on the floor. There are no pictures on the wall to distract him. The doors of the room are closed, and in the room is only one desk, located in the room's center, and pointed toward a corner rather than a wall. Any recording equipment in the room is located behind the desk so that it remains out of his view. Tom has just completed a "cool down" period that settles his mind, and he sits down at the desk and begins writing on pieces of plain white paper. Approximately one hour later, Tom emerges from the room with, say, 20 pieces of paper containing detailed descriptions of the target. The descriptions include accurate sketches of the target, plus verbal descriptions of people, activity, and things that are at the target location. He did this without being told anything at all about the target. Only after Tom completes his written description is he told what the target actually is.

If the above scenario is not mind-boggling enough, consider the fact that Tom is able to do this same feat even if the target has not yet been chosen at the time he is writing his descriptions of the target! That is, he not only is describing the target accurately, he is describing the target that will be chosen only in the future. Moreover, the person who will choose the target will be given no information regarding Tom's description of the target. Both will be "blind" to one another. What Tom is doing is "remote viewing." What he is also doing is forever changing the way humans conceive of their own existence.

The study of remote viewing is a relatively new scientific field, and there has been tremendous controversy about it in recent years. It would be wrong for me to disparage those who have doubts about even the possibility of remote viewing. There are real reasons for such doubts. I can say this even though there is no doubt in my mind that remote viewing is a real phenomenon, and that the widespread recognition of this phenomenon will bring fundamental change to science and society. But before discussing the legitimacy of doubt, it is important to define what we are talking about when we discuss remote viewing.

What Is Remote Viewing?

Remote viewing is a psi-based mental process. People who know much about remote viewing agree on at least that much.   But beyond that there is considerable disagreement. The term "remote viewing" was used by the United States military in defense-related research projects from the 1970s through much of the 1990s. Probably because of this, the term appears to have developed a permanent place in the public's vocabulary of psychic phenomena. However, remote viewing can mean different things to different people. It typically involves the ability of a person to perceive and describe some thing or place that is separate from him or her in space and/or time. Not surprisingly, because remote viewers were often called upon to describe and draw visual information, visual concepts often dominated the early discussions of this phenomenon. But remote viewing is not limited to visual information. Some scientists have desired to use other more general terms to describe psi functioning, such as Dr. Edwin May's recent and useful coining of the term "anomalous cognition." Nonetheless, the term "remote viewing" is likely to remain the term most widely recognized by many people as referring to the apparently psychic ability to describe distant places and events.

Pioneering researchers at a few scientific laboratories, such as SRI International, Science Applications International Corporation (SAIC), Princeton Engineering Anomalous Research (PEAR), and elsewhere have spent years investigating the remote-viewing phenomenon. A significant and growing number of scientific papers have been published in distinguished peer-reviewed outlets that describe the investigations of the researchers in these laboratories in considerable detail. Within this field, there is no single method of remote viewing that is universally accepted as dominant, or even preferred. A recent book by the talented remote viewer, Joseph McMoneagle, *Remote Viewing Secrets: A Handbook*, contains good descriptions of the remote-viewing methods and controls that have been used in many of these laboratories. Some of the remote-viewing methods have military origins, have become quite standardized, and are known by specific names, such as "HRVG Protocols," "Extended Remote Viewing" (ERV) and "Controlled Remote Viewing" (CRV). (See McMoneagle 2000, pp. 95-101.) Some remote viewers have developed their own individualized methods that seem to work for them. Others have simply followed instructions as given to them by the primary investigators of a given project. The overall range of these methods varies from simply trying to "sense what's out there," to more structured processes involving meditation, detailed procedures, and other techniques. What is common among most of the laboratory experiments is not so much the remote-viewing methodology used by the test subjects, but the scientific procedures used to evaluate the existence of psi phenomena. These procedures tend to be highly sophisticated, and they address a large variety of scientific ideas, such as blind vs. double-blind testing environments and statistical controls.

The remote-viewing methodology that is used in all of the experiments described in this volume is a set of procedures known as "Scientific Remote Viewing." Scientific Remote Viewing evolved originally from Controlled Remote Viewing, procedures often used by U.S. military remote viewers. Scientific Remote Viewing (SRV) is the primary remote-viewing methodology that is used in experiments conducted at The Farsight Institute. SRV has not been used in experiments conducted by the U.S. military, at SRI International, SAIC, or PEAR.

To avoid confusion among the general public regarding the methodological procedures that are used and developed at The Farsight Institute, "Scientific Remote Viewing" was registered as a service mark of Farsight Inc. Without such protection, others would undoubtedly use the same term, and the ability to explain what we do at the Institute would become nearly impossible. The placement of the word "scientific" in Scientific Remote Viewing does not imply that these procedures are superior to or any more scientific than other structured methods of data collection that may be used elsewhere. Originally, the use of the word "scientific" reflected my own desire to investigate the remote-viewing phenomenon using a single standardized methodology. One of the key elements in scientific research is the desire to control as many variables as possible to enable one to isolate significant influences on a phenomenon, and working with a single standardized remote-viewing methodology is one way of controlling for variations in data collection techniques. Similarly useful and equally valid structured data-gathering processes are the Hawaiian Remote Viewers' Guild (HRVG) methods, Controlled Remote Viewing (CRV), Extended Remote Viewing (ERV), and some other remote-viewing methodologies that have been developed by an increasingly diverse collection of remote-viewing research groups. But from the perspective of the results presented in this volume, it is useful to point out that a single standardized methodology of data gathering was used in all of the experiments presented here, and this standardization is an essential element of scientific control.

In the next section, and again in parts of chapter 2, I make some observations about Scientific Remote Viewing. But this is a book about remote viewing, not Scientific Remote Viewing. These observations are necessary in order to explain how the experiments discussed in this volume were conducted. These comments should not be interpreted as limiting the relevance of the conclusions that I present here to remote viewing as it is performed using the Scientific Remote Viewing methodology. It is my view that these results are equally valid for remote viewing as it is performed using all other structured remote-viewing methodologies. Indeed, I fully expect that the results presented in this volume will be replicated by others using CRV, HRVG, and other remote-viewing methodologies.

Scientific Remote Viewing

Scientific Remote Viewing (SRV) was developed – and continues to evolve – at The Farsight Institute, a nonprofit research and educational organization that is dedicated to the development of the science of intuitive consciousness as it can be researched via the remote-viewing phenomenon. SRV procedures have a historical link to CRV procedures developed by Ingo Swann while he worked at SRI International as a remote-viewing test subject.

By using a standardized set of remote-viewing procedures, it has been possible to isolate explicit aspects of the remote-viewing phenomenon that appear both repeatable and robust. We have found that persons proficiently trained in the use of a structured data-collection methodology can use these procedures to obtain surprisingly accurate and detailed descriptive information about distant locations and across time.

As performed at The Farsight Institute, remote viewing is a controlled shifting of awareness that is performed in the normal waking state of consciousness. In a sense, remote viewing uses the human nervous system (with all of its five senses) in a way analogous to how an astronomer uses a radio telescope. Using remote viewing, the human nervous system acts as a tuning device that apparently connects us to an underlying field of nature through which knowledge of many things is possible. But before going further, let us be sure to identify what SRV is not.

- SRV does not involve an out-of-body experience.
- SRV does not use hypnosis.
- SRV does not involve an altered state of consciousness.
- SRV is not channeling.

SRV has a number of distinct phases that the viewer performs sequentially. Each phase is designed to allow the viewer to perceive various aspects of a target. A "target" is the location, structure, person, or event about which information is desired. In each phase, different types of information are extracted about the target, and the overall result typically includes a wide variety of descriptive data, including sketches.

Complete descriptions of all of the mechanics of Scientific Remote Viewing are available for free on the web site for The Farsight Institute (www.farsight.org). This web site offers a large collection of free instructional materials, as well as recordings of remote-viewing sessions (recorded live) and many examples of remote-viewing work. Free file-sharing technologies are sometimes used to aid in the distribution of these materials. Again, The Farsight Institute is a nonprofit research and educational organization, and the materials offered on the web site are free to anyone 18 years of age or older.

While I do not rule out the possibility that someone may one day discover a normal three-dimensional physical basis underlying the remote-viewing phenomenon, my own view is that the ability to train someone to remote view supports the idea that humans have a nonphysical aspect (that is, a soul), since in the absence of such an aspect, it is not clear how remote viewing would be possible. Yet I must be very clear here. "Nonphysical" does not mean that the science of physics does not operate on the level of the soul, and readers will note that chapter 8 in this volume addresses this issue directly. Remote viewing is clearly a phenomenon that works on the physical level, and we will eventually understand with certainty the physical laws underlying its manifestation. But when I state that remote viewing supports the idea that humans have a nonphysical aspect to themselves, I mean that whatever allows the phenomenon of remote viewing to occur does not depend on our five physical senses of hearing, touch, sight, taste, and smell.   Moreover, the remote-viewing mechanism cannot be limited to our current physical understanding of three-dimensional space plus time. Remote viewers do not physically go to a target location to observe with their eyes and other physical senses whatever is there — the information is apparently perceived through a nonlocal mechanism only. (In particular, see my comments regarding entanglement in chapter 8.) I look forward to the day in which we may all understand more about the physics of the soul, and as readers will note upon finishing this volume, my view is that this issue involving physics has a relevancy that vibrantly speaks to many academic fields.

Proof Versus Process

In this volume I do not attempt to "prove" that remote viewing is a real phenomenon.   In my view, this has already been accomplished by others elsewhere. (In particular, see Utts 1991, 1996.) The accumulated statistical evidence presented in the literature of this field would have been broadly accepted long ago for a less controversial subject. Proof-oriented research will continue in a variety of settings, and in my own mind I am certain that the eventual universal acceptance of the phenomenon is inevitable.

My aim with this volume is to present the results of a set of experiments that are directed at improving our understanding of the process of remote viewing. I fully expect the results to be widely applicable regardless of the remote-viewing methodology used.   With the exception of the chapter concerning the public demonstration of remote viewing, the general approach that I have followed in these investigations is not quantitative, but rather qualitative. With proof-oriented research, quantitative approaches are normally used. This often involves large batches of psi trials, followed by statistical evaluations of the resulting data. Statistical significance is the normal goal of such research, and it is used to establish evidence that the psi phenomenon under investigation did in fact occur. While the quantitative approach is useful in other contexts, my own research plan involves the design of a variety of experiments that might shed light on specific mechanisms influencing the remote-viewing process. Some truly enigmatic phenomena have been reported in the scientific literature on remote viewing, and these puzzles have lent themselves well to carefully designed experiments that exploit the designs' characteristics. Nonetheless, some readers may first want to deal with the matter of whether or not remote viewing is a real phenomenon prior to entertaining arguments relating to subtleties involved in the process of remote viewing. This addresses the issue of doubt, and it is important for me to spend a moment defending the legitimacy of such doubt.

The Legitimacy of Doubt

It is easy to understand why many may find it difficult to believe that remote viewing is a real phenomenon. Remote viewing relies on a level of perception that is quite alien to our normal means of perceiving the reality that surrounds us. Much of this perception has often been described as intuitive in nature. We normally rely on our five senses of hearing, touch, sight, taste, and smell. Indeed, these five senses dominate our physical waking state of consciousness. All humans have experienced intuitive senses to some degree, but intuition is rarely as reliable as direct perceptions using one or more of the five physical senses. For virtually everyone, there are moments when our intuitive senses seem remarkably accurate. But when we begin to rely repeatedly on these intuitions for practical situations, more often than not they eventually fail us.

For example, most parents have experienced situations in which they perceived intuitively that a child may have been in a difficult or dangerous situation. The parents sometimes telephone the school or house where their child may be, or they may even get into their car and drive to their child's location to check on the youngster's well-being. In some cases the parents' intuitions are very accurate, while in other situations the intuitions seem wildly misplaced. In another example, some people have claimed that their intuitions help them in betting on the stock market, while others say that their intuitions are useless in this regard. When those who rely on their intuitions for purchasing stocks are asked to demonstrate the method of their success for the benefit of others who may be watching, the previously reliable intuitions often leave the stock purchaser with egg on the face. Why do these experiences occur? Are those who are guided by their intuitions simply lucky from time to time? Or is there something else going on that is very real but simultaneously very misunderstood by mainstream modern science?

To complicate matters, there have been many examples throughout the ages of charlatans who have taken advantage of others by claiming that they have strange and powerful psychic capabilities. Some of these charlatans have been skilled in the art of magic tricks, and some have even purposely attempted to mislead scientists who are conducting honest investigations into psychic phenomena. Indeed, some have done this precisely to discredit the investigation of such phenomena. The problem of the charlatans (variously defined) has led to a broad cultural bias in our human society in which authentic scientific investigation into the realm of psychic phenomena is strongly discouraged. Probably the single most important factor in explaining the relative scarcity of scientists willing to investigate the psi realm is the fear of professional ridicule.

Given such territory, why should scientists risk their reputations on a phenomenon that has seemed so difficult to demonstrate "on-demand," and in an arena in which scientific investigations can be threatened by the skills of tricksters? Why also should other scientists believe the claims of their few colleagues who do run the risk of professional criticism by conducting psi experiments? The fear of guilt by association is strong and has found parallels even in ancient texts, such as St. Peter's famous denial of his mentor.

To proceed further, we need to suspend the factor of fear and to maintain open minds. If remote viewing is to be demonstrated as a real phenomenon, then we must treat it as we would treat any other scientific puzzle. We must fear neither the charlatans nor our scientific colleagues who might denounce us. If remote viewing is a real phenomenon, no amount of denunciation will make it otherwise. There are puzzles to unravel for sure. Psi phenomena in general depend significantly on subjective perceptions. The fact that this subjectivity does not blend easily with laboratories filled with precision equipment of the type used to measure merely physical phenomena should not dissuade us from conquering the challenges that do exist. Indeed, there are ways to make the study of psi more objective, a point argued forcefully and by example throughout this volume.

What we have not yet fully accepted as a society is that we already have a physical device that can be utilized in laboratory settings to investigate psi phenomena generally, and remote viewing in particular. This physical device is the human nervous system. Our difficulty to date has been caused by our failure to understand how to use this device properly. This book seeks to advance our understanding of the human nervous system and its interaction with psi phenomena.

The History of Remote Viewing

Remote viewing has been a focus of research for many decades. For example, some of the earliest research directly relevant to this volume was published in 1948 by René Warcollier, which includes a detailed report of individuals who attempted to mentally transmit images and other thoughts from one person to another (Warcollier, 2001). A separate application of this same type of idea was published in 1951 by Sir Hubert Wilkins and Harold M. Sherman involving a riveting account of thoughts and images conveyed between individuals separated by thousands of miles (Wilkins and Sherman 2004). Montague Ullman, Stanley Krippner, and Alan Vaughan extended this theme in 1973 by working with thought transference involving nocturnal experiments with dreams (Ullman, Krippner, and Vaughan, 2002). More directly applicable to the current volume, Charles T. Tart, Harold E. Puthoff, and Russell Targ edited a seminal volume of research published in 1979 that details the results of various investigations into psi phenomena generally and remote viewing more specifically occurring both in the United States and abroad (Tart, Puthoff, and Targ, 2002).

The work presented in this volume follows most clearly from a recent history of research that dates back to the 1970s. At Stanford Research Institute (now SRI International), a remote viewing laboratory run by luminaries such as

Harold E. Puthoff, Russell Targ, and Edwin C. May, produced some remarkable results involving a number of early remote-viewing test participants. Some of these test participants developed their own remote-viewing methodologies that complemented their intuitive capabilities. Big breakthroughs occurred with talented viewers such as Pat Price, Ingo Swann, and Joe McMoneagle. These viewers developed histories of making amazingly accurate remote-viewing descriptions of locations and events that were otherwise unknown to them. After the remote-viewing lab at SRI International closed in 1989, Dr. May moved the program to Science Applications International Corporation (SAIC).

The U.S. government [through the Defense Intelligence Agency (DIA) and to some extent the Central Intelligence Agency (CIA)] funded some of the early research into remote viewing (see especially Puthoff 1996). But proper funding was always an issue of contention between the principal scientists and their sponsors. It was clear from the beginning that advances in this field would come only after a great deal of research into the basic science of the phenomenon. But the government's primary interest in the phenomenon was operational in nature. The government wanted to know if remote viewing could be useful as a data gathering procedure for espionage. The government was also worried that a Soviet/US "remote-viewing gap" could emerge if research was abandoned entirely. The pressures to make remote viewing quickly operational as an espionage methodology led to inadequate funding tied to short-term projects subject to regular evaluations. A good description of the funding tensions in this regard can be found in a report by Kress (1999), a CIA operative with first-hand knowledge of these matters. This report was published in the *Journal of Scientific Exploration*, currently one of the most important publication outlets for research dealing with remote viewing. Indeed, the *Journal* dedicated an entire issue (1996, Vol. 10, Spring) to an evaluation of the early remote-viewing research, an issue that contains remarkable historical and analytical information written by many of the original investigators as well as others.

A careful reading of the extant literature relating to remote viewing suggests that remote viewing is a real phenomenon, albeit fickle. It has sometimes been used to produce remarkable results, while at other times there have been problems. This has left remote-viewing researchers in a state in which they know that the phenomenon is real, but they are unable to demonstrate this adequately to a skeptical audience that looks at apparent inconsistencies not as evidence of puzzles yet to solve, but as proof that the phenomenon itself is nonexistent (see especially the debate between Utts 1996 and Hyman 1996).

I decided to write the current volume when I became convinced that recent research conducted at The Farsight Institute filled some of the gaps in our understanding of remote viewing. Although I present the Institute's research and findings here as new, none of this work could have been accomplished in the absence of pioneering research done elsewhere by participants in this field who were more attracted to the possibility of scientific discovery than they were afraid of scorn from their scientist colleagues.

My Own Background in Remote Viewing

My personal and scholarly interest in the subject of consciousness began when I learned the Transcendental Meditation (TM) technique. TM is a mechanical process designed to relieve stress and produce a heightened state of awareness. It is not, as is commonly misperceived, attached to any particular belief system. For me the TM experience proved to be a profound one, especially as I progressed through the more advanced TM-Sidhi Program, and the practice of TM remains an integral part of my daily life. Along the way, it also indirectly nurtured my growing interest in and desire to explore consciousness in general, and remote viewing in particular. In addition to TM, I also gained a valuable exposure to alternative approaches to the exploration of consciousness at The Monroe Institute, an institution established in Faber, Virginia by the late Robert Monroe who was deeply impressed early in his life with personal experiences that he described as having "out of body" characteristics.

My initial experience with remote viewing began in the early 1990s with a limited exposure to a basic version of CRV that had been renamed by a former military remote viewer. The more I practiced and studied remote viewing, including the examination of other remote viewing methods — some of which were used by a variety of mostly former military remote viewers, the more convinced I was that this is a very real and potentially significant phenomenon that deserved a wider forum among scholars, scientists, and the general public. Unfortunately, obtaining that wider forum beyond the narrow set of researchers who study parapsychology was and still is a difficult proposition. The relative absence or obscurity of scientific research on remote viewing that is published in mainstream outlets meant that the intellectual establishment looked upon the subject with a great deal of skepticism. That dominant view also controlled public opinion, to the extent that the general public was even aware of the subject.

Nevertheless, I felt compelled to communicate what I had learned, even though my conclusions remained necessarily tentative and hypothetical at that stage. My hope, of course, was to promote greater awareness of and research into remote viewing, and it was certainly not to promote myself as some kind of definitive authority or guru. (Actually, my experiences with this phenomenon have encouraged within myself a much greater rather than lesser degree of humility.) I realized, however, that my research and knowledge at that time had not progressed far enough for me to produce a formal scientific study that would be accepted in the academic world. And so I pressed on with the research.

Serendipitously, perhaps, my work in this area happened to converge with another growing interest of mine — the search for extraterrestrial life. Long the domain of astronomers (including the much-publicized SETI program), that subject has unfortunately also attracted a variety of crackpots and cult figures over the ages. The latter, sad to say, have been visible enough to undermine the more legitimate efforts to investigate the possibilities of other life forms in our solar neighborhood and beyond. So, perhaps my decision to link my remote viewing and extraterrestrial interests was not a safely conservative choice as seen from an academic point of view. But when I research anything, it is my nature to write down my experiences in an on-going fashion, and I prefer to publish records of my work as markers of my own intellectual development rather than to file them in dust-covered cabinets.

Pursuing these twin interests, I wrote and published *Cosmic Voyage* — a work of speculative nonfiction. All remote-viewing data are speculative in nature when they are recorded. Such data can sometimes be profoundly accurate, but one can never know this until the data are compared with the known facts about the target for each remote-viewing session. In laboratory situations involving basic science experiments, the target for a remote-viewing session can often be known in just minutes, and the remote-viewing data can be evaluated with respect to accuracy right away. But with esoteric applications of remote viewing, the data must remain only speculative for however long it takes to obtain verification of the data with respect to the targets. Thus, remote-viewing data can by themselves never prove that something exists. However, such data collected by a remote viewer who has a proven track record with respect to accuracy can be of sufficient interest to warrant the expenditure of significant resources to learn if the data are indeed correct. But until that happens, the data are only speculative no matter who the remote viewer may happen to be.

As it turned out, and perhaps predictably, *Cosmic Voyage* was a popular success, although it did not significantly impact the academic establishment. That was followed by my second book on the subject of remote viewing, *Cosmic Explorers*. While this new book also delved into matters pertaining to extraterrestrial life, it marked a significant advance in my knowledge of the phenomenon and practice of remote viewing, which I think is where its primary contribution resides. Again, in terms of their extraterrestrial content, both of these books were written as speculative nonfiction, and I look hopefully forward to a day in which there may be an ability to obtain verification one way or the other for some of the data presented. Until such verification is obtained, the books should probably be loosely described as-yet unproven "hypotheses" based on my own perceptions. As a matter of interest, I might also add that I am not the only remote viewer who has published remote-viewing data relating to the subject of extraterrestrial life. (In particular, see McMoneagle 1993, pp. 155-174; Swann 1998.)

Both books, of course, clearly chart the development and evolution of SRV as a methodology. Despite the interest in remote viewing sparked by *Cosmic Voyage*, after its publication I remained uncomfortable with the basic remote-viewing methodology to which I had originally been exposed. I felt there were inconsistencies and some incoherence in its structure and application, even though it seemed to work fairly well as a basic data-gathering tool. I felt the procedures could be improved, but I needed a space (a "laboratory" in effect) where I could pursue improvements in a much more focused and deliberative fashion. Other psi laboratories existed (and still exist), such as the University of Amsterdam Anomalous Cognition Group, The Boundary Institute, The Cognitive Sciences Laboratory, Consciousness Research Laboratory, Koestler Parapsychology Lab (University of Edinburgh), Princeton Engineering Anomalies Research, Rhine Research Center (Institute for Parapsychology), and James Spottiswoode and Associates. But these other prestigious laboratories and gifted researchers tended to work on a variety of diverse approaches to psi phenomena, generally following the interests of the principal researchers involved. As important as these other approaches were (and remain), I wanted to pursue a different orientation by working with a limited set of remote-viewing procedures, allowing the procedures to evolve incrementally as a consequence of experimentation, trial and error. The space needed to do this, once secured through the creation of The Farsight Institute, provided the foundation for continued research into the SRV methodology and the remote-viewing phenomenon.

In its early years, the Institute provided an infrastructure for research, as well as instruction for many individuals who were interested in learning more about the remote-viewing phenomenon. Courses conducted at the Institute did not focus on the extraterrestrial question, although a few students happened to share my personal interest in that controversial subject. Instead, the sole mission of the courses was to provide a basic introduction to remote viewing.

As our research and teaching progressed, SRV continued to evolve away from its CRV roots, always based on changes that were the result of a great deal of trial and error. Yet I was concerned that we might never be able to reach a wide public audience if we continued to teach only small groups. It was due to this concern that I decided to publish a complete text for Scientific Remote Viewing that has been freely available on the Institute's web site since 1997. We have continued to expand our (now very large) library of free instructional materials ever since. I have never taken any financial compensation from The Farsight Institute, so all of our financial resources were plowed back into training an expanding and increasingly talented group of remote viewers as well as research into the basic science of the remote-viewing phenomenon. This was a period of significant growth for The Farsight Institute.

I should also mention that a number of other very capable remote-viewing instructors and organizations emerged during this period as well, and they too were evolving and improving their own methodologies and approaches in new and interesting ways. For example, Glenn B. Wheaton, a talented instructor and former military remote viewer, founded the Hawaii Remote Viewers' Guild (www.hrvg.org), an energetic group which has remained both active and highly productive. Also, I have long admired the careful development work and educational efforts of Lyn Buchanan (www.crviewer.com), a former military remote viewer with solid educational instincts. F. Holmes "Skip" Atwater, another former military remote viewer, has additionally made very significant advances while working at The Monroe Institute (www.monroeinstitute.org) in the development and application of sound technologies that enable and/or enhance the remote-viewing experience. I have also heard positive reports from students of Paul Smith, yet another former military remote viewer. More recently, a number of people who began their training at The Farsight Institute and elsewhere have emerged as creative innovators and instructors of their own evolving versions of remote-viewing methodologies. Still others (some former military and some not) have also begun to make methodological and instructional contributions in this rapidly expanding field.

As time passed and the initial public interest in remote viewing seemed to subside, we used some quiet years at The Farsight Institute to design and execute a lengthy series of experiments that would allow us to better understand what we considered to be a few puzzling yet crucial aspects of the remote-viewing phenomenon. All of our experiments involved basic science questions relating to the remote-viewing phenomenon itself, rather than applied or esoteric topics such as extraterrestrial life. Simply, we wanted to find out more about why remote viewing actually worked, and how to make it work better. This volume is a report of our findings.

How to Place the Contribution of this Book

All investigators have their own approaches to the way they think research should be conducted, and many passionately defend these approaches. One need only look at the blistering review by Hansen, Utts, and Markwick (1992) of remote-viewing experiments conducted at the Princeton Engineering Anomalies Research (PEAR) program to see just how passionate these opinions on how to conduct research in this field can be held. It is not my intent to side with past debates regarding programs or approaches, but I do want to make a case for why people should consider the results presented in this volume seriously regardless of how individual psi researchers may want to conduct their own experiments.

Most psi laboratories are run by scientists who are not typically subjects of their own experiments. That is, these scientists find others to act as subjects in their experiments. The scientists themselves are trained in the scientific method, statistics, experimental design, and so forth. But they are usually not highly trained users of psi. In the case of remote viewing, the scientists often work with remote-viewing subjects of various capabilities, from stellar professionals like Joe McMoneagle to ordinary college students who have had no previous training. But the scientists themselves typically do not publish papers about their own attempts at remote viewing.

After years of reading scientific papers of psi phenomena in general, and remote viewing in particular, I began to sense that there was sometimes a disparity between the way many researchers set-up and conducted their remote-viewing experiments and the experience of remote viewing itself that I — and others with whom I have worked — have had. For example, in a report by May, Utts, Humphrey, Luke, Frivold, and Trask (1990), they present an interesting and original approach to analyzing remote-viewing data using a fuzzy set coding scheme. In this report, they code targets drawn from pictures from *National Geographic Magazine*. But as part of their approach, they define these targets to be exactly what is in each picture, *and nothing except what is in each picture*. Quoting from the article, "Implied visual importance was ignored. For example, in a photograph of the Grand Canyon that did not show the Colorado River, water, river, and so on would be scored as zero. By definition the target was only what was visible in the photograph" (May, et. al., 1990, p. 200). From the perspective of trying to limit the target definition to only that which is definitively known, this seems at first glance like a reasonable scoring procedure. But it is generally recognized by many remote viewers with whom I have worked that remote-viewing data are not limited to that which may be visible in a target photograph. Indeed, a target photograph tends to locate a viewer at a specific location, but the viewer is then free to perceive (or fail to perceive) anything that is at that location, and it is hard to imagine a situation in which a viewer would be *expected* to miss the Colorado River if the target was the Grand Canyon. Any scheme that fails to take into account this apparently inescapable reality of the remote-viewing phenomenon seems — from an experiential point of view — to be trying to bend the phenomenon to meet the scientific method rather than adapting the scientific method to match the parameters of the phenomenon.

As another and similar example, I once saw a report of a remote-viewing session (not one reported by May or his colleagues) that was scored as a miss when the viewer failed to perceive the vegetables on a plate that constituted the target. The session in fact gave a good description of the house and people that surrounded the vegetables, but alas, the vegetables were not in the data. Again, I saw this as an example of how the analytical methods used did not match the reality of the remote-viewing phenomenon. (I discuss in more detail the problems associated with this type of "embedded" target in the appendix to this volume.)

Another (and more important) example of how a commonly applied element of the scientific method conflicts with characteristics of the remote-viewing phenomenon itself is with what has become a standard experimental set-up for many researchers. In this set-up, comparisons are made between remote-viewing data and a set of potential targets, one real and the others decoys. The set-up normally uses five potential targets, and judges are used to make the comparisons between the possible targets and the remote-viewing data to see how well the remote viewer describes the real target. (The set-up to which I am referring does not utilize an "outbounder" in the data collection process, a term which I describe later in this volume.) Much of this volume is dedicated to explaining a nearly obsessive series of experiments that we ran at The Farsight Institute to understand what is in fact going on with this procedure, and our conclusion finds that the procedure itself deeply conflicts with the psychic targeting process of remote viewing, leading to the near total corruption of the data-gathering process. The reason underlying this conclusion is not simple, and I ask readers to hold off on their judgment of these statements until they have read the remaining chapters in this volume. Our initial suspicions regarding the "pick the correct target out of the bunch" idea came because of our own personal experiences with this procedure. Certain phenomena occur when this procedure is used, and the phenomena are so repeatable that we concluded that the fault was not with our remote-viewing capabilities, but rather with the experimental set-up. Speaking from a personal level, I am a scientist who has invested years learning how to remote view, and repeated remote-viewing experiences have taught me to trust that these experiences are real. Something was happening with the "pick the correct target out of a bunch" experimental set-up that made my own remote-viewing experience go awry, and it was because of my long experience as a remote viewer that I decided to question how elements of this routinely used experimental design might influence the remote-viewing experience in an unexpected fashion.

The fundamental substance of this volume delves into the problem of defining what makes a target a target. That is, why should a remote viewer perceive one place or location rather than another? Is it because a picture of a place was put in an envelope that the remote viewer will be given after a session is completed? Is it because someone will eventually analyze the remote-viewing data with respect to a particular target? Is it because someone chooses a picture and tacks a set of remote-viewing "coordinate numbers" on it? Is it because a computer randomly picks a target out of a pool of targets? The question of what makes a target work with respect to remote viewing is obviously an important one, and any potential answer to this question deserves to have a hearing. But this volume does not present a "cookie-cutter" collection of experiments with a twist. Our approach to investigating the remote-viewing phenomenon is different from much of what has been reported elsewhere, and it is within that differentness that the true value of the contribution of this volume can be found.

This is an exploratory volume that presents research conducted by remote viewers. In constructing the experiments presented here, we consciously tried not to stop ourselves from questioning some things that other scientists were doing when their procedures or experimental conditions seemed to conflict with our experience of the remote-viewing phenomenon. We have designed our experiments such that they find correspondence with the years of our own remote-viewing experiences. That is, in my attempt to answer the questions that I raise in this volume, I have tried to maintain as delicate a balance as possible between my role as a scientist and my role as a remote viewer. As a result, the information presented in the pages that follow is the result of a different internal dynamic than that which sometimes occurs in other remote-viewing laboratories. This is not a study conducted by scientists who observe how others remote view. Rather, this is a scientific study of remote viewing that has been guided by the personal remote-viewing experiences of the researchers themselves.

It is important to understand that I am not criticizing other remote-viewing laboratories. I think any reader of this volume will see that I have obviously gained tremendously from the reports that these laboratories and their associated researchers have issued over that past few decades. Rather, I am arguing that the efforts presented in these pages can add to the public dialogue regarding the remote-viewing phenomenon precisely because of the differentness of these efforts. It is certainly true that I deeply desire for other remote-viewing laboratories to attempt to test and/or replicate the findings presented in this volume. Indeed, I am counting on this to happen. Moreover, I fully expect that other remote-viewing researchers will add their own approaches and methods to their tests of our findings. If some researchers disagree with a particular procedure or set of controls that we have used and reported in these pages, then these same researchers will certainly make the changes that they find appropriate when they conduct their own experiments. But in the end, I feel certain that if the fundamental ideas presented here are tested honestly in an uncompromising fashion, these same researchers will find that the primary results presented in this volume are indeed correct.

This is not the "definitive" volume of remote-viewing research, and a definitive work may not even be possible in such a rapidly evolving field. Rather, these are a collection of ideas and experimental results. Here we have not eschewed the scientific method, by any means. But we have tried not to let certain practices that have been accepted as routine elsewhere confine our ability to investigate the compatibility of these practices with the reality of the remote-viewing phenomenon as we have experienced it. I ask not that anyone accept the findings presented here with blind faith. But I do ask that researchers consider the possibility that what is presented in these pages is correct, and that the modifications suggested here to the way many think about and study the remote-viewing phenomenon may be justified. Indeed, I am asking only that readers have an open mind and consider without prejudicing bias the possibilities that I present below.

The Structure of this Research

In chapter 2 of this volume I present the basic theory of remote viewing as it is researched at The Farsight Institute. This is not a detailed description of the mechanics of the basic SRV process, which is available elsewhere (Brown 1999, and for free at www.farsight.org). Chapter 2 presents a theoretical overview of the remote-viewing process itself, together with an explanation of the "subspace hypothesis" which is central to all of the discussions in this volume.

Chapters 3 through 5 each address a specific process-related research question regarding the remote-viewing phenomenon using data collected at The Farsight Institute. A particular empirical test has been used for decades to evaluate the descriptive accuracy of remote viewing. In this test, remote-viewing data are compared with a short list of possible targets, one real and the rest decoys. Curious phenomena have occurred when using this procedure which have left raging debates in this field. Chapter 3 presents results that address this controversy. The bottom line is that the evaluative methodology seems to interfere with the delicate mental remote-viewing process. Fixing the experimental design fixes the problem, and repaired experiments morph in the direction of profundity.

A number of experiments conducted at The Farsight Institute allowed us to probe the structure of time, which is the subject of chapter 4. The questions addressed revolve around what truly is the beginning of anything. The results of these experiments and others that are presented in this volume stretch our understanding of reality.

Chapter 5 presents results of an experiment which tests a potential problem inherent with experimental psi methods in which subjects are asked to obtain remote-viewing perceptions repeatedly in order to amass sample sizes large enough for statistical evaluations of psi functioning. In this experiment, controls are used to avoid the potential for contamination of psi phenomena via the thought processes of human analysts. To accomplish this, a computer program and system are used to evaluate the remote-viewing data and completely eliminate the threatening contamination. The results of the experiment suggest that the process of remote viewing batches of targets can potentially destroy the psychic targeting mechanism of remote viewing.

For approximately six months, The Farsight Institute sponsored a public demonstration of Scientific Remote Viewing on its web site, www.farsight.org. The demonstration was fascinating from at least two points of view. First, clear and solid scientific controls were maintained throughout the demonstration, and literally thousands of individuals from all over the world both watched and participated in the process. Targets were chosen by an outside person of significant reputation, and the results were verified by literally everyone watching. The second point of intense fascination was that we dovetailed our public demonstration project with an experimental design involving future time. All of this is presented in chapter 6.

Chapter 7 is where I more fully explain the underlying mechanism that determines how and why a remote viewer maintains a perceptual focus on a specific target. Also in this chapter, I explain why the role of uncertainty in the remote-viewing process further complicates the targeting mechanism and perceptual focus of the remote viewer. Figures with visual approximations of mentally accessed visual imagery are also presented.

For remote viewing to be fully accepted within the scientific community as a real phenomenon, it will be important to explain how it could be possible from the perspective of theoretical physics. Cosmological, relativistic, and quantum physics do not yet have fully developed theories that can explain how the remote-viewing phenomenon might occur. Modifications to the way we understand physical reality will be necessary for us to place remote viewing within a proper scientific context. This does not mean that remote viewing is impossible, for clearly it is possible, as I believe any reasonably unbiased reader will conclude after examining the extant field closely. Rather, it means that our theories of the physical universe need to change in order to allow for the remote-viewing phenomenon. In chapter 8, I outline a theory of physical and nonphysical reality that corresponds with the nature of the remote-viewing experience, and this discussion is aimed at assisting physicists and cosmologists who work with such theories.

I develop in chapter 9 some additional theory regarding consciousness, and discuss the profound philosophical implications of this research to our understanding of physical reality and the human condition. I also further address the broader issues of time and its implications with regard to free will.

To perform remote viewing, one has to acquire the skill of having a truly open mind, in the full spiritual sense. To understand remote viewing and its implications intellectually, one needs to have an open mind of a different sort. This is the challenge to the reader: maintain an open mind while considering the data, analyses, and interpretations offered here. One is always free to reject an idea once it is considered fully. But if one never gives the idea a chance by rejecting the possibilities in the idea, who is the loser, the idea or the mind?

We live in a universe of change. History has demonstrated that nothing changes more profoundly in this universe than the ideas we have about it. We are more of an open society than we previously could have imagined. No mind is a truly closed system, however privately sealed to the universe it may consider itself. We live in a time in which we can show that consciousness is not limited to our physiology. We live in a time in which we may be able to know that consciousness is more than private thought. In a very real sense, consciousness *is* an open mind, a mind of expanding boundaries with as yet undetermined limits.

CHAPTER 2

A Theoretical Perspective of Remote Viewing

In this chapter I outline some theoretical considerations that help us frame the empirical results presented in subsequent chapters. It would be understandable if some readers first want to see proof that there even is a phenomenon that needs to be considered before tolerating a discussion on a possible theory that could help explain this phenomenon. But it is not my wish to present the empirical part of my research prior to any mention of the theoretical. To do so risks placing a premature emphasis on a narrow physical interpretation of the data, which in my view would be inappropriate. Thus, I offer a compromise. This chapter sketches some of the essential ingredients of my theory of the remote-viewing process. Following this chapter I dive into the experimental results with enthusiasm. I later return to the theory building process as the implications of the empirical sections become more demanding in terms of an explanation. This theory-data-theory "sandwich" approach to explanation also allows for a more gradual consumption of the overall picture presented here.

The Subspace Hypothesis

One of the first questions that arises when considering the possibility that remote viewing is a real phenomenon addresses the causal mechanism by which the process can occur. Research at The Farsight Institute has always been based on the proposition that if the remote-viewing process is real then there must be a nonphysical component to all humans. Again, I am not arguing that we exclude the possibility that a normal three-dimensional physical basis may one day be discovered as the remote-viewing causal mechanism. But it seems consistent with the remote-viewing experience that we consider the more daring proposition that there is a nonphysical root to this experience. By "nonphysical" I mean that the remote-viewing phenomenon is essentially nonlocal, such that remote-viewing perceptions do not rely on any of the five physical senses (i.e., the body parts associated with hearing, touch, sight, taste, and smell). If there is a nonphysical component to existence, then we need to have a name for it. Unfortunately, there is no universally accepted name for such a nonphysical realm wherein all such nonphysical "stuff" is located. Other scholars have made various attempts to label this as part of a realm of consciousness. Carl Jung's idea of the "collective unconscious" is one such attempt. His idea is that humans have ingrained into their existence archetypal ideas that are consistent across the entire human race. These archetypal ideas are akin to deeply imbedded human instincts that condition all of our perceptions of reality in extremely subtle ways. (See especially, Jung 1960, pp. 310-311.) But it is not clear from Jung's perspective whether this idea of the collective unconscious can be applied to a theory of mind that explicitly extends beyond the boundaries of the physical brain. It depends on how one interprets Jung.

One of the most useful attempts to outline and label a nonphysical extension of consciousness has been described in transpersonal psychology. The basic idea is that there is a physical level of existence that is defined by our physiologically-based experiences, and then there is a universal level of existence, or simply, "the universe." To connect the physical level of existence which encompasses brain physiology with the remainder of the universe, there are "transpersonal bands." Within these transpersonal bands can be found Jung's understanding of the collective unconscious, as well as various psi-related experiences, such as remote viewing, astral projection, out-of-body experiences, ESP, and the like. The transpersonal bands are considered "supra-individual," and arguments have been made that many philosophies have identified these bands in various ways. For example, Ken Wilber argues that the Vedanta psychology of sheaths can be understood from the perspective of distinct levels of awareness that extend from a middle-ground of the transpersonal bands. (See especially, Wilber 1977, pp. 120-1, 168-9, and 266-8).

Transpersonal psychology is a large field these days, and important contributions have been made by many, including Wilber (1977, also numerous articles in the *Journal of Transpersonal Psychology*), Stanislav Grof (for example, 1983), Roger Walsh (2000, 1993), and Frances Vaughan (1991). Most understandings of transpersonal psychology address a desire to merge western psychology with ideas originating from various flavors of eastern mysticism. Some transpersonal psychologists suggest that this explicitly embraces the idea of a nonphysical realm of consciousness, but others do not necessarily argue that this is a requirement, or even that transpersonal bands must exist. Thus, there are mixtures of ideas here, and the ideas related to transpersonal psychology are deeply connected to the various views held by theorists and practitioners in the field. Moreover, theorists and practitioners of transpersonal psychology often develop their own methods of helping people grow on the level of consciousness. For example, Stanislav Grof uses a combination of music and breathing techniques, sometimes mixed with mandala drawing and other things, in a practice he calls "Holotropic Breathwork." Similarly, Roger Walsh (2000) suggests other practices to help in personal growth.

Physicists typically use their own specialized terminology to address ideas of multiple dimensions. In particular, the term "hyperspace" refers to a multidimensional view of the universe that includes the normal four dimensions as a subset of a larger number of dimensions, the total number of which is not yet resolved. The mathematics behind much of this is sometimes referred to as "fiber bundle theory." String theorists are working on additional aspects related to this, in the sense that they are trying to develop theories that will explain all of existence from one unified perspective. But the basic idea that is important in the current context is that consciousness may be related to the dimensions that extend beyond the normal four of our common experience. Physicists are not certain of how this might play out, but important contributions along these lines have been made by Saul-Paul Sirag (often collaborating with Jeffrey Mishlove), Michio Kaku (1994), Fred Alan Wolf (1998, 1988), and others.

The trouble with using any of the existing terminology in the context of the research presented in this volume is that the existing terminology is already associated with explicit meanings that may not be appropriate here. "Collective unconscious" is inappropriate for two reasons. First, there is no definitive understanding of how to interpret or extend Jung's usage, especially with regard to a nonphysical interpretation of consciousness. Second, it seems awkward to label an aspect of awareness that seems very much awake as "unconscious," as if it is knocked out. With regard to transpersonal psychology, its associated terminology has been used with explicit reference to alternative psychological frameworks that may or may not apply here. For example, Wilber argues that transpersonal bands can be located within a Vedantic scheme of carefully identified layers of consciousness — the so-called Vedanta psychology of sheaths (Wilber 1977, pp. 168-9). Also, others have associated very specific psychological or spiritual practices with their interpretations of transpersonal psychology, as with Stanislav Grof's Holotropic Breathwork. It is unlikely that the current users of such terminology would welcome alterations in the meanings of their language, especially if explicit remote-viewing procedures are associated experientially with those meanings.

The concept of hyperspace is not wedded to a specific psychological or spiritual framework, nor is it associated with specific psychological or spiritual practices. But hyperspace has a distinct meaning among physicists, and their mathematical approaches to this meaning are crucial to its definition. Hyperspace can extend to a theoretical infinite number of dimensions, and theorists usually argue that it collapses to a smaller set of numbers, as per their mathematical theories (such as 192, then down to 96, then 48, and then 12 dimensions, and so on). These dimensional collapses are called "projections." Our four-dimensional reality is a further projection (some might say "subprojection").

The idea of a projection is a mathematical concept that is not entirely intuitive, but one could approach its usage through a related analogy. Within a dimensional hyperspace of whatever number of dimensions can exist a hypersurface. A hypersurface has one less dimension than the dimensions of the hyperspace within which it resides. For example, a line is a one-dimensional hypersurface in a two-dimensional plane, and a sphere is a two-dimensional hypersurface (since it has no thickness) in a three-dimensional space. The idea here is that you develop a set of mathematical rules that you apply within a defined hyperspace to collapse a certain number of dimensions into a fewer number of dimensions. An entity living on or in a hypersurface with fewer dimensions theoretically might not be aware of the larger hyperspace within which it lives, such as an ant might not be aware of its larger 3-dimensional surroundings if it is only walking around on the surface of a sphere. This, of course, references the theme in the well-known story *Flatland: A Romance of Many Dimensions* by Edwin A. Abbott. In a sense, consciousness can have various layers, one for each hypersurface layer, so to speak. This re-addresses the Vedantic sheath concept where the conscious mind perceives one layer of awareness while the other layers of consciousness might be associated with other-dimensional hypersurface realms.

Again, the problem with using the language of hyperspace in the current context is that the language already has explicit meanings, both mathematical and philosophical. Any usage of the hyperspace terminology would have to be correspondent with existing usages, and that might potentially confuse the language further. More specifically, hyperspace terminology is used to delineate a large variety of potential dimensions, with subtleties of form and structure being associated with the various dimensional categories. This is not unlike the situation with some existing spiritual terminology in which various terms are used to describe different levels of a highly structured spiritual realm.

What is needed here is a term that works in more of a binary fashion, separating the physical from the nonphysical realms without imposing a more rigorous view of dimensional complexity on either of those realms. We know from our own experience that there are three physical dimensions plus one time dimension. We also know from the remote-viewing phenomenon that information appears to be transferable through means that circumvent the limitations of the known four dimensions. This supports the idea that other dimensions in fact may exist, since at least one added dimension is normally required to escape the limitations of an otherwise fixed dimensional structure (in the sense that you need to add a third dimension in order to escape from a two-dimensional plane). Furthermore, we do not want to be too specific and use language that binds us prematurely to a scheme with a complex specified structure with regard to extra dimensions, however many there may be. We simply want to say that there appear to be other dimensions, and we want to have a word that identifies those other dimensions separately from the already well-known four dimensions.

When I wrote my first book on remote viewing, *Cosmic Voyage*, I searched for a word that would capture this meaning of the other potential dimensions. The ideal word would be one which other people knew, but that was as yet undefined. The word "subspace" was such a word. It was used in the Star Trek television series, nearly everyone knew it, and it was not yet defined. It contained within it the concepts of "inner" or "within" as well as "space," thereby connecting the inner psychic world with the external universe. Moreover, the television usage seemed to capture the idea of dimensions exclusive of the known four dimensions. I began using the word "subspace" in *Cosmic Voyage*, and again in *Cosmic Explorers*, to mean all those dimensions outside of the known set of four dimensions. It is useful to emphasize that this two-fold typology is different from the more general concept of hyperspace, which includes the known four dimensions as a subset of a larger pool of dimensions.

In this volume, I continue to call the set of all dimensions outside of the known four dimensions "subspace." The border between physical reality and subspace is apparently permeable, since it seems possible to access the physical universe in a nonlinear fashion from subspace. We note this since remote viewing seems to have no known physical or distance limitations. On the level of consciousness, it may be that the border between the physical and subspace realms corresponds with what Wilber and others refer to as the transpersonal bands. Beyond this, subspace may indeed be a complex realm, although we impose no structure on it at this point.

In a parallel fashion, we label the nonphysical component of all humans that makes the remote-viewing process possible the "subspace aspect." Others have called this subspace aspect the human soul. However, I do not typically use this term in the current context due to the multiplicity of meanings which it conveys, depending on who is speaking and who is listening. The term "subspace aspect" is more precise and less laden with theological meaning. It simply denotes a part of ourselves that originates from — and resides dominantly within — subspace.

Critics of this line of thought may object to the fact that there appears to be no evidence for the existence of subspace or of a human subspace aspect. Such critics might argue that I am putting the cart before the horse by claiming the existence of a subspace dimensionality before conclusively ruling out a physical explanation of the remote-viewing phenomenon. I will not dismiss such criticism entirely, since I do accept the possibility that someone may one day find such a physical explanation for psi functioning. But I personally consider this possibility remote, and in order to flesh-out a more complete alternative hypothesis that explains the remote-viewing experiences that both I and others have had, it is necessary to use appropriate terminology that allows an accurate portrayal of the relevant ideas. In my view, there is ample evidence supporting the possibility of both the subspace realm and the human subspace aspect from within psi research generally, and remote-viewing research more specifically. This volume is indeed a presentation of some such evidence.

From the theoretical perspective of the research presented here, the human body is merely a machine. This idea of a biological machine is not meant as an analogy, but as a fact that claims its status of "real" due to a large and increasing body of scientific evidence. The human body appears to be little more than a device through which the consciousness of a person's subspace aspect achieves a focus of awareness within the physical universe.

Our understanding of the remote-viewing process is now sufficiently advanced that we can use the human body (actually, its nervous system) as a scientific mechanism or tool with which to conduct subspace experiments. I am convinced that we will one day develop machine-based technology that will greatly enhance our ability to conduct subspace research. But for now, the human nervous system is the most highly refined piece of hardware available to us. As will become clear throughout this volume, our understanding of how to use this biological technology within scientific settings has developed to the point that we can conduct experiments with greater precision than ever before.

Our subspace aspect is our connector between the physical and subspace realms. Current remote-viewing evidence suggests that the human subspace aspect is not localized. That is, it appears to be omnipresent (everywhere at once). One does not leave one's body (in a spiritual sense) and "fly" to a different location to describe a target. Rather, with remote viewing, one shifts one's attention from one location to another, just as a person would look (with the eyes) from one corner of a room to another without having to move one's body. But the remote-viewing experience ultimately becomes a physical experience, since all that is perceived and reported must eventually end up as conscious thoughts, spoken or written words, and sketches. The subspace aspect must thus have some mechanism by which these perceptions interface with physical (brain-based) consciousness.

Remote-viewing evidence argues forcefully that the human subspace aspect focuses its awareness of the physical universe through the five sensory channels of the human nervous system. It appears that the output strength of these five sensory channels with regard to physical consciousness is strong relative to the ability of a person to perceive direct subspace information. That is, it is easier by far for a human to perceive information originating from the five senses than it is for a person to perceive subspace information.

The nature of the physical/subspace interface is not well understood. Science will eventually understand this interface as research continues in the years and decades that follow. Indeed, researchers such as Hameroff, Penrose, and others are already exploring areas of inquiry that may soon allow us to understand the nature of this interface on the molecular level. (For example, see Hameroff 1998, 1994; Hameroff and Penrose 1996.) But we nonetheless now know some of the characteristics of this interface.

On the level of perception, the physical/subspace interface appears to act as a low-bandwidth connector between physical and subspace consciousness. Some may argue that the interface is more like a juggernaut than a helpful connection. Again, this is due to the low-bandwidth characteristic of the interface. By "low-bandwidth" it is meant that the interface appears capable of transferring only small amounts of information in a given time when compared with what is possible using the physical senses. To explain, consider that information sent to the brain from either the physical/subspace interface or the five senses arrives as "signals" (with the word used analogously in the sense of a radio signal or any other constant flow of coded information that requires translation upon reception). There are two issues relating to signals that are relevant here: amplitude versus quantity.

Experientially, remote viewers typically report that signals coming from the five physical senses feel like they are being received by physical consciousness (that is, the brain) at much higher levels of amplitude than those coming through the physical/subspace interface. Again, these are the subjective feelings of the remote viewers. It is unknown at this time whether amplitude is really the issue or whether the relative disparity in signal strengths is due to something else, such as the overall quantity of information. For example, if one tunes in a radio station with a radio receiver, the signal can be weak or strong, depending on the distance between the receiver and the transmitter as well as the power of the transmitter. But the quantity of information received (defined in terms of the number and variation of frequencies in the signal) is the same regardless of the strength of the signal. For the quantity of information to matter, the signal would have to be interrupted or suspended through some means. With regard to remote viewing, it is unknown whether the information that is received through the physical/subspace interface is lacking in amplitude (that is, signal strength) or information quantity, or perhaps both amplitude and quantity. It is likely that both amplitude and quantity differentials would be experienced similarly by remote viewers, and so they would not be able to tell the difference between the two.

Other remote-viewing experiences add further insight regarding the capabilities of the physical/subspace interface. Remote viewers often experience very clear momentary perceptions of things at a target, including visual images. These images and other perceptions are often perceived "in a flash," so to speak. This experience would suggest that the physical/subspace interface is capable of rapid information transference at certain times when optimal conditions exist. The obvious conclusion to draw from this would be that something is interfering with the signal under more "normal" situations, and that only when the interference is stopped or circumvented – even if only momentarily – can the subspace originating data be transmitted more completely. This observation does not resolve the amplitude versus quantity issue discussed above, since it is still not known whether any interference with a signal transmitted through the physical/subspace interface would affect either the amplitude or the quantity of information, or both.

Overcoming the Low-bandwidth Limitation

Remote viewing is possible because methods have been developed which essentially overcome the limitation of the low-bandwidth connection of the physical/subspace interface. Before discussing these methods, it is useful to make some observations regarding another approach that has been utilized to overcome what might generally be termed "limitations in awareness." Most remote viewers who conduct research at The Farsight Institute meditate. I practice Transcendental Meditation (actually, the more advanced TM-Sidhi Program). I do this twice each day. The observations that I make below regarding meditation refer only to my own thoughts and experiences (as well as my interpretation of the thoughts and experiences of some other remote viewers) as they relate to the remote-viewing phenomenon. These personal comments do not reflect official or unofficial views, endorsements, or support for remote viewing or meditation by anyone other than myself. Neither do these comments reflect support for the research or other activities of myself or The Farsight Institute by any spiritual movement or leader of such a movement.

In my own experience, and the reported experience of some others, meditation acts to "quiet" the effects of the five physical senses on the mind. In a sense, the mechanics of meditation act to put the conscious mind into a "vibrational loop," occupying its attention in the process, and consequently freeing a person's awareness to gravitate naturally to the signal that arrives through the physical/subspace interface. By "vibrational loop" is meant that the sounds (mantras) involved in the practice of meditation seem to adjust the consciousness of meditators so as to focus or tune their perceptual awareness. In the lingo of the day, this acts to enhance the "mind-body connection." The concept of a "loop" addresses the idea of repeating the sounds internally, thereby creating a mental state experiencing a desired periodic event. These sounds have apparently been developed through a trial and error process over a period of potentially thousands of years. Over the ages, people have been so impressed with the abilities of these sounds — properly utilized — to expand their awareness to the subspace realm that they have personified them as the names of deities in some cultures. This would be an expected occurrence for a traditional society that did not offer any other explanations as to why meditation would extend one's perceptions beyond physical reality.

A very useful treatment of the entire subject of meditation and spirituality from a "vibrational" or "wave-length" perspective can be found in Wilber (1977). In his book, *The Spectrum of Consciousness,* Wilber examines a broad range of spiritual traditions, and he synthesizes from them commonalities in experiential themes. Indeed, these are precisely the themes that I re-examine here from the perspective of the human physical/subspace interface of consciousness.

Two initial examples (both utilized by Wilber) are useful here. In the first,

Erwin Schrödinger comments on the typical human reaction to the notion of a nonlocal nature of consciousness. He notes that "we have entirely taken to thinking of the personality of a human being ... as located in the interior of its body. To learn that it cannot really be found there is so amazing that it meets with doubt and hesitation, we are very loath to admit it. We have got used to localizing the conscious personality inside a person's head – I should say an inch or two behind the midpoint of the eyes.... It is very difficult for us to take stock of the fact that the localization of the personality, of the conscious mind, inside the body is only symbolic, just an aid for practical use" (Schrödinger 1969, p. 133).

In the second example, a student of the guru Ramana Maharshi once made a remarkable observation that has striking similarities to the experiences reported by many remote viewers. He claimed that he had "flashes" of awareness from what he perceived as coming from outside of himself. Maharshi's response was to claim, "Outside! For whom is the inside or outside? These can exist only so long as there are the subject and object.... On investigation you will find that they resolve into the subject only. See who is the subject; and this enquiry leads you to pure Consciousness beyond the subject" (Ramana Maharshi, 1972).

Some spiritual masters have gone so far as to argue that the physical universe is not entirely real. From this perspective only the spiritual realm — which we can translate as the subspace dimension in the current context — is the only "firm" reality. For example, when Swami Sri Yukteswar (the guru of Paramahansa Yogananda) translates the ancient Sanskrit sutra, "Ignorance is the perception of the nonexistent, and the nonperception of the Existent," he is arguing (using my current terminology) that the subspace realm is closer to the origin of all existence, and that the physical universe is an artifact that is created due to something that occurs on the level of subspace (Swami Sri Yukteswar 1949, p. 47). Paramahansa Yogananda also has written extensively about this, noting that our observations of physical reality are inseparable from illusion, or "maya" (literally, "the measurer," a meaning that will connect pointedly with the quantum idea of observation as described in chapter 8 of this volume). (See particularly, chapter 30 "The Law of Miracles," in Paramahansa Yogananda 1946[1974]. See also the highly relevant account from the physicist, Amit Goswami 1993.)

Many such spiritual masters have employed techniques by which their disciples have been able to capture glimpses of an expanded reality. But since these subjective glimpses have always been reported anecdotally, they have typically been dismissed by modern science as delusions. This would include accounts from the historical masters of the Judaeo/Christian traditions. Indeed, it is not too far-fetched to imagine that in some situations Jesus would be at risk of institutional confinement if he lived in today's world. If one tried with any reasonable effort, would it be hard to find a psychiatrist who would certify that such a modern-day Jesus is schizophrenic and in need of medication to suppress his delusional perceptions of both beings and objects that do not exist in the physical world? I think not. And even if he was left alone to roam the streets, would Western science take such a person seriously when he talks of other realms?

All this points to the difficulty which humans have interacting with their physical/subspace interface. Special techniques are needed to overcome the limitations of this interface, and those who do not utilize such techniques are simply at a loss to explain the perceptions of those who do.

Meditation is a particularly interesting technique that aids in expanding a person's awareness. It both sidetracks the conscious mind (by throwing it into a mantra loop) and settles the mind's conscious mental activity for a period ranging from a few minutes to an hour or more. When doing so, a person's awareness soon shifts to perceive information arriving from the physical/subspace interface, and that is when the probability of conscious recognition of perceptions from the subspace realm increase. For beginning meditators, meditation typically gives an experience of calmness. But it is not rare to hear advanced meditators report perceptions of otherworldly realms. Indeed, the more consistently one practices meditation, the more regularly these perceptions seem to occur. In my view, it would be wrong to dismiss all of these reports as merely delusions, even though there is currently no way to confirm these perceptions.

What we gain from meditation is the suspicion that there is something real behind the veil of consciousness. What we gain from remote viewing is both the confirmation that a larger reality does exist, and an ability to mediate our interactions with that reality. More specifically, remote viewing adds a level of control to perceptions made through the physical/subspace interface that is not available through any other known means. It is a way to minimize interference from the conscious mind, to re-direct a viewer's attention to the subspace signal, to record perceptions in a systematic fashion, and then to evaluate these perceptions using objective criteria. It may not be easy to remote view accurately, but for those who are willing to work to attain the required proficiency, the rewards to both the individuals and science can be great.

The question of proficiency thus becomes an issue. If it were easy to remote view, books such as this one would have been written long ago. Indeed, the difficulty inherent in the process is one of the primary reasons skeptics of remote viewing have been so successful in the past with arguments suggesting that the phenomenon is not real. It is just too easy for someone to demand, "If you can remote view, then tell me now what is in the next room." Others listen to these demands and are often influenced or intimidated by them. But if we truly want to understand the remote-viewing phenomenon objectively, we must learn to tolerate the conditions under which remote viewing can be effectively accomplished. There are two important conditions that we consider first: training and environment.

It is true that many people have experienced what is known as "spontaneous remote viewing," a phenomenon in which something is perceived as a "flash" in consciousness (such as a momentary image), to be revealed later as an authentic and previously unknown reality. While no prior training is needed to have this type of experience, this phenomenon is not controllable and is of little interest in our current setting. Here we are interested only in remote-viewing experiences that can be controlled in experimental settings with clearly established evaluative parameters. To do this, a person needs training.

Just as playing the piano to a high level of skill does not come naturally — it takes years of hard work and practice — similarly, remote viewing requires patience and effort to do well and consistently. Evidence currently suggests that all (or at least nearly all) normal people can learn to remote view to some extent. People can even have powerful experiences with only a brief exposure to the procedures, as long as the educational environment is properly structured. But to become really good at this is just as hard as anything else in life. Becoming "really good" means having the ability to consistently produce useful data that accurately describe a target. This does not mean that every remote-viewing session must be perfect. But most sessions should reveal obvious target descriptions, with some of the sessions containing truly profound levels of target contact.

The remote-viewing environment is equally important in consistently obtaining experimentally useful results. Research at The Farsight Institute clearly suggests that remote viewing is much more effective if it takes place under the following conditions:

1.   The remote viewer should ideally conduct a minimum of two remote-viewing sessions per week. Three sessions per week is better, four can be tiresome if the viewer's life is filled with other activities as well, such as a job and family. But remote viewing every once in a blue moon is clearly not conducive to obtaining consistently useful results, especially results with profound levels of target description.

2.   The viewer should have a relatively peaceful domestic environment. If one is highly stressed at home, it is difficult for the mind to relax sufficiently so as to allow for an effective perception of the signal traversing the physical/subspace interface. One needs to experience a truly open mind to remote view, and openness cannot be obtained if one is feeling on-guard.

3.   The remote-viewing session should be conducted in a quiet environment. Ideally, this should be a room specifically set aside for remote viewing. A square room is best with nothing on the walls and few furniture. The colors of the room should be bland or neutral. A desk is needed to write, of course. An inexpensive six foot table with folding legs of the type sold in office supply stores is fine. The desk should be placed in the middle of the room facing diagonally toward a corner. If the corner toward which the desk is facing contains a door, this is fine, but the door should be closed

during the session. One should avoid situations in which the desk is flat up against a wall and the viewer is facing the wall. There is a psychological component to all of this, and facing a wall two feet in front of one's face gives the impression of a block, which is the last thing one needs in this process.

4.   The viewer needs to be deeply calm before beginning a remote-viewing session. This implies more than just being relaxed. The viewer needs to already be in contact with the physical/subspace interface at the moment when the session begins. At The Farsight Institute, we do one of two things. We either schedule our remote-viewing sessions to immediately follow our morning meditation, or we perform a procedure called the "Consciousness Settling Procedure" for 15 minutes prior to beginning a session. The first option is the best, but sometimes our schedules dictate the second as the only possibility. My own meditation program lasts for approximately one hour and fifteen minutes, and I normally consider this my personal prerequisite for remote viewing. It is impossible to overemphasize the importance of this "cool-down" step. Remote viewing simply does not work well (or at all) with a noisy mind.

5.   The viewer should be given absolutely no prior knowledge of the target. This requirement is not to "prove" that remote viewing is a real phenomenon, even though any test of the phenomenon would require this. Rather, the remote-viewing process itself works best if the viewer does not have even a hint of what the target might be. Any prior information only corrupts the viewer's ability to distance the conscious mind from the perception of subspace originating information. Experience has demonstrated that the conscious mind can generate ideas that mimic the feel of information coming from the physical/subspace interface. It is difficult enough for the viewer to avoid such false signals. Giving the conscious mind a lead on the type of information expected makes it nearly impossible to obtain anything useful from the remote-viewing process.

6.   Except under special conditions involving the use of what is called an "outbounder" (discussed in a later chapter), the remote viewer should probably never be given a target from a pool of other targets if the data from the session is to be compared by human judges (that is, not a computer) with these other targets to test if the viewer accurately describes the "correct" target. (That is, one target is correct, and the others are decoys.) Among scientists who study remote viewing, this may initially seem like a controversial statement since this method of judging remote-viewing data is almost universally practiced in many psi laboratories. But the idea addresses what I believe to be a fundamental — and until now poorly understood — problem that has plagued research in remote viewing for decades. More specifically, the experimental design which I suspect to be deeply flawed is for a viewer to conduct a session, and then for the data

to be given to judges who have a list of, say, five targets. They are then to decide which is the correct target based only on the data delivered by the remote viewer. The "correct" target is typically determined by some external random event and is not known to the judges when they are making their evaluations. Evidence that I present in this volume suggests that this seemingly obvious experimental design has serious problems that essentially invalidates the data, even though it has sometimes worked sufficiently well to produce statistically significant support of psi functioning in experiments at SRI International, SAIC, and elsewhere. It will take more than this paragraph for me to explain my reasons for stating that this experimental design is flawed, and I begin my treatment of the issue in the next chapter of this book. I return to these ideas in the remaining chapters of this volume as well.

The Remote-Viewing Process

Below is a treatment of the remote-viewing process from a theoretical perspective that relates the process to a viewer's interaction with the physical/subspace interface. For heuristic reasons, some of the discussion below relates to how SRV is taught to new students. Yet it is important to note that instructional settings are different from the experimental conditions used for the research reported in this volume. For example, with remote-viewing instruction, it is typical for a student to work with a person called a "monitor" who listens to and watches a student during a session, offering nonleading procedural advice when needed. But the remote viewers participating in the experiments discussed in this volume already were proficient with the remote-viewing process and monitors were not used at all in any of the research presented here. That is, all of the research presented in this volume is based on remote-viewing conditions in which the viewers were alone (solo) when the sessions were conducted, and no monitors or other individuals were ever nearby who could have interfered with, led, or influenced the results of the sessions. Also, for all of the research presented in this volume, all viewers were given absolutely no "front-loading" with regard to advance knowledge of a target's characteristics.

As with other structured remote-viewing procedures, SRV is designed to minimize the limitations of the low-bandwidth capabilities of this interface. The specific details of the SRV process are readily available elsewhere and thus are not discussed here. (See the first 100 pages of Brown 1999, as well as a free online text, and many other free resources on the web site of The Farsight Institute — www.farsight.org.)

Remote viewing always focuses on a target. A target can be almost anything about which one desires information. Typically, targets are places, events, or people. But advanced viewers also work with more challenging targets.

A remote-viewing session normally begins by executing a set of procedures using target coordinates. These are two randomly generated (by a computer) four-digit numbers that are assigned to the target. Other structured remote-viewing procedures (such as the HRVG procedures) sometimes use tags containing letters rather than random numbers for the target coordinates, but there is no inconsistency here. The important point is that the remote viewer's conscious mind does not know what target the numbers (or other tag) represent. The target coordinates are used just to get the remote-viewing process started, and extensive experience has demonstrated that the subspace mind instantly knows to perceive the correct target even if it is only given its coordinate numbers. The remote viewer is not told the target's identity until sometime after the session is completed.

In introductory training sessions, an instructor typically has a piece of paper in a closed folder or envelope. The paper in the folder or envelope has a description of the target written on it. The instructor often writes the target coordinates on the outside of the envelope and then tells the students these coordinates so they can use it for their sessions. With training sessions using novice viewers (and only in such training situations, never in research situations), the instructor knows (and mentally focuses on) the target while the session is taking place. Experience has shown that this process is psychically helpful to novice viewers as they attempt to focus for the first time on correct target perceptions. (The reason for this will become clear after reading this book.) When conducting research experiments at The Farsight Institute using advanced viewers, the viewers normally work without a monitor, instructor, or anyone else in the room, and they are simply informed via an email or a fax that there is a target (or that there will be a target ... see below). Depending on the experimental design being used in a specific instance, the target can be determined by either a person who has no contact with the viewer or a computer, the latter of which selects a target at random from a pool of targets. The viewers then use a computer to generate their own set of random target coordinate numbers for this target. The sessions are conducted using these coordinate numbers.

Outside of instructional settings, the target is often not determined at the time that the session is conducted. We have made many experiments to explore the nature of time using remote viewing, and we are now certain that it makes no difference whether or not the target is decided upon after or before the remote-viewing session is conducted. This phenomenon is completely explained later in this book, and due to the complexity of the issue, it is best if I postpone any further discussion of this matter until these later chapters.

Let me give a typical example of how I would be given a target to remote view. The only thing I am given prior to the beginning of my session is a fax or an e-mail from my "tasker" or project coordinator telling me that I can view a target as soon as I have an opportunity. If the target is chosen randomly by a computer from a large batch of targets, then it is the project coordinator who informs me that a session is needed, and the project coordinator would not know the identity of the target chosen by the computer to avoid any possible contamination. If the target is chosen by a person, then that person is called a "tasker" whose job it is to "task" or assign a target. Taskers are sometimes used in slightly less formal exploratory situations in which certain types of process experiments are conducted. In more formal conditions in which stricter controls are needed, computers choose the targets and a project coordinator is used who remains blind to the target choices. Regardless of how the target is determined, I am not told at that time of viewing whether or not the target is already chosen, or if the target will be chosen after I complete my session. I then generate my own set of target coordinates. I do not transmit these coordinates to my tasker or project coordinator. (The tasker need never know them.) Finally, I would normally conduct a remote-viewing session in isolation, that is, without the assistance of a monitor. If a monitor is ever used for any reasons required by an experiment (no such situations occurred for the research presented in this volume), then the monitor would have to remain blind as to the identity of the target throughout the session.

Why am I told absolutely nothing about the target when I conduct a remote-viewing session? Let us say that the target ends up being the Taj Mahal. It would be disastrous if I were told in advance that this is the target, since this would cause my conscious mind to remember everything I know regarding this structure, and I would have a near impossible time differentiating the remote-viewing data originating from the physical/subspace interface from my memories or imagination. Not knowing if the target is decided upon before beginning the remote-viewing session additionally inhibits the viewer from wondering what the tasker would likely be using for a target based on any recent conversations that may have taken place with this person. In general, human taskers require a significant level of training so that they carefully avoid choosing targets that might be suspected by a remote viewer, and the best taskers have well-deserved reputations for consistently designing diverse and unpredictable targets. Using a computer to pick a target at random from a large pool of diverse targets adds a level of insurance in this regard, and this process is used in experimental designs needing the highest level of scientific controls.

It is helpful to explain further why computers are sometimes used to task a viewer. During remote-viewing training as well as in some process-oriented experiments, tasking is typically done by humans, not computers. There are both convenience and heuristic reasons for this. But when experiments are designed to supply proof of psi functioning, or which require the most rigorous controls for other reasons, computers are normally used to select a target at random from a large pool of diverse targets. This is to avoid any experimental contamination that may result from either human taskers picking targets that they know or suspect viewers tend to describe, or viewers describing targets that they know or suspect the taskers like to task. In process-oriented experiments that are designed as preliminary explorations into the mechanisms of psi functioning, no attempt is normally made to prove the existence of psi functioning, and less stringent requirements for target selection processes typically cause no harm as long as target selection is done carefully by a trained tasker who avoids any pattern in tasking. Indeed, sometimes the requirements of exploratory experiments require that a human tasker be used, such as the situation described in chapter 3 of this volume. In this volume, research is presented using both human and computer taskers, where the method chosen depends on the needs of the experiment.

Continuing with my example showing how a remote-viewing session would proceed, knowing nothing about a target, I would only work with the numbers, say, 1234/5678. My conscious mind would not know what target is associated with these numbers, but my subspace mind would know the target immediately. A productive session would then include good sketches of the structure, or at least aspects of the structure, together with written descriptive data of the building and its surroundings, including people who may be in or near the building.

The reader may at this point wonder what then connects the target coordinates to any particular target? This addresses a much broader and fundamental question, one which only recently has had an answer. This question is, "What makes a target a target?" Much of this volume is dedicated to answering this question. A short (but very unsatisfactory) answer to this question is that the thoughts of one or more critical individuals at a crucial point in time act to establish the target. But in truth, the answer to this question is not at all obvious, so I ask the reader to be patient with this point, allowing me to explain both a more extended version of this question as well as its answer in the chapters that follow.

When a remote-viewing session begins, the viewer systematically works through at least four different sections of the SRV procedures. These sections are called "phases," of which there are five. The fifth phase contains special procedures and is not normally used in research designs. In each phase the viewer is brought into either a closer or an altered association with the target. Remote viewing is performed by writing — on pieces of plain white paper with a pen — sketches, symbols, and words that describe aspects of the target. Here is a rough outline of the five phases of the "Basic SRV" process (as compared with more involved sets of procedures, such as "Enhanced SRV" and "Advanced SRV" — see the glossary):

- Phase 1. This establishes initial contact with the target. It also sets up a pattern of data acquisition and exploration that is continued in later phases. This is the only phase that directly uses the target coordinates. Once initial contact with the target is established, the coordinates are no longer needed.

Phase 1 essentially involves drawing and decoding an "ideogram" in order to determine basic descriptive characteristics of various components of the target. ("Decoding" and "ideogram" are defined below.) Phase 1 also includes drawing sketches of these components.

- Phase 2. Information obtained in this phase explicitly employs all of the five senses: hearing, touch, sight, taste, and smell, in that order. This phase also obtains initial magnitudes that are related to the target's various dimensions.
- Phase 3. This phase is a sketch of the target.
- Phase 4. Target contact in this phase is more detailed. This phase involves the use of an informational matrix that is designed to allow the viewer to gather a broad range of information about the target, as well as to probe particular aspects of the target to obtain more specific information when needed. Additional sketches are also made in Phase 4.
- Phase 5. In this phase the remote viewer can conduct some guided explorations of the target that would be potentially too leading to be allowed in Phase 4. For example, one Phase 5 procedure is a locational sketch in which the viewer locates a target in relation to some geographically defined area, such as the United States. The leading idea here is that the viewer is told that the target is located in the United States. Again, Phase 5 procedures are not normally used in basic-science research experiments at the Institute, and no Phase 5 procedures have been used in the experiments presented in this volume.

Shifting the Awareness to the Physical/Subspace Interface

If one were to simply command the mind to perceive something via the physical/subspace interface, the attempt would likely fail. The conscious mind initially acts as if it is threatened in some way by the presence of the interface. When given a chance, the conscious mind typically goes to enormous lengths in order to maintain the focus of perception, even to the point of mimicking the "flavor" of information traversing the interface. That is, if allowed, the conscious mind can trick virtually anyone into thinking that they are perceiving something accurately through their subspace connection, whereas the reality is that the information is nothing more than the fraudulent consequences of conscious-mind trickery. Analogously, having the conscious mind say, "Now I will perceive something through the physical/subspace interface" is comparable to having a thief say that he will now call the police; the stated activity simply does not occur, pledges of intent notwithstanding. Since the conscious mind still controls the decision to contact the interface, it remains in control of the mind's center of awareness. To break this lock on a viewer's perceptions, something needs to happen to allow the subspace mind direct access to the awareness potential of the viewer. That is, the subspace mind needs to get some uncorrupted information through the physical/subspace interface which can then lead the viewer to a firmer grip on the correct stream of information.

This uncorrupted (or at least, hopefully, less corrupted) piece of information is called an "ideogram," and it is the first thing done in Phase 1 of SRV. An ideogram is essentially a written squiggle. The viewer writes the target coordinates on a piece of paper, and then immediately places the point of the pen to the right of the coordinates, and a momentary movement of the pen creates a drawing. This drawing is the ideogram, and the subspace mind of the viewer is trying to use this drawing to convey information about the target to the conscious mind of the viewer without giving the conscious mind an ability to intercept and alter the information.

The subspace and conscious minds of remote viewers eventually learn to cooperate smoothly between their relative spheres of activity. But new viewers nearly always report a tension as the conscious mind learns to "let go" and the subspace mind learns to "jump in." Habits die hard in the competition for the mind's perceptual focus. But eventually a happy state is developed in which the subspace and physical minds of a viewer feel more as one, rather than as different entities separated by a narrow bridge (the interface).

The subspace mind of the viewer is normally very eager to establish a communicative link to the conscious mind. To this end, remote viewers train the subspace mind to deliver certain ideogram shapes that are predetermined to mean certain things. For example, there are certain ideograms for structures, other ideograms for water, others for subjects, and so on. Properly executed, ideograms are often some of the most reliable pieces of information about a target. Individually, they contain an absolute minimum of information about the target, but at least they give the viewer a foothold from which further explorations of the target can occur.

The process that follows the drawing of the ideogram is standardized in the sense that it is repeated throughout the session in all phases. Some extra vocabulary is needed at this point to describe this process. The process is to move gradually from describing what is called "low-level" information to "higher-level" information. All of this is done by "decoding." Decoding is the process of translating intuitive feelings about a target component (such as land, a structure, a subject, etc.) into descriptive words. In Phase 1, this is done by placing the point of the viewer's pen on the ideogram and "feeling" the target through the ideogram. This is called "probing the ideogram."

Remote viewers train to decode ideograms. After practice, they become able to recognize the shape of the ideogram, and to combine this recognition with the feeling of the target component that the ideogram represents. For example, if the ideogram represents a structure, it will likely have a shape that is one of the predetermined shapes for structure ideograms. Moreover, when the viewer probes the ideogram, the viewer will be able to tell that the structure itself (not the ideogram) feels hard. The initial impressions that the viewer obtains from the target through the ideogram are nearly always "low-level." Low-level information is always the most basic type of information that is possible about a target component. A typical type of very low-level information is whether or not the target component feels hard, soft, wet, or mushy.

After probing the ideogram to perceive this very low-level of information, and after decoding this from the probe and writing this description down, the viewer probes again, this time reaching for a slightly higher level of information, such as whether or not the target component is natural or manmade. With these two pieces of information (the first slightly lower-level than the second), the viewer makes a stab at trying to decode a basic description of this target component. This is where the viewer would write that the component feels like a structure, or land, or water, or a subject, and so on.

It is important to emphasize the low-to-higher progression of information decoding that has just been described. In terms of the progression, if the target component is a structure, then the viewer would first draw an ideogram representing a structure (the lowest level of abstraction for remote-viewing data). Then the viewer would probe the ideogram and most likely feel that the target component represented by the ideogram feels hard, and then after probing again, manmade. Only then does the viewer state that the target component is a structure, which is information at the highest level of abstraction.

After this, the viewer continues to probe the ideogram repeatedly to obtain more descriptive information about the target component. All of this information remains at a low-level of overall abstraction, but it is likely to be at a relatively higher level than simply hard or soft. For example, the viewer may feel that the target component is tall, made of natural materials (such as rock or wood), that it is on land, that it has a flat top, and so on. All of this is recorded, and the process of probing the ideogram and decoding the perceptions continues until the viewer feels that a visual image is beginning to form. At that point, the viewer attempts to sketch the target component. All of this, from the ideogram to the sketch, goes on one page of Phase 1.

The viewer repeats the above process typically five times, resulting in five pages of data, five ideograms, five lists of descriptive words, and five sketches. That ends Phase 1. In each pass through this process, viewers move from the lowest to the higher levels of abstraction with regard to their decoding attempts. They never begin a decoding process with a higher-level attempt. For example, a viewer would never draw an ideogram and immediately claim it represents a structure or a subject or anything else. It is always necessary to probe the ideogram for information that is at the lowest level of abstraction before moving on to the higher levels.

The above discussion of lower and higher levels of abstraction is totally relative. None of the information obtained by a remote viewer is actually at a high level of abstraction. A truly high level of abstraction would be if the viewer was trying to explicitly identify the target component. For example, a viewer may perceive a structure, and the viewer should describe this target component as a structure. Viewers are encouraged not to name things, such as the "Empire State Building in Manhattan." That would be too high a level of abstraction, and such a statement would normally be a result of the viewer's conscious mind making a conclusion regarding the subspace perceptions, not a result of the perceptions themselves. (Although, viewers sometimes do identify targets explicitly.) Thus, all good remote-viewing data are low-level. All truly high-level data are suspect of being conscious mind inventions. But within the ranks of acceptable low-level data, there are relative degrees. Some data can be at a higher level than others, and yet all of the data can still be low-level generally.

Here is an example of a data stream that is entirely low-level, but which progresses from the lowest levels of abstraction to relatively higher levels: structure ideogram ➔ hard ➔ manmade ➔ declaration of structure ➔ tall, tan, natural materials, thin, multi-level, pointed top, rectangular patterns on side ➔ a sketch of the structure. All of this falls within the idea of low-level data, but there is clearly a progression from the lowest possible levels of abstraction to higher levels, which is not the same as truly "high-level" data.

The distinction between truly low-level and high-level data (not relative gradations within the low-level category) is sufficiently important that I make a special effort to distinguish the two. Skeptics of the remote-viewing phenomenon often demand high-level descriptions of a target, and this demand is simply impossible to satisfy for reasons that I will describe later. Remote viewing, thus far, only works reliably with viewers describing their perceptions only in low-level terms. The best way to understand the differences between low- and high-level data is through examples. Below is a list of examples of each.

Low-level Data	High-level Data
explosive energy	bomb blast
sand, water, salty tastes, waves, perfume smells	beach
large waves, water	tidal wave
squirmy, primitive animal life, thick skin	dinosaurs
tall structure with many floors	skyscraper

wooden structure near animal life	barn with farm animals
booming sound	explosion
sloping dry land with energetics or intense heat at top	volcano
many rooms side-by-side in multi-floor structure	hotel
gathering of subjects	world meeting of heads-of-state
slow moving structure, air above and water below	boat
fast moving metallic structure	spacecraft
gathering of subjects in uniforms	Pentagon briefing meeting
structure on dry land	The White House
a long structure with two parallel lines with regularly spaced cross-hatching	railroad tracks
moving metal structures with subjects inside	cars
people, vapor, difficult breathing	gas attack
high energy expelling outward	explosion
hard, cold, floating, ice	iceberg
hard to breath, pain, gasping	suicide drowning
one subject in trouble due to intentional force	Kennedy assassination

holding small metal things for defense	guns
many groups in allegiance to a central authority	United Nations

Nearly all of the examples of low-level data above are actually at the higher end of the low-level category. But they are nonetheless clearly distinguishable from the truly high-level data listed along side. Thus, Phase 1 proceeds from the very lowest possible levels of abstraction to the higher levels of acceptable low-level data. But truly high-level data are never allowed in SRV at all. The following discussions of the process of moving from lower to higher levels of data abstraction are all intended to remain within the context of generally low-level data. When higher levels are discussed, I am referring to relative levels within the overall low-level category.

The key to maintaining a steady stream of data transfer across the physical/subspace interface is to continue a wave-like flow of moving from lower to higher levels of abstraction in the decoding process. This is done on each page of Phase 1. When the viewer shifts in Phase 2 to perceive a set of sensory data related to sounds, textures, temperatures, visuals (such as colors), tastes, and smells, this is done with a mixture of descriptions that span the range of acceptable low-level data, with the greater weight on the lower end of this range.

After completing Phase 2, the viewer attempts to sketch the target. This is an important assembly stage in SRV. In each pass through the target in Phase 1 (remember, there are five such passes), a sketch is hopefully obtained for each component addressed by each ideogram. In Phase 3, the viewer attempts to put these separate components together by drawing a more complete sketch of the target. This is the first such attempt to assemble the parts of the target. The viewer continues this assembly process in Phase 4. But again, the Phase 3 sketch is a useful reminder of the overall pattern of moving from lower to higher levels of abstraction in a gradual way. The Phase 3 sketch is a more complete sketch than the previous Phase 1 sketches, and it is by definition a sketch made at a higher level of abstraction. Thus, one can see that the process of moving from lower to higher levels of abstraction is repeated not only within each page of Phase 1, but also across the entire SRV session generally.

Ideally, the description of the target more fully comes together in Phase 4. Again, the descriptions of the target always fall within the range of low-level data. But the breadth and depth of the low-level descriptions of the target in Phase 4 can often be profound. Phase 4 can include sketches of the target or some of its components. Phase 4 also can contain sentences or phrases that allow the viewer to describe the target with a greater latitude of expression.

Subspace "Thinking"

The subspace mind does not "think" the way the conscious mind thinks. Remote-viewing data do not come across as words, or even ideas that are directly comparable to words. Rather, perceptions made using remote viewing are best described as direct and passive perceptions. An example is useful here. If one were to remote view a boat, one would not mentally see a high resolution image of a boat and then write, "I see a boat." Rather one might perceive an object with an irregular shape. It might feel metal (if it is a metal boat), and the viewer may perceive it to have a curved bottom and a flat top. If the boat has a sail, the viewer may perceive a triangular shape on top of the metal object. Finally, the viewer may perceive water below the object. As a last stage in the process, the viewer may conclude that this description matches that of a boat, but there would be no direct conscious recognition that the object is a boat.

The direct perceptions of the subspace mind have to be translated into words that represent ideas. Ideas are conscious mind artifacts. Ideas are used by the conscious mind to organize perceptions into templates that allow a person to navigate day-to-day life. But the ideas themselves are not directly perceived. A person can feel a rock, and note that it has a rough texture. The person can also feel that it is heavy, and that its color is brown. But the idea that it is a rock is a conscious mind intellectual invention that organizes these perceptions into a useful packet that can be utilized repeatedly in any similar situation in which a person "interacts" with a rock. Thus, the words "rock" and "boat" are labels that organize collections of perceptions. When saying that something is a rock and that another thing is a boat, the person is accessing memories that associate the correct direct perceptions for each object.

The subspace mind has no known ability to work on the level of ideas. Current research indicates that the subspace mind cannot directly inform a viewer that a target component is a boat or a rock or anything else. Rather, the subspace mind can only feed direct perceptions into the conscious awareness of the viewer, and the viewer must then collect these conscious perceptions and try to sort out the nature of the target. This is the reason for the decoding process in remote viewing. A viewer decodes a target by trying to translate the direct perceptions into words that describe the perceptions with the lowest level of intellectual abstraction. Truly low-level descriptions must reflect the nature of the direct perceptions as closely as possible. Only after a sufficiently large number of perceptions are decoded at the lowest level of abstraction can the viewer venture into modestly higher-level descriptive territory.

Thus, subspace "thinking" is awareness without idea processing. But for this awareness to be useful in a remote-viewing session, there must be some interaction between direct awareness and the conscious mind thinking process. The key is to operate the conscious mind thinking process so that it most closely parallels the awareness capabilities of the subspace mind. Words that describe the direct perceptions using the lowest levels of intellectual abstraction are optimal for accomplishing this.

The Remote-Viewing Experience

When remote-viewing sessions begin, remote viewers typically perceive a target with a clarity characteristic of, say, understanding the meaning of a fog horn on a misty night. While there may always be difficulty discerning the precise direction and distance of a fog horn under such conditions, it is nonetheless clear that a sound like a fog horn is perceived. With experience and skill, a remote viewer decodes perceptions of a target in the same way that a yachtsman decodes the signs associated with the fog horn. Upon hearing the fog horn, the yachtsman soon discerns the direction of the horn, the outline of the nearby coast, and the identity of the lighthouse from which the shrouded beacon shines.

"Remote viewing" is actually not an entirely appropriate term. This is because all of the senses—hearing, touch, sight, taste, and smell—are active during the remote-viewing process. More accurately, one might call the experience "remote perception." Nonetheless, since "remote viewing" has been widely adopted in the scientific as well as the popular literatures, it makes sense simply to continue the use of the current term with the proviso that the experience is not limited to visual pictures. But visual images are a part of the remote-viewing process, and it is useful to explain the nature of these images.

When one looks at an object, the light reflected off of that object enters the eye, and an electrochemical signal is generated that is transmitted along the optic nerve to the brain. Scientific studies have demonstrated that this signal is "displayed" on a layer of cells in the brain analogous to how an image is projected from a movie projector onto a movie screen. The brain then interprets this image to determine what is being seen. When someone remembers an object, the remembered image of the object is also projected onto that same layer of cells in the brain.

If one remembers an object and visualizes it while the eyes are open and looking at something else, then the same layer of cells in the brain contains two separate projected images. The image originating from the open eyes is the brightest, whereas the remembered image is relatively dim and somewhat translucent, since one can see through the translucent image to perceive the ocular originating image. For those readers who would like to read an accessible but more in-depth treatment of the physiology of visual and remembered images, I strongly recommend an article in *The New York Times* by Sandra Blakeslee titled, "Seeing and Imagining: Clues to the Workings of the Mind's Eye" (*The New York Times*, 31 August 1993, pp. B5N & B6N).

A remote viewer also perceives an image, but it is different from the remembered image or the ocular image. The remote-viewing image is dimmer, foggier, and fuzzier. Indeed, one tends to "feel" the image as much as one visualizes it. It is not easy for the subspace minds of humans to transmit high-resolution, bright images to the brain, and this fact is useful in the training process for remote viewing. If a student states that he or she perceived a clear, bright image of a target, this image almost certainly originated from the viewer's imagination rather than from the subspace connection.

This does not mean that the relatively low-resolution remote-viewing experience is inferior to a visual experience based on eyesight. Remember that all of the five senses — plus the sense of the subspace realm — operate during the remote-viewing process. Thus, it is actually possible to obtain a high-quality collection of diverse and penetrating data. The remote-viewing experience is simply different from, not superior or inferior to, physical experiences of observation.

A remote viewer's contact with a target can occasionally be so intimate that a new term, "bilocation," is used to describe the experience. Approximately halfway through a remote-viewing session, the viewer sometimes begins to feel that he or she is at two places at once. The rate at which data come through from the remote viewing signal at this point is typically very fast, and the viewer has to record as much as possible in a relatively short period of time.

At this point it is important to explain that it is impossible to demand that any two remote viewers report the exact same perceptions for any given target. Skeptics of remote viewing have in the past complained that variations in remote-viewing results across remote viewers are proof that the phenomenon does not exist. But this demand reflects not a failure of remote viewing, but a misunderstanding of the remote-viewing process. Remember that the remote-viewing process involves direct perceptions of a target that get decoded into descriptive words. There is no guarantee that any one viewer will focus his or her perceptions on the exact same thing at a target. Moreover, since the perceptions have to be decoded, there may be variations in the decoding experience as well. Thus, two remote viewers can collect two different but accurate sets of descriptive data for the same target, depending on the interplay between the focus of perception and the decoding process. The question then turns to why some viewers focus on one aspect of a target while others focus on another?

Experience has shown that viewers tend to be attracted to certain aspects of any particular target, and not all viewers are attracted to the same aspects. Thus, one viewer may perceive the psychological condition of people that are at a target location, whereas another viewer may focus on their physical health. Yet another viewer may spend most of a session describing the physical attributes of the local environment within which the target subjects are located. For example, I once assigned a target of a World War II bombing to a group of remote viewing students. One of the students was a doctor and another a photographer. After the session was completed, I reviewed each student's work. The entire class perceived the bombing incident to some degree, with some students having more complete descriptions than others.   But the doctor described the physical characteristics of the bombing victims closely, including their medical problems resulting from the bombing.   On the other hand, the photographer's session read more like a detailed description of the physical characteristics of the event, including an accurate characterization of the geographical terrain where the bombing took place.

"Closing" the Session

The idea of "closing" a remote-viewing session is relatively new in the development of the Scientific Remote Viewing methodology. It is more than just giving a remote viewer target feedback, or letting an analyst see a remote-viewing session. As is explained and illustrated in later chapters of this volume, closing a remote-viewing session is now thought to be one of the most important components of the remote-viewing process.

"Closing" a remote-viewing session is done by the first person who seriously examines the remote-viewing data obtained in a session. This person does not need to be the remote viewer. From work done elsewhere (SRI International, SAIC, and others), it has long been known that giving a remote viewer target feedback is not a requirement for successful remote viewing. But someone eventually does need to look at each remote-viewing session, and this person can be either the remote viewer (if the target feedback is given to the viewer first) or a separate analyst of the remote-viewing data (if the data are first examined by someone other than the viewer). When a session is closed, the relevant person examines the remote-viewing data while knowing the target. If the remote-viewing data are given to an analyst, then the analyst would also be given the target definition, and the analyst would compare the remote-viewing data with the known or suspected characteristics of the target as directed by the target definition. If the target is defined by a photograph, then the photograph essentially defines the target's qualitative parameters. However, if the target is a verbal description of a place or event, then the analyst normally obtains supplemental information to fully inform him or her as to the target's essential characteristics. The same process holds if the person closing the session is the remote viewer. Again, closing a session is the process of making the *first* comparison between the remote-viewing data and the target.

In research conducted at the Institute, we have found that the quality of the closing experience is enormously important to the quality of the remote-viewing process, and I explain this more fully in subsequent chapters. Although it is a bit analogous to putting the cart before the horse by discussing this subject in any depth before presenting the results of the chapters that follow, some comments seem essential to introduce at this point. In our experiments, we have asked our remote viewers what happens to them when they close one of their own sessions. In general, the response is typically that the viewers have subjectively experienced what can best be described as a "sinking" feeling when they review their data. As they examine their pages of data, they begin to feel like they are again remote viewing the target, as if they are reconnecting with themselves (in consciousness) when they originally viewed the target. To some extent, there is a sense of bi-location during the closing. When an analyst who is not the remote viewer closes a remote-viewing session, there is less of a sinking feeling, and less of the sense of bi-location, but there is nonetheless a sense of penetrating concentration that is very intense, as the analyst's mind shifts back and forth between the data in the remote-viewing session and the description of the target as given in the target disclosure. In general, we have found in our own work that the most successful remote-viewing sessions are accompanied by closings that follow one of these two patterns. We have also found that shortcuts or corruptions in the closing process can dramatically affect the quality of the session accuracy. In our current work, closing a session is now considered an essential element of the entire SRV process. It takes a minimum of half an hour to properly close a session, followed by a long break of at least an hour before beginning to work on another session. Again, I explain more about how I have come to these conclusions later in this volume.

The Experimental Conditions

The conditions under which remote-viewing experiments are conducted are crucial to understanding the results of such experiments. A useful set of criteria for setting up remote-viewing experiments has been outlined by McMoneagle (1998, pp. 24 & 30): (1) the viewers should not know anything about the target when they conduct their sessions, (2) the monitor of a remote-viewing session (if a monitor is used) should not know anything about the target, (3) the analyst of the remote-viewing sessions should not participate in other aspects of the experiment, (4) the tasker should not participate in the collection of information or any other aspect of the experiment, and (5) a monitor (if a monitor is used) should not work with multiple remote viewers within the context of the same experiment. Most psi experiments will likely have their own set of criteria that may modify or expand upon the above list, depending on the needs of the experimental design. Table 2.1 (located at the end of the chapter) summarizes the criteria that have been used for the experiments described in chapters 3 through 6 of this volume.

As can be seen from table 2.1, criteria (2) and (5) of McMoneagle's list are not applicable to the experiments described here since no monitors have been used to assist the collection of these data. A monitor is a person who works with a remote viewer while the remote-viewing session is being done. There are reasons for sometimes wanting to use a monitor during a remote-viewing session, and it has frequently been compared with a pilot wanting someone else to handle navigational tasks while he or she flies the plane. But monitors can also inadvertently lead or otherwise interfere with a remote viewer in ways that may be difficult to control, and the decision was made not to utilize monitors at all in these experiments. In all of these experiments, all remote viewers worked totally alone while conducting their sessions, and there were no other persons nearby who could have interacted with them in any way when they collected their data. These viewing conditions are described in table 2.1 as "solo and isolated."

Criterion (1) in McMoneagle's list is, of course, entirely appropriate for these experiments, and all of the remote viewers who participated in these experiments worked "blind," in the sense that they were given no information about the target prior to conducting a remote-viewing session. In some situations (none which apply to the research presented in this volume), working "blind" can also include a minimal level of "front-loading," which means that viewers might be told something about possible target parameters, such as that the target is a place or an event. When this occurs it is important to identify these parameters in the discussion of the results. Table 2.1 includes the amount of front-loading that occurred in all of these experiments. In all of the experiments described here, there was absolutely no front-loading of any kind. In the case of the experiment described in chapter 5, the viewer was aware that no flying targets were allowed in the target pool, but there were otherwise no restrictions in the target pool. Such a minimal restriction in the target possibilities is normally not considered front-loading. Nonetheless, for completeness, this information is included in table 2.1. Reasons for employing this minimal level of target restriction in this single instance are described in chapter 5 and follow suggestions made by other psi researchers with regard to limitations in "target bandwidth" that are applicable to that experiment.

Criterion (4) in McMoneagle's list addresses the issue of whether the tasker, or the person who chooses a target for a particular experiment, should be involved in any other aspect of the remote-viewing experiment. Obviously, the tasker cannot be a viewer in an experiment since he or she would then know the target in advance. The tasker should also not take part in the data collection process. Thus, the tasker should not be the monitor of the remote-viewing session (if the session has a monitor). Also, unless there is a particular reason for doing so (see below), the tasker should normally not also be an analyst in an experiment. This is particularly important in some situations in which a remote-viewing session is compared with a set of potential targets, one real and the others decoys. If the real target is determined (i.e., known) at the time of the analysis, and if the analyst knows the real target because he or she is also the tasker, then the analysis is corrupted since all targets would not be considered equally in the analyst's mind when the data are evaluated. There may be other reasons for wanting to compartmentalize each aspect of a remote-viewing experiment depending on the particular design and intent of an experiment, and it is normal for researchers to identify all the relevant conditions that apply in each situation.

From table 2.1 it can be seen that human taskers were used for the experiments presented in chapters 3, 4, and 6. For the experiment described in chapter 5, the tasker was a computer program that picked targets randomly from a large target pool, and McMoneagle's criterion (4) is certainly met in this case. With regard to chapter 6, the tasker was a respected individual with no previous contact or association with The Farsight Institute who did not participate in any other aspect of the experiment. For the experiment described in chapter 4, the tasker did not conduct the analysis, nor could he have done so while still satisfying the design of that experiment, as is described in that chapter.

A special condition exists for the experiment described in chapter 3, and in this single experiment, the tasker also shared the role of the analyst. This was done purposefully as part of the design of this experiment to help isolate all target identifying mental activity with one person, as is described in chapter 3. Conflicts of the sort described above in which the tasker and analyst are the same were avoided by having the experiment's test determinant (see below) occur *after* the analysis of the data (which means that the tasker/analyst was blind to the correct target among each set of targets both while determining target sets and while judging the remote-viewing data). The experiment was designed this way because other experiments similar to the one described in chapter 3 had been conducted previously at The Farsight Institute in which tasking was totally separated from analysis, and a particularly stubborn phenomenon occurred that did not lend itself well to causal identification. The decision was made in this case to try combining the tasking and analysis processes with one person in an attempt to isolate all thoughts which connect a target to remote-viewing data (and thus which might possibly interfere with the data collection process) as a means of keeping track of such potential influences. The result of this experiment was fruitful, in the sense that ideas were gleaned from the experiment that were later tested in situations in which the tasking and analysis processes were again isolated, as is described more fully in chapter 3 and later chapters.

McMoneagle's criterion (3) is similar in intent to criterion (4), and it involves isolating the analysis process in a psi experiment from other aspects of the experiment. Many psi experiments involve an event that determines some crucial element of the experiment. For example, a random number generator may be used to pick a target from a pool, or the activity of the stock market may determine the choice of a target. In this volume, the event that structures the outcome of a remote-viewing experiment is called the "test determinant." In general, it is important to separate the analysis from other aspects of an experiment because the analysis can be corrupted if it interacts with the test determinant. For example, if the test determinant is a lottery outcome, the analyst should not know the lottery outcome when analyzing the remote-viewing data since this would lead the analyst to weigh data more heavily that correspond with the lottery outcome.

Test determinants were used for experiments presented in chapters in 3, 4, and 5, but not chapter 6 [and thus McMoneagle's criterion (3) is not applicable for chapter 6]. For the experiment presented in chapter 5, there was no human analyst since a computer was used to obtain objective analysis of the remote-viewing data, and McMoneagle's criterion (3) is obviously met. For the experiment presented in chapter 3, the analysis of the remote-viewing sessions was done prior to the occurrence of the test determinant (which in this case was a future lottery outcome), and thus the analyst had no knowledge of — and was not compromised by — the outcome of the test determinant when he analyzed the remote-viewing data. With regard to the results presented in chapter 4, the test determinant was the time and date on which the tasker wrote each remote viewing target (see chapter 4 for an explanation of this). In this case, all analysis was done by someone other than the tasker, and who obviously had no knowledge of when the tasker wrote (i.e., determined) a target. The analyst did not become aware of when the tasker determined a target until all of the remote-viewing sessions were analyzed, as is explained in chapter 4.

Table 2.1 contains additional information that goes beyond the criteria discussed above, such as whether the person who closed a remote-viewing session was the analyst or the viewer, whether or not the viewers were aware of the test determinant when they obtained feedback for their remote-viewing data, and whether analysis was objective and computer-based as compared with subjective scoring done by a human. This table serves as a useful summarizing tool for the experimental conditions encountered in this volume, and it might be useful to refer back to this table from time to time as needed when reading the later chapters.

This concludes the introductory thematic treatment of the remote-viewing process. As mentioned previously, detailed descriptions of the mechanics of Scientific Remote Viewing (plus a large library of examples) can be obtained freely from the web site of The Farsight Institute (www.farsight.org). But this chapter has covered the remote-viewing process sufficiently well to allow readers to follow the experiments that are described in the subsequent chapters. These experiments — and the knowledge that we gain from them — are, indeed, the essential core of this book.

TABLE 2.1. Experimental Conditions for Research Presented in Chapters 3-6

	Chapter 3	Chapter 4	Chapter 5	Chapter 6
Viewer blind to target	Yes	Yes	Yes	Yes
Monitor used	No	No	No	No
Viewing condition	Solo and isolated	Solo and isolated	Solo and isolated	Solo and isolated
Tasking	Pairs of contrasting targets designed by human tasker	Targets chosen by human tasker	Targets randomly chosen by computer from large pool	Targets chosen by independent human tasker not associated with The Farsight Institute
Analysis	Subjective judging of RV sessions against target pairs using human analyst	Subjective numerical scoring using human analyst	Objective computer-based evaluation — no human analyst	Both subjective numerical scoring (human analyst) and objective computer-based evaluation (no human analyst)
Target Restrictions	None	None	No flying targets	None
Viewer Front-loading	None	None	No flying targets, otherwise none	None
Test determinant	Lottery outcome	Tasking time	Lottery outcome	None
Analyst kept blind of test determinant outcome during analysis	Yes — judging occurred before the timing of the test determinant	Yes — tasking times were not known to the analyst during analysis	Yes — no human analyst	Not applicable

Viewer given target feedback	Yes	Yes	Yes	Yes
Viewer aware of test determinant outcome when reviewing feedback	Yes	No	No	Not applicable
First person to review session data	Analyst	Viewer	Viewer	Viewer
Tasker different from analyst	No	Yes	Yes	Yes
Special conditions	Tasker and analyst the same	Analyst and one viewer the same	None	None

CHAPTER 3

Cross-Cutting Psi Channels in Remote Viewing

As is often the case with all fields of science, a puzzle emerges with experimental research that offers no simple explanation. Attempts to resolve the puzzle more often than not leads to years of frustration among scientists. This indeed was the early reaction of many physicists to the study of quantum mechanics, and in particular the phenomenon of entanglement. With remote-viewing research, there has similarly existed a puzzle, one that has plagued investigators in this field for decades. If a remote viewer is told to perceive a target — one that is chosen from a list of possible targets — why should the remote viewer so often describe one of the targets on the list, but not the chosen target (that is, the "correct" one)? The resolution of this puzzle has been a prime motivation for a great deal of research conducted at The Farsight Institute. As readers will see as they proceed through this book, the resolution of this puzzle leads us to an entirely new understanding of consciousness, and indeed physical reality, one that is as surprising as it is profound.

Due in part to the puzzle mentioned above, the history of remote-viewing research is filled with conflicting claims of success and failure. Previous work in the laboratories of SRI International, Science Applications International Corporation (SAIC), and elsewhere under the gifted leadership of Harold Puthoff, Russell Targ, Edwin May, and others suggest a clear pattern of remote-viewing capability. Laboratory results are sometimes striking in terms of descriptions of the manifested phenomenon as well as accumulated statistical evidence using repeated trials. There has also been considerable success in replicating evidence of psi phenomena across laboratories if you view the results in terms of effect sizes as argued by Utts (1996). But many attempts to replicate specific laboratory events, and sometimes statistical significance, have often proved more frustrating. Indeed, Targ (1999, 89) recently noted, "We sometimes hear psi is a weak and unreliable faculty," and to date there has been no breakthrough that has allowed researchers to understand the apparently fickle nature of psi phenomena generally, or remote viewing specifically.

Beginning in 1997, a determined effort was made at The Farsight Institute to isolate the cause of a remote-viewing event that seemed to be hindering efforts to remote view a target from a predetermined list of targets. This is a targeting process that has often been used in psi research. The basic and well-known problem involves having a remote viewer perceive a chosen target from a list of targets. The viewer does not know anything about any of the targets on the list prior to viewing. Also prior to viewing, a "correct" target is chosen by an outside agency or a random event. The data from the remote-viewing session is then given to a judge (or a panel of judges) who then tries to determine from the remote-viewing data which is the correct target. This is normally done by ranking the targets in the list in terms of their correspondence with the viewing data. Of course, the judge is not aware of the correct choice prior to making the ranking (i.e., the judge is "blind"). The specific problem investigated at the Institute is one in which the viewing data either clearly correspond with a target on the list, but the target is not the correct target, or the viewing data seem to contain aspects of two or more targets on the list. Here we are dealing with situations in which this phenomenon appears repeatedly — even systematically, and we are clear that we are not looking at remote-viewing data that simply match generic characteristics of other targets by chance. Indeed, this is precisely what this current chapter is attempting to sort out.

Again, this is not a new problem. Targ and Harary (1984) have, indeed, made an early reference to this problem, suggesting that targets on a list may be placed in a "psychic bubble" from which viewers draw their perceptions. In some of their experiments at Stanford Research Institute (later SRI International), they noted that some of their remote viewers would make excellent descriptions of other targets on a list, but not the correct target. This seemed to happen less often when geographical coordinates were used to identify targets, and more often when pictures were used, or when the targets were chosen from among a collection of objects on shelves. But the bottom line has always been the same. Sometimes viewers would make uncannily accurate descriptions of the correct target, whereas other times the remote-viewing data would correspond to another target (an incorrect target) on the list, and yet other times the data would seem to represent a mish-mash of various target aspects from more than one target.

Current Research Background

During my exposure to this phenomenon in experimental situations at The Farsight Institute, I became convinced that some as-yet-undetermined mechanism was causing the remote viewers to mix their perceptions across targets. The phenomenon acts as if there is a cross-cutting psychic connection between the viewer and various other known potential targets. Sometimes the connection would be clear, and the correct target would dominate the perceptions of the remote viewers, whereas other times the connection would cross-cut with perceptions of the other targets. In the former case, the result would appear nearly miraculous. In the latter case, the ultimate result would look like an "off" or poor session. Critics of remote viewing would use the "off" results to declare the general phenomenon invalid, while supporters bemoaned the fickle nature of the phenomenon (see esp. Hyman 1996, Jahn 1982).

In early experimental work at The Farsight Institute, we tried (usually successfully) to replicate some of the previous findings that were reported by the groups at SRI International and SAIC. In particular, we used lists of five targets and had viewers attempt to remote view a chosen target from the list. We later used lists of ten targets. To choose the correct target, each target would be associated with a single numerical digit from 0 to 9, and an outside event would be used to determine a chosen digit, and thus the correct target to view. We began using lottery drawings in the states of Georgia and Virginia to make these choices, since these events were clearly not controlled by ourselves, and because they were conveniently available daily events. Thus, if the first ball of, say, a Cash 3 lottery outcome in Georgia was the digit 8, then the correct target for that experiment would be the target that was associated with this digit in our list of targets for that experiment.

During these early experiments, we repeatedly witnessed the apparent cross-cutting of targets among our viewers. That some authentic psychic mechanism was involved in the remote-viewing phenomenon was clear to us since some of our sessions yielded unambiguous hits. But the problem of "off" sessions (sometimes referred to as "switched" sessions due to the way in which a viewer would apparently view the wrong target on a list) was a persistent phenomenon. We could not determine whether the problem was the list itself (causing the so-called "psychic bubble") or errors in the perceptions of the viewers. I do not describe the details of these early experiments here since they are referenced only to offer some historical background to the more revealing experiments described below. For the research presented in this and other chapters of this volume however, full details are included.

The Breakthrough

A breakthrough came when we began to notice that the thoughts that a judge or analyst had while examining the remote-viewing sessions seemed to correspond with the outcome of the sessions. We then began to systematically take note of the mental experiences of the analysts that were examining the remote-viewing data. We saw a remarkable pattern.

An example may be heuristically useful here. In one instance, a collection of three sessions were sent to an analyst. All the viewers were supposed to view a "correct" target from a set of two targets, with the correct target being determined subsequently (i.e., dynamically) by a future scheduled outside random event. The analyst was aware of the two target possibilities (in the binary set) for these sessions while (of course) the viewers did not know this. This analyst had a bias in favor of one viewer (call this viewer A), thinking that this viewer was always more accurate than others. This analyst also felt that another viewer (viewer B) ranked second, and yet a third viewer (viewer C) was ranked third, all in terms of their skill in viewing.

The analyst first examined the data obtained by viewer A. The analyst then examined the results for viewer B. But prior to examining the data obtained from viewer B, the analyst noted that he expected the data obtained from viewer B certainly to corroborate those obtained from viewer A. In this instance, one of the targets in the binary pair contained a large pyramid structure in a dry environment. Viewer A's data did indeed describe a large pyramid structure in a dry environment. Also, viewer B's data described a large pyramid structure in a dry environment.

The analyst then began to examine the data obtained from viewer C. The analyst noted that he thought that the large pyramid structure was such an easy target that viewer C would probably discern it as well. The first seven pages of session data obtained from viewer C did indeed contain a very clear description of a large pyramid structure. While examining page seven of viewer C's data, the analyst then noted that he did not think that viewer C was "good enough" to continue making such strong target contact with what must clearly be the correct target (based on the data from viewers A and B). The analyst then turned to the next page of the session and noted that the session from that point on departed dramatically from what was obtained previously in the first seven pages. Indeed, the new trend of the session was to describe a large crumpled and hollow metallic structure that was resting on the bottom of a large body of water. The analyst used this departure from the first theme of the session to confirm his suspicions regarding the viewing capabilities of viewer C.

As it turned out, the two targets for that experiment involved (1) a large pyramid structure in a desert and (2) the crashed remains of TWA Flight 800 on the bottom of the sea soon after the disaster. The "correct" target for that experiment (as determined by the outside random event) was the crashed remains of TWA Flight 800, and the "incorrect" target was the large pyramid structure. In retrospect, because of the observed timing between the thoughts of the analyst and the characteristics of the remote-viewing data, we began to speculate that the thoughts of the person examining the remote-viewing data might be guiding the perceptions of the viewers. Indeed, our cumulative research was beginning to suggest that it does not matter what is written down on a piece of paper to define a target. What seems to matter most is what is in the mind of the analyst when the remote-viewing data are examined. In the experiment described above, when the analyst "released" a viewer from prior expectations regarding what should or should not be viewed, then the viewer was psychically "free" to view the target differently. In this case, releasing viewer C was apparently done mentally by having the analyst think that the viewer was no longer going to be able to corroborate the results of viewer A. Viewer C then went on to remote view the correct target with considerable clarity. As mentioned above, these were early speculations on our part regarding what might be the mechanism causing the switched-session phenomenon. While we could not yet rule out other causes, we felt certain that we needed to investigate further what appeared to be a clear possibility regarding telepathically-mediated corruption of remote-viewing data by the analyst of a remote-viewing experiment.

The above example began to repeat itself in experiment after experiment as we continued to search for a pattern with the "off" sessions. This led to a desire to test the specific hypothesis that the thoughts of the analyst are indeed leading the viewer, and thus "creating" the target. To do this, we needed to create a new experimental design, one in which there would be separate and distinct target lists that the analyst would use in specific ways during different parts of the experiment. Using such separate target lists would allow us to localize the influence of the analyst's thoughts at any point in the experiment. In particular, we wanted to pull pairs of targets from a larger list of targets, and have the analyst focus only on one pair at a time when analyzing the sessions. We would then see if the sessions would describe targets from the mini lists of pairs that the analyst would be considering at the moment of analyzing each session, or if the sessions would describe targets that appear to come from the larger list. If the sessions described targets from the larger list, then we would reject the hypothesis that the thoughts of the analyst were guiding the sessions and conclude that some other mechanism is responsible for the "off" or "switched" sessions. But if the sessions described targets from just the binary pairs (i.e., the mini sub-lists of two target possibilities for each session), then we would conclude that the thoughts of the analyst were likely interfering with the data collection process while remote viewing.

At first this hypothesis that the thoughts of an analyst could corrupt the remote-viewing data collection process might seemed far-fetched. But remote viewing itself is a mental process that apparently involves a telepathic or clairvoyant component. Our own research has long been based on the working hypothesis that all humans are composite beings that have both physical and nonphysical components. The nonphysical components are defined as being all those external to the normal three-dimensional elements of reality. As outlined in the previous chapter, the physical component we call a body, and the nonphysical component we call a soul, or more formally, a "subspace aspect." Remote viewing seems to use the perceptive abilities of the subspace aspect to feed information into the electro-chemical physical mind using what appears to be a narrow bandwidth interface of some as-yet-undetermined nature. Saying that the thoughts of the analyst can interfere with the remote-viewing data collection process is no less bizarre than saying that remote viewing is possible in the first place. In both cases, a nonphysical mechanism is involved with information transference. The only additional ingredient needed to say that analyst-dependent corruption of remote-viewing data is possible is to assume that the subspace mind of the viewer is capable of knowing how the data are to be used in the end, and that the target becomes the desire to satisfy that use. If the thoughts of the analyst are what matters in defining the use of data resulting from a remote-viewing session, then it is possible that the viewer makes a mental telepathic link with the analyst when conducting the session.

The major problem with such a new experimental design would be that some of the sessions would likely still suffer from data corruption if the analyst-leading hypothesis is correct, since there would be at least two targets in the analyst's mind when he or she was examining the sessions. Based on past experiences, some of the sessions would result in a mixture of target descriptions that might make it nearly impossible to determine if such sessions were describing target A or target B. But the experiment would work if a sufficient number of very clear sessions appear in which viewers describe one of two targets in each set, and if there are a relative lack of sessions in which very clear results are obtained for what appears to be a target outside of the given pair of targets that are dominating the analyst's mind at the time when the sessions are examined.

The New Experimental Design

The purpose of the new experimental design is to allow us to identify the causative mechanism of the "switched" session phenomenon. An associative remote-viewing design was chosen in which targets were associated with numerical digits. However, in order to use pairs of targets to represent digits from 0 to 9, we needed to translate base-10 digits to binary values. In this new design, all digits from 0 to 9 were represented in terms of a binary combination of 0s and 1s. The exact code that was used for the base-10 to binary translations is presented in table 3.1. The table is equally balanced between the occurrence of 0s and 1s, and thus no single binary outcome is given preferential treatment in the analysis of any experimental outcome.

In this new setting, a collection of paired targets was created, with each target being as different from its paired counterpart as possible. Thus, for each pair, one target would be associated with the 0, while the other target would be associated with the 1. In order to identify one base-10 digit (i.e., a digit from 0 to 9), we would need to correctly identify four binary digits. This meant that a judge would have to use data from four remote-viewing sessions to identify each of the correct binary outcomes. After a number of trial runs, we set up an experiment involving a Cash 4 lottery outcome for the State of Georgia that would be drawn on 28 October 1998. To get four base-10 digits correct, we needed to correctly identify 16 binary choices using remote-viewing data.

Five remote viewers were used for this experiment. Each of the viewers had been trained to use an identical method of data collection (Scientific Remote Viewing). Not all viewers were of equal ability to use these procedures to remote view. Some of the viewers had histories in which they used these procedures to produce remarkable results quite regularly, whereas others had a

TABLE 3.1. Farsight Base-10 to Binary Numerical Code

First Binary Digit	Second Binary Digit	Third Binary Digit	Fourth Binary Digit	Target Number
1	0	1	0	0
1	0	1	1	1
1	1	0	0	2
0	0	1	1	3
0	1	0	0	4
0	1	0	1	5
0	1	1	0	6
0	1	1	1	7
1	0	0	0	8
1	0	0	1	9

somewhat more spotty record. Nonetheless, all viewers had at least a two-year exposure to these methods, and all had demonstrated a significant ability to use these procedures in the past to obtain at least some notable results.

To broaden the design of the experiment, the group of five viewers was divided into two groups. One group was given the task of remote viewing the "correct" target for each binary pair, whereas the other group was assigned the "incorrect" target. The correct and incorrect targets were determined by the lottery outcome and the code found in table 3.1. The sessions were all completed and analyzed prior to the date of the lottery. [Targ and Harary (1984) long ago noted that it does not seem to matter whether or not the target is determined prior to or after the remote-viewing session is completed, and our experiments as well as the experiments of others have repeatedly confirmed this. See also Nelson, Dunne, Dobyns, and Jahn (1996, 110), and Utts (1996, 13)]. All of the sessions were conducted solo, meaning that none of the viewers had a monitor to observe (and potentially lead) the session. None of the viewers were given any information regarding any of the targets on the list for the experiment until after the experiment was completed and the lottery outcome was known. The list of potential targets used in this experiment, as well as their binary numerical associations are given in table A3.1, which is found in the appendix to this chapter.

For the record, it is worthwhile to identify the viewers, the analyst, and pertinent aspects relevant to each of their general backgrounds. The participants in this experiment have a wide range of professional experiences, and they seem to have no obvious background commonality other than a similar interest and training in remote viewing. This information is as follows:

Viewers	Professional Background
Courtney Brown, Ph.D.	University professor
Richard Moore, M.D.	Internal medicine, licensed in Georgia, Arizona, and New Mexico, practicing in New Mexico
Denise Burson	Telecommunications specialist
Joey Jerome	Restaurant and farm owner and operator
Adele Lorraine	College instructor, flutist, member of a major symphony orchestra

Analyst	
Matthew Pfeiffer	Investment counselor working in the banking industry

It is important to note that this is an exploratory process-oriented experiment (as compared with a proof-oriented one), and the analyst who decides whether or not a remote-viewing session describes one target or another in a binary pair of targets is a person, not a computer. This is important for this experiment because we are attempting to isolate the influence of the analyst's thoughts during the judging process on the outcome of the actual session data. Thus, a human analyst is needed here. Different experimental needs require different experimental designs. For example, in chapter 5 of this volume, an experiment is described that used an alternative experimental design in which a computer program was used to analyze remote-viewing data.

It is also crucial to note that a decision was made to allow a target pool that had what May, Spottiswoode, and James (1994) call a large "target-pool bandwidth." (See also Lantz, Luke, and May 1994.) In studies comparing dynamic (such as video clips) to static (still photographs) target pools, these authors argue that limitations to the qualities of target pool characteristics allow the viewers to successfully edit-out false perceptions that are the result of the imagination if they know the range of perceptual possibilities, thereby producing a clearer description of actual target characteristics. For example, if all targets are limited to being on a surface (e.g. buildings, mountains, etc.) — as contrasted with flying targets — viewers are more successful at describing the targets that are assigned to them.

Our experience with remote viewing at The Farsight Institute has generally not supported this view. We have often found that limitations in the target bandwidth can sometimes worsen the quality of the remote-viewing data by encouraging the conscious mind to intervene more readily in the data collection process, essentially by giving the conscious mind some prior expectation of success in interpreting the remote-viewing data as it is being collected. Nonetheless, the "jury" seems still to be out on the topic, and for the experiment described in the current chapter, we are less concerned with increasing our "hit rate" than we are in observing clear patterns in the way targets are perceived incorrectly (i.e., viewers perceiving the wrong targets from a pair of targets). Thus, an "anything goes" orientation was adopted to target selection, including flying targets. The most important criterion for this experiment is that each target in each binary pair be as different as possible from the other target in each pair, especially in ways that would be relatively easy for an analyst to note.

To summarize the experiment, for each pair of targets in a binary set, the viewers are divided into two groups, one group of three (call that Group A) and another of two (call that Group B). The Cash 4 lottery of Georgia requires the correct pick of four base-10 digits, each ranging from 0 to 9. Each base-10 digit is represented as a set of four binary (0 or 1) digits, and each potential binary pair of digits is associated with two targets (one target for a 0, and the other target for a 1). For a Cash 4 lottery, there are thus 16 correct targets and 16 incorrect targets. For purposes of this experiment, the correct targets are referenced as "primary" targets, and the incorrect targets are referenced as "secondary" targets. Both the primary and secondary targets are equally valuable in determining an actual binary digit, since identifying a secondary target consequently identifies the primary target. For each binary pair of primary and secondary targets, viewers in one group are assigned the task of viewing the primary target, whereas viewers in the other group are assigned the task of viewing the secondary target. Prior to conducting their sessions, the viewers are sent only a fax telling them that they are to view either the primary or secondary target (one only, as specified in the fax) associated with a given winning ball and a given binary digit. The results are then sent to a judge or analyst who uses the data from a total of 80 sessions (five viewers with 16 sessions each) to attempt to identify the correct four base-10 digits. All this occurs *before* the date of the lottery.

More formally, there are 14 essential components to this experiment.

Viewers:

- A standard viewing methodology was used by all remote viewers to collect target data.
- Each of the viewers was trained in the use of these viewing methods over a period of at least two years to a satisfactory level of expertise with regard to the mechanics of the procedures.
- All the viewers worked alone under solo conditions.
- All viewers were given no prior information regarding any of the targets in the larger list of targets, or of those in any binary set of targets. The conditions also satisfy the definition for "double-blind" since viewers (who were blind to target possibilities) did their sessions alone and without any contact with anyone who knew anything about the target pool.

Target Organization:

- A target list of 32 targets was broken down into 16 pairs of targets in order

to uniquely identify each of the potential 16 binary outcomes.
- With all paired targets, one target was associated with a 0 and the other target with a 1.
- Each of the two paired targets was chosen to be as different from each other as possible. No limits were placed on the characteristics of the targets that could be used in any pair, which corresponds to a situation of maximum target bandwidth. The viewers were aware that there were no limitations placed on the range of target possibilities.
- Some of the viewers were assigned the primary target for each binary pair of targets (which is the target associated with the correct binary digit of 0 or 1), while the other viewers were assigned the alternate or secondary target. From ball to ball (there are four balls), four of the viewers rotated between the primary and secondary targets. One viewer (Dr. Richard Moore) viewed only the primary targets for each ball.

Judging:
- A human analyst (as compared with a computer program) was used to evaluate the sessions. Matthew Pfeiffer was the analyst.
- The analyst was totally blind to the correct target for each session since the correct target was determined by a lottery outcome that occurred after the judging took place.
- The analyst was initially assigned to make only a binary choice and pick the target that most likely resembled the session data, not to rank the quality of the session in a more detailed qualitative evaluation.
- The analyst was aware of which viewers were supposed to view primary targets and which viewers were supposed to view secondary targets for each binary pair of targets. The idea was that those viewers who were supposed to view the primary target in a binary set would tend to have data resembling one target in that set, while the viewers who were supposed to view the secondary target in that binary set would submit data resembling the other target. This way the analyst would be able to determine which target was the primary target as compared with the secondary target.

Connection to External Random Event:
- A code was used to translate the binary outcomes to base-10 digits.
- An outside event (a lottery) was used to determine the choice of correct targets within each pair of targets by using the base-10 to binary translation code.

Again, the overall motivation for this experimental design is to identify the cause of the so-called "switched" sessions by isolating the point at which an analyst's thought may "corrupt" the remote-viewing process. By taking the original list of 32 targets and breaking it into other lists (i.e., binary pairs) that are used separately in the experiment, the hope is to be able to isolate where the crossover of psychically perceived information is taking place, thereby aiding in the determination of the causal mechanism responsible for the crossover. It is crucial that readers understand that in this chapter I am not trying to describe an experiment in which the data from the viewers are judged in a statistically independent fashion (as compared with the results presented in chapter 5 in which true independence is designed into the experiment). Rather, in the current chapter's experiment we are attempting to track and isolate thought processes of the analyst in a situation in which we already know there is a lack of independence. We knew from our experiences with the switched-session phenomenon that some form of psychic contamination occurs in experimental designs that do not utilize an outbounder (explained in a later chapter) in which analysts compare remote-viewing data with a set of targets, one real and the others decoys. This lack of independence in such experimental designs seems to occur regardless of the level of experimental or statistical controls as long as human analysts are used. What we are attempting to gain from the current experiment is insight into the causal mechanism of this contamination.

Results

A summary of the results for all 80 remote-viewing sessions for this experiment are presented in tables A3.2a through A3.2d, all of which are found in the appendix to this chapter. Table A3.2a is for the four binary digits representing the number 3, which is the number on the first ball that was drawn on the Cash 4 Georgia lottery on 28 October 1998. All of the tables A3.2a through A3.2d identify the viewer groupings for the primary and secondary targets as well as summary information regarding each session.

After the name of each viewer are two numbers separated by a slash. The first number represents the binary choice (and thus the target) that the analyst decides corresponds with the session data. For example, in table A3.2a, the first number following J. Jerome in the third column is 0. This means that the data in Mr. Jerome's session describes the West Wailing Wall in Jerusalem more than the Marianas Trench (see table A3.1 in the chapter appendix, the first binary pair of targets). The second number after the viewer's name (following the slash) is a score representing the clarity of the session. The scale of the clarity score is from 0 to 3, with 0 being the worst and 3 being the best.

The session clarity scores are an additional qualitative measure that I have added to the original binary choices made by the experiment's judge. I do this for heuristic purposes to assist in explaining these results. Again, the experiment's judge only made binary choices with regard to his original evaluations of the remote-viewing sessions. But I feel it is useful in the current context to add an additional, albeit subjective, qualitative measure that describes the closeness of each session's data to the targets in each binary pair. Of course, if this were an experiment designed to offer proof of the remote-viewing phenomenon, this would not be an acceptable procedure since the claim could be made that I gave the sessions whatever score I wanted post hoc. But as I have stated previously, this is a process oriented experiment that is more exploratory in nature, and I take the liberty offered by this less rigid experimental design to offer this qualitative assistance in understanding these results. Post hoc ratings are not uncommon in remote-viewing research, and they serve a similar and valuable heuristic role in many situations in which complex results can be summarized numerically. (See, for example, May, Spottiswoode, and James 1994b.)

A session clarity score of 0 indicates that an analyst can find no discernable correspondence between the session data and the given targets. This does not necessarily mean that the viewer is not describing something relating to one or both of the two targets (see discussion further below). But it does mean that an analyst's prior expectations regarding either target do not match the session data in a way that is understandable to the analyst. A score of 1 indicates a discernable but weak correspondence between one of the targets in the binary set of targets and the session data. There may be numerous perceptual decoding errors in such a session, but not so many that an analyst cannot understand what is going on. (A decoding error is where the viewer describes something in a target one way, but the viewer misinterprets the actual perception. Sometimes an analyst can recognize such decoding errors and take them into account, such as if a viewer describes a pyramid as a pointy mountain with generally flat sides made of rock.) Clarity scores of 2 and 3 are for very clear sessions. A score of 2 indicates that the session data very clearly describe the chosen target (from the binary pair), although the description may not have been as complete as an analyst might have thought possible, or there could have been some minor decoding errors. A score of 3 in the clarity scale is reserved for very clear sessions that describe the given target with great depth and with very few, if any, decoding errors.

In some cases a question mark is placed in the primary target choice location. This normally happens when the session clarity score is 0, which means that an analyst cannot determine which target in a given binary set is represented by the session's data. However, if an analyst finds some correspondence between the data and both targets, but could not determine which target is represented more clearly, then the session clarity score represents how clearly both targets of a binary set are reflected in the data (as evidence by a clarity score greater than 0).

Following the clarity score for some sessions is an "S." The appearance of an S indicates that the session appears to be "switched" with regard to the appropriate target for that viewer. For example, notice that there is an S following the clarity score for viewer Burson for the first binary digit of the first ball (table A3.2a, row 1, column 4). Since the actual first binary digit for this

Table 3.2. Summary of Clarity Scores, "Switched" Sessions, and Undetermined (?) Sessions

Viewer/Score	0	1	2	3	"Switched"	?
R. Moore	2	4	5	5	4	3
C. Brown	5	3	4	4	2	6
J. Jerome	2	5	3	6	4	3
A. Lorraine	3	5	7	1	2	4
D. Griffith	2	6	6	2	2	4
TOTALS	14	23	25	18	14	20

ball is a 0, the primary target for this digit is the West Wailing Wall in Jerusalem (from table A3.1 in the chapter appendix). The secondary target for this digit is the Marianas Trench. Since the viewer Burson was assigned the secondary target for this digit, she should have viewed the Marianas Trench. Instead, her session describes the Wailing Wall in Jerusalem with considerable clarity. An S is not placed after the clarity score unless the clarity score is a 2 or a 3 so as to more definitively identify a session as "switched."

It is not possible to have won a lottery based on these remote-viewing results. Note from table A3.2a that the first ball is a 3, with a binary representation of 0011. There are switched sessions for all but one (the fourth) of the binary digits. Even if one uses a majority rule to decide on the appropriate digit choices, how would one decide on the third binary digit for that ball in which all but one of the sessions (both primary and secondary) corresponds to the same target?

Table 3.2 summarizes the results of tables A3.2a through A3.2d. Note that of the 80 remote-viewing sessions for this experiment, 43 have clarity scores of 2 or higher. Moreover, 37 sessions have clarity scores of 0 or 1. Finally, 14 sessions clearly appear to be "switched," meaning that the data for the sessions strongly correspond to the incorrect target. Those who criticize the validity of the remote-viewing phenomenon might quickly point to these results as "proof" that remote viewing does not work. But such a conclusion would be very premature. The more interesting story resides in the details behind these numbers.

Session Clarity and the "Switched" Sessions

To see what is really going on behind the numbers in tables A3.2a-d and table 3.2, it is necessary to grasp the level of target description that is being obtained with sessions that have a high clarity score. Even though it is not possible to display even one complete session here due to space limitations (each session runs approximately 15 pages), it is nonetheless possible to display the essence of a number of sessions using what is called a session "snapshot."

All session snapshots follow the same format. Since single word entries that describe a target tend to be repetitively scattered across many pages within a session, the central physical and concept descriptors (i.e., words that describe physical things and associated concepts related to those things) are gathered together under the category "Central Descriptors." Viewers often consolidate their perceptions of a target into one or more terms, sentences, or long phrases. These central consolidations are also gathered together under the category "Central Consolidations." Sometimes, one or more parts of even a very clear session may seem to be out-of-sync with the dominant remainder of the session. This can especially happen in situations similar to those found in this study in which two or more targets are being compared with data from a single session. In situations where the clarity score is high, these out-of-sync portions of a session are typically very small (say, one sketch out of 15 pages of data). These out-of-sync portions are gathered together and described under the category "Deviating Data." Finally, sketches that are drawn by viewers are displayed as part of the session snapshot. Since some sketches tend to be repetitious of other sketches, the sketches that are most complete in descriptive detail are included in the snapshot.

Four session snapshots are included in this report. All of the session snapshots are for the viewers Moore and Jerome (two each). The snapshots are for the second ball, third binary digit, and for the third ball, second binary digit. For the second ball, third binary digit, viewer Moore was supposed to view the Comet Shoemaker-Levy 9 impacting Jupiter, and viewer Jerome was supposed to view Lewis and Clark's first meeting with the Indians at Council Bluff. As it turned out, both viewers viewed the Comet Shoemaker-Levy 9 impacting Jupiter with clarity scores of 3. For the third ball, second binary digit, both viewers Moore and Jerome were supposed to view the moon Callisto. In this instance, both viewers viewed the other target in the binary pair, which was the Golden Gate Bridge, with clarity scores of 3.

Below are the session snapshots for the second ball, third binary digit:

Session Snapshot for R. Moore: Second Ball, Third Binary Digit
Central Descriptors: choking, swirling, sulfuric, whooshing, blasting, acrid, desolate, monitoring, watching at a distance, scientific
Central Consolidations:
- Comet
- Area of turbulence and intense energy
- possible that this structure represented something on Earth that was connected to the comet, such as an astronomical

observatory.
Sketches: Figures 3.1 and 3.2.

Session Snapshot for J. Jerome: Second Ball, Third Binary Digit
Central Descriptors: whooshing and hissing sounds, energy, motion, visible, falling, celestial event, hot, glowing, moving, friction,
Central Consolidations:
- Rock moving through air fast
- A falling star
- Comet
- Comet Hale-Bopp
- Shoemaker-Levy hitting Jupiter
- Seems small in relation to something bigger, yet has a big impact for something so small.
- Halley's Comet

Deviating Data: Initial data seemed to suggest a subject in a rapidly moving (flying) structure.
Comments: Deviating data dissipated quickly in the beginning of this session.
Sketches: Figures 3.3 and 3.4.

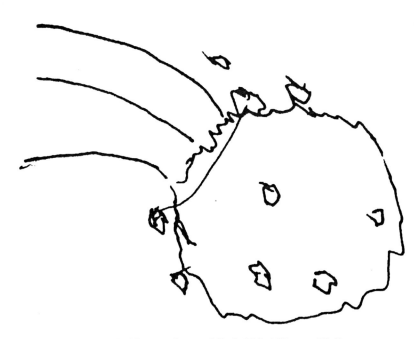

Figure 3.1. Viewer R. Moore, Second Ball, Third Binary Digit

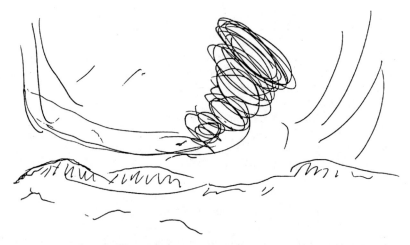

Figure 3.2. Viewer R. Moore, Second Ball, Third Binary Digit

These data for the second ball, third binary digit are exceptionally clear. Both of the viewers had concluded that the target involved an astronomical body such as a comet. One of the viewers (Jerome) even stated that the target resembled the Comet Shoemaker-Levy 9 crashing into Jupiter, which was an exact identification of the target. The sketches are also quite unambiguous. These are the approximate quality of all sessions that rate a 3 on the session clarity score.

Below are the session snapshots for the third ball, second binary digit:

Session Snapshot for R. Moore: Third Ball, Second Binary Digit
Central Descriptors: structure, water, windy, bird calls, cool, vehicles, structures, people, smog, tower, commerce
Central Consolidations:
- Like a busy intersection
- Harbor
- City
- Towering, tubular structure that turns at the top – good view.

Deviating Data: One sketch suggesting a flying structure such as a jet.
Comments: The deviating sketch does not re-occur beyond one sketch. This deviating sketch represents an insignificant quantity of data when compared with the remainder of the session. It is possible that the jet was perceived flying over the curved structure.
Sketches: Figures 3.5 and 3.6.

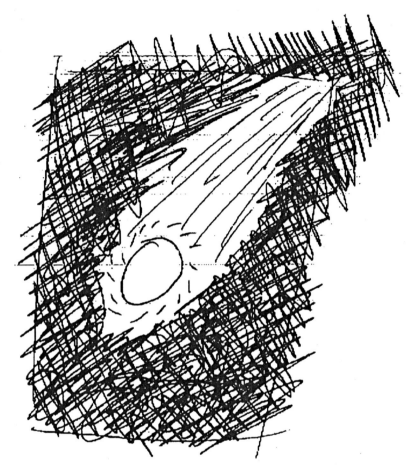

Figure 3.3. Viewer J. Jerome, Second Ball, Third Binary Digit

Session Snapshot for J. Jerome: Third Ball, Second Binary Digit
Central Descriptors: honking, voices, huge structure,
Central Consolidations:
- Cars
- Trucks
- Bridge
- Golden Gate Bridge
- Ocean smells
- Skyway bridge
- Car exhaust

- A massive, impressive structure
- Transportation
- People use this

Deviating Data: Essentially no deviating data.
Sketch: Figure 3.7.

As with the previous session snapshots, the data for the above two sessions are quite clear and unambiguous. The sketches of the harbor and bridge are indeed remarkable. Readers should be reminded that these data were obtained without the viewers being told anything about the targets prior to conducting the sessions. They were only sent a fax telling them to view either the primary or secondary target that is associated with a given ball and binary digit. Moreover, the viewers were alone when viewing. No one was present who could have led these viewers.

The quantity of clear sessions (43 out of 80 sessions rating a 2 or 3 on the clarity index) suggests that remote viewing is the most likely underlying mechanism for obtaining these data. (Although, and again, I am not attempting to "prove" this point here.) It is improbable that this quantity of clear sessions

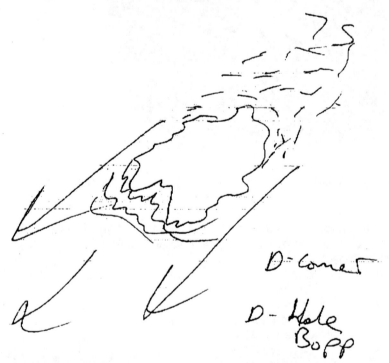

Figure 3.4. Viewer J. Jerome, Second Ball, Third Binary Digit

Figure 3.5. Viewer R. Moore, Third Ball, Second Binary Digit

could be obtained by chance, given the fact that the targets could be anything at all. However, if we work with just the 43 clear sessions, we note that getting only 14 or fewer switched sessions from this group instead of around 21 or 22 as predicted by chance is approximately .02, and this is free from arbitrary subjective "close-call" session evaluations from judges since we are only working with cases in which the sessions unambiguously describe only one of the two binary targets. We have repeated this same overall experiment four times with similar results (although with varying sample sizes), and so the actual probability is indeed much smaller. Thus there are two phenomena interacting here. First, we have what appear to be clear cases of remote viewing. Second, we have what seem to be unambiguous cases of target switching. Moreover, the target-switching phenomenon is not random, since an approximate mean proportion of switched sessions of 0.5 would result if this were the case. Indeed, it is the absence of the random factor that gives us leverage in suggesting an underlying causal mechanism mediating the remote-viewing phenomenon.

Some readers may be concerned that I do not correct for the "stacking effect" in the .02 probability mentioned above regarding the 14 apparently

Figure 3.6. Viewer R. Moore, Third Ball, Second Binary Digit

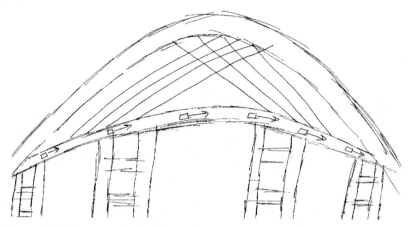

Figure 3.7. Viewer J. Jerome, Third Ball, Second Binary Digit

switched sessions by using methods suggested by Greville (1944) and others. (In particular, see the recent debate between Houtkooper, Vaitl, and Timm 2000 and Schmidt and Walach 2000.) The concern here would be that the results of the viewers may not be independent when they use the same target. There can be more than one reason for this. If one of the targets in a binary set is more amenable to viewer description than the other, then the data in the remote-viewing sessions may appear to resemble the "better" target. For example, if one of the targets is on a surface and another target is a structure flying over a surface, then viewers may tend to focus on the surface itself, and some viewers may miss the flying structure that is over the surface, leading the analyst to think that the correct target is the surface without the flying structure. Care was taken with determining the target pool used for this experiment to optimize the quality of the choices for each binary pair as much as possible, but one cannot rule out that target-dependent stacking may have occurred here.

But there is another reason for worrying about the stacking effect in the current context. With this experiment we are directly concerned about the role of an analyst's thoughts in psychically corrupting the independence of the remote viewing. In particular, if an analyst has an inner predisposition to want to know more about one target than another, it could be that the viewers could perceive this on a deep level and provide information that satisfies this informational need of the analyst. If this is the case, the results would not be independent at all, and you would expect a stacking effect due to this psychic mechanism.

There are two reasons for not controlling for the stacking effect with the .02 statistic given above. The first is that the number is offered here not as "proof" but rather as a heuristic aid in understanding the 14 apparently switched sessions *as if* they were independent (which we can assume they are not for the reasons outlined above). This does not make the number useless, since it has a comparative heuristic value, if nothing else. Remember that I am not trying to prove a psi effect in this chapter, thereby having to buttress my arguments with statistical controls that account for the stacking effect. Rather, we are using these data in the context of a highly structured experiment in a search for ideas that will allow us to determine how a remote viewer's perceptions are focused.

This leads us to the second reason for not controlling for the stacking effect through statistical means. We are expecting — indeed, hoping for — a psychically mediated stacking effect that will give us some insight into the mechanism by which a remote viewer's perceptions are focused. Thus, we do not want to make too much of the .02 number, other than to note it and then to focus on the strength of the more qualitative data as demonstrated in the sessions themselves as we search for a causal mechanism for the observed effect. If this study was designed around demonstrating in a proof-oriented manner that the 14 sessions in question are "switched" from a statistical significance point of view, controls for a possible target-dependent stacking effect would be needed, and the direction of this research would have to change to include a great deal of additional statistical analysis and a larger collection of data (presumably more than 80 sessions). But even then it may not be possible to segregate target-dependent stacking from psychic-dependent stacking using statistics. In the current context, I simply need to point out that 14 switched sessions appear to be unusual as a chance occurrence, and that non-independence among the viewers may be due (minimally) to psychic dependence as outlined above.

Using the four sessions portrayed above as heuristic examples with session snapshots, three of the four are "switched," meaning that the viewers recorded data that correspond with the target in the binary pair that is opposite the one that was supposed to be viewed. The target descriptions are so clear that the fact that these sessions are "switched" should be obvious to nearly everyone, and statistics should not be an issue here. That these sessions are qualitatively comparable in this regard with the other switched sessions leads us to the central question of this volume. With regard to the remote-viewing phenomenon, what makes a target a target?

A Theory of Focused Perception

Two key observations regarding these data allow us to suggest a mechanism by which the focusing of perception is achieved with remote viewing. The first observation is that only 14 of the 43 sessions that received a 2 or 3 clarity score are "switched." Thus, the targeting strategy of having the viewers attempt to perceive a particular target that is associated with a given ball and binary digit is somewhat successful, however imperfect. The second key observation is that in a post-experiment review of the remote-viewing data, we noted that in only one instance out of all 80 sessions did a viewer's data for a session strongly correspond with a target that was outside of the binary pair used in the analysis of that session. Thus, when there was target switching, it was almost entirely limited to switching between one of two targets. Moreover, we repeated this general experiment four times with modest variations in analysis procedures and found the general switching phenomenon to be quite replicable and robust. It will become more clear in the pages that follow that we ultimately find this to be due to the fact that when the analyst is judging the remote-viewing data, he or she is rarely thinking about targets in the pool that are not in the binary set being used to judge a particular session. The one exception in the current experiment of possible switching outside of a binary set of targets may fall into another category, as I explain later. In follow-up experiments, we were able to eliminate essentially all switching outside of the binary pair by more tightly controlling the mental analysis activities of the analyst — essentially by further distancing the times between the analyses of sessions with different target sets, thereby reducing "mental blending" from one target set to another.

What then makes a target a target? Does writing a target down on a piece of paper "create" the target? Does designing a set of procedures around which a target will be dynamically determined produce the target? Does the intent of the tasker (the person who writes or designs the target) determine the target? Do the thought processes of the person (or people) analyzing the session influence the focus of attention of a remote viewer? Why should a viewer's focus of attention be determined by one set of rules and not another? Indeed, why should a tasker's intent matter more than the rules determining a dynamically produced target, or more than the thoughts of the analysts, or any number of other influences? If remote viewing is a mental process involving more than simply physical brain computations, then why should a viewer's focus of attention be influenced more by any single thing among many that may be involved in an experimental setting?

The results of this experiment suggest that there are a number of influences involved in a remote viewer's ability to focus his or her perception on a target. Clearly, the experimental design of having a viewer focus his or her attention on a dynamically specified target has some influence on the ultimate result (since a large majority of the clear sessions were not switched). Such remote-viewing successes using a variety of targeting mechanisms — with or without associative components — are not new, even if replicability in the past has been problematic (Puthoff 1984; Puthoff and Targ 1979; Targ and Harary 1984; Targ and Puthoff 1977; Utts 1996, Nelson, et al. 1996).

But what is striking about the results of the current experiment is that the dominant influence on the error rate for the clear sessions seems to be the thought processes of the analyst. That is, when an analyst is examining the results of a remote-viewing session, the analyst has preconceived ideas regarding what he or she is expecting to see in the session. These data suggest that remote viewers are guided by these informational expectations of the analyst. For reasons that I propose below, viewers tend to focus their attention on one of the two targets that the analyst is holding in his or her mind. Much of our research indicates that viewers can also mix target perceptions together under such circumstances, finding, say, a stone structure at the bottom of the sea when in fact the two targets in the binary set are the sinking of the Titanic and the Parthenon building. But in many cases, the viewers abandon one of the targets and hone in on the other. Again, the fact that little if any target switching occurs outside of each binary set seems to suggest that the causal mechanism for the switched-session phenomenon is the analyst's initial mental processes when analyzing the remote-viewing data. Thus, the same analysis-related mental processes are likely to be the link that determines a remote viewer's focus of attention more generally.

One of the great puzzles in the history of remote viewing is why the laboratory results of repeated remote-viewing experiments have been so inconclusive, and yet anecdotal reports involving the intelligence services of the United States government have suggested spectacular successes using remote viewing for operational purposes (see, Kress 1999, May 1996, Puthoff 1996, Schnabel 1997, Targ 1996, 1999, and Utts 1996). Our current results may shed light on this tension. In experimental settings, a panel of judges are typically used to evaluate the accuracy of remote-viewing work. The results of the current experiment strongly suggest that having even one judge with more than one target in his or her mind may seriously corrupt the data collection process involved with remote viewing. Having more than one judge further complicates the situation. Indeed, it may be that the ability of the experimental design (i.e., the formal designation of a "correct" target) to also have some influence over how viewers focus their attention is the only reason scientific studies have had any success at all when using such judging methods.

Intelligence work is another matter, however. Intelligence agencies are not interested in whether or not a viewer's data can be used to pick a correct target out of a pool by a panel of judges. Rather, intelligence people have specific informational needs that they want addressed as effectively as possible. Their use of remote-viewing data would be totally different from those uses found in remote-viewing laboratories. In an intelligence agency, a single target would normally be assigned to a viewer. There would be no pool of targets from which a comparison would later be made. Rather, the remote-viewing data would be compared with what is already known about the given target. Field operatives would then search for confirmation regarding any new leads that originate from the remote-viewing data. In short, the intelligence agencies exploit remote-viewing data in a way that does not corrupt the data collection process. Indeed, some of the most noted anecdotal evidence in support of the general remote-viewing hypothesis originating from some scientific laboratories occurs in reports of clearly stunning results using notable remote viewers (e.g. Pat Price,

Ingo Swann, Joseph McMoneagle and others) in situations employing only one (that is, no pool of targets combined with blind analysis conducted by human judges).

A Conceptual Model of Remote-Viewing Perception

We now have the basis to develop a general model of how remote viewers may focus their attention on a given target. In my view, and in light of the results of the current experiment, any successful model will need to incorporate the idea of competing attractors. This is a subject of nonlinear systems theory, and I extend my discussion in this direction not by way of analogy, but rather by an explicit incorporation of the vocabulary and concepts that are inherent in the evolution of nonlinear and interdependent dynamical systems. In part, I do this because the vocabulary and concepts of such theories are natural to my way of thinking, and I have published a number of academic books addressing the theory and applications of such systems in the social sciences. Thus, in the remainder of this chapter, I briefly outline a model of the remote-viewing targeting mechanism that seems appropriate given the results of the current experiment. Since this outline is by necessity brief, it is less specific than one would require of a fully specified model of the targeting process. But I extend this discussion more fully later in this volume (in chapter 7) after the results of additional experiments are discussed. My later discussion also includes an algebraic specification of the process that may serve as a first approximation model of the psychic targeting mechanism. Because of the more general nature of the remaining discussion in this current chapter, if readers wish to look at these initial comments below as tentative connections between nonlinear systems theory and remote-viewing processes, no harm is done as long as one recognizes that I ultimately do frame the modeling problem using explicit language that is much more qualitatively correspondent with the remote-viewing targeting mechanism.

Beginning this discussion in a loose and interpretive fashion, let us say a remote viewer conducts a session, and let us assume that the targeting mechanism for this session is tied to the thoughts of the analyst who is examining the session data at a later date in an attempt to decide if the results resemble one or another of two potential targets. The subspace aspect of the remote viewer is aware of ideas in the analyst's mind that correspond with both of those targets, potentially making the perception of either target possible for the remote viewer. In a sense, the viewer's mind has to decide which set of perceptions to follow (dynamically) for the remainder of the session. If the viewer's mind chooses one target, then the session data will resemble that target. But if the viewer's mind chooses another target, then the viewer's attention will have abandoned the first target and will be attracted to the other, and the session data will reflect the perceptions of the second target. The remote-viewing session itself takes place during an approximate time period of between one-half hour to one hour, depending on the speed of the viewer in resolving target characteristics. Thus, the session itself is a dynamical event, with one perception leading to another, and so on. Remote-viewing sessions tend to become more focused as they proceed, and the experiential sense is that one's perceptions become stronger as one makes closer target contact in the latter parts of each session.

In the language of nonlinear systems theory, each potential target would correspond to what is called an "attractor" in phase space. Phase space is a mathematically defined region that has a certain number of dimensions which correspond to variables of relevance to a system. A nonlinear system can have variable values that place the state of the system at a certain point in the system's phase space. The values of these variables change as the system evolves, which in practice means that the system variables assume values that follow what is called a "trajectory" or path in phase space. In general, the movements of trajectories are dominated by the placements of the attractors in the system. Each attractor has what is called a "basin" of attraction, and any trajectory that falls into an attractor's basin risks becoming trapped by that attractor. The situation is analogous to a satellite that becomes trapped in orbit after passing nearby a planet.

If we are to apply these ideas to the remote-viewing experience, it appears as if we can assign the initial state of the system to the quality of the perceptions that are obtained by a remote viewer as a remote-viewing session begins. If guided by the thoughts in the mind of the analyst, a remote viewer's perceptions may or may not be initially "trapped" in the basin of one or the other target-defined attractors. But as the session proceeds, the viewer's perceptions tend to lock on to one of the two potential targets, and in such a situation the trajectory of the viewer's perceptions would become trapped in that attractor's basin. No single and clear decision rule yet exists that would describe why one attractor would win over another in this struggle between the two attractors, although it is not difficult to imagine the factors that would be involved in determining such a rule.

To summarize, remote viewing involves a situation of mental competition between various competing attractors, all of which influence the perceptions of the remote viewers. I argue here that in the experiment described in this chapter, each target in a binary pair of targets helps define an attractor in a two-attractor model. Each attractor can affect the focus of a viewer's attention in favor of one target or another. For heuristic purposes in the current setting, one can think of each attractor as one of the targets in a binary pair or set of targets. All of the attractors are housed in a topographically defined phase space of the entire system that is defined by the structure of the experiment, the choices of the targets, and all other relevant variables.

Given such a conceptual framework, the basin for each attractor has a certain range within the system's phase space. At the outset of a remote-viewing experiment, a more highly weighted attractor would have a larger influence over a viewer's initial perceptions, and topographically this would correspond with a larger size or a more advantageous strategic location in the phase space for this attractor's basin. If during a remote-viewing session a viewer's awareness follows a perceptual trajectory in the phase space, then the more influential attractor exerts a greater "pull" on the direction of the viewer's perceptions. Idiosyncrasies in the conscious and/or subconscious preferences of the judge or judges with regard to one or another target in the pool will crucially affect the topology of the system by influencing the location and shape of each target's attractor and basin. At this point, it is also useful to note that we are just beginning to understand the range of psychic influences that may exist during the collection of remote-viewing data, and we should be prepared to discover greater complexities in the above scheme as we continue to research these issues. For example, there may also be the issue of whether or not the viewers themselves have post-experiment target preferences that influence the strength of an attractor and the shape of its basin.

As discussed above, a typical remote-viewing session begins with less focus and ends with more focus. That is, a viewer normally perceives initial impressions of fragmentary elements of a target or targets (if there is a pool of targets). A great deal of experience with this phenomenon suggests that remote viewers often go through an initial period of struggle in deciding which aspect of their perceptions on which to focus (especially with targets from a pool). This struggle is often resolved about one-third of the way through the session, but it can at times continue throughout the session. In terms of the current model, the viewers's initial perceptions originate from an area within the system's phase space in which there is a competition among two or more basins of attraction. What happens next is determined by a variety of chance and deterministic factors. One of the chance factors is the initial placement of the viewer's perceptions relative to the competing basins of attraction. But one can assume that the trajectory of the perceptions wanders through the phase space as each viewer tries to decide on what to focus, and thus the size and shape of each basin relative to the other basins affect the ultimate outcome. In many cases, the viewer's focus of attention is eventually "captured" by one of the attractors, and the perceptual trajectory "falls" into an irrecoverable descent into its basin. From that point on, the session data become "clear."

The theory of such competing basins of attraction is complete, and empirical evidence of such phenomena elsewhere is not in dispute (see Thom 1975; Brown 1995a, 1995b; Zeeman 1972). What is new is the apparent recognition of such dynamics in connection with the remote-viewing phenomenon. My own observations and experience suggest that either the application of this conceptual model to the dynamics of remote-viewing perception is correct, or the remote-viewing phenomenon itself behaves as if it is correct. This "as if" criterion is minimally sufficient to apply nonlinear systems theory to the remote-viewing phenomenon, and, indeed, it is the primary threshold consideration in applying any modeling strategy to any process or relationship.

The above conceptual model of the remote-viewing process also sheds some light on remote-viewing data that are not at all clear (in this report, those rating a 0 or 1 on the clarity scale). I suggest three possible reasons for remote-viewing sessions to yield seemingly inaccurate or incomprehensible data. First, even skilled viewers can make errors in the decoding of their intuitions into descriptive words and phrases. Any court of law will demonstrate that various witnesses describe strikingly different things even though they apparently "saw" the same thing. Should remote-viewing perceptions be any different given the more difficult nature of the process as compared with physical sight? Using untrained, "off-the street" viewing subjects would greatly amplify this type of error, as our experience has demonstrated that viewers can improve dramatically in their perceptual abilities given long periods of systematic practice and guidance. However, to chalk all remote-viewing inaccuracies up to decoding errors would be a serious mistake in my view, as the situation can be much more complex.

A second primary reason for remote-viewing error can reside with the phenomenon of competing basins of attraction. In situations of perceptual conflict, one of two things can occur. A viewer can continue throughout the entire session in a state of perceptual confusion due to the fact that his or her focus of perception may never be completely "captured" by one of the competing attractors. In such situations, a viewer's perception may remain in the neighborhood of the boundary (i.e., the bifurcation set — however discrete or "fuzzy" that may be) that separates the two attractors, glancing one way and then the next as chance or as other factors may allow. (Indeed, on an experiential level, virtually all viewers at The Farsight Institute have reported some remote-viewing experiences in situations of binary target sets in which more than one focus was perceived and no resolution was achieved to the very end of the session.) But it is entirely possible that another more complex dynamic may occur, and the viewer's perceptions may oscillate between the various basins of attraction in a fashion not too dissimilar from the often depicted trajectory behaviors of chaotic attractors.

The third primary possibility for error in situations of competing target-defined attractors would be for the viewer's perception to abandon the conflict entirely and shift to a completely different location and time that may have some conscious or unconscious interest for the viewer. On a psychological level, humans often retreat in the face of conflict. Why should remote-viewing perceptions vary in this regard from physical perceptions? If a viewer's subspace mind cannot resolve a target conflict easily, there is no known reason why the viewer might not "look" at something else, thereby abandoning the conflict.

Much more research is needed to resolve these issues of perceptual conflict, and indeed, more is presented later in this volume. But the current experimental results do point us in a direction that seems likely to bear fruit. Cross-cutting psi channels in remote viewing are a very real possibility. These cross-cutting channels of information result from conflicts within the perceptual space of the viewer's targeting arena. The remote-viewing process appears to be highly sensitive to cross-pressure mental influence, often making it susceptible to corruption due to factors inherent in the experimental process itself. In particular, analyst contamination in the remote-viewing process may play a causative role in the indeterminate nature of many laboratory findings that utilize panels of "blind" judges who examine and evaluate remote-viewing data with respect to target pools. The use of remote viewing for intelligence gathering purposes by, say, governmental agencies, avoids such contamination by not using target pools that are employed judgmentally in post-session evaluations.

APPENDIX TO CHAPTER 3

•

TABLE A3.1. The Target Set

Ball 1	Binary Digit: 0	Binary Digit: 1
First Binary Pair	The West Wailing Wall / Jerusalem	The Marianas Trench
Second Binary Pair	The main lobby of the Jefferson Hotel / Richmond, Virginia	The detonation of the hydrogen bomb code-named "Bravo" at Bikini Atoll (1 March 1954)
Third Binary Pair	Hindenberg / destruction event (6 May 1937)	Stonehenge / England (27 September 1998, 3 a.m. Stonehenge local time)
Fourth Binary Pair	Times Square / New York City (17 October 1997, 9 p.m.)	Mt. St. Helens / Washington (18 October 1998, 2:15 p.m. Mt. St. Helens local time)
Ball 2		
First Binary Pair	Corfu Castle / England (2 June 1977, 2 p.m. Corfu Castle local time)	The kitchen within the restaurant known as "Agnes & Muriel's" / Georgia (4 September, 8 p.m. Georgia local time)
Second Binary Pair	The naval battle between the Spanish and the English near Gravelines (8 August 1588)	The Temple of the Magician / Uxmal (15 September 1858)
Third Binary Pair	Lewis and Clark's first meeting with the Indians at Council Bluff (30 July 1804) / event	Comet Shoemaker-Levy 9 impacting Jupiter (July 1994)
Fourth Binary Pair	Ayers Rock / Australia (22 September 1657)	The U.S. Space Shuttle Discovery (27 August 1985)
Ball 3		
First Binary Pair	Windsor Bay Deli / Ohio (22 October 1998, 12:30 p.m. Ohio local time)	The Great Pyramid of Khufu / Egypt (20 October 1998, 4 a.m. Egypt local time)

Second Binary Pair	The Golden Gate Bridge / California (16 November 1998, 5 p.m. California local time)*	The moon Callisto (29 September 1998)
Third Binary Pair	The prison known as "Alcatraz" / San Francisco Bay, California (9 January 1998)	Mt. St. Helens / eruption event (18 May 1980)
Fourth Binary Pair	The most recent Spice Girls concert / event	Hiroshima / nuclear destruction event (9 August 1945)
Ball 4		
First Binary Pair	The General Assembly building of the United Nations Headquarters / New York (27 August 1963, 1 p.m. New York local time)	Tunguska, Siberia / destruction event (30 July 1908)
Second Binary Pair	Assassination of Abraham Lincoln / Ford's Theater, Washington, D.C. / event (14 April 1865)	The largest crater in the Sea of Tranquility / the Moon (27 July 1998)
Third Binary Pair	The summit of Mt. Fuji / Japan (24 October 1998)	Japanese General Yoshijiro Umezu Signing the surrender document aboard the USS Missouri / event (2 September 1945)
Fourth Binary Pair	Lyndon B. Johnson taking the oath of office as President of the United States of America / event (22 November 1963)	The area known as the "Cydonia Region" / Mars (24 October 1998)

* A future date (post the lottery date) was used for this target. The assumption made by the tasker was that the bridge would still exist a month after the lottery was over. Fortunately, this was the case.

Table A3.2a: Session Summary Scores for First-Ball Results

Ball: First
Number on Ball: 3
Binary Code: 0011

Binary Digit Placement	Actual Binary Digit	Primary target choice / session clarity score	Secondary target choice / session clarity score
First	0	J. Jerome:0/1 A. Lorraine: 0/2 R. Moore: 0/3	C. Brown: ?/0 D. Burson: 0/2S
Second	0	J. Jerome: 0/2 A. Lorraine: 1/2S R. Moore: 0/1	C. Brown: 1/3 D. Burson: 0/1
Third	1	J. Jerome: 0/2S A. Lorraine: 1/2 R. Moore: 1/3	C. Brown: 1/2S D. Burson: 1/1
Fourth	1	J. Jerome: 1/2 A. Lorraine: 1/1 R. Moore: 1/2	C. Brown: ?/0 D. Burson: 0/3

Note: An "S" following the session clarity score means "switched," and indicates that the data clearly correspond with the other (incorrect) target in the binary pair.

Table A3.2b: Session Summary Scores for Second-Ball Results

Ball: Second
Number on Ball: 6
Binary Code: 0110

Binary Digit Placement	Actual Binary Digit	Primary target choice / session clarity score	Secondary target choice / session clarity score
First	0	C. Brown: 0/1 D. Burson: 0/2 R. Moore: ?/0	J. Jerome: ?/0 A. Lorraine: ?/0
Second	1	C. Brown: 1/1 D. Burson: 1/2 R. Moore: 1/2	J. Jerome: 1/1 A. Lorraine: ?/0
Third	1	C. Brown: 1/2 D. Burson: ?/1 R. Moore: 1/3	J. Jerome: 1/3S A. Lorraine: 1/2S
Fourth	0	C. Brown: 0/2 D. Burson: 1/2S R. Moore: 0/1	J. Jerome: 1/3 A. Lorraine: 1/1

Note: An "S" following the session clarity score means "switched," and indicates that the data clearly correspond with the other (incorrect) target in the binary pair.

Table A3.2c: Session Summary Scores for Third-Ball Results

Ball: Third
Number on Ball: 4
Binary Code: 0100

Binary Digit Placement	Actual Binary Digit	Primary target choice / session clarity score	Secondary target choice / session clarity score
First	0	J. Jerome:0/1 A. Lorraine: 1/1 R. Moore: 1/3S	C. Brown: ?/0 D. Burson: 1/2
Second	1	J. Jerome: 0/3S A. Lorraine: ?/0 R. Moore: 0/3S	C. Brown: ?/0 D. Burson: 0/2
Third	0	J. Jerome: 0/3 A. Lorraine: ?/1 R. Moore: 0/2	C. Brown: ?/1 D. Burson: ?/1
Fourth	0	J. Jerome: 0/1 A. Lorraine: 0/2 R. Moore: 1/2S	C. Brown: 1/2 D. Burson: ?/0

Note: An "S" following the session clarity score means "switched," and indicates that the data clearly correspond with the other (incorrect) target in the binary pair.

Table A3.2d: Session Summary Scores for Fourth-Ball Results

Ball: Fourth
Number on Ball: 8
Binary Code: 1000

Binary Digit Placement	Actual Binary Digit	Primary target choice / session clarity score	Secondary target choice / session clarity score
First	1	C. Brown: 0/3S D. Burson: 0/1 R. Moore: 0/1	J. Jerome: 1/3S A. Lorraine: 0/3
Second	0	C. Brown: 0/3 D. Burson: ?/0 R. Moore: 1/2S	J. Jerome: 1/3 A. Lorraine: 1/2
Third	0	C. Brown: 0/3 D. Burson: 0/3 R. Moore: ?/1	J. Jerome: ?/1 A. Lorraine: 1/1, possibly higher depending on determination of viewer perspective in session
Fourth	0	C. Brown: ?/0 D. Burson: 0/1 R. Moore: ?/0	J. Jerome: ?/0 A. Lorraine: 1/2

Note: An "S" following the session clarity score means "switched," and indicates that the data clearly correspond with the other (incorrect) target in the binary pair.

CHAPTER 4

The Question of Time:
The Alpha Project

Humans do not yet understand time. Early debates contrasted Newtonian with relativistic understandings about time. In the pre-relativistic period, Newton's description of absolute time dominated intellectual thinking, and there were few dissenters throughout the years. Ernst Mach was one of those few who questioned the validity of absolute time, and he argued strongly that Newton's logic failed to prove its existence, and that it was indeed nothing more than an illusion (see Born 1962, p. 84). Mach argued that since only relative positions, motions, and time could ever be observed, only these relative things could be real. Einstein, of course, changed all of this with his special and general theories of relativity. With relativity, we now understand that Newtonian principles apply only within a subset of more general conditions. Departures from these special conditions, due to high relativistic velocities and the like, cause phenomena to occur which require relativity to explain. This addresses time streams that slow down or speed up, in the sense that astronauts returning from a high-speed trip to the moon would be slightly younger than they otherwise would have been when compared with their relatively stationary Earth-based counterparts.

Psychic functioning raises new questions about time. A significant amount of work has already been done in the area of precognition and time with regard to psychic functioning. One of the earliest efforts can be found in a book that combines experimental evidence with a dimensional theory of time written by J.W. Dunne, originally published in 1927 (Dunne 2001). Also, Bierman and Radin (1997; see also Radin 1997, chapter 7) have demonstrated that subjects in a laboratory can experience physiological changes in apparently psychic anticipation of cognitive experiences, such as being shown disturbing photographs. May, Utts, and Spottiswoode (1995a and 1995b), as well as May, Utts, Spottiswoode, and James (1995), have discussed how subjects may use anomalous cognition to perceive into the future when making decisions, thereby choosing futures that are optimal. Joe McMoneagle has written a book from a remote viewer's perspective on the subject of time (McMoneagle 1998). Also, a helpful review of important studies of precognition and time (including Honorton and Ferrari's 1989 meta-analysis) can be found in the book chapter by Radin cited above (again, 1997, chapter 7). Clearly remote viewing addresses a level of experience that is not explained by either the Einsteinian or Newtonian paradigms.

Remote viewers perceive events, places, and subjects that are located at different time points. That is, a remote viewer conducts a session at time A, and the target is at time B. We can call time A the "viewing time" and time B the "target time." The viewer appears to perceive and describe the event at time B directly. There is no evidence of an intermediary device or mechanism that would operate as a link to the target at time B. That is, remote viewers do not perceive a hologram or movie somehow stored in a cosmic library of everything. Rather, the prima facie evidence is that the perceptions are directly obtained by the viewer from the actual target, and thus there is some type of real interaction between the observer and that which is observed in the remote-viewing process.

Thus, we have a problem with the Einsteinian paradigm. The two events (the viewing and the target) that occur at times A and B must both exist simultaneously in order for remote viewing to function. This is not a question of relative time, but rather an argument for the nonexistence of time that concerns us. Indeed, just as Mach complained that the Newtonian concept of absolute time was an illusion, we must similarly wonder if relativistic time is merely an intellectual template that accommodates certain inconsistencies within the Newtonian model that is applicable under certain circumstances, but which is inadequate to explain events that depend on subspace dimensionality.

Let us return to the remote-viewing problem in which there is a viewer at time A and a target at time B. With all remote-viewing experiences, there is also a time at which the target is assigned or "tasked." This is a moment when a person, computer, device (such as a radiation counter, or a coin that is flipped), or event (for example, a lottery outcome) assigns a target for the session. Let us call this time C, or the "tasking time." In most remote-viewing situations, the tasking time is after the target time and before the viewing time. In situations in which target times are simultaneous with the viewing times (that is, viewing some location or event that exists at the time the viewing takes place), the tasking times would occur first, which would mean that a target would be determined prior to the viewer doing a session. Having the target already determined at the viewing time produces no time-based inconsistencies other than that the target may be a historical target, which would require the viewer to "travel" back in time to view the target.

But the matter can be more complicated, and this chapter focuses on another situation in which the tasking time occurs after the viewing and target times. That is, a viewer perceives a historical target that is not determined until after the remote-viewing session is completed. These various scenarios are depicted in figure 4.1. In part, we are concerned here with experiential differences that may exist between the situation in which the tasking time precedes the viewing time and the alternative situation in which the reverse is true. But as will become obvious by the end of this chapter, these experiments also raise the more fundamental question of the structure of time to a level at which one must ultimately wonder if the Einsteinian notion of space and time is incomplete.

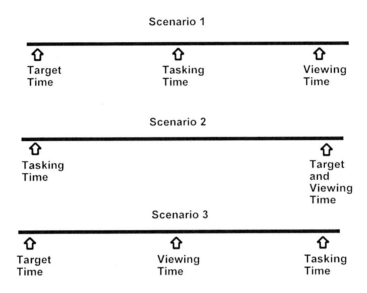

Figure 4.1. Three possible scenarios of time with respect to remote viewing

Before discussing the experiments themselves, it is best to more fully flesh out the problem of time which is being addressed. It is heuristically useful to restrict the current discussion to elementary Newtonian mechanics.

For the purposes of this discussion, let us say we have a target which is a particle at a location x at time t (using normal Cartesian three-space). (On a practical level, an atomic "particle" is actually not a good remote-viewing target for reasons that I will not discuss here. But this example places our current discussion in a more fundamental physical context.) Let us also say that there is a force which acts on this particle, and we can call this force $F(x)$. Due to this force, the particle moves from location x to the new location $F(x(t))$. Thus, F can be thought of as a map that assigns a destination point $F(x)$ to the starting point $\mathbf{x}$. To keep things simple, from a physical perspective let us say that the force on this particle is gravity, and F is the force that is applied to the particle at location x.

The "potential energy" of this particle is determined by its position only.

As an example, we can say that the particle at location x is pulled toward the source of gravity, such as the Earth. The potential energy is essentially defined by how much work the particle can do because of its position. If the particle is pulled toward the Earth, it travels to the Earth's surface and impacts that surface. The impact is the physical manifestation of that work. The strength of the impact is determined by the particle's potential energy before it begins its journey to the Earth's surface.

The "total energy" of the particle is the sum of the particle's potential energy and its kinetic energy. Its kinetic energy is the amount of energy it has that is due to its motion, which is related to the particle's mass and speed. If K is our kinetic energy and P is our potential energy, then our total energy, E, would be $E(t) = K(t) + P(t)$ (see also Hirsh and Smale 1974, pp. 17-9). Note that $E(t)$ is a function of time, as is $K(t)$ and $P(t)$.

Now, let us say that this particle travels from position x to the surface of the Earth. Let us also say that the remote viewer perceives the particle at its original position, its motion, and its impact on the Earth's surface. Call this entire sequence "the target event." Due to the law of the conservation of energy, the total energy of the event (in our conservative system) is constant across time (or independent of time, depending on one's choice of words). That is, the total energy in the target event stays the same, even though the potential energy and the kinetic energy may vary as separate items as the particle moves from one point to another. This means that $K(t) + P(t)$ equals a constant, and that $E(t)$ never changes across time, making the time subscript pointless.

The tradeoff between $K(t)$ and $P(t)$ can be easily visualized with an example of a ball thrown vertically upward. When the ball is first tossed upward most of the energy is kinetic. But as the ball gets higher, its kinetic energy diminishes and its potential energy increases. By the time the ball reaches its peak height, it has no more kinetic energy and its total energy is comprised of only potential energy. This process reverses when the ball begins to fall due to gravity, of course.

For our purposes here, the point of interest is that the total energy in the target event is a consequence of two separate energy components that vary over time in a coordinated fashion. As P gets smaller, K gets larger, the sum total being the same at all times. But remote-viewing evidence suggests that the movement of the particle from its starting point to its impact with the surface of the Earth is also independent of time. That is, the particle both in its state of movement and its state of collision exist simultaneously. Just as the total energy of the target event remains constant across time, the actual event itself appears to be free from time as well. In a very real sense, the internal components of total energy seem distributed spatially, not with respect to time. What seems to change is the sequential perception of the event such that a process emerges in which both the particle's position and its energy distribution appear to change in a continuous fashion. But with respect to the remote-viewing phenomenon, it appears that it is the measurement of the event as a sequential process that creates the perception of time, not the event itself. This is an idea that has been gaining considerable and serious attention in the physics community in recent years. [In particular, see "Physics' Big Puzzle Has Big Question: What Is Time?" by James Glanz, *The New York Times*, 19 June 2001, p. D2(N).]

On the surface, the idea of time being an illusion of perception seems impossible, of course. But mathematics can be used productively to describe this situation of simultaneity for seemingly nonconcurrent events, and I ask readers to bear with me a bit longer as I develop a more general example that can properly frame the issue of time as it appears from the perspective of the remote-viewing phenomenon. I am a mathematical modeler by training and profession, so the use of mathematics is a normal extension of my thinking process, especially when ideas require a level of organization that is difficult to achieve with words alone. Some readers may wish to skip a few pages ahead to the next section in this chapter if the following brief mathematically-oriented presentation seems cumbersome. But my hope is that most readers will continue reading through the next few pages to gather insight from my verbal arguments, perhaps glossing over some of the more technical explanations. It is my expectation that some readers will find the next few pages illuminating on both verbal and technical grounds as well. I return to a more completely verbal presentation in the next section of this chapter.

To clarify the language used here, I shall refer to the situation in which events that appear to be separated by intervals of time but which in fact may be occurring concurrently as "sequential simultaneity." I do not attempt here to use mathematics to prove sequential simultaneity in the sense of a formal logical proof based on theorems. Rather, as a mathematical modeler I am using a mathematical representation of the hypothesis of sequential simultaneity to more fully expose the scope and implications of what is being proposed.

Let us extend the above discussion of a moving particle to a situation that addresses a more general set of variables. These more general variables can be anything that changes with respect to time. Indeed, let us say that we have two such variables, X and Y, and that the algebraic descriptions of their changes over time are:

$$dX/dt = aX - bXY - mX^2 \qquad (4.1)$$

$$dY/dt = cXY - eY - nY^2 \qquad (4.2)$$

where a, b, m, c, e, and n are constant parameters for this interdependent set of two first-order differential equations. For those readers who follow such things, these are the more generalized versions of the classic predator-prey equations of Lotka and Volterra (see Koçak 1988, pp. 121-2; Hirsh and Smale, 1974, pp. 258-65; May 1974). However, in the current context, one can think of the variables

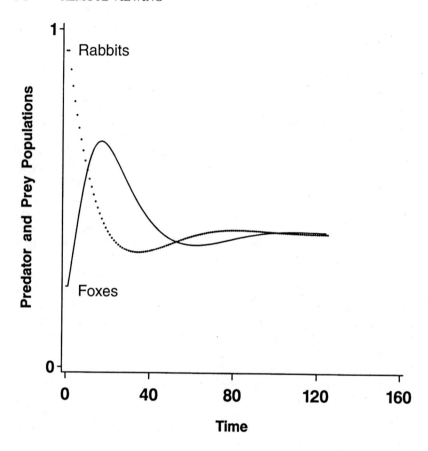

Figure 4.2. Time plots of two populations

X and Y as representing anything at all, from position vectors to quantitative variables (such as the numbers of foxes and rabbits in an ecosystem).

Both X and Y depend on time in the above representation. In the classic predator-prey scenario (where X represents rabbits and Y represents foxes), the number of rabbits increases exponentially (aX) until they are either eaten by the foxes ($-bXY$) or they die off due to their own large numbers while over-exploiting their food resources ($-mX^2$). The population of foxes grows only when there are rabbits to eat (cXY). Fox populations decline due to natural causes ($-eY$) or due to their own crowding and over-exploitation of their available resources ($-nY^2$).

One way to represent the interactions between these two variables is with a time plot, as is done in figure 4.2. Note here that the fox population "chases" the rabbit population in terms of overall quantities, there being a lag as the number of foxes adjusts to changes in the number of rabbits.

If we divide equation 4.1 by equation 4.2, we can eliminate time, as is done with equation 4.3.

$$dX/dY = (aX - bXY - mX^2) / (cXY - eY - nY^2). \qquad (4.3)$$

We can also use a phase portrait to portray graphically the sequential dynamics of the variables X and Y while suppressing time. One such phase portrait of this system is presented as figure 4.3.

In figure 4.3, note that the time axis no longer exists. Rather, we now have a representation of the sequential changes in X and Y independent of time. If time were to be included, a third axis would be required that would project off the page toward the reader's face. The curve in the figure is called a "trajectory," and this trajectory is located in the "phase space" of this system with two variables. If time were included, the trajectory would spiral outward from the page in the manner of a rocket's smoke trail rather than be a curve on a flat surface.

The characteristics of the trajectory portrayed in figure 4.3 closely parallel the generic phenomenon of sequential simultaneity that is experienced by remote viewers. From a sequential perspective, the trajectory has a beginning and an end, and the beginning happens before the end with respect to time. The trajectory in figure 4.3 ends inside an "equilibrium marsh," which is an area in the phase space of the system where change in the system slows down to a near stop (Brown 1995a, pp. 72-3). But the figure does not portray a time scale, and given the absence of Newtonian absolute time, it is possible for us to set this time scale arbitrarily. Indeed, we can say that the phase portrait is created as we compress the change in time toward a limit of zero (that is, compressing the time axis to the point of nonexistence), which would imply sequential simultaneity. One can conversely think of this as speeding up the movement along the trajectory until the trajectory's velocity approaches infinity. In such a world, the beginning of the trajectory in figure 4.3 would occur at the same moment of time as the end, which might conceivably parallel a situation in an Einsteinian sense in which an outside observer of the system exists within a singularity with respect to the relativistic space containing the system.

What we now need is a means of describing the direction and magnitude of change without reference to time in the global region of the phase space that houses the system. This is determined by the characteristics of a modified directional field portrayal for the system. Normally a directional field diagram contains information about the direction of change without including the information relating to its associated magnitude (i.e., the rate of change, or speed of a trajectory at a location in phase space). But we can easily include the information for magnitude as well (often called a "vector field"), and such a

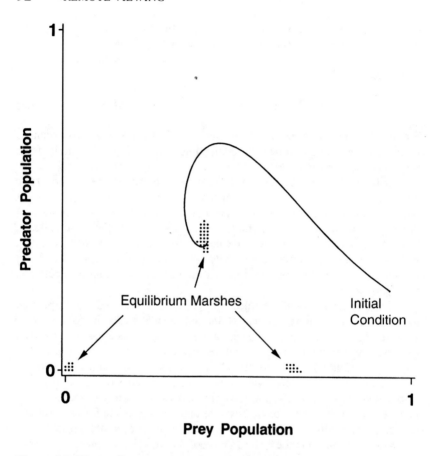

Figure 4.3. Phase diagram of two interacting populations

diagram for the above system is presented in figure 4.4.

Note that the direction of the trajectory in figure 4.3 follows the directional field lines in figure 4.4, and the length of each line in the vector field diagram reflects the rate of change in the state variables at any given point in the phase space. Any trajectory in this deterministic system, regardless of its starting point, will follow these directional lines as long as the trajectory passes near them. Note that the rate of change in this representation is with respect to the state variables, not with respect to time, which means that these directional lines do not depend on time but rather the values of the state variables. Thus, the directional lines that contain both direction and rate of change information structure much of the internal distribution of what we can call a trajectory's total "phase energy," and thus the nature of the evolution of a system, and nowhere

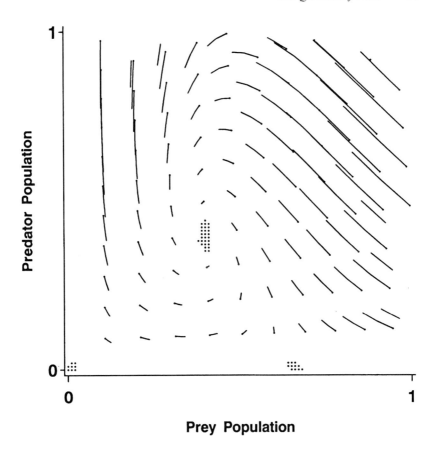

Figure 4.4. Vector field diagram for two interacting populations

is the description of this evolution now dependent on the inclusion of a time dimension.

By focusing the current discussion on the internal distribution of total phase energy rather than time-structured system dynamics, we can represent any internally varied system as one that is independent of time. The point here is that describing the changing internal distribution of total phase energy as a time-structured phenomenon only makes sense if we insist on observing the evolving system from a perspective that adds time to the dimensionality of the space housing the system. But in the absence of time — as we conveniently portray by repressing this dimension in the phase space representation of the system — the direction and magnitude of the directional lines in figure 4.4 reflect a distribution of phase energy that depends not on time but on the values of the state variables, and we can describe variation in the internal distribution of the total phase energy of a system as an alternate means of characterizing change in that system.

To summarize, one need not return to a description of time-structured dynamics in order to understand system evolution. That is, a system can evolve with respect to its principal variables (often called "state variables," or X and Y in the previous example), not with respect to time. Time is an additional dimension that further complicates the description of change within the system. But it is not mathematically necessary always to include time in the analysis of the system's evolution. On a practical level, this in part requires us to substitute words such as "change with respect to the state variables" for "change with respect to time" in all or nearly all circumstances where we describe the evolution of a system. Also, "rates of change" must refer to characteristics of the internal distribution of a system's total phase system rather than time-structured velocity dynamics.

If we consider the above representation in a context of the complete and real suppression of time, sequential events become a spatial distribution of simultaneous events in phase space. Their sequential nature is translated into spatial terms by the nature of the suppression of time. What then stops us from looking at the world in this way? The answer is that we (humans) organize our sequential events along a dimension that we perceive as time. In a sense, for humans, time can be thought of as an illusion of perception. It need not be that time exists in a real sense, but that our conception of sequential events allows no other organization of this material. This in turn is tied to the way our brains store information that is perceived point-by-point in a sequential mapping process that occurs in phase space. This mapping process creates time by adding this perceptual dimensionality.

On a biological level, what is needed to accomplish this illusion is a built-in limitation of our physical/subspace interface. If our physical minds are constructed to allow only the perception of one point in phase space, and the perception of this point must be jettisoned (actually, moved to memory) in order to perceive a different point, then time would automatically emerge as a necessary dimension to organize any given sequence of points. If one limits the physical/subspace interface such that it is exceedingly difficult to perceive more than one point in phase space, then we would be left with physical memory as the dominant means of organizing point sequences in one direction. As a side comment, it is unclear at the current time why our minds would choose one direction over another to organize our memories. In such a world, it might be just as possible to construct a mind that did the reverse, in which case the future would reside in "memory" and the past would appear not to exist yet. This odd idea is actually one of the major problems and theoretical possibilities with which cosmologists currently struggle.

How then is it possible for remote viewers to temporarily escape from this perceptual blockade that hides the past and future from us? Are we then to assume that the physical/subspace interface involves a singularity — or a collection of singularities — through which perception across the divide can transit from one state to another, from a state in which time does not exist to one in which time structures all recognition of the physical universe?

Singularities arise out of a complete collapse of the normal rules that govern a system. In a technical sense, a singularity is an area in phase space which is not differentiable, and rules need to be applied that are specific for the condition of a singularity but which do not apply in areas outside of its boundaries, such as the application of Maxwell's convention in the case of catastrophe theory (Thom 1975). Most people think of singularities as products of black holes that reside in the center of galaxies. But singularities that could mediate consciousness would instead probably need to be accessible on some molecular/quantum level in the brain. Because of this I find interesting the evolving developments of quantum biology, and especially the research of scientists such as Hameroff, Penrose, and others who are both developing theories and collecting physical evidence that suggest that singularities with characteristics correspondent with those pondered here may in fact be at the root of consciousness. (See discussions of "orchestrated objective reduction" and "quantum collapse" in Hameroff 1994, 1998; Hameroff and Penrose 1996.)

The Alpha Experiment

There is little that is intuitive or "normal" in this discussion of sequential simultaneity. But there is also nothing "normal" about time as it relates to remote viewing. To make all of this more real in the current context, we need to proceed to our experiments. The experiments presented below are called the "Alpha Project" because they address the question of what actually is the beginning of anything. Of course, I do not suggest here that this chapter is the first of its kind to present anomalous cognition data that challenge contemporary theories of time, and I have already mentioned a subset of the theorists and experimenters who have previously explored this issue. But the experiment discussed in this chapter yields another perspective on this complex and evolving subject that complements those ideas and results presented elsewhere by others. Its primary value can be found in how evidence of the simultaneity of events is reflected in the timing of remote-viewing taskings as they have been done at The Farsight Institute.

To set up the Alpha experiment, remote-viewing sessions were conducted using two types of tasking. In the first type, the tasker assigns a target for a remote-viewing session prior to having a viewer conduct the session. This is called a "tasking-prior" condition, and it follows scenario 1 in figure 4.1. For the second type, the tasker assigns a target for a remote-viewing session after the session is already completed. This is called a "tasking-post" condition, and it follows scenario 3 in figure 4.1.

Ten targets were assigned for the Alpha experiment, five of the tasking-prior type and five of the tasking-post variety. Two viewers completed all ten session for all of the targets, for a total of twenty remote-viewing sessions used in this analysis. All sessions were conducted "solo and isolated," which means that no one was present when the remote viewers conducted their sessions (see table 2.1). All targets for this experiment were determined by Matthew Pfeiffer, and that was his only role in this experiment. Before the experiment began, Matthew wrote the five tasking-prior targets. After all sessions were completed, Matthew then wrote the five tasking-post targets. Records were maintained as to the time and date that each target was determined. The prior and post targets were randomly matched with the sessions (1 through 10) for both viewers so that the viewers and analyst would not know which sessions were of the tasking-prior type and which sessions were of the tasking-post type when target feedback was given. Feedback was given to the viewers only after all sessions were completed by both viewers. Thus, at no time during the duration of the entire experiment (from viewing through feedback for all sessions) did the viewers know whether or not a particular session was of the tasking-prior or the tasking-post type.

After all sessions were completed for the Alpha Project, Matthew Pfeiffer gave the target specifics to the viewers to examine. The viewers themselves were the first ones to compare their data with the target specifics (which are the descriptions of the targets), although faxes of all sessions were transmitted to (and stored at) the Institute's central office prior to the viewers being sent the specifics. Matthew Pfeiffer did not have access to any of these faxes (or any other form of session content) until after all sessions were closed and analyzed. All analyses of the sessions for this chapter were done using these faxed copies. To conduct the analysis, I scored each session using the same scoring method used in the previous chapter. Since the timing of the tasking is the test determinant for this experiment, I was necessarily kept blind when the analysis was done as to the time and date on which each target was determined.

Table A4.1 (located in the appendix to this chapter) contains the list of all targets used for this project. Note that each target has an "essential cue" and three "numbered aspects." As the name suggests, the essential cue identifies the target in the broadest way. The numbered aspects are three components of each target that contain information desired for the experiment. The first numbered aspect normally is a repeat of the essential cue with the addition of time and date information, if relevant. This is the numbered aspect that guides the viewers' initial approach to the target based on the viewing instructions they are given prior to the beginning of the experiment. The second and third numbered aspects normally require a shift in perspective for the viewer. This shift can be in time, space, or both. The viewers are aware that three numbered aspects exist for each target, but nothing more. They sequentially conduct movement exercises during their sessions in order to relocate their perceptual focus to the next numbered aspect for each target until all three are completed. Of course, the viewers are given no prior leading information regarding what the perceptual focus may be for any numbered aspect.

For example, with regard to target 5, the essential cue is the ruins of Machu Picchu in Peru. This identifies the general parameters of the target, and everything else in the target specific must relate to these general parameters. This would exclude having a numbered aspect in the target specifying something unrelated, such as the sinking of the Titanic. The first numbered aspect repeats the essential cue, but it specifies a time and date. The viewer's initial data should correspond to this numbered aspect. The second numbered aspect shifts the viewer's perspective to another time and date. The perspective is also shifted to a person at the target site on that new time and date. The third numbered aspect re-locates the viewer's perspective to a point 20 feet away from the highest point at Macchu Picchu, and in this case a date is not specified. The goal of the session is to follow the numbered aspects as one moves from the beginning of the session to the end. Again, the viewers perform specific exercises to shift their perspectives at certain points during each session to those specified by the numbered aspects.

Project Limitations

This project has certain limitations, as is common of all scientific experiments of any type, and it is important to understand these limitations so that our expectations are clear from the outset. The goal of this project is to determine if choosing a target before a remote-viewing session has begun as compared with after the session is completed makes a difference in the quality of the session. We are not trying to determine fine distinctions that may become apparent as target-writing dates are strategically placed, say, at weekly or monthly intervals over the course of a year prior to and again after the sessions are completed. We are rather interested in the gross question of whether or not tasking-post situations actually work, and whether there is any apparent major quality difference between tasking-prior and tasking-post experimental conditions.

The first limitation of this study is that the analysis is limited to 20 sessions. Scientists love large sample sizes, and many more sessions would allow more detailed statistical analyses. But this utopian situation is not possible now, nor may it ever be possible to obtain so many sessions of the type used here. Thus, given the existing sample size, we need to focus on our primary objective for the project as stated above. On the positive side of this limitation, the viewers used in this experiment have extensive experience using the SRV procedures, and thus the quality of the data can be expected to be rather high. Indeed, the strategy applied throughout all of the analyses reported in this volume is the same in this regard, which is to use a few individuals who have identical specialized training using a standardized data-collection methodology rather than many individuals who have little or no training. This produces a more controlled experimental setting with higher quality output but at lower quantitative levels.

Another limitation of this study is that each viewer conducted only one remote-viewing session for each target in the Alpha Project. While there may be some variations across viewers, experience has generally demonstrated that it is optimal for viewers to attempt at least two remote-viewing sessions using the same target if the goal is to obtain the richest collection of descriptive material for the given target. Often the viewer has a better grasp of the essential target components during the second attempt with the target. The second viewing attempt also allows the viewer another chance to put many or all of the target pieces together. The situation is a bit like asking someone to go into a building for a few minutes and then to emerge and describe everything that was in the building. The person would remember, say, the staircase, the size of the building, and perhaps some parts of the interior of a room. But if the person has a second chance to go into the building after making the first report, the person is likely to offer a more detailed and accurate description of the structure's interior, including how rooms are connected, colors of paint, furnishings that exist, and so on.

But this limitation of one session per target for each viewer is also a required strength in the design of this study. The purpose of the Alpha Project sessions is not to obtain the best possible collection of information for the given targets, in the sense that an intelligence analyst in a spying agency would require the most complete collection of data possible to satisfy operational demands. Rather, the purpose here is to make one reasonable pass at each target — the same for each target and each viewer — and then to examine the sessions with respect to their tasking-prior and tasking-post conditions. If variations in the number of viewing attempts for each target are allowed, we would not know if the improved target descriptions are due to the number of attempts or the time that the target is chosen. Controlling this and other factors allows us to more clearly isolate the causal mechanisms of the observed phenomena.

Results

The results of Alpha Project sessions are summarized in table 4.1. The "scores" that are reported in this table (columns two and three) are determined in the same manner as the scores reported in the previous chapter. Again, a score can range from 0 to 3, where a 0 indicates that the session contains little or no information that clearly describes the target, a 1 indicates a discernable but weak correspondence between the session data and the target, a 2 indicates that the session data very clearly describe the given target, and a 3 indicates a superb description of many or most of the essential target elements. Some of the scores in table 4.1 are fractional, and this tends to occur in situations in which most of a session would be scored at the level of the higher integer, but the data for one

Table 4.1: Project Alpha Session Scores and Targeting Dates (month/day/year)

TARGET	Viewer 1: Courtney Brown	Viewer 2: Roma Zanders	Viewing Dates	Tasking Date	Target-Prior or Target-Post
1	0	1	V1: 11/1/99 V2: 9/28/99	11/19/99	Post
2	2	2	V1: 11/8/99 V2: 9/29/99	09/21/99	Prior
3	1	2	V1: 11/15/99 V2: 9/30/99	09/21/99	Prior
4	3	2	V1: 11/22/99 V2: 10/1/99	12/09/99	Post
5	3	1.5	V1: 11/26/99 V2: 10/2/99	12/14/99	Post
6	1	1.5	V1: 12/5/99 V2: 10/4/99	03/29/00	Post
7	1	1	V1: 12/9/99 V2: 10/5/99	09/21/99	Prior
8	1	1	V1: 12/13/99 V2: 10/9/99	09/22/99	Prior
9	2.5	Indeterminate	V1: 2/4/00 V2: 10/10/99	03/29/00	Post
10	1	1	V1: 2/18/00 V2: 10/11/99	09/21/99	Prior

of the latter target aspects (usually aspect #3) begin to deviate from the previously recorded (and more accurate) data. Experience has shown that this is sometimes a consequence of fatigue. If viewers are a bit tired before starting a session, by the time they near the end of the session their perceptions may begin to lose focus.

The date that each viewer conducts a session is reported in the fourth column of the table. The fifth column contains the date of tasking, which is the date that Matthew Pfeiffer wrote that target specific. The final column summarizes whether the tasking was a tasking-prior or a tasking-post situation.

Table 4.2 contains some summary information relating to table 4.1. The first two rows of the table contain the average scores for each viewer with regard to the sessions' tasking-prior and tasking-post experimental situations. For viewer 1, the average score for all five tasking-prior sessions is 1.2, whereas the average score for the same viewer for all five tasking-post sessions is 1.9, with a total difference of 0.7 favoring the tasking-post situation. For viewer 2, the respective prior and post means are 1.4 and 1.5, with a total difference of 0.1, again favoring the tasking-post situation. Averaging all sessions across both viewers with respect to prior and post situations, the average score for all tasking-prior sessions is 1.3, whereas the average score for all tasking-post sessions is 1.7, a result that favors the tasking-post situation.

Table 4.2: Summary Information

	Viewer 1	Viewer 2	Two-Viewer Average
Target-Prior Mean	1.2	1.4	1.3
Target-Post Mean	1.9	1.5	1.7
Target-Prior Number of 3s	0	0	
Target-Post Number of 3s	2	0	
Target-Prior Number of 2s	1	2	
Target-Post Number of 2s	1	1	

It is also useful to examine the distribution of the best sessions for each viewer. For viewer 1, two tasking-post sessions scored a 3, whereas no tasking-prior sessions scored similarly. One additional tasking-post session (for target 9) would have also scored a 3 as well, had it not been for deviating data late in the session. While none of the sessions for viewer 2 scored a 3, two of the tasking-prior sessions scored a 2, while one of the tasking-post sessions scored a 2. This "high-end" result for this viewer seems to slightly favor the tasking-prior situation. But this is balanced out by the two tasking-post sessions for this viewer that scored 1.5, indicating significant session clarity in at least major sections of these sessions as well.

The results in tables 4.1 and 4.2 are quite striking. These results should not be interpreted to suggest that tasking-post situations are superior to tasking-prior situations for remote viewing. But the results clearly indicate that tasking-post situations do not impede the remote-viewing process in any way. That is, even when the target is not yet determined at the time that the viewing occurs, there is no discernable difference in the quality of the remote-viewing experience! Put differently, the time at which the tasking occurs appears to be independent of the results of the remote-viewing outcome.

Session Snapshots

The above numerical analysis needs to be supplemented with session snapshots to more fully appreciate the quality of these results. In this collection of remote-viewing sessions, two sessions from viewer 1 received scores of 3. Both of these sessions are also tasking-post situations. Since the primary concern here is to investigate this seemingly "impossible" situation, I focus on the session snapshots for these two targets.

Session Snapshot for Viewer 1, Target 4 (the football game in the stadium)
Central Descriptors: large and heavy structure on land, vigorous subjects, subjects engaged in activity, shouting, yelling, intense emotions, anger, crowd, talking, chattering, leader
Central Consolidations:
- The structure seems prominent, isolated, or separate from surrounding in some way.
- (There are) subjects in an open area in a large structure.
- There appears to be lots of subjects engaged in much activity.
- This looks like subjects in an open area inside a structure, like a courtyard, outside but contained.
- This is like a riot or demonstration. People are shouting.
- [Aspect #2] It is as if the subject (a male leader) needs to control something or others.
- [Aspect #3] Like the hum of a crowd when everyone is talking.
- [Aspect #3] I am slightly above these subjects, looking downward.
- [Aspect #3] Now I feel far away, looking at some large structure.

Shifts in Perspective Matching Numbered Aspects: Yes
Deviating Data: Few if any.
Sketch: Figure 4.5

Session Snapshot for Viewer 1, Target 5 (Machu Picchu)
Central Descriptors: sloping land, feels both natural and manmade, structures, rocky structure, hollow, primitive structures on dry land, bird noises, outdoors sounds, rocky, outdoors, primitive, foliage, rounded mountain, cliff face, stone structures, tourist place now, ruins, old, ancient Indian burial ground, mountain, adobe house, settlement, village, Machu Picchu (The target was named in the session.)
Central Consolidations:
- Dry land with small things on top that feel manmade

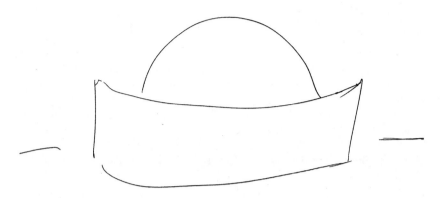

Figure 4.5. Sketch of a football stadium

- Multiple low-level structures on what appears to be flat or gently sloping land.
- The structures appear small, like one-room houses.
- There is some type of large land formation nearby, like a rounded mountain.
- (There is) a large heavy structure on dry land.
- This feels like a large stone structure.
- It feels like people used to live here, or come here regularly.
- It feels like there are periodic visits to this place still.
- There is a set of structures below me in what seems to be an open area. There also seems to be some kind of mountain or other elevated area.

Shifts in Perspective Matching Numbered Aspects: No (Aspect 2), Yes (Aspect 3)
Deviating Data: Few if any.
Sketches: Figures 4.6, 4.7, 4.8, and 4.9

The sessions for targets 4 and 5 described above are very clear descriptions of the respective targets. In the second example (Machu Picchu), the target was actually named on more than one occasion in the session. Again, the point of showing these session snapshots is to demonstrate unambiguously that the nonconcurrent existence of the targets for these sessions did not impact on quality of the results.

Conclusion

The ideas that remain at the focus of the research presented in this chapter

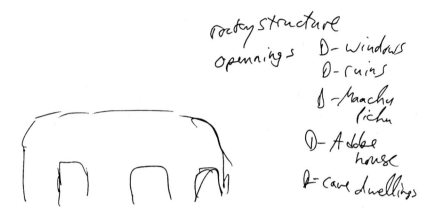

Figure 4.6. A sketch of a structure

involve the influence of time in mediating remote-viewing outcomes. Since we live an existence that appears (on the surface at least) to be structured by forward-moving time, we can frame the ideas that we want to test as hypotheses that are wedded to our normal time-based experiences. At a most basic level, our first hypothesis must deal with the possibility of future events being able to influence current events.

Null Hypothesis #1: Events that exist in the future do not yet exist and thus cannot influence past events.
Alternative Hypothesis #1: Events that exist in the future can influence current events, and thus future events must in some way exist simultaneously with current and past events.

Tasking-post situations do work, and there is no evidence presented here that indicates that they work any less well than tasking-prior situations. Thus, the null hypothesis #1 is clearly wrong and we must reject it in favor of the alternative hypothesis #1. If we define the "current" as the time that the remote viewing takes place, then the future time of tasking (following scenario 3 in figure 4.1) must exist concurrently with the current time of viewing. Following this same logic, we can state our next hypothesis.

Null Hypothesis #2: Time is relative to the observer as specified by the special and general theories of relativity, and it always exists at some relative rate of forward progress as a real and fixed dimension of physical reality that fundamentally structures and separates the sequencing of events such that a future event at one time point cannot exist concurrently with, nor can it influence, another event that exists at a previous time point.

Figure 4.7. A sketch of a structure

Alternative Hypothesis #2: Future events which are clearly separated in time from past events can influence past events as if they are both concurrent entities, and thus time must be an illusion of perception that does not fundamentally separate the sequencing of events.

The results presented in this chapter clearly support rejecting the null hypothesis #2 in favor of accepting the alternative hypothesis #2. Time appears to be only a perceptual phenomenon, not a real separator of sequential development. Apparently, as humans, we can only experience the reality of sequential simultaneity via perceptual information which traverses the physical/subspace interface. But the data presented here indicate that the phenomenon of sequential simultaneity is real, and it seems impossible to escape the conclusion that our "normal" assumption that only the instant of the present exists is wrong. The idea that only one point in time can exist, and that the past ceases to exist, and that the future does not yet exist, does not seem to be supportable in light of these data. Interestingly, science writer James Glanz has noted that an increasing number of physicists are also beginning to accept (for

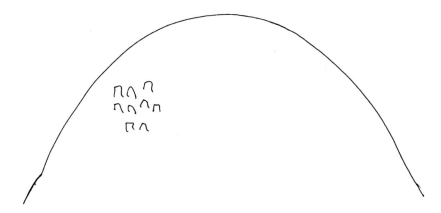

Figure 4.8. Locational sketch of structures on a mountain

their own reasons) the alternative hypothesis #2 as a real possibility [*The New York Times*, 19 June 2001, p. D2(N)].

These are bold conclusions to make from any set of data. I have no illusions in thinking that these conclusions will be accepted easily. Ultimately physicists with cosmological interests will need to explain better than I have done here how sequential simultaneity is possible from some theoretical perspective. Already there is progress in demonstrating in experiments with radiation that the future can be witnessed before the past. In particular, some scientists have already managed to produce waves that travel faster than the speed of light, and Dr. Lijun Wang has recently demonstrated that under certain circumstances light can be made to travel approximately 300 times faster than its previously considered limit ["Faster Than Light, Maybe, But Not Back to the Future," by James Glanz, *The New York Times*, 30 May 2000, pp. D1&3(N)]. In Wang's experiments, the light traveled so fast that it exited the experimental chamber before it entered. The issue here is not that these radiation experiments prove the remote-viewing results. Of course, the results presented in this volume must stand by themselves. But it is important to point out that our prior assumptions about time are likely to be addressed in a variety of different forums, and the remote-viewing results offer us extra insight with respect to our pursuit of a more suitable theory of time.

The conservative skeptic is correct in pointing out that all of this makes sense only if remote viewing itself is a real and demonstrable phenomenon, and in this situation quantity and quality are important. I address this issue in chapter 6 where I discuss the results of a long series of experiments in a publicly monitored demonstration of remote viewing that was conducted under highly controlled conditions. With interest to the subject of the current chapter, all of the experiments conducted in the public demonstration are of the tasking-post

Figure 4.9. Locational sketch of structures showing foliage

variety. But first I move onto yet a different remote-viewing experiment, one designed to investigate whether remote-viewing investigations can successfully incorporate large numbers of sessions processed in batches, a common characteristic of many previous experimental designs.

APPENDIX TO CHAPTER 4

TABLE A4.1. Target Specifics for the Alpha Project

Target 1
Essential Cue
The Imperial Garden / The Forbidden City, Beijing, China (1901)

Numbered Aspects
1. The Imperial Garden / The Forbidden City, Beijing, China (9 July 1901, 5 p.m. Beijing local time)
2. The Pavilion of 10,000 Spring Seasons / The Imperial Garden / The Forbidden City, Beijing, China - perspective: viewing the Pavilion of 10,000 Spring Seasons from 40 feet away, 6 feet above ground level (9 July 1901, 5 p.m. Beijing local time)
3. The structure atop the Hill of Accumulated Elegance / The Imperial Garden / The Forbidden City, Beijing, China - perspective: viewing the Emperor and Empress within the structure atop the Hill of Accumulated Elegance (at the time of visitatin by both the Emperor and the Empress)

Target 2
Essential Cue
Haughton Crater / Devon Island, Canada (26 July 1997, 4 p.m. GMT)

Numbered Aspects
1. Haughton Crater / Devon Island, Canada (26 July 1997, 4 p.m. GMT)
2. Emeral Lake / Haughton Crater / Devon Island, Canada (26 July 1997, 4 p.m. GMT)
3. The Slope of Woe / Haughton Crater / Devon Island, Canada - perspective: as seen from 100 feet above the Slope of Woe (26 July 1997, 4 p.m. GMT)

Target 3
Essential Cue
Io (13 August 1999, 3 p.m. GMT)

Numbered Aspects
1. Io (13 August 1999, 3 p.m. GMT)
2. The highest elevated point on the volcano known ad "Pillan Patera" / Io (13 August 1999, 3 p.m. GMT)
3. The center of the inner core of Io (13 August 1999, 3 p.m. GMT)

Target 4
Essential Cue
The football game between the Washington Redskins and the New York Giants / Fedex Field / Landover, Maryland (21 November 1999)

Numbered Aspects
1. The football game between the Washington Redskins and the New York Giants / Fedex Field / Landover, Maryland (21 November 1999)
2. The Washington Redskins players playing on the field during the 37th play of the game Fedex Field / Landover, Maryland (21 November 1999)
3. Fedex Field - perspective: as seen from 100 feet directly above the center of the stadium

Target 5
Essential Cue
Machu Picchu / Peru

Numbered Aspects
1. Machu Picchu / Peru (1 September 1983, 7 p.m. Peru local time)
2. Hiram Bingham / at the moment of initially "discovering" Machu Picchu (24 July 1911)
3. The highest elevated point of the peak of Machu Picchu - perspective: as seen horizontally from 20 feet away.

Target 6
Essential Cue
Waikiki, Hawaii

Numbered Aspects
1. Waikiki, Hawaii - perspective: from 35 feet above Waikiki Beach, looking down upon the beach and the subjects on the beach (4 July 1994, 1pm local time)
2. The extinct volcano known as Diamond Head/Waikiki, Hawaii – perspective: as seen from the shore of Waikiki Beach, looking directly upon Diamond Head (4 July 1994, 1pm local time)
3. The area of land now known as "Waikiki", Hawaii (4 July 1835)

Target 7
Essential Cue
Mir Space Station (23 September 1997, 8am GMT)

Numbered Aspects
1. Mir Space Station (23 September 1997, 8am GMT)

2. The subjects within Mir Space Station (23 September 1997, 8am GMT)
3. The main sleeping area within Mir Space Station (23 September 1997, 8am GMT)

Target 8
Essential Cue
Great Pyramid of Khufu/Egypt (11 September 1999, 6pm Cairo time)

Numbered Aspects
1. Great Pyramid of Khufu/Egypt (11 September 1999, 6pm Cairo time)
2. The largest chamber within the Great Pyramid of Khufu/Egypt (11 September 1999, 6pm Cairo time)
3. 400 feet above the Great Pyramid of Khufu - perspective: looking downwards at the Great Pyramid of Khufu/Egypt (11 September 1999, 6pm Cairo time)

Target 9
Essential Cue
Times Square, New York City

Numbered Aspects
1. Times Square, New York City – perspective: from ground level (1 January 2000, 12:01am EST)
2. Times Square, New York City – perspective: from 2,000 feet above ground level (1 January 2000, 12:01am EST)
3. Times Square, New York City – perspective: from ground level (3 June 1930, 2pm EST)

Target 10
Essential Cue
The USS Missouri (2 September 1945)

Numbered Aspects
1. The USS Missouri (2 September 1945, 5am GMT)
2. General Yoshirjiro Umezo during the signing of the "surrender document" (2 September 1945)
3. The water 30 meters directly below the USS Missouri (2 September 1945, 5am GMT)

CHAPTER 5

The Repeated Trial Problem:
The Lottery Revisited

I spent one summer in the late 1990s in Vermont with my family. During my stay up north, I developed many of the ideas relating to binary analysis that are presented in chapter 3 of this volume. Over the period of about a month, in the early morning hours in my apartment, I conducted hundreds of trials in which I would use a computer to give me a target that was selected randomly from a pool. The targets were typically shapes with curves, angles, straight lines, and so on, but I also used other types of "real-world" targets. In each trial, I would attempt to describe that target. The sessions would be very short, each one lasting only a few minutes. The choice of the correct target for each trial was determined by a binary event, such as when a computer would randomly pick a 0 or a 1. I often conducted many trials for each binary event in an attempt to use a "majority-rule decision" to determine the correct outcome of the binary event.

This type of experiment has been repeated seemingly countless times with variations in numerous psi labs. I was not trying to be original that summer. Mostly, I was having fun trying to do something that others had also tried. Sometimes researchers in psi labs report results using large numbers of trials that seem to offer statistical significance supporting the hypothesis of psi functioning. But other times the results are more ambiguous, and statistical significance seems nowhere in sight.

My own attempts with these experiments in Vermont were not successful. Indeed, I failed utterly in being able to predict a binary event, regardless of how hard I tried, or which variation of procedure I used. On one hand, I was surprised with these results since I had worked so long learning how to remote view. That I had developed some level of mastery of the remote-viewing process was not in doubt in my mind. I was able to use the SRV methodology to describe arguably unique characteristics of randomly chosen verifiable targets, and I expected that this learned skill would be transferable to other procedures in other experimental situations. If I could do it once, why would there be any difficultly doing it hundreds of times, or thousands? Moreover, even if I made occasional mistakes, if I performed a sufficient number of trials, would not the correct answer eventually become apparent?

On the other hand, I was aware that my short sessions with these binary targets were considerably different from my normal longer sessions. Moreover, the binary targets were symbols typically distinguishable by whether or not they had curves, angles, parallel lines, and so on. I was not used to these types of symbol targets, and it has long been demonstrated by other researchers that remote-viewing quality degrades in forced-choice situations in which the viewer knows the possibilities. My normal remote-viewing targets were more open-ended real-world targets, like structures, mountains, oceans, islands, significant human activity, aircraft, and generally anything. They were targets about which I did not know all of the possibilities. Ultimately, I decided that my failure with these binary experiments was due to both the relatively predictable nature of the symbol targets as well as the short nature of the sessions. I assumed that long sessions with complex targets were needed to keep the interest of the mind, thereby enhancing the accuracy of the trials. The binary experiment described in chapter 3 of this volume is a result of this type of thinking.

But there were other elements in my experiences of that summer in Vermont that bothered me, even though I did not know how important they might be at the time. I was particularly concerned about the repetitive nature of the trials themselves. I had long known that the conscious mind was able to interfere with psi experiments, especially if the experiments became predictable. Repetitive trials seemed to offer a perfect opportunity for conscious-mind meddling, and I saw no reason why the conscious mind could not offer a mental image that looked just like an acceptable remote-viewing image, especially if what was required was curves, angles, parallel lines, and so on. But I also considered the possibility that boredom might play a role. If a subject's conscious mind could become bored while looking for certain characteristics of a target, could not the subject's subspace mind similarly become bored, perhaps refusing to cooperate, perhaps mischievously perceiving the wrong target? I did not have answers to these questions. I just knew that the long sessions to which I was accustomed seemed to work, and the short sessions with the symbol-based binary targets did not work for whatever reason.

After completing the experiment presented in chapter 3 of this volume, I began to re-evaluate the binary problem based on what had been learned with the new results. In particular, I felt that successful remote-viewing experiments relating to binary methodologies would require eliminating the potential for telepathic mental contamination originating from the human analysts. But I still did not know if eliminating such contamination would be enough to "guarantee" success if there was also a problem with large numbers of trials, as discussed above. Thus, a new experiment was designed, one which used a computer program to eliminate the human analyst entirely, but which allowed the use of a large number of trials in a binary associative remote-viewing scheme. I decided to call this computer program the "Session Analysis Machine," or simply SAM.

In many respects, SAM's development is not unlike similar efforts by Nelson, Dunne, Dobyns, and Jahn in the Princeton Engineering Anomalies

Research (PEAR) Remote Perception program to develop computer-based analytical judging methods to replace the human judging process (see for example, Nelson, Dunne, Dobyns, and Jahn 1996). Also, May, Utts, Humphrey, Luke, Frivold, and Trask (1990) published a paper describing a creative approach to coding remote-viewing data using "fuzzy set" technology that was designed to enable computer-based analysis. It is useful in the context of the current chapter to explain how our approach differs from that used by May and his colleagues. While some of the ideas in the paper by May, et al. are intriguing (especially the use of fuzzy set technology), other parts of their approach are deeply troubling to us, and our concerns relate specifically to our own experience with the remote-viewing phenomenon.

From our perspective as remote viewers, many of the coding items used to construct the "universal set of elements" used by May, et al. are intolerably too high level. For example, there are items such as fort, castle, palace, church, mosque, pagoda, and coliseum as possible codings for structures. Yet for us, if a viewer finds, say, a structure, it is fine to say that the structure is made of natural materials such as stone, that it has multiple levels, that it has openings in the sides that have curved or arched tops, and so on. But for the viewer to conclude that this is a castle — or even like a castle — would entail a huge violation of our viewing procedures. A castle is a label of a very high-level object. It involves all sorts of interpretation, and any viewer that said that there is a castle at a target site would very likely continue with a story-line in the session that could include anything from knights of the roundtable to Mozart concerts in Salzburg. We require our viewers to keep their descriptions at the lowest possible level, and this means avoiding many labels of the type used by May and his colleagues. Similarly, we would never expect a remote viewer to be able to tell the difference between a church and a mosque. If the viewer describes a structure that has the same shape as the target structure, we are satisfied. If the viewer also perceives that this structure is associated with a religious idea, all the better. Some remote viewers might perceive a specific idea of a mosque or a church, but we require that such ideas be listed as deductions (not data) since they are so high-level, and thus prone to conscious-mind interpretation.

We have similar problems with the idea of May, et al. (even as analysts) coding psychically perceived data in terms of high-level and clearly defined structure parts (or elements) rather than describing these parts with low-level terms. Such high-level elements in their report include boats, pier, motorized vehicles, column, spire, fountain, fence, arch, wall, monument, and roads, with some parts unexplainably listed in plural and others singular. In our experience as remote viewers, we simply would never want ourselves or any viewers to code (and thus interpret) their data in such high level terms. A flat wooden structure that begins on land and extends over water is fine to describe, but to have the viewer label this as a pier would likely initiate a storyline that just might have the old man of the sea fishing in an idyllic setting while watching a beautiful sunset. That is, we want the viewer to describe (not label) with low-level terms the structure and its elements. We carefully avoid using high-level labels in these descriptions. At best, this is a post-session job of a remote-viewing analyst who knows something about the target. But even as an analyst there is the potential for creating a false target influence due to the telepathic transmission of such high-level interpretive thoughts (see below).

In defense of May et al., they argue that a blind analyst (or a consensus of blind analysts) should do these codings, and that the analyst(s) is using the fuzzy set idea of examining the remote-viewing data only to see if they reflect a part of the idea of the coded term. But our experience with experiments such as that described in chapter 3 suggests that it is not possible to separate the analysis from the targeting process, and any attempt to use such high-level terms in such an analysis would result in an interpretation of the remote-viewing data that would corrupt the targeting and closing process. This would be particularly troublesome in situations in which the analyst(s) did not know the identity of the actual target (i.e., blind analysis) and was trying to fit the remote-viewing data into the given high-level coding scheme. The analyst(s) would unavoidably need to interpret the data, and this interpretation would by itself create a target, or at least create a biasing influence on the real target in the viewer's mind. Using more than one analyst in a consensus framework would only further confuse matters by creating a competition of targeting ideas within the minds of the group of analysts.

I do not have the space here to describe each problem for each of the structure element terms mentioned above from the report by May et al. But one more example might illustrate the depth of the problem of using high-level labels in a situation that most people might at first consider nonproblematic. When we remote view, we try to describe things like boats as structures on water rather than as boats simply because we do not really know if every structure on water is a boat. It could be a crashed airplane, or a house blown into the sea by a hurricane, and so on. It is also possible for a viewer to make a decoding error and place a structure on water when it is actually on land but near water. If the viewer calls it a boat, he or she will probably get nothing right in the remainder of the session. But if the viewer calls it a structure, we leave open the possibility of the viewer fixing the decoding error with regard to its placement later in the session. After all, the idea that it is a structure is correct. The only problem is where it is located. If the viewer calls it a boat, then it is doubtful that he or she would ever re-locate the "boat" on land, which is where the structure actually is. Further examples of labels used by May, et al. that we find too high-level to be useful include port or harbor (we would say a land/water interface with nearby structures), oasis (we would say water surrounded by flat dry land), agricultural fields or orchards (we would say flat land with uniform vegetation), and so on.

We also have low-level problems (as compared with the high-level problems discussed above) with some of the other codings used by May and his colleagues. For example, they spend a lot of space coding various colors (14 of them). We would not want to have a viewer attempt to perceive that level of precision with regard to colors. Viewers typically run into all sorts of colors at a target, and we have not spent much time trying to train them to differentiate between various hues at a target site. Indeed, if they spend much time on hue differentiation, they will risk having the conscious mind intervene with these subtle distinctions, and they will not have much time left to go after the more important things, like structures, activities, land forms, and so on.

I should add at this point that I do not find all of the codings used by May and his colleagues problematic. Some of their interface ideas are useful (like land/water), as are some ambience ideas (such as ordered or aligned, disordered or jumbled, open, and congested). Similarly, some of their geometry ideas are interesting (such as parallel lines, horizontal lines, diagonal lines, etc.), and we have similarly employed many of these. Yet perhaps I might characterize our general or overall impression with the report by May and his colleagues as an interesting set of ideas (fuzzy set technology, coding concepts, etc.) that is oriented toward using computers to analyze remote-viewing data more from a logical and conscious-mind perspective than from the perspective of the remote-viewing experience itself, or at least our experience of the remote-viewing process. It is what we see as their misunderstanding of what controls the remote-viewing process in the first place that leads to an analytical framework that ultimately corrupts that very same process.

Finally, I note that May and his colleagues initially used their approach post hoc by having themselves code sessions (i.e., create "response fuzzy sets") that were conducted previously and used for prior experiments, and thus they did not encounter the coding problems that we expect to occur if viewers or blind analysts are to enter the remote-viewing data into a computer using their coding scheme. In a real experimental situation they would not use their approach post hoc. Yet as stated previously, we do not trust the idea of using another person — or persons, if a consensus judgment is used — who does not know something about the target to examine the sessions and interpret and code the viewers' data because of the problem of allowing analyst-originating thoughts to interfere with the targeting process as per the discussion presented in chapter 3. This problem arises with the May et al. scheme because the codes themselves require significant interpretation, and since they are otherwise so alien to the remote-viewing experience as we understand it. To avoid such problems, a coding scheme would be needed that used lower-level descriptions that employ viewer-acceptable language and a minimal degree of interpretation.

Thus, we designed SAM to reflect the remote-viewing experience as we know it. We also decided to attempt to make SAM as simple as possible, in the sense of having viewers make a minimal set of coding decisions that would capture their sessions as completely as necessary such that the results could still be used to differentiate one target from another. In the end, perhaps the most important aspect of the report by May and his colleagues for us is the idea of using fuzzy set technology with computer-based analysis. We have also experimented with fuzzy-set concepts using SAM, and these attempts led to derivative efforts to try a variety of novel weighting schemes as we worked to mold SAM into a substitute for a human analyst. (In particular, see the Russell procedure in the next chapter.) We are still experimenting with these ideas, and computer-based analysis may ultimately require a variety of formulas in a multi-directional approach that more closely approximates the diverse judging considerations of human analysts.

Session Analysis Machine (SAM)

The idea behind SAM is simple enough. A viewer would conduct a remote-viewing session for a target that would be chosen in the future by SAM. After conducting the remote-viewing session, the viewer would then input a description of the target into a computer in order to produce a data set of perceptions for that target. Then SAM would randomly choose two targets from a large pool of targets. Each target would be of high quality, including a picture as well as a verbal description, and the pair of targets would have many obvious opposing characteristics, such as a mountain scene versus an urban environment, or a collection of structures versus an island with only foliage, and so on. Each target would also have its own descriptive data set that corresponds in structure with the data set of perceptions produced by the remote viewer. SAM would then compare the data from the remote-viewing session with the descriptive characteristics for each target to determine which target correlates best with the session data. This would yield a prediction of a binary event. When the binary event actually occurs, the correct target that is associated with that binary outcome would be given to the viewer as feedback, and SAM would destroy the other target by erasing it from the computer hard drive. Thus, no human would ever know the opposite target that was used in the binary evaluations of the remote-viewing session. All of the remote-viewing sessions would be of the long variety as described throughout this volume, and the targets would all be real-world targets with as much diversity as possible.

In theory, this set-up would solve the human analyst problem as discussed in chapter 3. A viewer would receive a target for each session completed, just as would normally occur in any other remote-viewing situation. There would be no telepathic interference from human judges with thoughts of other targets. When designing this experiment, I discounted the possibility that the computer itself could produce telepathic interference, although evidence of this might be easy to spot if the switched-session phenomenon re-appeared in this new setting. This essentially isolates the issue of repetitive taskings (that is, trials) in this experiment. Such repetitions are necessary in order to add certainty to the choice of an associated binary outcome, and we wanted to know if large numbers of trials would work in situations in which the switched-session phenomenon is eliminated.

The Target Pool and Straining the Sessions

To produce a data set for each remote-viewing session, a questionnaire was designed that contained a list of possible target characteristics. After each remote-viewing session, the viewer would use a computer and a web-based form to enter those characteristics that most closely fit the session data. The process of filtering out the essential elements from the remote-viewing data is called "straining the session," and care was made to ensure that the questionnaire was sufficiently complete so as to allow a representative data set to be constructed for a large variety of target types. The data variables (i.e., codings) are presented in table A5.1, which is located in the appendix to this chapter. General categories (called "elementals") of data types are in the first column, while the specific variables (called "expandables") are in the second column. To strain a remote-viewing session, the viewer clicks on a radio button that is located next to each of the expandables that are listed in the second column of table A5.1. (The radio buttons are not included in the table.) All this results in creating a data set for each remote-viewing session that is composed of a collection of 0s and 1s, where a 0 means that an expandable was not perceived while a 1 means that this characteristic was perceived.

For this experiment, a target pool of 238 highly varied targets was assembled. The targets were obtained by volunteers at the Institute who found them on various Internet resources. Some targets were also found using large photographic databases available in most computer stores. I was involved in assembling the target pool as well, and while this is not optimal, the target pool was of sufficient size and diversity that my knowledge of the targets in the pool was not a significant issue. "Purists" may disagree, of course. But a great deal of experience using remote viewing with such pools has taught us that if the pool is sufficiently large and diverse, the conscious mind maintains very little hope of guessing a target. We are looking at the problem not from the perspective of disallowing cheating, but from the perspective of maximizing the viewer's ability to describe a target well. In general, target pools with over 200 highly diverse targets are considered "safe," in the sense that viewers can avoid having their conscious minds interfere with the data collection process — and thus *lower* the chance of describing the target well — when using such a large target pool. Also, the current experiment is based on an objective test: a lottery outcome. This assures a randomized target choice from the pool.

A data set for each target was created using the same web-based form described above for straining a session. Thus, each target has its own data set of 0s and 1s to describe its essential characteristics. A decision was made to add a restriction to the target pool by following the advice of May, Spottiswoode, and James (1994a), and thus flying structures (e.g., airplanes, space vehicles, etc.) were not allowed. Nonetheless, other targets with great variety were allowed, including targets with surface-based structures of all types and in many settings, targets with mountains and other natural settings, islands without structures, and targets of great variety on both water and land. In general, this was a target pool with great variety even if it did not have flying targets.

Each target in the pool was also chosen to maximize the amount of meaningful information, which is related to the concept of "Shannon Entropy" as described by May, Spottiswoode, and James (1994b) as well as Watt (1988). May, Spottiswoode, and James (1994b) use this concept in connection to the physical characteristics of a photograph that identifies a target. (See also May, Spottiswoode, and Faith 2000.) These researchers have measured these characteristics in terms of the pixel color intensity. However, digital analysis of pixel characteristics was not used to construct the target set for this experiment. Rather, cognitive content was judged by choosing targets that had dramatic visual appeal, such as pictures of the Grand Teton mountains, or Palestinians rioting in Jerusalem, or the World Trade Center buildings in Manhattan, and so on. (Note that this experiment was conducted prior to 11 September 2001.) Experience has shown both at The Farsight Institute and elsewhere that such targets more often elicit correct descriptions from viewers than do more boring targets, such as a photograph of a telephone.

Collecting the Remote-Viewing Data

It was desirable in this experiment to control for viewing variations among viewers. For this reason, only one remote viewer was used, myself. To prepare for each remote-viewing session in this experiment, I meditated for approximately one hour. Normally, this was accomplished by conveniently scheduling my remote-viewing session immediately after my normal morning and afternoon practice of the TM-Sidhi Program. All remote-viewing sessions were conducted in the same setting, a square room specially designed for remote viewing. The room has no furniture visible to the viewer except a table in the center of the room, diagonally facing a corner. The color of the room is beige, including the carpet on the floor. There are no pictures on the walls.

Each remote-viewing session typically lasted from between 45 minutes to one hour. It takes about 15 minutes afterward to strain the session into SAM. If one includes the meditation time, the entire process takes from two to two and one-half hours to complete. For this experiment, 128 sessions were collected. These sessions were distributed over 16 binary digits representing four balls in a Georgia Cash 4 lottery, exactly as was done in the experiment described in chapter 3 of this volume. Thus, each binary digit was represented by eight remote-viewing sessions. SAM's goal was to use these sessions to determine whether each binary digit will be a 0 or a 1, as determined by a future lottery.

Comparing the Remote-Viewing Data with the Target Data

After straining all 128 sessions into SAM, the program assigns two targets at random to each session. For each pair of potential targets, SAM searches to find targets that are "opposites" in terms of essential characteristics. Thus, no two targets both have mountains, or structures, or islands, and so on. SAM then compares each session with both opposite targets for each binary set. SAM works with both raw counts of session/target matches as well as a variety of weighted counts and statistics, and then makes a decision based on these calculations. That is, SAM begins its analysis by counting the raw number of matches between each session data set and the data sets for the two targets in the pair for that session. SAM also calculates and utilizes (1) the proportion of total session characteristics that are unique matches for each target (as compared with overlapping characteristics for both of the potential targets), and (2) the proportion of total target characteristics that are unique matches for a session. In the former case, SAM divides the total unique matches by the total number of session characteristics identified by the viewer, while in the latter case, the division is by the total number of target characteristics. SAM also identifies matches for particularly important characteristics for each target and for the session, such as whether or not mountains are perceived, or large bodies of water, or many structures in an urban environment, and so on. After taking all of this into account in a weighting scheme that awards points to each target for each calculated advantage it has over the other target when both targets are compared with the session data, SAM then makes a prediction of whether the correct target in each pair will be associated with a 0 or a 1. SAM then tabulates all of this information and makes a prediction of which ball will be chosen for a given Cash 4 lottery.

Part of the design of this experiment is the continual inclusion of doubt at all levels such that no human ever has any solid information regarding the lottery prediction process. For example, from the Farsight Base-10 to Binary Numerical Code (table 3.1), there are 10 combinations of 0s and 1s out of a total possible of 16 combinations (2^4). Thus, there is a 6/16 probability of SAM not coming up with a ball choice for any given run if the SAM-based process were to be considered comparable to a random draw. Also, there can be situations in which the eight sessions for a binary digit do not resolve into a clear choice for SAM, so the actual probability of not having a prediction for a ball is still higher. Thus, the design of the experiment is such that participants in the experiment will never be able to "fix" in their minds what the eventual SAM lottery outcome will be, thereby minimizing the possibility of telepathic leakage that might corrupt the data collection process.

When SAM is finished, a text file that contains the lottery ball predictions is created and given to someone who purchases lottery tickets. This person must not know how successful SAM was in making its lottery predictions. If this person sees that SAM could not make a prediction for a ball, then he or she would know that the remote-viewing experiment did not succeed, and we want to rule out the possibility that this information could influence the closing of the sessions by the viewer through any telepathic means. That is, we do not want anything to potentially influence the loop in time that contains the viewing and the session closing, and any person having advanced (with respect to the closing time) information that the process did or did not work could potentially corrupt the integrity of the loop. To solve this potential problem, SAM first evaluates the remote-viewing sessions with regard to their ability to produce a lottery prediction, and then SAM produces a random number as a ball choice for all situations in which the remote-viewing sessions did not resolve into a lottery prediction. Thus, the person who is buying lottery tickets does not know if a predicted ball number is a random number or a number based on the evaluation of the remote-viewing data.

Testing SAM

Before using SAM in a full lottery, the SAM system was put through a number of preliminary tests, and five formal tests. In each of the tests, the goal was to attempt to predict one binary digit for one ball. Some refinements were made to the SAM system along the way, but the basic system remained intact throughout the five formal tests. There was one major difference in one of the formal tests, however. In the fourth test, the closing process was shortened to more closely approximate that which would be possible in a situation in which many sessions had to be closed in a short period of time, as I explain more thoroughly below.

When closing remote-viewing sessions in the context of SAM, it is important to examine whether or not each remote-viewing session contains information that is unique or deeply descriptive of the target's characteristics, not merely the correct prediction of the binary digit. For example, in the third test, one remote-viewing session was used. The target was the Wailing Wall in Jerusalem. In this session, clear descriptions of the Wailing Wall were obtained, including descriptions of many subjects packed closely together with an open structure surrounding them. The viewer described many subjects in a "sunken or depressed area, an area surrounded by something raised, like a border." Appropriate sketches were also made that closely characterized the target's essential characteristics.

For the preliminary tests, SAM was simply used to pick targets one at a time from the target pool for single sessions that were done by myself and others at the Institute. The preliminary tests were not associated with a lottery outcome. All of these tests were essentially identical to practices that we have long and routinely used when employing a computer to pick targets from a pool, and the preliminary tests using SAM in this regard worked fine. Nearly all of these tests produced remote-viewing sessions with solid and obvious target contact.

The five formal tests of the SAM system using batches of sessions associated with a lottery outcome were by and large successful, with the exception of test 4. For the first test, SAM predicted the correct binary digit using 3 out of 5 sessions, with the two missing sessions producing data that resulted in SAM not being able to make a decision (which is different from making an incorrect decision). Thus, the two missing sessions did not predict the incorrect binary digit. Their data were simply insufficiently focused for SAM to be able to make a definitive choice of targets for each of the two binary pairs of targets for those two sessions. For the second test, SAM predicted the correct binary digit using 2 out of 2 sessions. For the third test, one session was used with excellent remote-viewing results obtained, and that session is described above with regard to the Wailing Wall in Jerusalem target.

For the fourth test, SAM missed terribly. Two sessions produced data with which SAM could not make a definitive decision. Of the other three sessions, SAM predicted the incorrect binary digit. What is more telling of these results is that the remote-viewing data themselves were of a very poor quality, in the sense that the sessions generally did not reflect any of the essential target characteristics. As it turns out, the major difference between this test and the other tests appears to have been the shortcuts made in the closing process. All of the sessions for the fourth test were closed in a period of about 45 minutes (total for all sessions), and essentially no break was taken between the closing of one session and the closing of another session. Again, these conditions more closely paralleled what we expected to occur in a full lottery experiment in which many sessions needed to be closed in a short period of time. I discuss this more thoroughly below.

Following the fourth test, a fifth test was run. In this case, SAM predicted the correct binary digit using 3 out of 5 remote-viewing sessions. The sessions were closed a bit more slowly than with the fourth experiment, with a minor break of a few minutes taken between each closing. A short break was not optimal, but it was felt necessary to try to attempt some process that would be compatible with a full lottery experiment in which a large number of sessions needed to be closed in a relatively short period of time. In this batch of sessions, two were of excellent quality, one was satisfactory with regard to SAM criteria but not exceptional with regard to describing target subtleties, and two sessions were of very poor quality.

In general, the SAM process seemed to work very well in situations in which all sessions were closed normally, which (for SRV) means taking about one half-hour to close each session, followed by a long break of at least one hour (sometimes a day) before looking at any other target or remote-viewing data. The SAM process worked poorly if the closing process was too brief and done without a break between each closing, and it seemed to offer the potential for working satisfactorily if the closing process was slightly longer with short breaks (of a minute or so) taken between closing each session. Isolating the target in the closer's mind is the key, and mentally mixing too many target ideas by closing multiple sessions in a short time may never be a good idea. But this is precisely what we needed to test, and it was necessary to work with the realities of the lottery situation and the need to close a number of sessions in a relatively short period of time. These were not a lot of tests of the SAM system prior to working with a full lottery. But these tests were very expensive in terms of viewing time, and it was not possible to continue with partial tests indefinitely. Recall that each session consumes about two and one-half hours of time if one includes the meditation period prior to viewing (one hour), the actual viewing time (one hour), and the computer time used to strain the session into SAM (15 minutes to half an hour). Moreover, we knew that the only way to fully test the system was to do it on a full lottery. Feeling that the SAM system was as ready as it was going to get in the absence of a full lottery test, the decision was made to proceed with a full lottery experiment.

The Results of the Full-Lottery Test

In part to help compensate for the effects of a shorter closing process, the decision was made to use eight sessions for each binary digit. This required 128 sessions for a full lottery test involving 16 binary choices required for four ball numbers.

The SAM analysis for the full lottery experiment was completed on the 19th of June 2001. SAM made four ball predictions by writing these numbers in a computer file that was given unopened to a person who then opened the file in private and bought a number of lottery tickets for the mid-day lottery of the 20th of June. All tickets purchased were for the same predicted 4-digit number. After the time of the lottery, I then obtained the correct lottery numbers for all four balls and input them into SAM. All of the correct targets (for each binary pair of targets) for all 128 sessions were retained by SAM, and all of the incorrect targets were eliminated from the computer's hard drive. Still ignorant of whether or not SAM had correctly predicted the lottery outcome, I then began to close the 128 sessions using the correct targets for each session. Due to scheduling requirements, it was necessary to close all sessions over a period of two full working days. It was possible to take a break of a few minutes, plus a walk around my basement, between closing each session.

As it turns out, the process did not work. I will begin with a numerical summary, but the more interesting story resides in the description of the actual closing process as I discuss below. Of the 16 binary digits, SAM correctly predicted 4 of them. SAM made incorrect predictions for 7 binary digits, and was unable to make any prediction for 5 binary digits. With regard to the actual lottery ball numbers, SAM was unable to predict a single ball, and as a result, all four ball numbers offered by SAM were simply random numbers as drawn in situations in which no choice could be made using the remote-viewing data.

Before continuing, it is necessary to point out that SAM's failure to predict the correct lottery number cannot be the result of simply using a computer to choose targets, as compared with having a human choose targets as is done with other experiments discussed in this volume. It has long been a routine and successful experience among Farsight remote viewers to have computers choose targets for viewing from a large pool. There has never been a noticeable qualitative difference in the quality of remote-viewing sessions when computers have been used to pick targets as compared with using human taskers. The fact that human taskers were used for the other experiments presented in this volume is simply a consequence of the nature of the experimental designs used for those particular experiments. The reason behind SAM's failure in the current experiment resides elsewhere, and the recognition of the actual problem is crucial in the current context.

As mentioned above, the more interesting story resides with the description of the closing process. In terms of remote-viewing sessions, SAM was able to correctly place 58 of the sessions. 70 of the sessions resulted in incorrect SAM predictions. Clearly, and from a numerical perspective, SAM did not work successfully in this experiment. But there is more to this story. When closing the sessions, I was struck by the poor quality of the data for the correctly placed sessions (as per SAM criteria). That is, only three of the 58 sessions which SAM correctly placed (with respect to the lottery outcome) contained good descriptions of the essential characteristics of the targets. That is, in 55 cases out of those 58 cases, the session data were terrible. In practical terms this means, for example, that targets that had structures on a flat surface were correctly matched by SAM with sessions that indeed had structures on a flat surface, but the descriptions of the structures in the remote-viewing data had very little resemblance to the structures in the actual targets. Extending the example, there is a big difference between an Apollo spacecraft on the surface of the moon and downtown Chicago. The same can be said with non-structure targets/sessions. Of the three sessions that did match their targets closely, one can assume that in a collection of 128 sessions, a few would inevitably closely match their targets simply by chance. Thus, one must conclude that the SAM results for this experiment were entirely random and not the product of successful remote viewing.

How can we explain this? It would be very wrong to conclude that this is evidence of the impossibility of remote viewing. I have to compare this experience with what I am normally used to when I close a remote-viewing session. Subjectively (and intuitively), when I was closing the 128 sessions, try though I did, I was not able mentally and subjectively to "connect" with each target the way I normally do when I close a session. There was no "sinking" feeling that is common to the closing experience. I sensed that there were too many targets for me to process, and that I could not spend the time each target required to let its essential nature "sink" in a unique way into my consciousness. Indeed, after the closing process was over for all sessions in the experiment, I began to ask myself why anyone would expect any particular target to be a target for any session regardless of how carefully the viewing part of the experiment is conducted if the closing process is seriously truncated. If the results of the switched-session analysis presented in chapter 3 are correct, then the thoughts of the session closer are crucially important to the successful conclusion of the remote-viewing experience. But in this experiment, there were too many targets in my mind, and over the period of two days, they all blended together. In short, there was not a sufficient isolation of each session's closing experience from that of all other remote-viewing experiences, and target isolation (mentally defined) seems to be one crucial factor in achieving success with remote viewing.

These results contrast dramatically with the remote-viewing results presented in the next chapter. In that chapter, 13 public demonstrations of remote viewing done by myself and two other viewers are discussed in detail. The "hit rate" for these public demonstrations appears very high, measured both in terms of subjective descriptive clarity as well as SAM-based objective statistical analysis, and I encourage all readers to examine the results presented in that chapter closely. But in all of those cases, the viewing was accompanied by a slow and calculated closing process. No shortcuts were taken in closing sessions. Moreover, all remote-viewing experiences (either closing or viewing) were carefully isolated from one another. No contamination across demonstrations occurred in part because these 13 public demonstrations took place over a period of six months. With regard to the current lottery experiment, it would not have been possible for us to spread 128 remote-viewing sessions out in a similar fashion.

If my reasoning here is correct, then it may be impossible to use remote viewing to win any lottery. The reason is that the lottery takes a level of precision that requires too many remote-viewing trials to be practical. It is not that the viewing cannot be done, but that the viewings must be coordinated with the closings, and it would simply take too long to both properly view and appropriately close the required number of remote-viewing sessions. Indeed, it is even possible that the time required to close the sessions properly could extend beyond the time limit of the individual lotteries to claim winning tickets if large numbers of sessions are required. Moreover, it may not be advisable for viewers (or analysts) to close sessions in large batches under any circumstances. Closing sessions in large batches reduces the remote-viewing experience to a tertiary role. One is not remote viewing to learn about the target, but rather to determine the outcome of a binary digit, which in turn is needed to win a lottery. If the viewer or analyst knows this when closing a session, it may interfere with the closing process in a manner for which there may be no recovery since the intimate purpose of the remote-viewing process was never to perceive the target, but rather to determine some other desired information. Profoundly successful associative remote-viewing experiments may have to more fully disguise the process so that the binary associations are secondary to the real purpose for conducting the remote-viewing exercise.

But there is more that can be learned from this experiment that is of potential importance to other psi researchers. It is very common for psi researchers to design experiments that use large numbers of trials, normally with minimally trained subjects. For example, in an article by Stanford and Stein (1994), 25 studies of ESP are examined, and the minimum number of trials in each of these studies is 100. The maximum number of trials in these studies is 5200, and the average number of trials is 1500. These studies tend to address the more general issue of ESP, and not remote viewing specifically. But remote-viewing laboratories have also used multiple trials (even if with much lower numbers than those cited above) in experiments designed around establishing evidence of psi functioning. Multiple trials are needed in order to achieve sufficiently high levels of statistical significance in these experiments. Meta-analysis is often used to assemble even greater statistical power by combining multiple studies (see Utts 1996; also Radin 1997, chapter 4). In the absence of meta-analysis, demonstrations of psi functionality are sometimes statistically significant, and other times they hover not too far from chance. Also, it is possible that many experiments designed to test for psi functioning may not have been published due to the researchers' failure to produce statistically meaningful results that positively demonstrate the existence of psi, a special concern for those who conduct meta-analysis using published studies. This is the old "file drawer" phenomenon, and it still requires a bit of faith among some to be convinced by the sometimes energetic arguments suggesting that parapsychology is not affected by it. Yet it is not my intent to weigh into the merits of the "file drawer" issue here, but simply to observe that one reason why parapsychological experiments sometimes may not demonstrate more clearly the effect of psi is due to the problem of working with multiple trials as discussed in this chapter. Thus, even if one concludes that the extant statistical evidence of psi functioning is clear regardless of the file drawer issue, my suggestion is that such evidence could be made even more convincing by restructuring the experimental design that includes the processing of multiple trials in a short period of time.

To summarize the conclusions presented in this chapter, an experimental design that utilizes large numbers of trials that are processed in an insufficient period of time interferes with the functioning of remote viewing, and perhaps psi functioning more generally. At The Farsight Institute, much of our research has been in the area of enhancing the effectiveness of remote-viewing methodologies. We have found that profound target contact can be achieved in many, and sometimes most, instances of remote viewing when the viewers are trained over an extensive period in the use of an appropriate methodology (SRV,

HRVG, CRV, etc.), and if the sessions are evaluated and closed with regard to their content on a session-by-session basis, with care being taken to isolate all mental activity relating to each target until the tasking/viewing/closing loop is entirely complete. Processing sessions quickly in large batches destroys this capability.

How large is a "large" batch of sessions? Ideally, our experience suggests that viewing three long sessions per week is a comfortable rate for many viewers. More than that becomes tiring both physically and psychically. Closing these sessions works best if they can be spaced out to be no more than one per day. Except for the experiments discussed in this chapter, all of the other research presented in this book involves sessions that were conducted and closed under such conditions that allowed for sufficient trial separation. The general issue thus becomes not so much the number of trials in an experiment, but how compactly these trials are spaced. Two or three in a day can be too much in some situations (especially if the sessions are long). It would be helpful if all psi studies published how many trials are processed daily, how long each trial takes to conduct and close, and how much time is given to separate each session and each closing. Stating that there were, say, 40 trials in an experiment is not really sufficient to know how quickly those trials were processed from beginning to end (for example, see Utts 1996, p. 18). The more we learn about the psychic targeting mechanism, the more this extra information becomes important to us. (Again, see especially the next chapter in this volume in which results are presented for a long series of public demonstrations which were conducted under appropriate conditions.)

This success in using highly trained viewers to produce long, descriptive sessions for a target combined with a proper closing strategy is not unique to The Farsight Institute. There are now a number of individuals who have become proficient with an effective remote-viewing methodology and who can regularly produce remarkable remote-viewing results under such conditions. For example, Joe McMoneagle has conducted a number of very public and successful demonstrations of remote viewing, at least some of which have been covered on television in locations all around the world. While Mr. McMoneagle has worked under a large variety of conditions both within and outside of laboratory environments, with these public demonstrations he sometimes works with protocols that utilize a person called an "outbounder." (See McMoneagle 2000, 1998, 1993.) An outbounder is a person who is physically at the target at the time that the remote-viewing session takes place. The instructions given to Mr. McMoneagle are for him to remote view the target that is being witnessed by the outbounder. These public demonstrations sometimes also utilize a short potential list of targets, with one target being the correct one and the others decoys. From the perspective of the research presented in this volume, the outbounder experimental design establishes a psychic link between Mr. McMoneagle and the outbounder that enhances contact with the correct target, and this minimizes the potential of encountering a switched session of the type described in chapter 3 of this volume in which the remote-viewing data are compared against a pool of targets. However, if an outbounder is not used in such settings, research presented in this volume suggests that the switched-session phenomenon cannot be prevented entirely regardless of how talented the remote viewer may be.

The Hawaii Remote Viewers' Guild, led by Glenn Wheaton, also regularly publishes the results of remote-viewing experiments on their very active web site (www.hrvg.org). That group of remote viewers uses a remote-viewing methodology that originated from within the military (Glenn Wheaton's background), but which is not CRV. The highly trained members of that group have excellent track records with regard to consistently being able to describe a randomly selected target using a long session followed by a proper closing period. However, it is interesting to note that they once tried to work with a large batch of sessions analyzed in advance of a Keno gambling experiment conducted in Las Vegas during the summer of 2001. In that situation they were not able to move beyond chance when they extended their method of working with single targets into settings with batches of sessions tied to rapidly occurring random events that require shortcuts in the closing process. The current chapter offers a reason to explain their difficulty in that experiment, and this difficulty had nothing to do with their ability to remote view a target under properly structured conditions.

The reason I am emphasizing the ability of highly trained remote viewers to consistently produce accurate descriptions of targets when the sessions are conducted and closed properly is because the availability of such viewers in significant numbers is a relatively new phenomenon in psi research. Most psi research depends on relatively inexperienced viewers to participate in laboratory experiments that are designed around large batches of trials. Our research suggests that this method of testing for psi may be self-defeating. The testing process itself appears to destroy the effectiveness of the psi phenomenon. I suggest that it might be much more fruitful for psi researchers to utilize in their experiments the growing number of highly trained remote viewers that now exist. These experiments should not be designed around large numbers of trials, but rather around content analyses of individual remote-viewing cases. Statistics can and must still be used, of course (especially, see Utts 1999). But it would probably be more fruitful to use statistics in content related research that focuses on isolated remote-viewing experiences rather than on collections of many trials processed with a rush-order mentality in a batch.

This is an important point in part because one of the primary complaints that skeptics of remote viewing have raised is that psi researchers have utilized statistics to demonstrate a phenomenon for which the skeptics claim there is no other evidence. Consider Hyman's statement in his report arguing that current evidence does not support the existence of paranormal functioning.

•

"Parapsychology is unique among the sciences in relying solely on significant departures from a chance baseline to establish the presence of its alleged phenomenon. In the other sciences the defining phenomena can be reliably observed and do not require indirect statistical measures to justify their existence. Indeed, each branch of science began with phenomena that could be observed directly" (Hyman 1996, p. 37). I believe that it would be incorrect to casually dismiss Hyman's complaint, and, indeed, it is not necessary to do so.

Psi is a delicate phenomenon, and remote viewing is no different in this regard. Our research suggests that it can reliably be performed to produce profound results only under a limited set of conditions. There are many factors that can destroy the remote-viewing capability. The research presented in this volume suggests that using human judges to compare remote-viewing data with targets in a pool can corrupt the targeting process itself via a mechanism of telepathic contamination. Other evidence reported here and elsewhere suggests that psi functioning works relatively poorly at best when experiments are designed using large numbers of trials. Indeed, psi functioning is a bit like a very temperamental technical device that malfunctions when you stress it. While it only works well when certain conditions are met, we are beginning to understand those conditions. Due largely to the existence of an expanding number of highly trained remote viewers, it is now possible to replicate the remote-viewing phenomenon more readily.

Personally, it makes less sense to attempt to force delicate psi functioning to fit inside existing laboratory approaches than to modify the laboratory and statistical approaches to fully accommodate the settings under which profound remote-viewing experiences can be obtained. Lots of trials compressed into a short space of time numbs the mind and eliminates the possibility of observing profound evidence of psi functioning. Slowing the entire process down to the evaluation of one remote-viewing session at a time produces a context that more fully allows the paranormal functionality to manifest. In short, this means that we now know the conditions under which we can repeatedly observe this phenomenon directly, and Hyman's complaint can be addressed.

What Makes a Target a Target?

We can now return to the matter of what makes a target a target. This question is more thoroughly explained later in this volume, but it is worthwhile summarizing what we know, or at least suspect, up to now in these discussions. So far, the research presented in this volume suggests that a successful remote-viewing experience depends crucially on the intersection of two things. The first is the actions of the remote viewer. Remote viewers use various procedures to obtain perceptions of a target. But for those perceptions to be accurate, the remote-viewing activity of the viewer at the time that the remote viewing takes place needs to be coordinated with the mental activity of the person or persons for whom the remote viewing is being performed in the first place. That is, there is a psychic/mental loop that exists between the viewer and the closer of the session. That closer can be the viewer, or it can be a separate analyst. But the closer is the person who first evaluates the remote-viewing data with respect to the actual target, and the thoughts of that person are the thoughts that predominantly determine the target that the viewer actually perceives. Anything that degrades the mental experience of closing, similarly degrades the quality of the target and the ability of the remote viewer to accurately describe the target. If the closer has a list of targets (one supposedly real and the other decoys) on his or her mind when analyzing the remote-viewing data, then all the targets on the list become real targets, and the remote viewer can end up describing anything on the list. In such a situation, there are no decoys.

At this point it is necessary to move the discussion to a series of generally successful demonstrations of remote viewing that follow the criteria established above. This is the point of the next chapter. I subsequently summarize and extend the above theory to more fully explain the remote-viewing targeting mechanism.

APPENDIX TO CHAPTER 5

TABLE 5.1: SAM Straining Instrument Categories

ELEMENTALS	EXPANDABLES null : characteristic observed
surface	surface level topology irregular topology
land	land manmade natural level topology irregular topology steep peak(s)
water	LIQUID water INTERFACE land/water interface SOLID ice or snow
atmospherics	natural smells manmade smells smoke or burning (natural or manmade) cloud dynamics

structure(s)	SURFACE STRUCTURE(S) surface structure(s) one multiple city subjects inside subjects on base surface outside MATERIALS natural materials manmade materials GENERAL LOCATION on land on/in water on a flat surface not located on a surface NONSURFACE STRUCTURE(S) nonsurface structure(s) one multiple subjects inside subjects nearby outside noticeable relative movement stationary silent movement emitting energetics
natural object(s)	natural object(s) on a surface not on a surface
subject(s)	subject(s) male female one/few many/crowd focused gathering
mountain	mountain(s) one multiple

environment	urban natural harsh natural harsh manmade extensive foliage distant or no base surface
energetics	explosive, swirling, or multi-directional movement kinetic (fast or slow, one direction) fire or heat
activity	activity or movement by subject(s) activity or movement by object(s)
light	bright dim/dark glow
sounds	talking, shouting, voices booming or roaring wind-type sounds loud noticeably quiet music, rhythm, or pulsing
temperatures	hot moderate cold
Dominant Session Elements Complete only with Phase 4 entry. No more than two entries!	structure(s) on a surface structure(s) not on a surface lots of subjects movement/activity/energetics natural environment natural object not on a surface

Sketches Describe only the dominant sketch elements. Use for all Phases.	structure(s) structure(s) on a surface structure(s) not on a surface natural object on a surface natural object not on a surface subjects(s) subject(s) in a structure subject(s) on an outside base surface horizontal base surface sloping or peaking base surface(s) object totally below a surface significant motion of primary object(s) radiating or explosive energetics extensive foliage extensive water

CHAPTER 6

A Public Demonstration of Remote Viewing

In October of 1999, The Farsight Institute sponsored a public demonstration of remote viewing that continued for approximately six months. Many people from all over the world were able to watch and participate in this demonstration over the Internet via our web site, www.farsight.org. However, the demonstration was designed to do more than merely show people how remote viewing worked. We wanted to continue our experiments with time also, and we decided to combine our public demonstration with a series of time experiments. This multipurpose strategy allowed visitors to our web site to witness an interesting set of experiments oriented around a novel idea pertaining to time as well as to watch the more general remote-viewing process.

As a follow-up to the design of our Alpha Project, we decided to conduct all remote-viewing sessions for the public demonstration under conditions in which the tasker would assign a target after the sessions were already completed. Working out all of the logistics so that the public could be certain that everything was legitimate was the great challenge of setting up the public demonstration. The overall plan turned out to be much more complicated than simply doing remote-viewing sessions, getting a target, and then telling people what happened. Yet the plan was not so complicated that others had trouble following and participating in the process.

The Design of the Demonstration Experiments

Key to the success of the public demonstration process was finding a person to choose the targets who was not associated with The Farsight Institute in any way and who had both a credible reputation and a sufficient interest in the subject matter such that he or she would participate in the project seriously. Scientists demanding "proof" of remote viewing as a real phenomenon might argue that a computer should be used to pick a target at random from a large pool of targets in such a demonstration. But in my view, a human tasker is currently a real requirement for any public demonstration of remote viewing. A public demonstration is different from a proof-oriented laboratory experiment. The public would have no reason to trust that a computer program was not written to give targets that were known to the remote viewers. The widespread problem of hackers manipulating computer files has created an additional layer of public cynicism with regard to computer "trustworthiness" in a way that would adversely affect the acceptance of a public demonstration such as the one discussed here. In short, when public demonstrations of remote viewing are concerned, the public really wants to know something about the personality and reputation of the tasker before considering to take seriously the results of the experiment. It may be that future public demonstration experiments will be designed to incorporate computer assisted targeting, but for this experiment it was felt that a human tasker with a credible reputation was a requirement.

When we were beginning to set-up the demonstration project, I was contacted via email by John David Berryman, M.D., a professor of medicine at George Washington University Medical School. His reason for initially contacting me had nothing to do with the public demonstration, which had not yet been announced anywhere. I wrote back to him and explained that we were about to begin a long-term public demonstration of remote viewing, and I asked if he would be interested in choosing targets for us, to which he readily agreed. When the public demonstration began, we posted the following description of Dr. Berryman's credentials:

> *Dr. John David Berryman is a clinical associate professor of Obstetrics and Gynecology at the George Washington University School of Medicine. He has a background in basic sciences and in the law through graduate school and law school. Dr. Berryman is also on the Board of Columbia Hospital for Women, and chairs the Legal and Rules Committee.*

From October 1999 through March 2000, we attempted 15 remote-viewing demonstrations. Of the 15 attempted experiments, two were scrubbed (#2 and #13) due to procedural errors. Dr. Berryman was the tasker for all 13 of the successfully completed experiments. The first of the scrubbed experiments (#2) involved a different tasker (not Dr. Berryman) to whom we did not adequately explain the parameters of the experiment. This resulted in the tasker submitting a target that involved some esoteric content, which was not allowed for this demonstration. We realized at that point that it would be best to work with only one outside tasker so that we could more easily manage the internal flow of instructions and other communications. The second of the scrubbed experiments (#13) was corrupted when our experiment facilitator at the Institute received one target from Dr. Berryman but then mistakenly forwarded an incorrect email attachment with yet a different target to the viewers. This error was not discovered for 24 hours, which resulted in an incorrect target being associated with the remote-viewing data, thereby corrupting our experimental process. All other 13 experiments went smoothly.

The basic process for each of the public demonstration experiments followed the same sequence of events:

1.   Two remote viewers each conducted at least one remote-viewing session for each experiment.

2.   Each viewer typed a verbatim transcript of his own session(s), including a written description of the sketches. There was one transcript per session. If a viewer did two sessions for the same target, then two transcripts were prepared.

3.   Each viewer then encrypted his transcript(s) using the widely respected encryption software PGP (Pretty Good Privacy) which is publicly available from the web site www.pgp.com. Each viewer chose a password to encrypt their session transcripts. These encrypted transcripts could not be de-encrypted and read without this password. The viewers did not divulge the passwords to de-encrypt the transcripts to anyone until after Dr. Berryman submitted his choice of a target for the given experiment.

4.   After the transcripts for the remote-viewing sessions were completed, the Institute then published on its web site (www.farsight.org) a link to download these transcripts. At that point, anyone connected to the Internet could download these encrypted transcripts and store them for safekeeping on their own computer's hard drive (or anywhere else).

5.   Dr. Berryman was then told (via email) that the encrypted remote-viewing session transcripts were available for download from our web site. He could then download the encrypted transcripts and store them. Since he did not have the passwords to de-encrypt the transcripts, he could not read them, just like everyone else. Dr. Berryman would then begin the process of deciding on a target for the experiment. Anywhere from a few days to two weeks after the encrypted session transcripts were initially made available for download from the Institute's web site, Dr. Berryman would email us a target. The target was sent to a contact person at the Institute (our "experiment facilitator"), who would then forward it to the viewers.

6.   After receiving the target from Dr. Berryman, each viewer would "close" their sessions. This is a process by which the viewer closely examines his remote-viewing data and compares them with the target specific for the given experiment. (This is explained more thoroughly below.)

7.   The viewers then revealed the passwords that they used to encrypt their session transcripts, and the passwords were posted on our web site together with scans of the original session pages and the target specific that was submitted by Dr. Berryman.

8.   Visitors to the Institute's web site would then use the passwords to de-encrypt the session transcripts which they had previously downloaded. The de-encrypted transcripts could then be read and compared with the newly posted scans of the remote-viewing sessions to ensure that the posted scans matched the previously downloaded transcripts.

9.   Once the visitors to the Institute's web site were convinced that the scans of the original sessions were authentic and not altered, they could then

study the scans of the sessions to evaluate them for accuracy with regard to the target specific. A brief evaluation of each session was also posted on the web site to help describe the sessions.

For the first 10 public demonstration experiments, the remote viewers were myself and Joey Jerome. The experiment facilitator was Matthew Pfeiffer. For the next five experiments, the viewers were myself and Matthew Pfeiffer, while Joey Jerome assumed the role of the facilitator. People participated in the demonstration from all over the world by downloading the encrypted transcripts and then waiting to see the actual sessions when Dr. Berryman sent his target choice. This continued for six months until we were all a bit exhausted and had to turn to other matters. All of the public demonstration results remain on the Institute's web site, and readers are encouraged to examine them closely.

In general, the experimental design described above allowed for visitors to the Institute's web site to participate in the experiments as if they were in a remote-viewing laboratory themselves. The modern technologies of encryption combined with the distribution capabilities of the Internet now allows the possibility of extending the boundaries of remote-viewing laboratories into everyone's home and office. It is no longer necessary to take a researcher's word on faith that a certain experiment had a certain result. Researchers are needed to interpret the results, such as to point out an interesting sketch and some accompanying written data, but others can watch the process and come to their own conclusions from any other location, secure in the knowledge that the results are real. This capability is enormously important for situations such as this in which skeptics have often claimed that remote-viewing results have been fabricated. But this capability is also important for heuristic reasons as well. If the remote-viewing hypothesis is to be sustained, important implications to virtually every human being on this planet will soon become transparent. Given the significant transformative role that remote-viewing research may potentially have for everyone, it is important that as many people as possible be given the opportunity to follow this research.

The aspect of time as it relates to the public demonstration experiments also added an unusual twist. Using a tasking-post experimental design in which the target was chosen after the sessions were completed allowed us to more fully document the results of the Alpha Project that are described in the previous chapter. The tasking-post situation also added a bit of public drama to the overall project. While it is not a new observation that tasking-post conditions are viable, it is not something that most people visiting the Institute's web site would be expecting in a public demonstration of remote viewing. This time-based "oddness factor" supplemented the already challenging proposal that remote viewing is real in the first place and added to the overall appeal and interest of the project.

It is crucial to note an important difference between the public demonstration experiments and those of the Alpha Project. The experimental design for the Alpha Project specified that only one session would be conducted by each viewer, thereby controlling for the amount of contact time each viewer has with each target, a factor that could influence the quality of the sessions. Varying the degrees of target contact time across viewers and between tasking-prior and tasking-post sessions could vary the quality of the remote-viewing data in such a way that would make it difficult to determine the influencing role of time in structuring the results. But the design of the public demonstration experiments is different since all of the sessions are conducted with a tasking-post situation, and thus our only remaining concern is to obtain the highest degree of descriptive accuracy possible.

While it would always be ideal for all viewers to conduct at least two sessions for each target with such a set of public demonstration experiments, this was not always a possibility due to other professional and family responsibilities that faced the viewers. Nonetheless, one viewer (myself) was fortunately able to conduct two sessions each for 9 of the 13 successfully completed experiments. For all other situations, one session per viewer was conducted.

We have also found that it is ideal if viewers can always meditate regularly twice each day, especially during periods in which they are engaged in remote viewing, and it is optimal if they can conduct their remote-viewing sessions immediately following one of their daily meditations. Finally, it is best if remote viewers conduct at least two sessions each week (three is better) in order to perform optimally. It is a bit like playing the piano — one needs to do it regularly if one is to do it well. While all viewers attempted to do all of this during the six months of the public demonstration, there were some unavoidable snags along the way, nearly always involving competing commitments with everyone's time.

All of the viewers who were involved in the public demonstration experiments volunteered their time and energies amidst various demands on them, and there were inevitable compromises with regard to their ability to do everything. These external demands on the time and other resources of our volunteers — however trained they may be — are the greatest challenge that we have faced as an Institute, and we look forward to the day in which we may be able to work with full-time remote viewers who are able to dedicate all of their time and energies to enhancing their skills. Among all of the viewers, I was perhaps best able to satisfy fully all of my professional responsibilities while not cutting corners with regard to the public demonstration process. Nonetheless, everyone did what they could, and the results, however impressive they may appear, should be seen not as a portrait of peak performance beyond which no human could achieve, but rather as a baseline level of performance that is currently possible under reasonable and commonly available conditions. Without doubt, given greater resources, superior results would be possible.

Closing a Session Revisited

Based on earlier research presented in chapter 3 of this volume, it became apparent to myself and others that a mental connection appears to occur between a remote viewer and the first person who examines and analyzes the remote-viewing data. Again, in our experiments using binary targets, if the analyst has two targets in his or her mind, then the viewer can be guided by the thoughts of the analyst so as to perceive elements of either or both of the targets.

This subject is discussed further from a theoretical perspective in the following chapter, but the essence of this phenomenon is also the essence of what makes a target a target. The thoughts of the analyst at the moment that the analyst examines the remote-viewing data play a dominant role in structuring the perceptual behavior of the remote viewer. Since the analyst could have other thoughts in his or her mind as well during the analysis of the data — including prejudicial thoughts about the remote viewer — we concluded that it was safest to allow the viewer to be the first person to analyze the data, thereby "closing the loop," so to speak. After the viewer closes the session by comparing the data with the target specific, it would be safe (or at least safer) for others to subsequently examine the results without the risk of playing a corrupting role in the viewing process.

In all of the public demonstration experiments, the viewers always closed their sessions prior to having anyone else look at their data. Again, this was possible in our experimental design due to the fact that encrypted transcripts of the sessions were already available and widely distributed. Thus, there was no possibility that the viewer could alter the data in any way during the closing process.

The Criteria for the Targets

Dr. Berryman was given the following set of criteria for determining his choice of targets for the public demonstration experiments:

1. All targets for this public demonstration experiment must be real and immediately verifiable.
2. Information about all targets must be easily obtainable by the general public.
3. No esoteric targets, or targets containing known esoteric content, are permissible.
4. All targets should have prominent topological features that can be easily identified (by both the viewers and the analysts of the remote-viewing data).
5. Activities at the target site (if any) should be significant.
6. The numbered aspects for acceptable targets should be designed to move

each viewer's perspective around one physical central target location and not used to answer complex plot or story questions. The purpose of the numbered aspects is to offer alternative viewing perspectives for one primary target, in the way a camera is moved from place to place around a primary object of interest.

7. Perspective statements should be used for either or both of the second and third numbered aspects.

Most of these requirements are of an obvious nature and need no further explanation. These requirements correspond in large part with suggestions made by May, Spottiswoode, and James (1994a, 1994b), May, Spottiswoode, and Faith (2000), as well as Watt (1988). However, we decided against imposing greater restrictions on the types of targets allowed, such as prohibiting flying targets such as airplanes or spacecraft. The reason for not limiting the target bandwidth in this way was due to the fact that at The Farsight Institute (similarly as with other remote-viewing groups, such as the Hawaiian Remote Viewer's Guild) we normally do not restrict our target possibilities, and we wanted this demonstration to parallel more closely the type of remote viewing that we do. The numbered aspects for the targets (mentioned in point 6 above) are the same as those used in the Alpha Project, where each target specific has an essential cue followed by three numbered aspects that act strategically to place the viewer's perspective in time and space. "Perspective statements" (from point 7 above) are new to the current discussion and require a note of explanation.

A perspective statement is an explicit instruction to shift the viewing perspective to an alternate point of view. Perspective statements are normally restricted for use in the second and third numbered aspects. For example, a perspective statement may require that a viewer perceive a target from 200 feet above the center of a particular scene, or from four meters directly in front of a particular person, and so on. It is of interest to analysts of remote-viewing data to observe how closely a viewer's perspective follows the explicit instructions given in such perspective statements.

Target content is always important to any demonstration of remote viewing, and we gave Dr. Berryman the suggestions listed below. The goal was not to limit the choice of targets, but rather to encourage the broadest possible range of targets. We have found that remote viewers tend to perform best if the targets have no anticipated components, which means that the targets should be as diverse as possible for any given set of targets. We suggested that he may wish to consult this list from time to time to see if a different type of target from a different category may add more variety to his own target ideas.

1. Train, aviation, and maritime events (of all types)
2. Monumental stone structures, with or without activities
3. Manned space flight events of all types

4.   Mountains, waterfalls, and other large and significant natural formations, with or without human activities
5.   Major wartime battles, riots, terrorist incidents
6.   Natural disasters of all types involving significant topological features and activities
7.   Notable and topologically distinct structures of all types
8.   Governmental leaders and other significant persons within significant and topologically distinct settings (such as within or near major structures)
9.   Adventurist events, successes, and disasters of all types

Readers should note that the above instructions emphasize targets that are similar in only one respect. That is, it was important for all targets used in these public demonstration experiments to be "easy" targets. Easy targets are those that have very distinctive features, such as lots of activity or notable topology. For example, one of the targets chosen by Dr. Berryman was the opening ceremony for the Eiffel Tower. This target fits the above criteria well since the Eiffel tower has a distinct topological shape, and there were many people engaged in diverse celebratory activities on the day chosen.

Inappropriate targets, on the other hand, would have been those for which there is very little topological variety and/or very little activity. For example, an inappropriate target for the purpose of these demonstrations would have been "one kilometer below the surface of the Atlantic Ocean" at a given latitude and longitude. In this case, the only thing at this target location would be water, and the viewer would have tried for about one hour to find more to the target than water, which in turn might have led to a bit of concern about not perceiving more than the sense of being wet, leading to conscious mind intervention with the viewing process and possibly the development of a fantasy story line.

Another example of an inappropriate target would be, say, "Richard Nixon," or only the name of any person. Such a target does not specify where or when one would perceive this person. Anything from birth to death in any setting would be accurate.

Thus, easy targets are "easy" for two reasons. First, the data can be interpreted in a direct way. For example, everyone knows what the Eiffel Tower looks like, and we would hope to see a sketch of a structure that resembles the Eiffel Tower plus other obviously descriptive information in a convincing remote-viewing session for this target. Second, certain targets can be easier than others for remote viewers to describe, especially those targets with very distinct topological variety, such as a satellite in space, a mountain event, a notable structure, a wartime event with lots of activity, and so on. Sometimes we call these "punch you in the face" type targets, as compared with, say, the lawn in someone's backyard in which there is only grass on a flat surface. Viewers spend a lot of time with a target, and an easy target offers viewers lots of stuff to describe during that time, thereby maintaining the interest and accuracy of the viewers.

Ultimately, while any target can be a good target given an appropriate setting, for these public demonstration experiments we wanted targets that had diverse and obvious features that the public would be able to recognize in the remote-viewing data. Table A6.1 contains the list of all targets chosen by Dr. Berryman for the public demonstration experiments, and it is located in Appendix I for this chapter. It is worthwhile for readers to review this list of targets to appreciate the variety of subject matters that are addressed by these experiments. The targets on the list are quite diverse, and it is not likely that we (or anyone) could have predicted in advance the type of targets chosen by Dr. Berryman through any known means other than remote viewing. Again, it is useful to remind readers that this is a process-oriented discussion, as compared with a "proof of remote viewing" discussion. If this were a proof-oriented experiment, the proper procedure would be for a computer to pick all targets at random from a large pool of targets. But having humans pick targets for remote viewers is both heuristically useful and inevitable in many situations, especially with regard to public demonstrations of the remote-viewing process. The fact that no one at The Farsight Institute had ever met Dr. Berryman personally at the time of the public demonstration, and that contact with him was minimal and conducted via email and only with regard to this public demonstration, helps to establish his independence as a tasker.

Results

Two types of results are presented here with regard to the public demonstration remote-viewing data. The first is a subjective analysis of these data based on session clarity scores. But the second is an objective statistical analysis that is based on the use of the SAM computer-based analysis process.

A summary of the subjective analyses for the results of the series of 13 experiments is presented in table 6.1. The first column of this table lists the number of the experiment, and readers will note that experiment numbers 2 and 13 have been omitted due to the reasons discussed above. The second column contains session clarity scores for all remote-viewing sessions conducted by viewer #1 (Courtney Brown) while the third column presents clarity scores for remote-viewing sessions conducted by Joey Jerome and Matthew Pfeiffer. Note that in the third column the scores for experiments #1 through #11 are for Joey Jerome's sessions while those for experiments #12 through #15 are for those of Matthew Pfeiffer.

Since viewer #1 was able to conduct two remote-viewing sessions per target for 9 of the 13 experiments in the series, it is useful to offer a combined session score for those instances. This combined session score is more than simply an average of the scores for the two sessions in each pair. It is common in these situations for such sessions to compliment each other with new material

TABLE 6.1: The Public Demonstration Session Scores

Experiment Number	Viewer 1 Courtney Brown Actual: Opposite	Viewer 2 Joey Jerome (1-11) Actual: Opposite
1	One Session — 2: 2	One Session — 1: 0
3	Session #1 — 2: 0 Session #2 — 2: 0 Combined Session Score — 3	One Session — 1: 0
4	One Session — 2: 0	One Session — 0: 0
5	One Session — 0: 0	One Session — 1: 0
6	Session #1 — 2: 0 Session #2 — 3: 0 Combined Session Score — 3	One Session — 1: 0
7	One Session — 2: 0	One Session — 2: 0
8	Session #1 — 2: 0 Session #2 — 2: 0 Combined Session Score — 2	One Session — 2: 0
9	Session #1 — 2: 0 Session #2 — 2: 2 Combined Session Score — 2	One Session — 1: 0
10	Session Score #1 — 3: 0 Session Score #2 — 3: 0 Combined Session Score — 3	One Session — 2: 0
11	Session Score #1 — 2: 0 Session Score #2 — 1: 0 Combined Session Score — 2	One Session — 2: 0
		Viewer 3 Matthew Pfeiffer (12-15)
12	Session Score #1 — 3: 0 Session Score #2 — 3: 0 Combined Session Score — 3	One Session — 2: 0
14	Session Score #1 — 3: 0 Session Score #2 — 2: 0 Combined Session Score — 3	One Session — 2: 0
15	Session Score #1 — 1: 0 Session Score #2 — 1: 0 Combined Session Score — 1	One Session — 1: 0

rather than simply to duplicate the same material. Thus, it is possible for two sessions to more fully describe a target than any one session accomplishes alone. For this reason the combined session scores more adequately represent the total informational content of the two sessions in any pair.

It should also be noted that the session clarity scores are produced post hoc. That is, no session clarity scores were used during the six-month course of the public demonstration. The goal of the demonstration was to let people see real remote viewing done under real and controlled conditions under which they could participate. We wanted people to look at the remote-viewing data themselves and not to rely on a single number to tell them that the remote-viewing phenomenon is real. Indeed, later in this chapter I discuss many of the details for the individual demonstrations, and it is important for readers to carefully examine these results themselves. Moreover, the original sessions are available in their entirety to examine for free on the web site for The Farsight Institute (www.farsight.org), and those who are able will benefit from looking at the raw data with their own eyes. But in a chapter such as this, a heuristic aid is needed to summarize the results of the demonstrations, so the session clarity scores are used here. Interested viewers are encouraged to compare the session clarity scores presented in this chapter with scores that they might have assigned after looking over the raw data for themselves. This continues the theme of interactivity that is so useful for public demonstrations.

For each session and for all viewers in table 6.1 there is both an "actual" score and an "opposite" score, always separated by a colon. The actual score is the score for the given session when compared with the target specific as listed in table A6.1. The opposite score is for each session when compared with a false target that is chosen such that all or nearly all of its essential characteristics are opposite that of the actual target. The reason for doing this is to help demonstrate that these remote-viewing data are not a product of a random process. But the process of comparing remote-viewing data to a pair of targets, one real and the other false, is similar to what was done in the lottery experiment described in chapter 3 using primary and secondary targets to determine the correct binary digits. It is natural to ask why the problems that were encountered and discussed in that chapter would not similarly plague the current analysis. If we analyze the remote-viewing data in this series of public experiments against two distinct targets, should we not again find examples of good sessions for the wrong targets?

This is a new field of inquiry, and it is not possible for us to know in advance of conducting these experiments all of the possible things that could happen. However, given the results of our earlier experiments, two conclusions seem reasonable. (1) Since the first person who compares a remote-viewing session's data with the target (that is, analyzes the sessions) has the dominant mental link with the remote viewer's perceptions during the time when the remote-viewing session is taking place, if the viewer closes his or her own sessions prior to the analysis, the contamination of the data caused by the analysis should be minimized. (2) If there is going to be a contaminating influence in the analysis presented in this chapter, it will most likely be with my own sessions, since I both close my own sessions and compare them with the opposite targets (explained below). If contamination does occur, it would hopefully be minimized due to the session closing process. Closing the sessions prior to the analysis of the remote-viewing data is important not because of the barrier quality of time, which we see from the results presented with regard to the Alpha Project is no barrier at all. Rather, closing a remote-viewing session prior to analysis eliminates any conscious or subconscious mental influences on the thoughts of the remote viewer during the closing process that might result from his or her knowing something about the results of the analysis that may have been conveyed directly or indirectly to the viewer.

Contamination with regard to my own sessions might be more possible since there would be a similar mental flavor (that is, my own) in each instance of closing and then re-examining the data with regard to the opposite targets, all of which may affect the attracting qualities of the correct target with regard to my remote-viewing perceptions. If my subspace perceptions are influenced by my own mental activities associated with closing the sessions, then those mental activities would probably feel psychically very similar to the mental activities that I have when doing the comparisons with the opposite targets. Separating the two events (closing the sessions and opposite comparisons) in time may not be enough to stop these influences, especially given the results of a previous chapter (The Alpha Project) with regard to the illusory nature of time. Nonetheless, closing the sessions might be expected to offer at least some buffering to the contamination process. Since the comparison with opposite targets offers the potential for yielding some useful theoretical insight, it seems worth the risk to try it. Thus, with the spirit of "we will not know unless we do it," I did it.

An interesting point with regard to the use of opposite targets in this analysis is that I did not decide on making comparisons with opposite targets until the experimental series was completely over and all the sessions had been closed. This raises the interesting question of the degree to which cross-cutting psi channels are open-ended with respect to time. Can doing something relating to a psi experiment have a contaminating influence on a psi experiment done long ago? While no one currently knows the answer to this question, I suspect the answer addresses the intent of the viewer when the session data are being collected. If the remote viewer is intending to satisfy the informational needs of a particular analyst, then the potential for contamination due to the analysis activities of that analyst may be greater over a longer period of time, perhaps until there is some sense of intellectual closure with respect to the original intended use of the remote-viewing data.

The opposite targets for this experiment were chosen by Matthew Pfeiffer. He did not refer to the remote-viewing data in the public demonstration experiment series when deciding on these opposite targets. He was asked to write such targets for another experiment that we were conducting in which we needed pairs of opposite targets, and I suggested that he use the public demonstration targets as one member of each pair. He was not aware until after the opposite targets were written that I was going to use them in an analysis of the data collected for the public demonstration experiments. The list of all opposite targets used in this analysis is presented in table 6.2. Table 6.2 also contains the essential cues of the actual targets used in the public demonstration experiments.

Returning to table 6.1, note that in general the clarity scores for all viewers are higher for the actual targets than for the opposite targets. For viewer #2, there are only two instances in which the clarity score for the actual target equals that for the opposite target, and that is for experiment #4 in which both scores are zero. In no other instance for viewers #2 or #3 do the clarity scores for the opposite targets equal (or surpass) those of the actual targets. For viewer #1, there are only two instances (experiments #1 and #9) out of 22 sessions in which the clarity score for an opposite target equals that of the actual target. These results by themselves strongly argue the case for the reality of the remote-viewing phenomenon. If session data are the consequence of random processes, then these results would not be possible. But these results are real facts.

At the bottom of table 6.1 are the averages of the session clarity scores for each viewer with respect to both the actual and opposite targets. The ratios of average actual to opposite session clarity scores for the three viewers are 2.01:0.18 (Courtney Brown), 1.3:0 (Joey Jerome), and 1.6:0 (Matthew Pfeiffer). In each case, the session clarity score averages are much higher for the actual targets than for the opposite targets.

The Objective Statistical Analysis

Tables 6.3 and 6.4 present a summary of objective statistical analyses for all of the remote-viewing sessions conducted in the public demonstration process. To calculate the statistics in these tables, the SAM data sets were constructed by coding both the remote-viewing session data and descriptive information for all targets used in the public demonstration. These session and target SAM data sets are all parallel in structure to those used in the previous chapter.

A detailed description of the statistics presented in tables 6.3 and 6.4 can be found in Appendix II for this chapter. These two tables also contain the session clarity scores for all sessions to allow for a comparison between the subjective and objective evaluations of the remote-viewing data. The tables contain three tests. The first test is a chi-square test for each experiment of the fit of the remote-viewing data to the target attributes. To calculate the chi-square statistic, a 2X2 table is constructed that calculates the matches and misses between the remote-viewing data and the target attributes, as is described in

TABLE 6.2: The Public Demonstration Primary and Opposite Targets

Experiment Number	Actual Target	Opposite Target
1	TWA Flight 800/crash/event (17 July 1996)	Hillary on Mt. Everest
3	The assassination of Abraham Lincoln/event	Blake Island, Alaska (12 Noon, 1 June 99)
4	The Battle of Gettysburg (July 1863)	Downtown Tokyo, Japan
5	The Great Chicago Fire / Chicago, Illinois / event (October 1871)	Greer Spring, Missouri (12 Noon, 1 June 1999)
6	The Eiffel Tower / Paris, France (during the inauguration ceremony at the Paris International Exposition, March 31st, 1889)	Monteverde Cloud Forest Preserve
7	The White House / Washington, D.C. (August 1814)	Largest Crater on the Moon
8	The battle between the Bon Homme Richard and the HMS Serapis / event (23 September 1779)	Largest Crater on the Moon
9	Mount Everest	Downtown Tokyo, Japan
10	The Leaning Tower of Pisa, Italy	Blake Island, Alaska
11	The USS Missouri (2 September 1945)	Largest Crater on the Moon
12	The edge of the Polar Plateau / Antarctic Continent (28 November 1929)	Downtown Tokyo, Japan
14	The eruption of Mt. Vesuvius / near Pompeii, Italy (24 August 79 A.D.)	Hubble Space Telescope
15	The Statue of Liberty / New York Harbor (4 July 1976)	Death Valley, California

greater detail in Appendix II. Various significance levels are possible for this test, as are also described in Appendix II. In general, any chi-square statistic in tables 6.3 and 6.4 equal to or greater than 3.84 is statistically significant at the .05 level (with 1 degree of freedom).

The second test is named after (and due to) the physicist John Russell, and it has two parts, both of which are explained in detail in Appendix II. The first part utilizes the binomial distribution to test whether or not the number of matches between a remote-viewing session and a target is based simply on chance. Confidence intervals are calculated to test the significance of the number of matches between the remote-viewing data and target attributes. This is done a second time utilizing a weighting procedure that emphasizes the remote viewing and target matches that are generally rare or unique relative to the attributes for a large baseline collection of 240 highly diverse targets (see Appendix II). This allows for an evaluation of how uniquely the remote-viewing session characterizes its target, as compared with simply matching commonly occurring attributes found in many targets.

Part II of the Russell Procedure evaluates the remote-viewing session from the perspective of how many random SAM entries would be needed to describe the target as completely (as per the number of session/target matches) as is done by the actual session. To conduct this test, the SAM Program constructs pseudo sessions composed of random SAM entries, with each entry being added one at a time until the total number of matches with the actual target equals that achieved by the actual remote-viewing session. The mean and standard deviation for the total number of SAM entries for each pseudo session are computed from a set of 1000 Monte Carlo samples. Confidence intervals are again constructed, and this test evaluates the efficiency of the remote viewer (as per proportion B used in Test #1) in describing the target. When the total number of actual session SAM entries is outside of (that is, less than) an appropriate confidence interval, then the remote viewer's perceptive efficiency is outside of chance, and the null hypothesis is rejected.

The third test presented in tables 6.3 and 6.4 also has two parts that utilize the idea of correlation, both of which are explained in detail in Appendix II. The heart of this test is "correspondence numbers" that characterize the proportion of a target that is described by a remote-viewing session. (See the discussion of the average of proportions *A* and *B* with regard to test #1 in Appendix II.) Correspondence numbers can be calculated with respect to a session's data and the session's target, but they can also be calculated with respect to a session and all other targets in a pool. Ideally, the correspondence number should be higher for a remote-viewing session and its target than for the same session and other targets. But since many targets have overlapping characteristics (structures, mountains, subjects, etc.), it is useful to calculate the correlation coefficient that evaluates the comprehensive collection of correspondence numbers with respect to each target and all other targets. In tables 6.3 and 6.4, two pools of targets are used for this evaluation. In part I of this test, the pool is the targets used in the public demonstration. In part II, the pool is a separate collection of 240 highly

TABLE 6.3: Objective Statistical Tests of the Public Demonstration Data, Viewer — Courtney

Experiment Number and Session (if more than one)	Subjective Session Clarity Scores	Test #1: Chi-square 1 d.f.	Test #2: Russell Procedure Part I - Maximum Significant C.I., Unweighted and Weighted	Test #2: Russell Procedure Part II - Maximum Significant C.I.	Test #3 Part I - Correlation Coefficient N=13	Test #3 Part II - Correlation Coefficient N=240
1	2	2.797	UW: 90% C.I. W: 98% C.I.	N.S.	-0.034	-0.433
1, Session #1 second half	3	27.581	UW: 98% C.I. W: 98% C.I.	98% C.I.	0.767	0.900
3, Session #1	2	84.545	UW: 98% C.I. W: 95% C.I.	98% C.I.	0.922	0.995
3, Session #2	2	36.620	UW: 98% C.I. W: N.S.	98% C.I.	0.908	0.944
4	2	37.010	UW: 98% C.I. W: 98% C.I.	98% C.I.	0.880	0.966
5	0	2.292	UW: N.S. W: N.S.	N.S.	-0.790	-0.853
6, Session #1	2	59.392	UW: 98% C.I. W: 98% C.I.	98% C.I.	0.889	0.985

6, Session #2	3	40.958	UW: 98% C.I. W: 98% C.I.	98% C.I.	0.877	0.968
7	2	45.054	UW: 98% C.I. W: 98% C.I.	98% C.I.	0.868	0.958
8, Session #1	2	20.738	UW: 98% C.I. W: 98% C.I.	98% C.I.	0.639	0.895
8, Session #2	2	13.017	UW: 98% C.I. W: N.S.	98% C.I.	0.457	0.825
9, Session #1	2	26.522	UW: 98% C.I. W: 98% C.I.	98% C.I.	0.762	0.818
9, Session #2	2	0.077	UW: N.S. W: N.S.	N.S.	-0.707	-0.723
10, Session #1	3	67.323	UW: 98% C.I. W: 90% C.I.	98% C.I.	0.915	0.994
10, Session #2	3	46.968	UW: 98% C.I. W: N.S.	98% C.I.	0.879	0.985
11, Session #1	2	37.405	UW: 98% C.I. W: 98% C.I.	98% C.I.	0.866	0.925
11, Session #2	1	34.433	UW: 98% C.I. W: 98% C.I.	98% C.I.	0.858	0.973
12, Session #1	3	44.938	UW: 98% C.I. W: 98% C.I.	98% C.I.	0.827	0.855

12, Session #2	3	41.518	UW: 98% C.I. W: 98% C.I.	98% C.I.	0.797	0.842
14, Session #1	3	44.795	UW: 98% C.I. W: 98% C.I.	98% C.I.	0.759	0.891
14, Session #2	2	25.634	UW: 98% C.I. W: 98% C.I.	98% C.I.	0.597	0.782
15, Session #1	1	31.541	UW: 98% C.I. W: 90% C.I.	98% C.I.	0.875	0.971
15, Session #2	1	20.778	UW: 98% C.I. W: 98% C.I.	98% C.I.	0.847	0.954

TABLE 6.4: Objective Statistical Tests of the Public Demonstration Data, Viewers — Joey and Matthew

Experiment Number	Subjective Session Clarity Scores	Test #1: Chi-square 1 d.f.	Test #2: Russell Procedure Part I - Maximum Significant C.I., Unweighted and Weighted	Test #2: Russell Procedure Part II - Maximum Significant C.I.	Test #3 Part I - Correlation Coefficient N=13	Test #3 Part II - Correlation Coefficient N=240
Viewer: Joey						
1	1	18.511	UW: 98% C.I. W: 98% C.I.	98% C.I.	0.413	0.733
3	1	29.728	UW: 98% C.I. W: N.S.	98% C.I.	0.789	0.932
4	0	2.288	UW: N.S. W: 98% C.I.	N.S.	-0.452	-0.521
5	1	43.960	UW: 98% C.I. W: 98% C.I.	98% C.I.	0.872	0.985
6	1	32.936	UW: 98% C.I. W: 98% C.I.	98% C.I.	0.897	0.988
7	2	28.830	UW: 98% C.I. W: 98% C.I.	98% C.I.	0.855	0.972
8	2	0.043	UW: N.S. W: N.S.	N.S.	-0.634	-0.444

9	1	0.290	UW: N.S. W: N.S.	N.S.	-0.698	-0.688
10	2	2.948	UW: 90% C.I. W: N.S.	N.S.	-0.339	-0.376
11	2	25.486	UW: 98% C.I. W: 98% C.I.	98% C.I.	0.488	0.861
Viewer: Matthew						
12	2	29.374	UW: 98% C.I. W: 98% C.I.	98% C.I.	0.814	0.813
14	2	2.652	UW: N.S. W: N.S.	N.S.	-0.116	-0.185
15	1	32.888	UW: 98% C.I. W: N.S.	98% C.I.	0.812	0.959

diverse targets (that do not include the public demonstration targets). In general, the correlation coefficient calculated for both parts of this test will be high (nearer unity) when the remote-viewing session closely describes its actual target as compared with other targets in the pools. Correlation coefficients that are low (near zero or negative) indicate that the remote-viewing session did not describe the target well.

These three tests (with their various parts) are intended to offer a broad statistical evaluation of these data. Other tests could also be performed as well, of course. But the included tests are sufficient to indicate minimally whether or not a given remote-viewing session describes the essential characteristics of its target. Combined with the subjective evaluations available with the session clarity scores, it is possible to obtain an overall perspective of accuracy of these remote-viewing data for this public demonstration.

Detailed statistical breakdowns for all of the results presented in tables 6.3 and 6.4 can be found on the Institute's web site (www.farsight.org). To summarize these results beginning with table 6.3, it is clear that the subjective and objective criteria used to evaluate these remote-viewing sessions closely correspond. There are some cases in which a session clarity score suggests a level of accuracy that is substantially higher or lower than that indicated by the objective statistical measures, but such deviations are generally rare. For example, with respect to experiment #1, the session clarity score is 2 while the objective measures are very weak. But this is caused by the fact that this remote-viewing session changes dramatically in the middle when its descriptive accuracy improves markedly. The second half of this session is analyzed separately in the second row of table 6.3 (the only instance in which this is done), and in this case the subjective and objective measures correspond closely.

Table 6.3 contains evaluations for 22 remote-viewing sessions conducted by myself (Courtney Brown), and using the combination of both the subjective and the objective measures of session accuracy, these results suggest that 17 of these 22 sessions described their targets well. This can be seen by counting the number of sessions that achieve a session clarity score of 2 or better combined with significant statistical evaluations in all or all but one test (or part of a test). Table 6.4 contains results for Joey Jerome and Matthew Pfeiffer. There are 13 sessions evaluated in table 6.4, 10 for Joey and 3 for Matthew. Two of Joey's sessions obtained session clarity scores of 2 combined with significant statistical evaluations, while one of Matthew's sessions achieved high subjective and objective evaluations. As a personal note, it is useful to note that both Joey and Matthew were experiencing significant stress in their job-related working environments during the time of this public demonstration, and in my opinion these results do not truly reflect their capabilities as viewers due to the shortcuts and strains that affected their remote-viewing experiences. This is not to excuse these results, but just to offer a more complete picture of the less-than-ideal conditions under which some aspects of the public demonstration were conducted. Nonetheless, the overall picture from the results of tables 6.3 and 6.4 is one of very significant success in describing these targets using remote viewing.

No matter how valuable numerical analyses are as summarizing tools, such analyses do not do justice to the profound nature of the data contained in many of the sessions for this public demonstration. As is so often the case, the really interesting story is in the details. Since there are too many sessions in this series to present in this volume due to normal space limitations, and since all of the sessions are available for examination on the web site of The Farsight Institute, I will limit my discussions of the content of these data to only my own sessions that had session clarity scores of 2 or higher, which is 17 out of 22 sessions. While this number in itself may at first seem excessive, discussions of many of the sessions can be combined since they exist in pairs for one target. Also, what actually occurs in each of these sessions is quite interesting and not repetitive, and it is worth telling this story fully given the importance of the claims being made here. To allow a more analytical approach, I use a narrative form of discussion rather than session snapshots.

EXPERIMENT #1: TWA Flight 800/crash/event (17 July 1996)

Returning to table 6.1, the ratio of actual to opposite session clarity scores for this experiment is 2:2. Indeed, after doing the opposite analysis for this experiment, I had serious doubts as to whether or not it was advisable to continue with the opposite analysis at all. The reason is that this session has two very clear themes. The first is a theme of an explorer climbing a mountain in a cold, icy, and snowy natural environment while the second theme is of a curved metallic structure with subjects being buffeted around as they crash into water. The first theme exactly matches the opposite target (Hillary on Mt. Everest) while the second theme exactly matches the actual target (the crash of TWA Flight 800). It is as if there are two sessions in one, and the viewer's perceptions flip half-way through the session from one target to the next. Indeed, had the two themes not been combined in a single session, and if the session had instead been divided in half, the first half of the session would have had a clarity score ratio of 0:3 while the second half of the session would have had a clarity score ratio of 3:0.

After seeing these results, I considered the possibility that this is yet another example of cross-cutting psi channels, as outlined in chapter 3 of this volume. Fearing that I might be corrupting the remaining experiments if I simply continued with my analysis, I decided to try something different from then on. Since I needed to re-examine the data twice to do this analysis (once for the actual target and again for the opposite target, all of which is occurring months after closing the sessions), for my first pass through the session pages I tried not to think about the opposite target. When I was ready to compare the data with the opposite target, I would quickly read the opposite target description and mentally repeat the notion that I should *not* find data relating to this target in the session. I continued to mentally repeat this as I examined the session pages while doing the opposite target analysis.

While this idea of trying to control my thoughts while doing the session analysis may seem strange at first, it nonetheless is a real concern here. Remember that remote viewing is a mental phenomenon that transcends both time and space. Thoughts matter in this realm. Again, since the opposite analysis would yield fruit if I could do it, I continued with my original plan to do the analysis, while trying to incorporate the safeguard of controlling my thoughts in the process. As readers will see, this seems to have worked. Only in one other experiment are the data apparently aligned with the opposite target as occurs with experiment #1, and there were special circumstances with that experiment (#9, see below). This again reaffirms the notion that it is the analyst's thoughts that help define the target for the viewer.

EXPERIMENT #3: The assassination of Abraham Lincoln / event

Experiment #3 has two sessions for this viewer, both of which have session clarity ratios of 2:0. However, the combined session clarity score for both sessions is a 3. The reason for this is that the sessions complement each other with information that is sufficiently varied such as to more completely describe the target. None of the data for either session describe the opposite target at all.

The first of the two sessions is very accurate with regard to location and environment. Descriptions of Washington, D.C. are very clear. Descriptions and sketches of various landmarks (such as the Washington Monument and what appears to be the Lincoln Memorial) in Washington, D.C. are also clear. Descriptions and sketches of what appears to be the Ford Theater are quite good, especially with respect to the long vertical lines on the facade and the existence of many short vertical and angular elements at the top of the structure. The session is also very accurate with regard to perceptions of the nature of the primary subject (a U.S. president). In this session I do not perceive the actual attack on President Lincoln, although I do report a mental despondency on the part of the President at the time of the assassination event.

The second of my two sessions for this target is also very accurate with regard to location and environment. Descriptions of Washington, D.C. are very clear. Descriptions of various landmarks (such as the Washington Monument and the Lincoln Memorial) in Washington, D.C. are also clear, and some of the sketches with identifying deductions are quite remarkable. (See figures 6.1, 6.2a, and 6.2b.) Descriptions and sketches of what appear to be the Ford Theater (or components of Ford Theater) are quite good. However, I do not perceive the actual attack on President Lincoln.

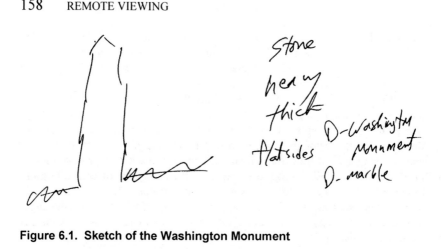

Figure 6.1. Sketch of the Washington Monument

EXPERIMENT #4: The Battle of Gettysburg (July 1863)

The session clarity score for this single remote-viewing session is 2, which indicates a high level of descriptive accuracy. The greatest faults of the session are on the level of overall completeness of the target descriptions. In general, I accurately portray the target as one of death and destruction, and I record detailed perceptions of explosions and a general wartime environment. Several deductions also suggest an accurate perception of the time period.

The problem with the completeness of the target description is that I do not report perceptions of subjects specifically engaged in fighting. Also, I note at the end of the session that I suspect I have made some decoding errors with regard to things on the land surface. This may or may not refer to decoding errors in which dead subjects and war paraphernalia on the ground are perceived

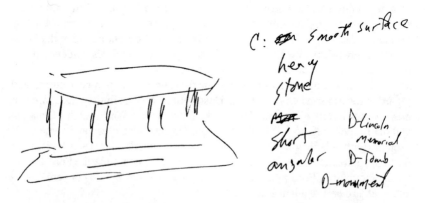

Figure 6.2a. Sketch of what appears to be the Lincoln Memorial

Figure 6.2b. Washington Monument and Lincoln Memorial. Source: IMSI's MasterClips/MasterPhotos(c) Collection, 1895 Francisco Blvd. East,San Raphael, CA 94901-5506 USA

only as burned and broken objects. After the session was completed, I verbally reported to Matthew Pfeiffer that I edited-out of this session (which means I decided not to write it down during the session) a perception of seemingly countless people dead on the ground since I considered the perception too clear to be remote-viewing data. Not to report all perceptions is a viewing mistake, and I make them too, regardless of my experience with this process. Nonetheless, the general tone of the session is remarkably accurate. Nothing in this session resembles a description of the opposite target.

EXPERIMENT #6: The Eiffel Tower / Paris, France (during the inauguration ceremony at the Paris International Exposition, March 31st, 1889)

The second session of the pair of sessions for this target has some extraordinarily accurate and complete descriptions (a clarity score of 3). But the first session is also quite useful, with a clarity score of 2. In this first session there are some decoding errors, although they are not overwhelming. The target itself involves a large pointed metallic structure and a huge celebration, complete with pyrotechnics (even a 21 cannon salute), lots of smoke, noise, and people. Our research could not establish whether or not there were fireworks at the target site sometime on that day, but it seems a reasonable assumption. In the beginning of this first session, many of the major components associated with the target site are addressed, particularly the cannons, booming sounds, smoke, and other pyrotechnics.

In later parts of the session, clearly a metallic, pointed object is perceived, and I produce two sketches that are exceptionally accurate (for example, see figures 6.3a and 6.3b), correctly observing that this is a tall building on land. The Eiffel Tower is also perceived to be in the context of other nearby structures in the city. I perceive the people watching the event. However, these perceptions are also mixed with the idea that a metallic, hollow, and silvery object is moving, which combines the ideas of the tower and the energetics surrounding the tower incorrectly.

The anticipatory nature of the event, in which people are waiting for the climax, is captured well near the end of the session. Also near the end of the session, I begin to wonder if the target involves the launch of a rocket, due to the energetics at the base (such as the cannon fire) and the tall pointed nature of the metallic structure. It is interesting to note that my perspective shifts correctly as specified in the third numbered aspect of the target specific. The third numbered aspect positions the viewer 100 feet above the tower looking downward, and this is precisely what I report at the end of the session.

The second session that I did for this target demonstrates unusual levels of what is often called "target penetration," which indicates the level to which a viewer perceives a complete description of the target. This session is a good example of the potential of remote viewing under optimal conditions. From the beginning of the session I clearly discern a pointed shape on land with people. In Phase 2 I note the smells of sulfur and burning associated with the gunpowder of the cannons. Later in the session I report that there is a tall, thin, manmade object that sits on flat land at the target site, and I again sketch a tall pointed structure similar to that of figure 6.3a, even deducting that this is a tower. On one page I note that the target involves "a tall manmade object with steep sides, slightly sloping."

The second numbered aspect involves a subject, Gustave Eiffel. When I shift to the second numbered aspect in this session, my perceptions correctly shift at the appropriate moment to this subject. I correctly perceive that the male subject is inside the structure and at an elevated altitude. I also state that the target structure is metallic, tall, and thin. Near the end of the session I begin to wonder if the metallic object may be floating (as in moving). But generally I seem to be focusing at this point on the smoke and energetics associated with the cannons and other pyrotechnics at the site.

EXPERIMENT #7: The White House / Washington, D.C. (August 1814)

This is the last time in this series of public demonstration experiments that I conducted only one session for a target, this time obtaining a session clarity score of 2. This target involves a British attack on Washington, D.C., and more

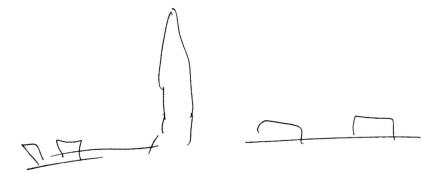

Figure 6.3a. Sketch of Eiffel Tower

specifically, the burning down of the White House. While this session is quite accurate, it does have some decoding errors, but none so great that they distract from the more obvious overall session accuracy.

In the early parts of this session I discern that the target involves a structure on dry land. I also perceive some of the elements of movement on land during warfare, and some of this seems to reflect the tumult of battle. Phase 2 data are very accurate, as is portrayed especially by the perceptions of sounds (roaring, booming), tastes (smoke), and smells (smoke and gunpowder).

The idea of a disaster comes through clearly in Phase 4 of this session. There is even a very interesting deduction of a house destroyed by a bomb. Some decoding errors appear to emerge early in Phase 4 when I begin to think that the target activity may take place on water. But we need to remember that the British troops arrived by boat, and the President even went to the coast to declare to his soldiers that the British were foolhardy to attack and were sure to be routed quickly. The American soldiers surprised him when they fled at the onslaught of rockets which they claimed to be "comets" being fired at them. Thus, the concept of activity being associated with or near water may or may not be a decoding error. There are also rivers and a bay near or at the target cite. (This is where a second session would have come in nicely!)

As the session continues I perceive aspects of war at the target site, particularly metallic "pebble-sized" bullets, rockets, and exploding debris flying through the air. I report, "It is like something is hitting me (the viewer), or striking me from the surrounding medium. Like many small things that sting me when they hit. It is like there is a strong force that is unleashed that has kinetic energy to throw things about. The things seem small, pebble-sized."

When I shift my attention to the second numbered aspect, I correctly direct my attention to a central target subject who is in command, even deducing that he is a leader and captain. I then begin to perceive the heat and fire that connects

Figure 6.3b. The Eiffel Tower. Source: IMSI's MasterClips/ MasterPhotos(c) Collection, 1895 Francisco Blvd. East,San Raphael, CA 94901-5506 USA

the target structure with the central target subject (General Ross). When shifting attention to the third numbered aspect, I correctly perceive the chaotic aftermath of the Washington battle, reporting that there are many people who have intense feelings about a now ash-gray structure.

EXPERIMENT #8: The battle between the Bon Homme Richard and the HMS Serapis / event (23 September 1779)

Both sessions that I did for this target receive a session clarity score of 2, and both are fairly comparable in content. The essential topological characteristics of this target are two triangularly shaped objects (the extensive sails of these boats form a triangular shape) on a flat surface, all of which are mixed with fighting/warfare activities. While I perceive these characteristics, it is clear from the decoding errors that exist in the session that my conscious mind does not totally recognize what is actually being perceived.

For both sessions there are two primary decoding errors. First, I perceive the flat base surface as hard land rather than water. This is a common error among novice viewers, but advanced viewers also sometimes make this mistake. The second primary decoding error is the perception that the triangular structures are all or mostly solid and hard. Thus, I miss the fabric nature of the sails on the boats (something that the other viewer, Joey Jerome, succeeded in perceiving together with the fact that they are wind powered). But I nonetheless do perceive the narrow and flat top of the boat's deck together with the general topology of the target.

For example, figure 6.4a is one sketch from the second of my two sessions in which I am trying to figure out some of the irregularities of the triangular shape for one of the sailboats. (Compare this with figure 6.4b.) In this sketch I perceive the overall topology and the irregularities of this topology due to the triangular arrangement of the sails, but I decode these irregularities as surface features of a hard structure. One problem from a decoding point of view is that part of the structure is hard (the bottom part of the boat) while the upper part (the sails) is fluffy and soft. It is perhaps due to this mixture of a triangular shape with a partially hard surface that the deductions that I make at the time I draw figure 6.4a lean in the interpretive direction of a stone pyramid with stepped sides. Later in the second session I note that the topology of the structure re-occurs elsewhere, stating "There are other similar structures nearby. They also seem to be shaped similarly with sloping sides." Again, we have accurate decoding of the general topology, but inaccurate decoding of the surface materials.

I also perceive the fighting at the target site in the latter parts of the first of my two sessions. Some of the atmospherics related to the fighting (such as the smoke from the battle) can also be found in early parts of this session. In the middle of the first session I begin to perceive the mass activity by the subjects at the target site, and as the session proceeds it is clear from my deductions that I suspect that this activity is related to a historical battle.

Of note with regard to the second of my two sessions, when I shift my perception to the second numbered aspect (Captain John Paul Jones), I do correctly perceive and sketch a male leader with a highly vertical hat. Although

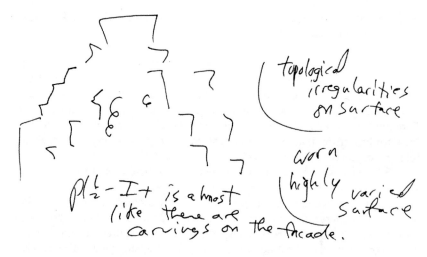

The handwritten annotations read:

topological
irregularities
on surface

worn

highly varied
surface

pl½ - It is almost
like there are
carvings on the facade.

Figure 6.4a. Sketch of a structure with triangular topology

the shape of the captain's actual hat is wider than the hat in my sketch, the sketch is not a bad approximation of its vertical dimension for a remote-viewing drawing, and at least I perceived that the captain wore a hat. (See figures 6.5a

Figure 6.4b. Bon Homme Richard battles HMS Serapis. Painting by James Hamilton (1819-78)

Figure 6.5a. Sketch of a subject with a hat

Figure 6.5b. John Paul Jones. Portrait by A. S. Conrad

and 6.5b.) Also in this second session, when I shift my perception to the third numbered aspect (the "Bon Homme Richard" at the bottom of the Atlantic Ocean), I at first think that I am perceiving fleshy immature bodies, but I later realize that these are essentially lifeless human forms, stating "It is almost like there are symbolic subjects here, almost like statues," and I deduce "dead."

EXPERIMENT #9: Mount Everest

The remote-viewing sessions for experiment #9 contain many very clear descriptions of the actual target, Mt. Everest. However, a mistake was made in the writing of the opposite target, and it was not possible for me to repair this since it was written by someone else and I had already looked at the opposite target just prior to doing the opposite analysis. The mistake was to use a large city as an opposite target for a mountain range. Even though a city and a mountain range may seem totally different to most people, both targets have a very similar topology with peaks and drops everywhere. It is not uncommon for viewers to wonder during a session if a target that is a mountain range is actually a city, and visa versa. But targeting mistakes do happen, and in this situation it was not easy for me to avoid thinking about (that is, worrying about) the opposite target of downtown Tokyo, Japan when doing the analysis presented below for experiment #9. Thus, contamination due to cross-cutting psi channels is a greater possibility for this experiment than for all of the other experiments except for #1.

Both sessions that I conducted for this target receive session clarity scores of 2, indicating essentially accurate data with some decoding errors. Despite some of the decoding errors, the first of the two sessions contains excellent descriptions of the mountainous topology of the actual target. On the second page of this session I even explicitly identify and sketch the target (deducting Mt. Everest). Nearly the entire focus of this first session is on the mountainous environment as defined in the first numbered aspect, while the other aspects are more clearly described in my second session for this target. In some parts of the first session, I wonder if the mountains are actually tall, pointed structures resembling a city skyline, but such decoding errors are infrequent and the shapes of the mountains are maintained in the sketches throughout the session.

In the middle of the first session I perceive what I think is some kind of structure that is high up and perhaps hovering, but I eventually end up repeatedly deducting ideas related to rock. I soon return to describing and sketching a rough mountainous environment. I also describe the reflective nature of the ice. The middle of the session is filled with highly accurate details of the target environment. I record "peaks, valleys, wild topology" made of rock, and I sketch the mountainous terrain. I also record, "This feels like a natural but rough surface...a large expansive natural environment...cold." (See figures 6.6 and 6.7)

Later in the session I again begin to wonder if the target may actually contain a tall pointed structure, but the sketch that I make at this point is still accurate for a mountain. Near the end of the session I correctly (from a procedural perspective) abandon the attempt to identify the target as either a set of pointed structures or a mountainous area, and instead correctly (again, from a substantive and procedural perspective) describe the irregular, tall, and pointed topology itself. I also continue to correctly describe the glassy and shiny nature of the surrounding icy surfaces while deducting higher-level ideas.

The second of my two sessions for this target compliments rather than repeats the data of the first session. In this session I describe the mountainous environment of the target less well than my first session for this target, and the first half of this second session is simply filled with decoding errors that suggest that the target is a capital city filled with tall structures. There are even two deductions that have oriental content, and the possibility of there being a cross-cutting psi channel with the opposite target of downtown Tokyo, Japan seems quite real in this context. But the second half of this session is quite good, and I do a better job here describing the emotional state of the subjects in the second and third numbered aspects, which is the reason the session scores as high as it does.

Examining the data for this second session at face value, I initially decode the mountain as a large structure with a curved facade, and these decoding errors continue through the initial pages of the session. However, when I get to the middle of the session I begin to discern more accurately the environment as a cold, harsh, wintry climate filled with snow. I then return briefly to thinking that the steep vertical topology is possibly that of a city with tall buildings, but I then begin to focus on the blustery energetics that are typical of the mountain summit. I both describe and sketch the rapid movement of clouds (describing a cloud as

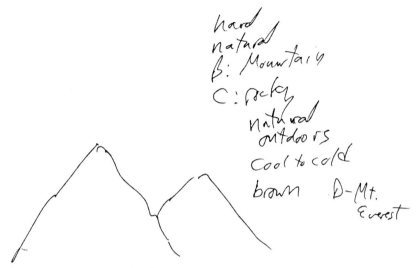

hard
natural
B: Mountain
C: rocky
natural
outdoors
Cool to cold
brown   D-Mt.
Everest

Figure 6.6. Sketch of Mt. Everest

a "puffy thing") that exist in that environment.

At this point in the session I begin to perceive some of the worrisome emotions of the target subjects. In the second numbered aspect, Edmund Hillary made a triumphal climb up the mountain. When I focus on the second numbered aspect, I initially make some decoding errors by describing some of the

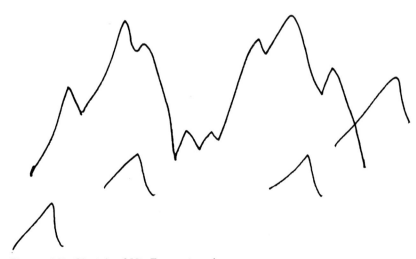

Figure 6.7. Sketch of Mt. Everest region

struggling movements of the subjects as possibly associated with fighting, which is undoubtedly a result of their difficulties with the environment. But these high-level concepts are soon dropped.

When I focus on the third numbered aspect, things change dramatically. In the third numbered aspect, Rob Hall was a guide of an ill-fated expedition in which he and many of his companions were killed in a brutal storm near the peak of Mt. Everest. The story of Rob Hall and his expedition is well covered by the IMAX movie, "Mt. Everest." When focusing on this aspect, I correctly perceive the emotional state of Rob Hall (and others). I report "despair, sadness." I state, "It feels like something is over or finished. It also feels like whatever happened was not good." I then end the session with the accurate statement, "It just feels like lots of people may have been hurt here, perhaps died."

EXPERIMENT #10: The Leaning Tower of Pisa, Italy

This target with its variously dated numbered aspects contains interesting complexities. 1179 is the year immediately following the first suspension of construction for the Leaning Tower of Pisa due in large part to a war that began in 1178 with Firenze (Florence). In 1179, only three floors had been completed for the Tower, and it took approximately 200 years to complete the project. (Interestingly, it began to lean after only the first three floors were built.) Again in 1179, next to the Tower was (and still is) the Duomo (a large cathedral) and other notable structures. The target as written contains many of the evolving components of the Leaning Tower of Pisa. The essential cue references just the Tower, which includes its present form, while the first and second aspects address its squatter manifestation as it appeared in 1179. The 1179 year tag is significant since it links the war to the target.

Sketches are the key element for describing this target, since the target is essentially a structure with an interesting topology in an urban environment. While my second session for this target contains some extraordinary sketches, the first session also contains highly accurate sketches and other descriptive information. For this first session, figure 6.8 is a very accurate drawing of the Tower as it appeared in 1179 (short and leaning). Another sketch from this session (figure 6.9) captures the compound on which the Tower resides. Note that the Duomo is clearly the structure on the far left and the Tower is the tall, thin structure next to it. There are many sketches in these two sessions, and in nearly all of the sketches that portray multiple structures, there is a large, wide structure near a tall, thin structure.

As I mention above, my second session for this target contains some extraordinary sketches. Figure 6.10 is a very good sketch of the Duomo, which is immediately next to the Tower. Other descriptive information (including sketches) suggest interiors with dim lighting that are very ornate with what appears to be gold and other rich colors. But the heart of all my efforts to

Figure 6.8. Sketch of the Leaning Tower of Pisa as it appeared in 1179 A.D.

describe the Leaning Tower of Pisa is figure 6.11a. (Compare this with figure 6.11b.) This sketch is about as perfect a sketch as one can usually get in remote viewing. Here we see the Duomo in the center, and the Tower immediately to the right of this. Other similar sketches appear elsewhere, but this is the clearest. The remainder of the session repeats the same theme of structures in an urban environment as found with the first session.

EXPERIMENT #11: The USS Missouri (2 September 1945)

This well documented and very interesting target involving the Japanese surrender to the American forces at the close of World War II is exceptionally complex. This is not just a boat with two men on it. Among many other things, this target is a very noisy event that includes squadrons of U.S. Navy carrier planes flying in formation over the ceremony, large numbers of enthusiastic and boisterous troops, and notably, two large SC-1 floatplanes hanging on catapults

structure on land
city
subjects

Figure 6.9. Sketch of Leaning Tower of Pisa and nearby buildings

on the USS Missouri just a few feet away from the location of General MacArthur, General Umezu, and the many other attendees during the signing ceremony.

Many of the components of this complex target are clearly evident in both of my sessions for this target, although I discuss only my first session here (due to its clarity score).   In the beginning of my session I perceive subjects, energetics and movement, and a hollow, dull silver colored metallic vessel, all of which strongly correlate with the USS Missouri on that day of celebration. The sketches are fine, although very elementary.   Early deductions of water-related vessels are notable as well. The data for energetics and movement are very appropriate for this target given the enormous amount of firepower as well as flying and sea movement displayed on that day. The sounds (voices,

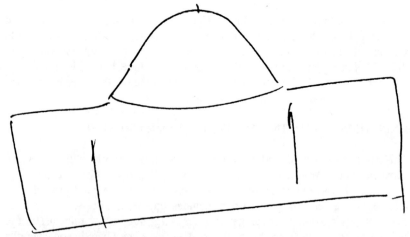

Figure 6.10. Sketch of the Duomo

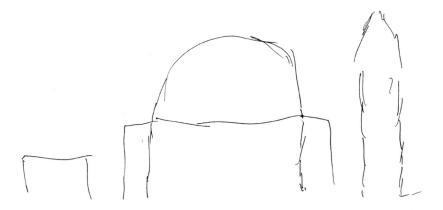

Figure 6.11a. Sketch of the Leaning Tower of Pisa, the Duomo, and a nearby structure (from right to left)

booming, thunder), tastes (burning), and smells (smoke and burning) are entirely appropriate for this target as well.

One of my sketches appears to have a decoding error that mixes the high levels of booming sounds and aerial displays into something that appears to be breaking up. On the other hand, this could represent some of the pyrotechnics that were available on that day. As the session proceeds I continue to have perceptions suggesting a metallic structure breaking up due to explosive energetics. This ceases by the middle of the session, however, and I then perceive simply a hollow, metallic structure. Then I focus on, describe, and sketch one of the two aircraft that are positioned just a few feet away from the signing ceremony on the deck of the USS Missouri.

When I shift my perception to the second numbered aspect for this target, I correctly perceive the central subjects (the military brass) at the center of the target, and I perceive that many other subjects are looking at a few subjects in the center of the target. Perceptions also suggest hand and arm motions that initially resemble fighting, but in retrospect are most likely the celebratory arm movements of cheering troops at the end of the ceremony. In this case I report,

Figure 6.11b. Leaning Tower of Pisa with Duomo. Source: 1911 Encyclopaedia Britannica

"It is as if the subjects are fighting among themselves. It is like they are swinging their arms and hitting one another. They seem to be standing up and surrounded by many or a few others who may be looking on.... The subjects are moving around quickly, mostly using rapid motions of hands, arms, and legs. Now it does not feel like fighting as much as just arms and legs flailing about."

In the middle of the session I continue to perceive a long, hollow, metallic structure. Following the third numbered aspect, I correctly shift my perception above the USS Missouri and begin to focus on the aerial activity at the target site (even sketching an airplane). I write, "It is like I am farther away from the center of the target structure as compared with earlier in the session." Again I report a "pointed object below and to the side of my current perspective," which would be the USS Missouri as per the instructions in the target specific.

EXPERIMENT #12: The edge of the Polar Plateau / Antarctic Continent (28 November 1929)

This very interesting target contains extraordinary imagery, and it produced one of my best pair of sessions for the entire public demonstration series. Both sessions received a 3 for their clarity scores. At approximately 8:15 p.m. on the date of the target, the Floyd Bennet flew over the ground-based companion geological team that was proceeding slowly using dog sleds. Mail and photographs of the surrounding terrain were dropped to the geological party by Byrd and June from the Floyd Bennet. The plane then headed directly toward the Polar Plateau, which Byrd and June needed to pass over in order to reach the South Pole. At approximately 9:15 p.m., the plane had climbed to 9,000 feet. In order to climb to 11,000 feet to attain the Polar Plateau, Byrd and June threw out of the plane empty fuel containers and 300 pounds of food. By 10:00 p.m. they were flying over the Polar Plateau on their way to their successful flyover of the South Pole.

The accuracy and descriptive detail in my first session is unusually clear, and even the deductions are highly insightful. On the first page of the session, I describe and sketch an ice mountain on water and deduct an iceberg (figure 6.12). On the next page I identify the target explicitly as Antarctica in a deduction, and again sketch and describe snow-covered terrain (figure 6.13). I then describe and sketch a male subject standing on ice and snow in a cold and hostile outdoor mountainous environment (figure 6.14).

The Phase 2 sensory perceptions are quite accurate, especially the temperatures (and even the smells of "cold"). I note that there is a "flat and sloping interface," which strongly corresponds with the Polar Plateau topology, and I sketch a mountainous terrain. The middle of the session contains exceptionally clear descriptions of the target terrain and subjects, including a second explicit identification of the actual target in a deduction. I also deduct the "Arctic" and a "sled" (a dog sled) when I perceive and record "a subject and

Figure 6.12. A sketch of an iceberg

what appears to be a small object about the size of the subject." Note that the historical record indicates that dog sleds were seen below from the Floyd Bennet at the approximate time of the target.

When shifting my perception to the second numbered aspect of the target, I accurately describe a healthy and vigorous male. Later I describe the "bulky" clothing of the target subject as well as his emotional state. Further descriptions of the surrounding environment appear at this point in the session, including

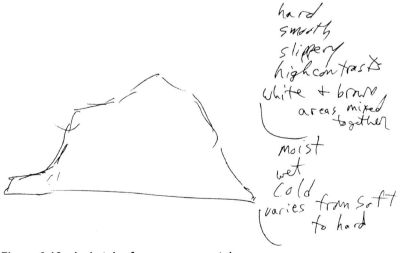

Figure 6.13. A sketch of a snowy mountain

Figure 6.14. A sketch of a subject on rough, snowy terrain

useful observations of the bright sunlight mixed with deep cold.

When shifting my perception to the third numbered aspect, I describe a cold sloping surface that matches the topology of the Polar Plateau, and I make the interesting deduction of a ski lift. My perspective of this sloping terrain is also "high up," as per the specification of the third numbered aspect in the target specific. Accurate descriptions of the surrounding environment continue on subsequent pages. Near the end of the session I make a particularly insightful deduction of "Perry on North Pole."

My second session for this target is nearly as profound a description of the target as the first session. Indeed, the data recorded in the second session complement rather than merely duplicate the prior observations. In this second session, there are descriptions of cold and mountainous terrain in bright sunlight. I then begin to perceive and accurately sketch some of the billowing snow that covers the mountains, and I note that it resembles a white cloth blowing in the wind that is wrapped around a person (figure 6.15). This theme of swirling energetics surrounding a mountainous topology re-occurs in later parts of this session.

Accurate environmental descriptions continue throughout the session. Throughout these pages are descriptions of cold and snowy, mountainous and sloping terrain. At one point I make a string of insightful deductions: "Alaska," "Arctic," "North Pole," and "Mt. McKinley."

When I shift my attention to the second numbered aspect for this target, I

Figure 6.15. Billowy snow blowing around a white mountain

perceive a subject dressed in very bulky clothing (figure 6.16). I execute a deep mind probe of the target subject that is particularly interesting. I report that he has a high level of emotional intensity, and that "there seems to be a one-minded level of thought going on, as if focusing on one thing." Continuing with the target description on subsequent pages, I do not perceive the actual plane, the

Figure 6.16. Sketch of subject with bulky clothing

Floyd Bennet, but rather the scenes that are witnessed from the plane by Byrd and June, including the mountainous terrain, the bright sunlight, and the bright and highly reflective snowy surface below.

EXPERIMENT #14: The eruption of Mt. Vesuvius / near Pompeii, Italy (24 August 79 A.D.)

My first session of the pair for this target has some very clear descriptions, which yielded a session clarity score of 3. On the first page of the session I perceive, label, and sketch the mountain (Mt. Vesuvius). Following this, the remainder of the session focuses mainly on Pompeii.

Structures are identified and sketched throughout the session, all of which have the appropriate architecture for the city and period, as evidenced by the ruins of Pompeii which are still standing today. For example, the sketch in figure 6.17 is of a structure with a domed or curved roof and arched openings in the facade. A deduction of the Parthenon on the same page as this sketch is also of interest due to the parallels in structural styles. Later I sketch a group of structures with appropriate architecture together with intense human activity that involves movement and smoke. Indeed, in one sketch I show smoke rising from between the buildings. (See figures 6.18a and 6.18b.)

When collecting Phase 2 sensory data I perceive sounds of voices and "booming," extreme variations in temperatures, smoke that "hurts the nostrils," and other items that are appropriate for this target. In the middle of the session I perceive all the shouting, subjects, and structures that are appropriate for this target, as well as the concepts of death. I note that "the activity itself is the center of my perspective," which is appropriate for a target with such a high level of activity.

Toward the end of the session I perceive a subject in a horizontal position inside a structure, and I suspect that the person may be dead. It is interesting to note that this is another good example of how a remote viewer can perceive something without understanding what is actually going on. In this case in which the subject is most probably dead, I write, "I seem to be inside a structure with one central subject who is in a state of sleep, or calm, or something, maybe even dead. He seems to be either sitting or resting, or perhaps lying down."

When shifting my perspective to the third numbered aspect, I correctly re-locate my perspective above Pompeii, looking downward, as specified in the target specific, and I sketch the city with the people moving quickly below. I again perceive intense emotions (although I make some decoding errors regarding some emotional types). I end the session perceiving an urban environment, death, and lots of activity. I record perceiving what amounts to pandemonium on the surface, many people moving about, a city, loud booming and popping sounds, and lots of yelling.

In the second session for this target, I again perceive and make numerous

Figure 6.17. Sketch of a structure in Pompeii, Italy

sketches of the structures in the city, all appropriate in terms of architecture. Some of the sketches contain more detail than those for the first session, but the themes are the same.   However, when I shift my attention to the second numbered aspect for this target, I make an interesting sketch of a person wearing period-appropriate toga-style clothing. (See figure 6.19.) I also perceive that the target event involves "many subjects that are connected to some type of social change that is significant," and I compare it to that of a revolution. While still collecting data for the second numbered aspect (the citizens of Pompeii trying to flee the eruption of Mt. Vesuvius), I follow one subject into a structure and report that the "structure seems to be complicated in the sense of being either large or with many rooms.... Somehow, the central subject feels protected inside this structure, as in the sense of a haven." This report can send a sad chill down my spine when I read it even now and remember how current day archeologists

Figure 6.18a. Sketch of Pompeii, Italy during volcanic destruction

have found so many bodies crouching inside buildings in the buried ruins of Pompeii, showing how people sought haven in their homes from the wrath of the volcano, all to no avail.

When I shift my perspective to the third numbered aspect, I again correctly

Figure 6.18b. Pompeii (Forum) and Mount Vesuvius. Photo by Leo C. Curran 1997. Placed in public domain by creator at http://wings.buffalo.edu/AandL/Maecenas/general_contents.html and http://wings.buffalo.edu/AandL/Maecenas/italy_except_rome_and_sicily/ pompeii/ac881723.html

move my observation point above the city, looking downward. From this bird's eye perspective, I perceive human activity, loud sounds, and structures, all appropriate for this target.

EXPERIMENT #15: The Statue of Liberty / New York Harbor (4 July 1976) and Parade of Tall Ships

This is a very interesting and complex target. The Statue of Liberty is a tall metallic (copper) figure that sits on a small island between Manhattan and New Jersey near the mouth of the Hudson River. During the U.S. Bicentennial celebrations in 1976, there was a huge parade of tall sailing ships in the waters around New York Harbor (near the mouth of the Hudson River). This included ships with powerful water cannons, and every other type of water vehicle imaginable (over 10,000 in all). There was also one of the most spectacular (and loud) fireworks displays ever, all of which could be seen from many vantage points in New York and New Jersey. The Statue of Liberty was essentially in the center of all of this activity. Verification of these events can be found in microfilm records of *The New York Times* for 5 July 1976, available in most libraries.

In the second session that I did for this target (the only one that had a clarity score of 2 or greater), I do not tie everything together, but many of the essential components of the target are described accurately. I begin the session by perceiving that the target involves a metallic structure standing on two legs, although my sketch is very crude. I then perceive a flying, tubular object shaped like a rocket, and deduct a "launch." There were an enormous number of rocket launches (fireworks) on that day near the Statue of Liberty. When I perceive a central target subject, at first I think that the subject may be reclining, although other words that I use suggest that I may be perceiving the Statue of Liberty itself, even noting that the subject feels "feminine or gentle."

When I focus on what I perceive to be the head of the target subject, I report that "something is around or on top of the subject's head that makes me think of long hair, but it may be different." The confusion increases soon afterward when I then suspect that the subject may be male with something spike-like projecting out of the top of the head. In retrospect it seems that I may have been trying to make sense out of the spiked crown that projects from the top of the head of the Statue of Liberty.

When collecting sensory data in Phase 2, I perceive the sounds of "rumble" and a "dull roar," as well as the smells of "sulfur," all of which are accurate for this target. It is of interest to note that I also report colors of "red, white, and blue," which were abundantly visible on this very patriotic day. Also, I note that there is something at the target that is "long, thin, heavy, part solid or filled and part empty or hollow," which is correct for the Statue of Liberty.

In the middle of the session I describe a metallic structure with an irregular shape, a subject (perceived now as male), and bright reflected sunlight. When I shift my focus to the second numbered aspect, I describe and sketch the smoke of the rocket launches at the target site (again, there were many). I then report the loud noises at the target site, writing, "It sounds like there is a loud roar or rumbling sound. It feels like the ground is vibrating or shaking." I also perceive the light of "high energy fire," which accurately describes the fireworks.

Later in the session I perceive and sketch boats at the target site. Many of these boats had cannons (water and otherwise), which are sketched. (See figure 6.20.) When shifting my attention to the third numbered aspect (the top of the Statue of Liberty), I perceive a subject that is "wearing something that is like a shell or hard covering," which is an entirely appropriate perception given that the statue is made of metal. The remaining pages of the session contain data and deductions that suggest a general water and water vehicle environment.

While the above discussion of selected remote-viewing sessions done for this public demonstration does not include sessions which received session clarity scores less than 2, there is one observation coming from the first session for the current Statue of Liberty target that I think is interesting to note. In the first session I also perceive a large metallic structure, and I also perceive a central target subject, although I never equate the two. But in the process of focusing on the central subject in this target I execute a deep mind probe of the subject. (Not knowing it was not a person, why not?) What resulted is not that uncommon for remote viewing. I perceive what the target person represents. In particular, I perceive concepts (not emotions) of "care, concern, protection." I then write that this person is a "caretaker." Finally, "(t)here is the idea of someone who is desiring to protect something or someone or others." These words in my session are remarkably correspondent with the words of Emma Lazarus's famous poem that speak for the statue and are graven on a tablet at the

Figure 6.19. Subject with toga-style clothing

Figure 6.20. Sketch of a boat with a canon

base of the Statue of Liberty, "Give me your tired, your poor, Your huddled masses yearning to breathe free, The wretched refuse of your teeming shore. Send these, the homeless, tempest-tost to me." The profoundness of the remote-viewing process surprises most people who look at it closely. It never ceases to surprise me.

Summary

In this chapter I have presented results of a six-month public demonstration of remote viewing that was sponsored by The Farsight Institute from October 1999 through March 2000. Rigorous scientific controls were used throughout this demonstration that utilized a tasking-post strategy of target assignment, and which was witnessed by thousands of people from all over the world. This discussion presents a numerical analysis of all of the remote-viewing sessions that appear in this demonstration that includes both subjective session clarity scores and objective computer-based statistical analyses based on SAM. Although the session clarity scores are assigned post hoc, others can compare these evaluations using their own judgments, and I suggest that the overall results (both subjective and objective) argue forcefully that remote viewing is a real and potent phenomenon that is repeatable. And for all of us who also desire to see examples of how the process works under controlled conditions, I have presented summaries and analyses of 17 of my own 22 sessions. Again, all of the original raw data for all of the sessions in the pubic demonstration series are available to view at the Institute's web site, www.farsight.org. No data (sketches or otherwise) have been omitted from the web site presentation.

In my own mind, I cannot see how a reasonable person can closely examine these findings and still doubt the existence of remote viewing as a real, trainable, and increasingly reliable mental phenomenon. As discussed in previous chapters, there are now many individuals associated with a growing number of professional remote-viewing organizations who are similarly proficient (or even more so than myself) in an effective remote-viewing methodology. This ensures that controlled public demonstrations of this phenomenon will become an inevitable part of our future, and it is possible that one day in the near future nearly everyone may accept that remote viewing is a real phenomenon in need of serious and properly funded scientific study.

APPENDIX I TO CHAPTER 6

Table A6.1: Targets Used for the Public Demonstration Experiments

Experiment #1:
    Essential Cue:
    TWA Flight 800/crash/event (17 July 1996)

    Numbered Aspects:
    1. TWA Flight 800/crash/event (17 July 1996)
    2. The explosion of TWA Flight 800- perspective: as seen from 50 feet above the explosion (17 July 1996)
    3. The cockpit of TWA Flight 800 during the moments immediately after the explosion event (17 July 1996)

Experiment #3:
    Essential Cue:
    The assassination of Abraham Lincoln/event

    Numbered Aspects:
    1. The assassination of Abraham Lincoln/Ford's Theater, Washington, D.C./event (April 14, 1865 circa 10:15 p.m. EST)
    2. The audience within Ford's Theater reacting to the shooting of Abraham Lincoln/Ford's Theater, Washington, D.C./event (April 14, 1865 circa 10:15 p.m. EST)
    3. John Wilkes Booth/arrival at Mary Surratt's Tavern/Surrattsville, Maryland/event (April 14, 1865, circa 11:59 p.m. EST)

Experiment #4:
    Essential Cue:
    The Battle of Gettysburg (July 1863)

    Numbered Aspects:
    1. The Battle of Gettysburg / event (July 1863)
    2. Pickett's charge / event (July 3, 1863)
    3. General J.E.B Stuart ordering the 1st Virginia to advance against the Union Calvary / event (July 3, 1863)

Experiment #5:
    Essential Cue:
    The Great Chicago Fire / Chicago, Illinois / event (October 1871)

    Numbered Aspects:
    1. The Great Chicago Fire / Chicago, Illinois / event (October 1871)
    2. The start of the Great Chicago Fire at Katherine O'Leary's barn / Chicago, Illinois / event (October 8, 1871, circa 9 p.m. Chicago local time)
    3. Chicago, Illinois - perspective: 200 feet above Chicago's City Library looking downwards (October 11, 1871, 11:30 a.m. Chicago local time)

Experiment #6:
    Essential Cue:
    The Eiffel Tower / Paris, France (during the inauguration ceremony at the Paris International Exposition, March 31st, 1889)

    Numbered Aspects:

1. The Eiffel Tower / Paris, France (during the inauguration ceremony at the Paris International Exposition, March 31st, 1889, 1:45 p.m. Paris local time)
2. Gustave Eiffel unfurling the French flag at the Eiffel Tower (during the inauguration ceremony at the Paris International Exposition, March 31st, 1889)
3. The Eiffel Tower - perspective: 100 feet above the Eiffel Tower, looking downwards at the tower itself (during the inauguration ceremony at the Paris International Exposition, March 31st, 1889, 1:45 p.m. Paris local time)

Experiment #7:
Essential Cue:
The White House / Washington, D.C. (August 1814)

Numbered Aspects:
1. The White House / Washington, D.C. (25 August 1814)
2. Major General Robert Ross / The White House / Washington, D.C. (25 August 1814, 4 p.m. Washington D.C. local time)
3. The White House / Washington, D.C. (26 August 1814, 8 a.m. Washington, D.C. local time) - perspective: as seen from 100 feet directly above

Note: Major General Robert Ross was the British officer who decided to burn the White House

Experiment #8:
Essential Cue:
The battle between the Bon Homme Richard and the HMS Serapis/event (23 September 1779)

Numbered Aspects
1. The battle between the "Bon Homme Richard" and the "HMS Serapis"/event (23 September 1779)
2. Captain John Paul Jones stating "I have not yet begun to fight"/event (23 September 1779)
3. The "Bon Homme Richard" at the bottom of the Atlantic Ocean (12 October 1779)

Experiment #9:
Essential Cue:
Mount Everest

Numbered Aspects
1. Mount Everest (29 May, 1953)
2. Edmond Hilary - perspective: from 3 feet away from Edmond Hilary (at the moment of reaching the summit of Mount Everest, 29 May 1953)
3. Rob Hall siting on an outcrop of rock - perspective: from 6 feet above Rob Hall (during his last radio communication, 11 May 1996)

Experiment #10:
Essential Cue:
The Leaning Tower of Pisa, Italy

Numbered Aspects:
1. The Leaning Tower of Pisa / Pisa, Italy (1179)
2. The Leaning Tower of Pisa / Pisa, Italy (1179) - perspective: from 200 feet directly above the Leaning Tower of Pisa
3. The largest chamber within the Leaning Tower of Pisa (8 p.m. GMT, 28 September

1774)

Experiment #11:
Essential Cue:
The USS Missouri (2 September 1945)

Numbered Aspects:
1. The USS Missouri (2 September 1945)
2. General Yoshijiro Umezu / signing the surrender document / event (2 September 1945)
3. The USS Missouri - perspective: from 20 feet above General Yoshijiro Umezu during the signing of the surrender document (2 September 1945)

Experiment #12:
Essential Cue:
The edge of the Polar Plateau / Antarctic Continent (28 November 1929)

Numbered Aspects
1. The edge of the Polar Plateau / Antarctic Continent (28 November 1929, approximately 9:00 p.m. Antarctic local time)
2. Richard E. Byrd and Harold June in the aircraft "Floyd Bennet" approaching the edge of the Polar Plateau on their way to the South Pole (28 November 1929, approximately 9:00 p.m. Antarctic local time)
3. The edge of the Polar Plateau - perspective: as seen by the occupants of the aircraft "Floyd Bennet" passing above the Polar Plateau on their way to the South Pole (28 November 1929, approximately 9:15 p.m. Antarctic local time)

Experiment #14:
Essential Cue:
The eruption of Mt. Vesuvius / near Pompeii, Italy (24 August 79 A.D.)

Numbered Aspects:
1. The eruption of Mt. Vesuvius / near Pompeii, Italy (24 August 79 A.D.)
2. The citizens of Pompeii trying to flee the eruption of Mt. Vesuvius / the port of Pompeii (24 August 79 A.D.)
3. The Forum / Pompeii, Italy - perspective from 100 feet above the Forum looking downward (during the eruption of Mt. Vesuvius, 24 August 79 A.D.)

Experiment #15:
Essential Cue:
The Statue of Liberty / New York Harbor (4 July 1976)

Numbered Aspects
1. The Statue of Liberty / New York Harbor (4 July 1976)
2. Parade of Tall Ships passing the Statue of Liberty / New York harbor (4 July 1976)
3. Parade of Tall Ships passing the Statue of Liberty - perspective: from the top of the Statue of Liberty looking down upon the passing ships (4 July 1976)

APPENDIX II TO CHAPTER 6

This appendix explains the statistical information discussed in chapter 6 of this volume. The data for the targets and for the remote-viewing sessions were coded into SAM post hoc in order to produce the data sets on which these analyses are based. The codings for both the sessions and the targets are available in tabular form for all sessions on The Farsight Institute's web site, www.farsight.org. Readers may also wish to compare these codings with the actual session pages, all of which are also available at the same web site. Detailed statistical analyses for all sessions are also available on the Institute's web site, and these analyses are broken into three thematically organized sections for each remote-viewing session, with each section containing a number of statistical tests of the relationship between the session and target data.

Test #1: Basic Counts and a Chi-square Test

On the web site, www.farsight.org, detailed lists of all of the data describing the perceptions recorded in the remote-viewing session are displayed together with the matches with respect to the SAM data set for the target. Those target attributes that are not observed by the remote viewer are also included. Following the description of the session and target data, a variety of counts are presented. Two important proportions (labeled "A" and "B") are then presented. Proportion A is the total matches between the session and the target as a proportion of the total number of target attributes. If one considers the total number of target attributes as representing the total variance in the target, then proportion A tells us how much of this variance is described by the session. When proportion A is high, then a session has described most of the variance in the target.

    Proportion B looks at this from a mirror perspective, and it is the total matches between the session and the target as a proportion of the total number of session entries (not target attributes as with proportion A). Proportion B tells us how efficient the viewer is in describing the target. Of course, in an extreme and offending case, one can always match all of a target's attributes by entering every possible attribute available in SAM when inputting session data. Inaccuracies in this dimension are revealed by proportion B. When proportion B is low, then a viewer did not do a good job describing the unique characteristics of the target, and the best one can say is that accurate target perceptions may be mixed in with erroneous perceptions. An ideal situation is when both proportions A and B are high, which means that a target was well described with very few erroneous perceptions. The average of proportions A and B is called the "correspondence number" for the session, and it is a general measure of the correspondence between the observed remote-viewing data and the actual target attributes.

Below proportions *A* and *B*, a chi-square test is presented that evaluates the general correlation or "goodness of fit" between the remote-viewing data and the actual target's attributes. To calculate the chi-square statistic, a 2X2 table is constructed (see below) that associates a 1 for every session entry or target attribute, and a 0 for the lack of a session entry or target attribute. Large numbers of matches between the session and the target attributes (i.e., values of 1 for each) lead to larger chi-square values.   The chi-square statistic is often referenced as an overall measure of deviation, and large values for this statistic indicate that the null hypothesis stating no relationship between the session and target attributes has little credibility (since the test under such circumstances indicates a large deviation from the null hypothesis).   An alternate and more conservative version of the chi-square test which is based only on the observed session entries (the first row in the table below) is also presented.   This effectively eliminates the influence of large numbers of 0/0 matches in the calculation of the first chi-square statistic.   The structure and interpretation for the chi-square test is as follows, and is applicable across all such analyses presented below:

	Target 0:	Target 1:
Session 1:	1/0 matches	1/1 matches
Session 0:	0/0 matches	0/1 matches

Chi-square Values:	Significance Level:
3.84	0.05
5.02	0.025
6.63	0.010
7.88	0.005
10.8	0.001

Interpretation of the Chi-square Statistic

1. If the value of the chi-square statistic is equal to or greater than the chi-square value for a desired significance level in the table above, and if the correlation between the session data and the target attributes is positive, then the session's data are statistically significant descriptors of the target.
2. If the value of the chi-square statistic is less than the chi-square value for a

desired significance level, then the remote-viewing data for the session are not statistically significant. This normally means that there are decoding errors in the data.

3. If the value of the chi-square statistic is equal to or greater than the chi-square value for a desired significance level but the correlation between the session data and target attributes is negative, then the session either has major decoding errors, or there may be conscious-mind intervention and/or invention in the data gathering process.

NOTE: The chi-square value does not take into account the direction of the relationship between the session data and target attributes. The chi-square value is a useful measure *only* if there is a positive correlation between the target's attributes and the session's SAM entries. (That is, there needs to be a reasonably high number of target and session matches.)

Following the chi-square analysis, a heuristic comparison is presented. With this comparison, a pseudo target is constructed that has the same number of target attributes as the real target. But with the pseudo target, the attributes are selected randomly. This heuristic comparison offers a general idea of how well the remote-viewing data correspond with the real target as compared with a bogus target. Of course, this heuristic comparison is an added procedure used for illustration, not a test.

Test #2: The Russell Procedure

The second section of the statistical analyses for each session presented here is called the "Russell Procedure," and is due to the physicist, Dr. John Russell. The test has two parts. Part I calculates the expected number of matches between a remote-viewing session and a target based simply on chance. This binomial mean is found by dividing the total number of attributes for a given target by the total possible number of attributes (93), and then multiplying this ratio by the total number of SAM entries for the corresponding remote-viewing session. A standard deviation is then calculated based on the appropriate hypergeometric distribution (see Feller 1968, pp. 232-3).

Confidence intervals are then calculated that determine if the actual number of session/target matches is different from chance. An actual match total that is outside of a given confidence interval is different from chance, which leads to the rejection of the null hypothesis.

Following this, a weighted number of matches between the session and the target is calculated. This weighted number is an alternative way of looking at this problem. Rather than simply counting the number of matches between a session and a target, weights are constructed for each SAM entry for the remote-viewing session based on how rare each entry occurs in general. To calculate the weights, a large pool of 240 very diverse SAM targets is used. The formula for determining the weights is derived as follows:

Let,

Ci = the total number of times a given attribute (i) occurs in a pool of targets
Q = the total number of targets in the pool

Thus, the probability of any attribute chosen in a remote-viewing session being represented in the pool is Ci/Q. Since we want a weight that is large when an attribute is relatively rare in the pool, and small otherwise, we use the reciprocal of Ci/Q, times a constant of proportionality (for scaling) for the weight. Thus, our weight is, Wi = weight for attribute i = kQ/Ci = V/Ci, where $kQ=V$ (a constant), and k is our constant of proportionality.

We now need to determine V, which we can do by solving for it in one particular instance (since it is always a constant). We know that under conditions that all Ci equal the mean of C, then the weight for attribute i is simply V divided by the mean of C, which equals 1 by definition since all weights must be equal to 1 under such conditions. Thus, V equals the mean of C, which will be true for all distributions of Ci (again, since V is a constant). This means that our desired weight, Wi, is the mean of C divided by Ci.

The weighted mean (called the "Russell Mean") is then the summation of all of the weighted SAM entries for a given remote-viewing session. The Russell Mean is then evaluated with respect to the same confidence intervals as with the unweighted mean to determine the significance of the session's SAM entries. This test is quite rigorous (perhaps excessively so), and it evaluates a remote-viewing session based on SAM entries that are relatively rare, and thus more or less unique to a given target.

Part II of the Russell Procedure evaluates the remote-viewing session from the perspective of how many random SAM entries would be needed to describe the target as completely (as per the number of session/target matches) as is done by the actual session. To conduct this test, the SAM Program constructs pseudo sessions composed of random SAM entries, with each entry being added one at a time until the total number of matches with the actual target equals that achieved by the actual remote-viewing session. The mean and standard deviation for the total number of SAM entries for each pseudo session are computed from a set of 1000 Monte Carlo samples. Confidence intervals are again constructed, and this test evaluates the efficiency of the remote viewer (as per proportion B used in Test #1) in describing the target. When the total number of actual session SAM entries is outside of (that is, less than) an appropriate confidence interval, then the remote viewer's perceptive efficiency is outside of chance, and the null hypothesis is rejected.

Test #3: Correspondence and Correlation

All targets have a variety of descriptive characteristics (that is, SAM target attributes). When comparing one target with another, both similarities and differences will be found between the two. The correspondence numbers are one measure of the degree of similarity between any two sets of SAM data, and these numbers can be used to compare one target with another target, or a remote-viewing session with a target. The correspondence numbers are calculated as per Test #1 (see above). Proportion *A* is the total matches between the session and the target as a proportion of the total number of target attributes. Proportion *B* is the total matches between the session and the target as a proportion of the total number of session entries (not target attributes as with proportion *A*). The average of proportions *A* and *B* is called the "correspondence number" for the session, and it is a general measure of the correspondence between the observed remote-viewing data and the actual target attributes. Again, correspondence numbers can also be calculated between any two targets to measure their degree of similarity.

Test #3 evaluates the correspondence numbers for each session. The better a remote-viewing session describes all of a target's characteristics, the higher will be the correspondence number between the session and the target. Used in this way, the correspondence number is called the "session/target" correspondence number. When correspondence numbers are calculated that compare one target with another, such numbers are called "target/target" correspondence numbers.

We want to do two things with these correspondence numbers. First we want to note the relative ranking of the session/target correspondence number for the remote-viewing session and its real target as compared with the session/target numbers for the session and other (bogus) targets in a pool of targets. If a session describes the actual target relatively well, then its correspondence number should be high relative to alternative correspondence numbers for bogus targets selected from a pool. Second, we want to compare the variation of both the session/target numbers and the target/target numbers with regard to the pool of targets. Since a pool of targets normally contains targets with a great variety of descriptive characteristics, comparing any given real target with other bogus targets will result in finding various collections of similarities across the comparisons.

For example, the real target may have a mountain and a structure. Comparing this target with another target that has only a mountain will find the similarity in terms of the mountain but not in terms of the structure. Comparing the same real target with another target that has only a structure will find the similarity with respect to the structure, but not with respect to the mountain. Using a number of comparisons in this way across a pool of targets allows us to account for all or most of the real target's important characteristics.

This returns us to wanting to compare the variation between the two sets of session/target and target/target correspondence numbers across the pool of targets as a means of evaluating the overall success of a remote-viewing session in capturing its real target's total set of attributes. When compared with other targets which in the aggregate contain many different attribute sets, both the remote-viewing session and its real target should have correspondence numbers that vary similarly. The correlation coefficient summarizes this relationship. The correlation coefficient can vary between -1 and 1. The closer its value is to 1, the more closely the remote-viewing session describes all of its real target's various characteristics.

To begin this comparison in Test #3, correspondence numbers between the remote-viewing data and all 13 targets that were chosen for the public demonstration of remote viewing are calculated. This allows for a comparison of correspondence numbers between the remote-viewing session and the real target as compared with those correspondence numbers involving the remote-viewing session and the other targets in this small pool. An accurate session should have a correspondence number for the real target that has a relatively high ranking as compared with the correspondence numbers involving the other targets. Correspondence numbers between the real target for an experiment and the 12 other targets in the pool are also calculated. The correlation coefficient for the session/target and target/target correspondence numbers is then calculated. A high correlation between the two sets of numbers indicates that the session data and the target attributes for the real target for the experiment are similar when compared with target attributes for other targets in the public demonstration pool.

In Part II of this test, correspondence numbers for the given remote-viewing session and all targets in a diverse pool of 240 SAM targets are calculated. Additionally, correspondence numbers calculated using the real target for the remote-viewing experiment and all targets in the SAM pool are also calculated. If the remote-viewing session describes the real target well, then the two sets of correspondence numbers (that is, one comparing the session with the SAM pool, and the other comparing the real target with the SAM pool) should vary similarly, and this should be reflected in the correlation between the two sets of numbers.

An Example of the Statistical Breakdowns That Are Available at www.farsight.org for All Remote-viewing Sessions Conducted in this Public Demonstration

Statistical Evaluations for Public Experiment #12

Here are three test procedures that evaluate the remote-viewing session with the target data. All of these tests utilize Farsight's Session Analysis Machine

(SAM).

Viewer: Courtney Brown
Session: Session #1

TEST #1: Comparing the Remote-viewing session Data with the Target
Attributes

The session data are:	Session/Target Matches:
surface: surface	match
surface: irregular topology	match
land: land	match
land: natural	match
land: irregular topology	match
land: steep peaks	match
water: water	match
water: land/water interface	match
water: ice or snow	match
atmospherics: natural smells	match
natural object(s): natural object(s)	match
natural object(s): on a surface	match
subject(s): subject(s)	match
subject(s): male	match
subject(s): one/few	match
mountain: mountain(s)	match
mountain: one	match
mountain: multiple	match

light: bright	match
environment: natural	match
environment: harsh natural	match
sounds: talking, shouting, voices	match
temperatures: cold	match
dominant session elements: natural environment	match
sketches: natural object on a surface	match
sketches: subject(s)	match
sketches: subject(s) on an outside base surface	match
sketches: sloping or peaking base surface(s)	match
sketches: extensive water	

The target attributes not perceived are:

Missed Target Attributes:
structure(s) materials: manmade materials
structure(s) general location: not located on a surface
nonsurface structure(s): nonsurface structures
nonsurface structure(s): one
nonsurface structure(s): subjects inside
nonsurface structure(s): noticeable relative movement
energetics: kinetic (fast or slow, one direction)
activity: activity or movement by object(s)
sounds: wind-type sounds
dominant session elements: structure(s) not on a surface
sketches: structure(s)

sketches: structure(s) not on a surface
sketches: subject(s) in a structure
sketches: significant motion of primary object(s)

The total matches between the session and the target are: 28
The total number of target attributes not perceived: 14
The total number of session entries is: 29
The total number of target entries is: 42
A. The total matches between the session and the target as a proportion of the total number of target attributes are: 0.667
B. The total matches between the session and the target as a proportion of the total number of session entries are: 0.966
General session/target correspondence (the average of A and B above): 0.816
The normal chi-square value with 1 degree of freedom testing the fit of the session to the target based on the table below is: 44.938
The alternative chi-square value with 1 degree of freedom based on only the distribution of chosen session attributes (the top row of the table below) is: 30.925
The correlation between this session's data and the target attributes is: POSITIVE
NOTE: The chi-square value does not take into account the direction of the relationship between the session data and target attributes. The chi-square value is a useful measure *only* if there is a positive correlation between the target's attributes and the session's SAM entries. (That is, there needs to be a reasonably high number of target and session matches.)

	Target 0:	Target 1:
Session 1:	1	28
Session 0:	50	14

Chi-square Values:	Significance Level:
3.84	0.05
5.02	0.025
6.63	0.010

7.88	0.005
10.8	0.001

Interpretation of the Chi-Square Statistic

1. If the value of the chi-square statistic is equal to or greater than the chi-square value for a desired significance level in the table above, and if the correlation between the session data and the target attributes is positive, then the session's data are statistically significant descriptors of the target.
2. If the value of the chi-square statistic is less than the chi-square value for a desired significance level, then the remote-viewing data for the session are not statistically significant. This normally means that there are decoding errors in the data.
3. If the value of the chi-square statistic is equal to or greater than the chi-square value for a desired significance level but the correlation between the session data and target attributes is negative, then the session either has major decoding errors, or there may be conscious-mind intervention and/or invention in the data gathering process.

HEURISTIC COMPARISON: Comparing the Session with a Target with Randomly Chosen Attributes

The total matches between the session and a target with randomly chosen attributes are: 13
The total number of session data entries is: 29
The total number of target attribute entries is: 42
The total matches between the session and the target as a proportion of the total number of target entries are: 0.310
The total matches between the session and the target as a proportion of the total number of session entries are: 0.448
The normal chi-square value with 1 degree of freedom testing the fit of the session to the target based on the table below is: 0.002
The alternative chi-square value with 1 degree of freedom based on only the distribution of chosen session attributes is: 0.001

TEST #2: The Russell Procedure

Part I.
The expected mean number of chance matches for this session is: 13.097
The standard deviation (hypergeometric distribution) for this mean is: 2.235
The 90% confidence interval for this is: [9.420, 16.774]
The 95% confidence interval for this is: [8.716, 17.478]

The 98% confidence interval for this is: [7.900, 18.294]
The unweighted (actual) number of matches between the session and the target are: 28
The weighted number of matches between the session and the target are: 36.829
Interpretation: If the unweighted and/or weighted number of matches between the session and the target are outside of (that is, greater than) the desired confidence interval, then the number of matches obtained in the session was not by chance.

Part II.
If the Session Data Were Random, How Many SAM Entries Would Be Needed to Describe the Target as Completely as Is Done by the Actual Session?

From 1000 Monte Carlo samples: The mean number of random session pseudo SAM entries that are needed to achieve 28 matches with the target is: 61.178
The standard deviation is: 5.059
Lowest number of pseudo attributes from sample = 46
Highest number of pseudo attributes from sample = 73
The 90% confidence interval for this is: [52.856, 69.500]
The 95% confidence interval for this is: [51.262, 71.094]
The 98% confidence interval for this is: [49.415, 72.941]
Compare these intervals with the actual number of session entries: 29
Interpretation: If the actual number of session SAM entries is outside of (that is, less than) the desired confidence interval, then the number of entries utilized by the remote viewer to obtain the number of matches between the session and the target was not by chance.

TEST#3: Correspondence and Correlation

Part I.
The correspondence data in the table immediately below are computed using the targets from the public demonstration only. The "Session/Target" correspondence numbers are calculated between the remote-viewing session for this experiment and all of the targets used in the public demonstration. The "Target/Target" correspondence numbers are calculated between the real target for this experiment and all of the other targets in the public demonstration pool.

Experiment Number:	Session/Target Correspondence:	Target/Target Correspondence:
Experiment #1	0.240	0.495
Experiment #3	0.292	0.325

Experiment #4	0.350	0.381
Experiment #5	0.291	0.333
Experiment #6	0.274	0.326
Experiment #7	0.265	0.313
Experiment #8	0.338	0.381
Experiment #9	0.930	0.821
Experiment #10	0.271	0.314
Experiment #11	0.327	0.513
Experiment #12	0.816	1.0
Experiment #14	0.632	0.546
Experiment #15	0.346	0.353

The correlation coefficient is: 0.827 with an N of 13.

Interpretation: All targets have a variety of descriptive characteristics. When comparing one target with another, both similarities and differences will be found between the two. The correspondence numbers are one measure of the degree of similarity between any two sets of SAM data, and these numbers can be used to compare one target with another target, or a remote-viewing session with a target. The closer a remote-viewing session is to describing all of a target's characteristics, the higher will be the correspondence number between the session and the target. Since a pool of targets normally contains targets with a great variety of descriptive characteristics, comparing correspondence numbers for the remote-viewing session and its target across a variety of other targets tests how closely the session describes all of the essential characteristics of its real target. When compared with other targets with many different characteristics, both the remote-viewing session and its real target should have correspondence numbers that vary similarly. The correlation coefficient summarizes this relationship. The correlation coefficient can vary between -1 and 1. The closer its value is to 1, the more closely the remote-viewing session describes its real target's various characteristics.

Part II.

The correlation coefficient is computed as in Part I above, but now using a large (240) pool of SAM targets.

The correlation coefficient is: 0.855 with an N of 240.
The lowest correspondence number for the session and pool is: 0.182
The highest correspondence number for the session and pool is: 0.838
The lowest correspondence number for the target and pool is: 0.277
The highest correspondence number for the target and pool is: 0.75
Interpretation: Similarly as with Part I above. The closer the value of the correlation coefficient is to 1, the more closely the remote-viewing session describes its real target's various characteristics.

CHAPTER 7

Modeling the Subspace
Perceptual Focus

Fundamental to the results presented in this volume is the finding that the thoughts of one or more individuals can influence the perceptual focus of a remote viewer. Of course, this is not the first report to argue that the thoughts of one person can mentally influence the thoughts of others, despite separations in space and time (see especially, Braud 2003, and Vasiliev 2002). Yet we now have some useful leverage on this idea by noting that the thoughts of the person who first examines and analyzes the remote-viewing data with respect to the target (or potential list of targets) dominantly influences the perceptual focus of the remote viewer through an apparent telepathic process.

In this setting we have what amounts to a mental dance in which the two partners are the viewer and the analyst. In a situation in which the analyst is confronted with data from one remote-viewing session and two possible targets, the focus of the remote viewer's perception often shifts (sometimes repeatedly) from one to the other of the potential targets, guided in part by the assumptions, conclusions, and general thought processes of the analyst. In turn, the thoughts of the analyst tend to wander from target to target as data are examined (during the post-session analysis of the data) that suggest a match one way or the other as per the analyst's evaluations of the data with respect to the two targets.

At this point it is useful to organize some of the observed behaviors of the subspace perceptual process as we have witnessed them in these investigations. One method of organization is to theorize more generally with respect to the observed phenomena. My own approach to theory construction often involves working with mathematical models. While this is not the place to fully flesh-out and estimate such a system, it is heuristically useful to outline some elements of the remote-viewing process that would need to be incorporated into an appropriately specified model of this process. Readers who do not want to wade through the details of such a mathematical model need not worry. I present only one such model in algebraic form, and I do this only in the appendix to this chapter. Moreover, I suspect that this chapter's more general (and non-mathematical) discussion of the subspace perceptual focus will be of keen interest to many readers.

Some readers may wonder why a mathematical model of the subspace perceptual process would be important. If one can remote view, why not just do it rather than use math to describe it? The answer is that mathematical models of physical and psychological processes often help us understand those processes more profoundly, and it is a truism in all of the sciences that such models add a significant layer of precision to our application of those processes as well. Moreover, I view it as inevitable that many scientists will want to see a mathematical representation of my theory of the remote-viewing targeting mechanism, and this is the appropriate place to make some comments in this regard.

The results of chapter 3 suggest that cross-cutting psi channels can create a multi-dimensional perceptual system in which there are multiple attractors (i.e., targets) that pull at the remote viewer's center of focus. If we are to model this perceptual process with respect to remote viewing, we need to begin with specifying (1) change in the perceptual focus for a remote viewer, and (2) change in the assumptive focus on the part of the analyst. We call the focus of the analyst "assumptive" because the analyst is making the assumption that reported remote-viewing data describe one or the other of the two targets.

Let us say we have a two-target remote-viewing problem in which one possible target is a house and the other is a lake. A non-mathematical heuristic analogy would be that of a round boulder that is delicately resting on the top of a mountain that has two steep-sloping sides, one of which leads to the house and the other to the lake (i.e., on the other side of the mountain). At any moment, the boulder could be dislodged due, say, to a strong wind, and it would then fall down the mountain on one of the two sides toward one of the two outcomes. The perceptual focus of the remote viewer behaves in a way that is somewhat comparable to the travels of the boulder, and we want to model this in a manner that leads to a greater understanding of the overall phenomenon.

There are a variety of ways to approach the modeling of such a system, and it is important for any approach used to incorporate the basic elements of the perceptual process. In essence, we have two attractors with significant "gravity," and each of these attractors are defined in terms of the mental attention given to each of the possible targets by the person (or persons) who is analyzing the remote-viewing data. The better the analyst is in keeping the essential characteristics of both targets in his or her mind, the more tension there will be in the overall system, and the greater difficulty the viewer will have in perceptually locking on to one of the targets (thereby abandoning the other target).

One way to model this would be to follow a strategy analogous to the three-body problem in celestial mechanics. In this problem there are two large bodies with significant gravity (such as the Earth and the Moon) and one additional body with insignificant gravity (such as a spaceship). There is a Lagrange point that is located on a line between the two large bodies at which the gravitational attraction of both bodies is in balance, and this point is known as an unstable equilibrium point in the overall system. (We can in this situation ignore the other Lagrange points that result from the rotation of the system.) In the language of dynamical systems, we have two significant attractors together with their basins of attraction, and a central bifurcation point on the separatrix that separates the two basins. If a spaceship is located precisely at this Lagrange point, it will stay put and not be pulled toward either of the two celestial bodies. However, movement away from this point for whatever reason will place the spaceship into the basin of attraction for one of the two attractors, and the ship will then fall toward the winning attractor (until it crashes into, say, the Earth or the Moon).

The mathematics of this type of system are well understood, and there is no need to derive the fundamental equations of motion here. But the useful point to make in the current context is that this system closely parallels that of our problem involving the perceptual focus of a remote viewer, where the perceptual focus of the viewer is (from a mathematical point of view) comparable to the location of the spaceship in this three-body problem. To operationalize this approach in our current setting, the model needs to be written such that the two large attractors are identified in a two-dimensional hyperspace, and equations of motion within that hyperspace are written that allow for the movement of the perceptual focus in the neighborhood of the separatrix separating the basins of the two attractors. The model must allow for stochastic (essentially random) movements in the neighborhood of this separatrix that can "bump" the perceptual focus of the viewer from one basin to the other to mimic the confusing leaps that occur when the analyst tentatively changes his or her focus from one target to another before an irretrievable spiral deep into the basin of one attractor has occurred.

Another approach to modeling this problem is to use a catastrophe model that identifies the tension between the perceptual focus of the viewer and the assumptive focus of the analyst in terms of a system of equations that explicitly specifies this tension as a product of a tug of war between the two attractors. This allows for the tension to vary incrementally, depending on how strongly the viewer and that analyst are mentally drawn toward the characteristics of one or the other targets. Thus, we can have a situation in which the tension can be relatively slight, which would be the case in which the analyst and viewer have not made any psychological commitments with regard to either possible target, as would be more common both in the beginning of a remote-viewing session and the beginning of the process of analyzing the remote-viewing data. As the session (and the parallel analysis) continues, the tension between the two attractors (and thus within the overall system) would increase as the data accumulate. The increase in the system's tension has the effect of increasing the gravity of each attractor, and thus increasing the speed of movement of the perceptual focus of the viewer toward one or the other attractor once the commitment to either has been made. This ability to vary the level of tension in the system is an advantage for this approach as compared with the three-body approach described earlier, since gravity in the celestial mechanics model is assumed to be constant for each attractor. For readers who are interested, I briefly sketch a catastrophe theory model as described above in the appendix to this chapter.

Let us re-state the basic elements of the remote-viewing perceptual process that have been described so far in this volume. First, perception through a remote viewer's physical/subspace interface appears to be influenced by the mental processes of individuals other than those of the remote viewer. The most important of such influences comes from those for whom the data are being collected in the first place. Thus, the intent of the remote viewer to satisfy the informational needs of the analysts is a crucial element in the mechanism of perceptually locating a given target. Second, if the analysts of the remote-viewing data are not clear as to one specific target in their minds when they examine the data, this lack of clarity will guide the viewer, even though the viewing may take place at another point in time. Crucially, we do not currently know if this phenomenon is due to the nature of the human subspace aspect itself, or if it is a side-effect of some other process related to the physical/subspace interface.

We can also infer from the general remote-viewing experience that the human subspace aspect is not bound by any closed system relating to a single fixed time or a single location in a three-dimensional space. Rather, it appears to extend everywhere at all times, and the physical/subspace interface allows for a focusing of awareness at certain loci in space and time. This allows for potentially contaminating influences with this process that may originate from various places and at various points in time. We need now, however, to see why the role of uncertainty plays so heavily in the mind of the remote viewer when the remote-viewing process is underway, and how this uncertainty influences the overall viewing result. Much of this uncertainty is due to the relative lack of clarity with regard to the actual psi-mediated visual perceptions, which in turn relates to the overall perceptual quality of the remote-viewing experience.

In general, there appear to be two levels of quality with respect to the visual impressions obtainable through remote-viewing. On the high end, very high quality and high resolution visual images have been reported by many remote viewers. But these high-quality visual images tend to be of extremely short duration, lasting only a fraction of a second. On the other hand, lower quality visual images seem to be more common fare among remote viewers, and many reports suggest that these lower quality images remain within the consciousness of the remote viewer for longer periods of time, often lasting a number of seconds, or even (very rarely) a minute or more. Every once in a great while, a competent remote viewer will report an experience in which high-quality perceptions with clear visual images were maintained for an extended period of time, but this type of experience seems to be exceptionally rare and difficult to replicate. Thus, the more general rule seems to be that either very short-lived high-quality or longer-lived low-quality visual impressions dominate a remote-viewing experience, where the high-quality images last only for a fraction of a second and the low-quality images last for a second or more. The overall remote-viewing session is made up of a great many of these fleeting images of various qualities, and the job of the remote viewer is to organize these images into a format that eventually makes some sense.

Both the lower and higher quality visual impressions present a problem of uncertainty for the remote viewer, since the shorter-lived high-quality images rarely last long enough for the remote viewer to make much sense out of them, and the longer-lived low-quality images are difficult to sort out due to the relatively poor level of resolution. How all of this interacts with the problems associated with a confused remote viewer/analyst telepathic loop due to the process outlined above is perhaps best described in terms of an example.

An Example with a Two-Target Attractor

On two separate occasions, I was given the following targets to remote view: (1) "The Shuttle Discovery Mission to Repair the Hubble Space Telescope (mid-February 1997)," and (2) "The Great Sphinx of Egypt (period immediately following the completion of the original construction event)." Here, I will synthesizing a heuristic example using the results of these two separate sessions to describe a remote-viewing process using both of these targets in a two-

S82E5937 1997:02:19 07:06:57

Figure 7.1. Hubble Space Telescope target

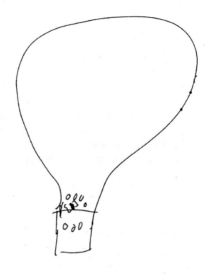

Figure 7.2. Remote-viewing sketch of Hubble Space Telescope target

attractor process in which an analyst would be judging the remote-viewing data against these two targets to determine which target is correct. This would be comparable to a situation in which the analyst is not told which of the targets is correct at the time of the analysis, and the determination of the correct target is made by some random process. Thus, we would have a classic situation in which there would be cross-cutting psi channels that would corrupt the collection of remote-viewing data.

For the Hubble Space Telescope target, some of the data in a reasonable session might be expected to resemble the image in figure 7.1. This is a NASA photo of the Hubble Space Telescope during the repair mission mentioned in the target cue. This is a very high-resolution image that would be easy to describe if seen with the naked eyes. However, the remote-viewing images that I "saw" during that session led me to draw the sketch found in figure 7.2. The sketch resembles a hot-air balloon flying over the surface of the Earth.

Someone not familiar with remote viewing might consider this to be an inaccurate depiction of the actual target. But consider the quality of the visual images that led me to make the sketch shown in figure 7.2. Using a graphical computer program to change the image in figure 7.1 to more closely approximate the quality of the mental visual impressions that I had of the target during the

Figure 7.3. RV visual approximation #1 of Hubble Space Telescope target

session, I produced the image shown in figure 7.3. This figure closely resembles what I "saw" during the session. Note that there is a vignetting effect, in the sense that a remote viewer normally does not see a clear wide-angle view of the target. More often than not, the visual impression is as if looking through a lens that "fuzzes out" at the periphery of the scene. Note also that the central image itself has very low resolution. It seems clear that there is a horizontal line through the image, and that the differing brightness above and below the horizontal divide suggest a horizon. There also seems to be some object that is both wide (and lighter in color) at the top and very narrow (and dark) at the bottom which appears to be floating above the horizon. This image is designed to closely approximate a typical low-resolution remote-viewing mental visual impression that might last for a second or longer.

Every once and awhile during the session in which I remote viewed that target, I perceived a near instantaneous higher resolution image that more closely resembled the image in figure 7.4. Note that this image has less of a vignetting effect, and that its resolution is somewhere between that of figures 7.2 and 7.3. The trouble with such relatively high-resolution images is that they remain so briefly in the consciousness (a fraction of a second) that a remote viewer really does not know what to make of them. Moreover, such high-resolution images do not normally return very often during the session, and many sessions end

Figure 7.4. RV visual approximation #2 of Hubble Space Telescope target

without the viewer having perceived any high-resolution images. Nonetheless, if this was the only target in the viewer/analyst loop, the level of confusion would be relatively minimal, and the viewer would have a long time to try to sort things out based on whatever images and other impressions present themselves.

Let us now shift to the second target in this heuristic example, the Great Sphinx of Egypt. With the Sphinx as the target, a good remote-viewing session might have some data that resemble the picture taken prior to 1905 and shown in figure 7.5. (The time of this photo is, of course, not the time of the target, but the Sphinx should be somewhat similar in its general parameters.)

During my own remote-viewing session of this target, I perceived mental visual impressions that resembled the low-resolution image in figure 7.6. Note the vignetting effect, and also notice the relative poor level of resolution for the image when compared with figure 7.4 for the Hubble Space Telescope. The outline of the Sphinx is still discernable in figure 7.6, and the pyramid is silhouetted in the background, but it is not easy to be sure what is actually going on with the image based only on the image itself.

In this particular instance, I was able to describe the target as is presented in figures 7.7 and 7.8. On both pages of this session, I was able to describe the target rather well after making a number of low-level perceptual observations that described the color, texture, substance, and other characteristics of the target structures.

Figure 7.5. The Sphinx and pyramids RV Target. Photograph taken in Giza, Egypt before 1905.

Now consider a situation in which the remote viewer is following the guiding thoughts of the analyst who has both the Hubble Space Telescope and

Figure 7.6. RV visual approximation of Sphinx and pyramids

the Great Sphinx targets in his or her mind, as would be the case when a judge is trying to determine which is the correct target based on his or her comparisons between the remote-viewing data and the physical characteristics of both targets. At some parts of the session, visual imagery resembling figure 7.3 will be perceived by the viewer. At other times during the session, the viewer will perceive images that resemble figure 7.6. There is tension in the viewer's mind as to which is the correct image. Moreover, the viewer does not even know if the images are actually of different places, or perhaps of different perspectives for one target location. If one only has a second to perceive the image in figure 7.3 and another second to perceive the image in figure 7.6, then the viewer may very well conclude that the images are the same, and that the fault lies in his or her ability to correctly remember the similarities in the impressions.

At some point during the session — as the analyst proceeds sequentially, page by page, through the remote-viewing data looking for evidence that the viewer has accurately described one of the two targets — the analyst is likely to conclude that the viewer has succeeded in describing one of the two targets correctly. The analyst then shifts his or her mental framework to look for confirming information in what remains of the collection of remote-viewing data produced by the remote viewer. The remote viewer subconsciously perceives this shift in mental guidance, and then discerns a new level of clarity in terms of a target's characteristics. At this point, the viewer might produce data that resemble either figure 7.2 or figures 7.7 and 7.8.

The ability to produce remote-viewing data such as contained in figures 7.2, 7.7, and 7.8 require that the viewer's perceptions fall irretrievably into the basin of one of the two target attractors. Sometimes this can happen at the outset of the session, especially if the session's analyst has a conscious or subconscious predisposition toward one or the other targets. But sometimes the session will drag on for awhile without any clear descriptions of either target, largely due to an ambiguity in the analyst's mind as to the correct target, as well as to the resulting confusion this causes the remote viewer as he or she tries to make sense out of the resulting chaotic imagery. It is only when one of the target attractors and its basin of attraction disappears from the tug-of-war between the two targets that the viewer has a reasonable chance of assembling enough low-level data so as to be able to organize those data into a coherent theme. As I have argued above, the thoughts of the analyst can cause this to happen, but it could also be that the viewer will at some point in the session simply decide to follow one of the impression lines, effectively giving up on sorting out the other conflicting impressions. Thus, one of two things can happen to resolve the conflict — the first led by the thoughts of the analyst and the second determined by a decision made (potentially arbitrarily) by the viewer.

This example outlines the basic parameters of the cross-cutting psi channels problem. Endless variations on this general idea are possible of course, as there is no limit to the variation that can be experienced between the telepathically-

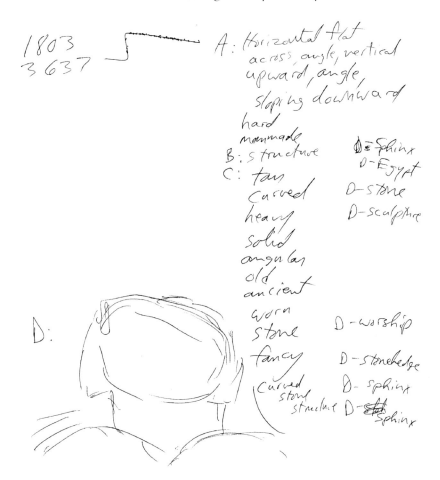

Figure 7.7. RV sketch of the Sphinx in Giza, Egypt

mediated mental dance that occurs between the remote viewer and the analyst. In my view, it is essential that future psi research control for this phenomenon. At least this characterizes all current and future work conducted in experiments done at The Farsight Institute. This indeed is why it is useful to design remote-viewing experiments such that the remote viewer can close his or her own sessions. Having the remote viewer close the viewing and analytic loop prior to allowing other human analysts to work with the data can minimize much of the contaminating influence caused by the creation of other competing attractors in the system. But it is also necessary to avoid experimental designs that employ the "pick a target out of the bunch" approach to blind judging.

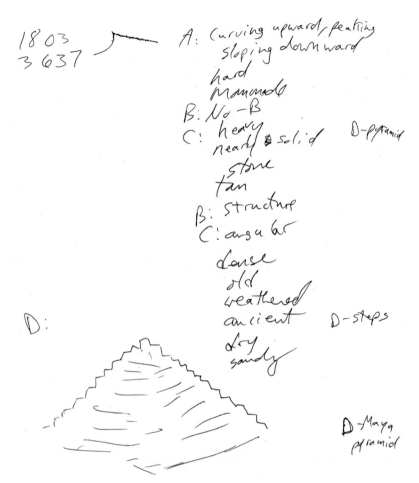

Figure 7.8. RV sketch of pyramid in Giza, Egypt

It is not certain at this point when a session may truly be independent of contamination resulting from the competition of alternative target attractors. At some point, it does seem clear that one can do whatever one wants with a session's data without the risk of telepathic contamination. But the exact parameters that specify the final point of closure remain to be determined. This is another reason why it is especially useful to have a computer program such as SAM do any analysis of the remote-viewing data during the periods when the viewing/closing loop may be most susceptible to contaminating influence.

To summarize, the theory presented here (and supported by data presented throughout this volume) suggests that the basic rule to follow when setting up a remote-viewing experiment is for the experimenters to do everything possible to eliminate in advance the risk of competing and telepathically-mediated multiple attractors which may influence the collection of remote-viewing data. This probably means that the experimental set-up commonly used in the past in which data are collected that are then evaluated by blind judges who try to determine the correct target from a list of, say, five targets (one real and four decoys) should never be used again. It is far better to set-up an experiment in which there is one and only one target for a session, and then the data for that session are evaluated with respect to a detailed list of characteristics for the one target. This process of comparing the data for a remote-viewing session to a single target can then be repeated five or more times in a series (with a new session and a new target each time, of course), eventually yielding any level of statistical significance desired. Subsequent to a session's closing, the remote-viewing data for any one target can be compared numerically with descriptive lists for any number of other highly different targets using computer programs similar to SAM, as was done in chapter 6 and described in detail in the appendix for that chapter under "Test 3 - Correspondence and Correlation."

But if an experimenter for whatever reason does not want to work with a series of sessions as described above, and instead insists on the need to utilize human judges to compare the remote-viewing data for a single session with a set of targets (one real and the others decoys), then such experiments should probably be designed such that the remote-viewing procedures employ an outbounder (someone who physically travels to a target at a specified time). Having the remote viewer perceive the target as seen through the eyes of the outbounder adds gravity to that target's attractor and its basin, and this is likely to significantly ameliorate the effects of the perceptual contamination caused by the other competing attractors.

APPENDIX TO CHAPTER 7: An Algebraic Specification

Our interest is in developing a model that specifies (1) change in the perceptual focus for a remote viewer — a quantity for which we will use the variable X, and (2) change in the assumptive focus on the part of the analyst — a quantity for which we will use the variable Y. I briefly sketch such a model here. This appendix assumes a prior familiarity with a mathematical theory known as "catastrophe theory." Interested readers may find my own introductory treatment of this theory useful (Brown 1995b).

The variables X and Y quantify the number of items or qualities at a target site that correspond with one target or another. Thus, if a remote viewer's perceptual focus is fixed on one target, then all of the perceptions that he or she may have will originate from only that target. On the other hand, if a remote viewer is simultaneously perceiving parts of two targets, then the perceptions will be a mix of items and qualities of these targets. A similar process is applicable with respect to the assumptive focus of the analyst. If the analyst is thinking about only one target when analyzing the remote-viewing data, then all of the items and qualities in the analyst's mind will relate to only that one target. However, if the analyst is careful to keep many of the items and qualities for both targets in his or her mind (perhaps by oscillating mentally between the two targets), then the assumptive focus of the analyst will not be fixed on any one target.

Let us say that there are two targets, A and B. One plausible model with a catastrophe theory flavor that would allow for the types of changes in the values of X and Y that have been reported in this volume would be as follows:

$$dX/dt = fX^3 + gTX - wY \tag{7.1}$$

$$dY/dt = e(pY - T)(Y - L_A)(U_B - Y). \tag{7.2}$$

This model is a multi-dimensional interdependent system of two dynamic (i.e., time-dependent) first-order nonlinear differential equations. In the above specification, change in the remote viewer's focus of perception (X) is dependent on the current value of this perception, following a polynomial specification with (minimally) degree 3 that allows for the perspective to be "captured" by one or the other of the target attractors. The parameter T represents the overall tension in the system of two interdependent mental processes as the two targets are variously perceived and judged, and is explained further below. In the above specification, the viewer's perceptual focus shifts (numerically upward as X increases — as structured by dX/dt) toward one of the targets unless it is pulled in the opposite direction by the assumptive intent of the analyst ($-wY$).

Changes in Y are dependent on the difference between the current state of the analyst's mental orientation and the overall tension in the system ($pY - T$). The more clearly the analyst holds the two targets in his or her mind as real possibilities that are evidenced by the recorded stream of data, the greater the tension in the overall system (and thus the higher the value of T). Experimentally, this tension manifests as the viewer tries to locate the "true" center of the target given the conflicting directional signals between the momentary content of the analyst's mind and the perceptual focus that may currently exist for the viewer. In combination with equations (7.1) and (7.2), this tension results in a "tug-of-war" between the viewer and the analyst.

The multiplicative terms $(Y - L_A)(U_B - Y)$ in equation (7.2) above allow for the setting of lower and upper bounds on the values of Y, as per a situation in which the analyst assumes that the "true" target is either A or B. In this case, the lower bound (L) is associated with target A and the upper bound (U) is

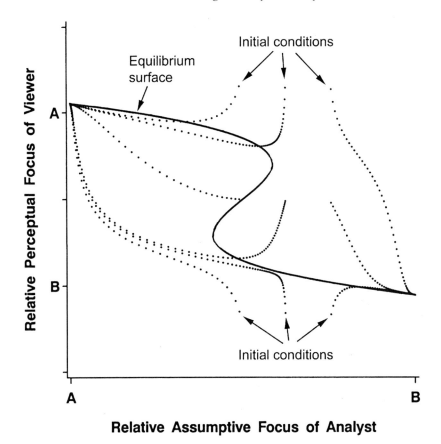

Figure 7.9. Two-target attractor model of competing remote-viewing perceptions

associated with target B. In equations (7.1) and (7.2) above, *f, g, w, e,* and *p* are parameters that allow for the specification of rates and scaling properties of the model.

The model as specified in equations (7.1) and (7.2) allows for a type of phenomenon known as a "catastrophe" to occur, such that multiple attractors and their basins can coexist, and trajectories moving through these basins can be "captured" by one of the attractors. The mathematical theory of such systems is complete, and empirical examples of phenomena that have been successfully modeled and fully estimated (by myself and others) using this approach exist and are not in dispute (Brown 1995a, 1995b; Danby 1985, pp. 89-94; Thom 1975; Zeeman 1987).

Following the maxim that a picture can sometimes say more than a thousand words, the workings of the above system can be explained using an example. Figure 7.9 is a phase diagram in which the system as specified above is given plausible parameter values. In this figure the two axes measure the relative perceptual focus of the viewer (the vertical axis) and the relative assumptive focus of the analyst (the horizontal axis). Targets A and B are located on each axis, and these positions on the respective axes mark situations in which the viewer or the analyst is focusing totally on one or the other targets.

The most significant catastrophe signature of the phase diagram in figure 7.9 is the reverse "S" shape. This shape is the equilibrium surface for the system. Systems specified with polynomial degrees higher than 3 will have more complex equilibria surfaces, but in our case of a binary choice of targets, the current shape is appropriate. There are two points on the equilibrium surface in figure 7.9 that represent attractors for this model, and they exist at the upper left and lower right corners of the surface. Each point resides at a location in which both the viewer's perceptual focus and the analyst's assumptive focus coincide.

The various dotted curved lines in figure 7.9 represent possible trajectories of perception and assumption for the system. Note that in this case, most trajectories move toward the resolution of target A in the upper left corner. Only if a viewer's and/or analyst's initial focus begins close to target B do the trajectories become captured within the basin of target B's attracting sphere of influence (from a mathematical point of view). The dominance of target A in this example is a consequence of the parameter values used to produce the plot, and this represents a situation in which there is some initial subconscious or conscious bias on the part of the analyst in favor of target A. Thus, this model is quite robust in its ability to reflect the aggregate effect of subtle psychological influences on the remote-viewing process.

From figure 7.9 it should be clear that a mathematical specification of at least one of the types of phenomena witnessed in these analyses (i.e., the cross-cutting psi channels) is indeed possible. Further analyses, of course, should make it possible to refine the above specification, and continued experience with these matters will allow for the estimation of parameter values more or less precisely, given an appropriate data set for a series of experiments. But the largest chunk of the work is already accomplished when we simply note that the existing data strongly support the given theory, and that a mathematical model that captures the witnessed dynamics exists.

CHAPTER 8

Remote Viewing, Cosmology, and Quantum Mechanics

What is a useful model of physical reality that allows for the remote-viewing process? The answer to this question is the focus of this chapter, and it is perhaps the most profound question ever posed to science. This attempt to place the remote-viewing phenomenon within the context of physics is not entirely speculative, since the reality of the remote-viewing phenomenon can by itself add greatly to the current debates as to the nature of physical reality. This is especially true with regard to the existence of dimensions other than the three known physical dimensions, as I explain later in this chapter. But I develop a theory of reality here that is more detailed than one might at first expect, and much of this is admittedly speculative. However, as I explain below, since my theory is based on the now better understood remote-viewing experience, I strongly suspect that any "final" theory of physical reality developed by physicists and cosmologists who specialize in such matters likely will at least have the general flavor of these ideas.

Experiential Cosmology

As I have mentioned in chapter 2 of this volume, physicists have developed both numerous and competing cosmological theories of physical reality. For example, string theory, the theory of relativity, loop quantum gravity, and brane theory are four heavily discussed sets of ideas (among others) that currently frame a great deal of debate in cosmology. Heated arguments abound regarding each theory, and specialists often variously weigh the potential of each particular approach to a "theory of everything." Complex mathematical solutions to theoretical questions often take years to resolve, if they are resolved at all. Indeed, it often seems that every few years a new and significantly different cosmological theory emerges from the debates, and then more solutions are sought, and so on. The one common thread that seems to link so many of these theories is that physicists often have very few practical ways to demonstrate their validity, and contemporary cosmology has occasionally been characterized as complex mathematical philosophy that will ultimately require physical experimentation to help sort through the competing cosmological ideas.

I strongly believe that remote viewing can offer an important contribution to the current debates in cosmology. Since I am convinced beyond any doubt that virtually any scientist who approaches the study of remote viewing with an objective and unprejudiced mind will arrive at the conclusion that remote viewing is a real phenomenon, it is possible to argue convincingly at this point that the remote-viewing experience must be incorporated into (as in, explained within the context of) any accepted theory of physical reality.

But it is also important to note that remote viewing can be used to help sort out differences in the various and competing theories of cosmology. A primary avenue for doing this is to use remote viewing experimentally to test whether or not certain cosmological ideas work. For example, Stephen Hawking has commented in his famous lecture debates with Roger Penrose that string theory has yet to predict anything about reality that can be observed (Hawking and Penrose 1996, p. 4). While the search for various traditional means to test cosmological ideas will always continue, it must be pointed out that physicists and cosmologists can now also use remote viewing to test at least some of their ideas. Remote-viewing experiments offer the possibility of making observations via carefully controlled experimental set-ups that might otherwise not be possible. The public demonstration experiments presented in this volume are an example of this in the sense that they can be seen as a test of whether future-time is truly permeable, since the tasker chose each target for those experiments after the remote-viewing sessions were completed (a tasking-post experimental set-up). Other types of experiments could be set-up to test a variety of other ideas drawn from many theories of cosmology.

To differentiate this type of experimental approach to cosmology from the more mathematically based approaches such as string theory, I prefer to give it the new label "experiential cosmology." More specifically, experiential cosmology is the use of remote viewing within experimental settings to test theories and theory fragments relating to the structure of physical and nonphysical reality, or simply, the universe. Experiential cosmology can never replace traditional cosmology. Rather, experiential cosmology — at its best — should complement and assist traditional cosmology. In my view, experiential cosmology should be used in tightly controlled experiments that allow traditional cosmologists to propose and test new ideas that can subsequently be incorporated into their more general theories. Experiential cosmology adds a new element that has never before been available to cosmologists who have traditionally worked with mathematically-based theories alone. The combination of both experiential cosmology with traditional cosmology brings with it the potential for truly great advances in our understanding of existence.

It is essential to emphasize that experiential cosmology can never occur outside of a properly structured experimental design. Thus, it is not possible for a remote viewer to have a subjective remote-viewing experience and for that subjective experience by itself to be considered an exercise in experiential cosmology. For example, a remote-viewer cannot be tasked with the target "the

Big Bang" and the results of this tasking be used by themselves to describe the nature of the universe at the beginning of time. Rather, experiential cosmology requires that remote-viewing subjectivity be packaged within an overall experimental design that allows for objective testing of explicit cosmological ideas. In practice this means that the results of the remote-viewing sessions need to be evaluated using either computerized or at least clearly defined means that minimize the degree of additional subjective ambiguity that might corrupt the interpretation of the results. It is important to recognize that all scientific experimentation is subjective to some extent, in the sense that experimental designs are created by human intelligence, and human intelligence is similarly used to interpret results, read dials, rank the importance of various streams of data, omit or include outliers, choose data-smoothing algorithms, and so on. Obviously rigorous science can still be pursued within the context of these latter forms of subjectivity. Intelligently structured experimental designs can similarly bridge the subjective nature of the remote-viewing data-gathering experience with the requirements of modern science such that the level of subjectivity that occurs on the analysis side of such experiments is minimized to enable the rigorous testing of important theories and theory fragments.

One objection to the idea of creating what is essentially a new field of experiential cosmology is that it is putting the cart before the horse, in the sense that cosmology may require that a theory be developed prior to experimentation such that testable predictions can be offered. But surely this critique can no longer be considered seriously given how long humanity has waited for such a theory to mature. It has been many years since Albert Einstein prefaced Upton Sinclair's 1930 book on telepathy by writing "(T)he results of the telepathic experiments carefully and plainly set forth in this book stand surely far beyond those which a nature investigator holds to be thinkable" [Sinclair, *Mental Radio*, 2001(1930), p. xi]. How many more years must the scientific community wait for physicists and cosmologists to think the unthinkable? Is it truly reasonable to demand that mathematical philosophy must resolve the nature of existence before experimentation within a "forbidden realm" can add significantly to these debates, especially when experiments within this realm may appreciably resolve such debates? Although the story of Newton's apple is most certainly apocryphal, exceedingly careful observations of the physical world is certainly a hallmark of physics. Remote viewing is now a sufficiently repeatable phenomenon such that it can be used reliably in many circumstances to conduct experiments that can assist our theory-building activities. The results of intelligently designed remote-viewing experiments are as real as any other physical observation, and we must no longer deny this.

In terms of the history of science, the significance of the remote-viewing experience is akin to the seminal experiment conducted in 1887 by the American physicists Michelson and Morley in which they attempted to decisively establish the existence of ether. Prior to then, most scientists believed that light waves traveled through a mysterious background fluid called "ether." They felt this was necessary since waves could not travel through a vacuum if there was nothing to vibrate. Since the Earth orbits the sun (and thus also travels through the ether), the theory of ether suggested that there should be an ether current through which the light in their experiment would have to travel. Travel through an ether current should affect the course of a beam of light (carrying it "downstream") much as the flow of water in a river would affect the path of a swimmer attempting to swim across the river. The result of the Michelson-Morley experiment established conclusively that there is no ether at all, a completely unexpected result at the time. There was no evidence that the beam of light was affected by any flowing current, regardless of what direction they aimed the light beam.

One comparable "big lesson" to draw from the remote-viewing experience relates to the number of dimensions that exist in reality. Physicists typically seek to determine how many dimensions exist by arguing how many are needed to explain all observable phenomena in the physical universe (see, for example, Hawking 1998, Chapter 11, "The Unification of Physics"). When physicists talk about dimensions, they are usually referencing geometrical dimensions that are represented graphically by perpendicular lines. However, other scientists and mathematicians use the term "dimension" differently to mean any quantity or quality that can vary within a system. For example, the number of foxes and rabbits in a predator-prey system are variables that define a two-dimensional system that is understood mathematically, not geometrically. Sometimes mathematicians like to use other terms such as a "control parameter" when describing a quantity that can vary but which may be seen as conceptually different from the other essential variables in a system under study. But even in such cases, the control parameter is often graphically represented by a mathematical axis that resembles the axes of the other dimensions. Thus, the use of a particular meaning for "dimension" is somewhat dependent on the person using the term. Since my own background is as a mathematician rather than a physicist, I prefer to use the term "dimension" more broadly to refer not just to geometrical dimensions, but also to mathematical ideas that may directly affect the way in which we perceive our universe. As will become clear in my arguments below, I sense that at least one such crucial dimension that affects our perception of physical reality may address the idea of frequencies, not just spatial geometry.

The essential question being posed here is whether we truly live in a 3-dimensional universe (for the moment excluding the time dimension)? Or do other dimensions exist outside of the three physical dimensions? Some cosmological theories predict such other dimensions, and there are continuing efforts to find evidence of them (for example, see Smolin, 2004, p. 68). Yet the fact that remote viewing is a real phenomenon appears to be consistent with the idea that there may exist dimensions other than the currently known three physical dimensions, since it is not clear how remote viewing could otherwise occur. Remote viewing is an anomaly with respect to the physical laws that govern the three physical dimensions. Remote viewing transcends not only time, but space as well.

The three physical dimensions have laws that work well when considering the three dimensions as a self-contained system. But anomalies to laws governing this system will occur whenever activities take place at least partially within the system that directly utilize dimensions outside of the three physical dimensions. Proof that such external dimensions exist (with respect to the three physical dimensions) is obtained by conducting an experiment that produces results that cannot be explained by any of the laws or combination of laws that govern all behavior within the three physical dimensions. As I explain later in this chapter, physical phenomena such as demonstrated by the so-called "two-slit experiment" and entanglement seem to satisfy this condition (see below). Remote viewing also seems to satisfy this condition.

By itself, this is an important contribution that remote viewing offers to physics. This does not say that we know how many non-physical dimensions actually exist. It only says that physical reality must exist in ways that we do not directly observe. Moreover, we still do not know if these extra dimensions are physical dimensions with spatially orthogonal characteristics or mathematical dimensions based on frequencies or something else entirely.

The problem now is to develop a general outline of a dimensional structure for overall reality that would allow for the existence of remote viewing as it has been repeatedly experienced under controlled conditions. The phenomenological theory described below does this in a very general fashion. This theory is probably not correct in all of its parts, and I would be most surprised if it did not require significant revision as we learn more. But, as I mentioned previously, I strongly suspect that whatever final theory does eventually emerge from the current cosmological debates about the nature of reality, the flavor of the theory developed below will most likely reside within that final theory.

Let us begin by considering the situation of altering time lines, an easily accomplished consequence of remote-viewing. This indeed is one goal of using remote viewing as an intelligence tool by a government (see especially, Kress 1999). If, say, a terrorist attack is perceived to occur in the future by a remote viewer, the government would want to use the remote-viewing data to intervene and to prevent the attack from happening. Contrarily, in public demonstrations of remote viewing, one goes to great lengths to prevent a change in the time line by encrypting remote-viewing results so that no one can see them prior to the time when the tasker decides on a target, as is the norm for tasking-post experiments in which the tasker chooses the target after the remote-viewing sessions have already been completed. Failure to do this would allow the tasker to see the remote-viewing results in advance of picking a target, and then to choose a target that differs from the remote-viewing data, thereby corrupting the experiment. Thus, it is easy to change a time line if one has information about the future. One simply has to use the remote-viewing data to cause a future outcome to change. In the case of a public demonstration of remote viewing, you do not want this to occur, and you must take stringent steps to avoid this from happening. In the case of intelligence work for a government, the opposite may be true if one wants to avoid a future unpleasant event. This raises the issue of alternate realities, since a remote viewer nonetheless perceives someone's "real" future even if it is subsequently "prevented." This apparent contradiction needs to be resolved in any theory of general reality.

The theory described below takes as a starting point the idea that Planck's constant may indeed be constant only within our current three-dimensional reality. For those who might object to this consideration, it is useful to remind the reader that this is not an entirely unheard of idea in cosmological debates, and that the theory which I am outlining here is designed to correspond with the remote-viewing experience rather than a single theory of cosmology. Indeed, John D. Barrow has written a particularly useful book from this perspective that focuses on a great many of the "constants of nature," explaining how such constants structure the fabric of the universe while at the same time often evading a theoretical explanation as to why they must be one value as compared with another (Barrow 2002). Again, while the theory presented below is without question speculative, it is expected that it nonetheless will shed some light on the nature of physical reality. I am assuming that physicists and cosmologists who specialize in more traditional approaches to cosmology will understand what I am outlining from a remote-viewing experiential basis and then reinterpret it to match their own approach to a theory of reality. Thus, while I focus on Planck's constant because it lends itself well to describing a universe that corresponds with my understanding of the remote-viewing experience, it may be that a cosmologist will re-structure my argument by focusing on some other constant, or perhaps on something else entirely, while maintaining a general consistency with the discussion presented here.

One reason for suspecting that Planck's constant may in fact not be truly constant across all possible dimensions is based on the idea that it is a ubiquitous measured quantity that is particular to our known universe, and whose value structures the interactions of all frequencies (and thus waves, and thus all matter) in our physical reality. For example, Planck's constant appears in formulas for quantum energy (of all sorts, including a photon's momentum), the de Broglie wavelength of a particle (which helps to establish the wave characteristics of matter), and Heisenberg's uncertainty principle. Among its most noted uses is to scale the mathematical application of frequencies in various quantum calculations, something which involves a multiplicative interaction between frequencies and Planck's constant. In one sense, this use of Planck's constant can appear as a convenience to make calculations work out such that physical observations of frequency and energy in laboratory experiments match formulaic expectations. But why such a scaling number should be one magnitude rather than another has never been established within physics. The primary connection between Planck's constant and frequencies from the perspective used here is the relationship, $E/h=f$, where f = frequency, E = energy, and h is Planck's constant. If Planck's constant changes, note that all frequencies (and thus all forms of matter) in the universe are affected. I later combine this idea with another that I call the "quantum step size" to yield ideas that closely match reality as it seems to be from the perspective of the remote-viewing experience.

What if Planck's constant could vary across different universes? Would this simply cause all colors to shift as one moves from universe to universe, or would something more fundamental occur? Moreover, if Planck's constant could vary, why would it be so difficult to find an example in which the constant is a different number? Finally, if Planck's constant can vary across universes, is it theoretically possible (even if we cannot do it currently) to vary it locally from within the context of one universe, and what would be the result if this could happen?

The other reason for me to focus on Planck's constant is that I do not see any means of explaining the remote-viewing experience without incorporating the idea of a "quantum step size." This idea is currently popular among some cosmologists. In particular, Lee Smolin has recently written a very accessible article in *Scientific American* in which this idea is explained in the context of a cosmological theory called "loop quantum gravity." The basic idea is that space and time may not be continuous. One might intuitively think of this in terms of an example in which the movement of a particle would be more closely analogous to a dotted line rather than a continuous one. Rather, reality is broken up into the tiniest of discrete chunks, typically measured in terms of a "Planck length," a quantity which in turn depends on a number of other things, including gravity and the speed of light. In my own remote-viewing conditioned experiential view of reality, it makes sense for me to connect Planck's constant with what one might call the "spacing" or "quantum step size" dimensional chunks that connect time and space. It is reasonable to suggest that in our universe Planck's constant would scale this discrete quantum step size much as it scales periodic or wave-type phenomena. Again, cosmologists will certainly modify these ideas, just as physicists later refined the surprisingly intuitive yet still primitive ancient Greek notion that matter was composed of smaller blocks (i.e., atoms). Nonetheless, my own theory posited here serves as a useful heuristic first step, since it allows me to explain reality as it is experienced from a remote-viewing perspective, which again is the point of this exercise.

Consider a situation in which Planck's constant may in fact be only one setting or fixed number along an otherwise continuous dimension that we will here identify as "Planck's dimension." At this point in this discussion, it should be clear that I am using the term "dimension" in a mathematical not geometrical sense. However, I later introduce the idea that a wave function may operate within Planck's dimension, and thus it may be that this dimension is ultimately a geometrical dimension. I nonetheless do not need to settle this issue now, as will become clear below. For now let us simply say that Planck's dimension identifies a quantity that can assume values along a continuum. (Some may want to call this a "control parameter" rather than a dimension, which is something I leave up to personal choice.) While there will always be an infinite number of variables in our universe (i.e., unemployment rates, stock market averages, etc.) nearly all of those variables will not affect the way in which we perceive our three physical dimensions. The key for considering a variable as a dimension in the current context is that it should at least in theory be able to fundamentally structure our perceptions of our universe with the same significance with which this is accomplished by a geometrical dimension. Thus, Planck's dimension would minimally be a mathematical dimension with such significance.

At this point it is worthwhile alerting the reader that my initial discussion regarding the value of Planck's constant as one point along a continuum suggests that any other value along that continuum could be chosen to create a new universe. This is not exactly my argument, as will become more clear later in this chapter. Further on (as I mentioned earlier) I introduce an important idea that there appears to be a wave function associated with the value of Planck's constant for any particular universe. Nonetheless, for this initial discussion, all that is needed is the idea that Planck's constant may indeed be different for different universes.

For heuristic purposes, let us consider a most simple one-dimensional universe that exists in a two-dimensional hyperspace as depicted in figure 8.1. There are two axes in figure 8.1. The horizontal axis represents Planck's dimension, and the value of Planck's constant (which is constant for our universe) is found on this axis. The vertical axis is a dimension of this simple universe, and is comparable to one of our three physical dimensions in our more complicated universe. The vertical line that intersects the value of Planck's constant (for our universe) on the horizontal axis represents the totality of this simple one-dimensional universe. In this universe, an imaginary being could travel up and down the line, effectively being cut off from anything outside of that line, such as another one-dimensional universe that could be represented by another line that intersects the horizontal axis in a different location.

We can, of course, add dimensions to this portrayal. In figure 8.2, an imaginary two-dimensional universe that is located within a three-dimensional hyperspace is represented. In this case, the shaded plane represents this universe, and it intersects Planck's dimension at the value it has for our universe. The universe is totally confined to this plane, and an imaginary being living on this plane would think that the existence of anything outside of this plane was impossible.

But now imagine a situation in which two universes existed in such a three-

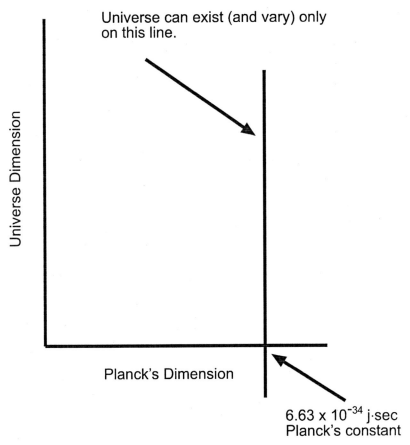

Figure 8.1. Simple one-dimensional universe in a two-dimensional space

dimensional hyperspace, something which is represented graphically in figure 8.3. The shaded plane to the right (Universe #1) intersects Planck's dimension at a value equal to that of our own universe, but the shaded plane to the left (Universe #2) intersects this dimension at a different value. If Planck's constant (as it appears to be a constant from the perspective of an imaginary being living in Universe #1) acts to scale all frequencies — and thus the periodic (wave) characteristics of all matter, including the quantum step size — then Universe #2 might not be visible to this being in Universe #1. The quantum step sizes of both universes would have to be the same for them to both appear simultaneously. Differences in the quantum step size would theoretically cause this in a fashion that would be analogous to watching a movie from behind a fan.

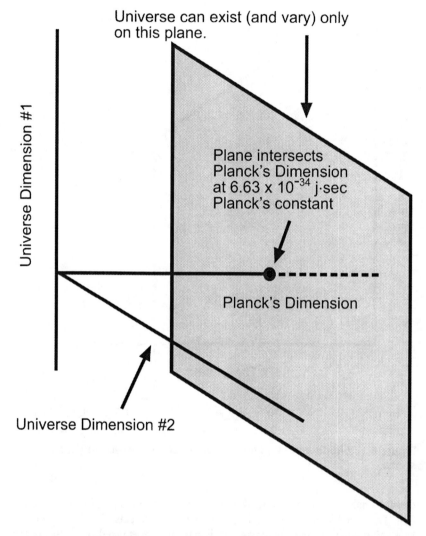

Figure 8.2. Two-dimensional universe in a three-dimensional space

If the blades of a fan spin at a certain rate such that the rotation of the blades (which acts to break the viewing experience up into discrete chunks) matches the frame rate of the projection system, the movie goer will not see the movie. The only way a viewer would see the entire movie unhindered by the fan would be if the spinning gaps between the blades of the fan perfectly match the flashes of light made by each frame in the movie's projector. In the case of figure 8.3, the

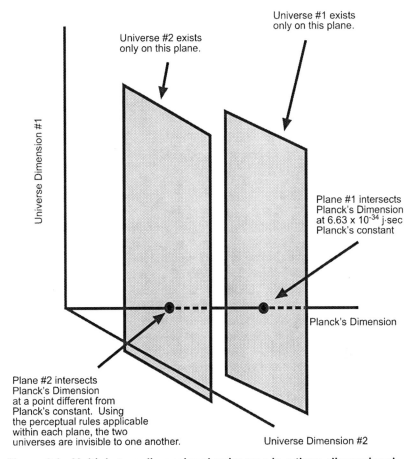

Figure 8.3. Multiple two-dimensional universes in a three-dimensional space

quantum chunks of existence must have the same quantum step size in order to be visible or they will slip past other quantum chunks even if they both occupy the same location in the overall hyperspace. Thus, elements from Universe #2 would have a unique quantum step size that would not intersect with anything in Universe #1. If it were possible to locally change the Planck's constant for something in Universe #1, it would seem to disappear from the view of an imaginary being living in this universe, but then simultaneously reappear in some other universe.

If such a dimension as Planck's dimension acts to separate universes, how many universes are possible? Some readers who may want further information about this general topic from the perspective of physics may find useful the exceptionally accessible treatment of the subject of parallel universes by Fred Alan Wolf (Wolf 1988). If certain cosmologists are correct and quantum step sizes of some sort do exist (even if they vary across and possibly within universes), then perhaps the existence of multiple universes is also discrete (i.e., not a continuum), and there are essentially gaps between the universes. If this is the case, there would effectively be an infinite number of universes, all of which would be invisible to each other. The differences in step sizes between the discrete quantum chunks of each universe would likely mean that the respective macro-objects in each universe (like planets and people) would not collide, even if the universes had relatively close Planck values. They could occupy the same general location in hyperspace yet pass right through one another invisibly, the way two different swarms of mosquitoes can pass through one another while traveling during the night (with each mosquito in each swarm both discrete and thus separate, like the quantum chunks in each universe).

But is each universe totally different from each other universe, or are there similarities between certain sets of universes? At this point I want to insert a new idea that is totally drawn from my own subjective interpretation of the remote-viewing experience. This idea is that universes (i.e., hypersurfaces) that are close together within a single hyperspace have increasing degrees of similarity in direct proportion to their mutual proximity within that hyperspace. That is, the closer one universe is to another universe within a hyperspace with respect to at least one important dimension, the more similar both universes will be when compared with more distant universes. In a sense, the quantum chunks of one universe seem to indirectly influence the quantum chunks in nearby universes, and I suspect that this happens if the universes are within a certain range of one another with respect to one or more subspace dimensions. Perhaps this is due to the way vector forces in one universe create work in the three physical dimensions of other universes due to the projection of these vector forces through the subspace dimensions. Universes in which the dimensions are more similarly aligned would also be more similarly affected by these projections, in the sense that the projections would be approximately equal (mathematically) among universes in which the dimensions and their alignment are nearly the same. In terms of the simplified depiction in figure 8.3, universes that have values of Planck's constant that are very close would be very similar. As the values of Planck's constant increasingly diverge as one extends from one universe to other universes along the Planck dimension, the qualitative characteristics of each universe in the direction of this extension would likewise diverge. This would imply that there may be a normal distribution of overall similarity across universes surrounding any given vector-defined point in any one universe.

Now let us focus on the issue of the added subspace dimensions. Imaginary beings living on Universe #1 in figure 8.3 would likely develop laws that "explained" phenomena that occur within that hypersurface. Since Universe #2 would not be visible to beings living in Universe #1, there would be no reason for them to suspect that other dimensions might exist that would intersect other universes. These seemingly external (subspace) dimensions would likely create anomalies in Universe #1, and beings living in this universe would certainly puzzle long over these anomalies.

The Two-Slit Experiment

From a remote-viewing perspective, it appears that multiple time lines can occur within one universe. When remote-viewing data involving a future event are used to change a time line (such as when a terrorist event is prevented), it appears that the new time line is actually a new sequential path of experiences on a hypersurface, and that sequential path differs from the one from which the remote-viewing data were drawn. One interpretation of this is that many possible time lines actually occur within one hypersurface (i.e., universe), but that we only remember one time line as our own. As will become clear with my argument below, I think this is not what is actually going on, but the remote-viewing experience nonetheless does resemble this perspective in some respects. More broadly, since experiments presented in this volume suggest that time is essentially little more than a artifact of perception that is sequentially structured, the question remains as to whether or not remote viewers are actually perceiving alternate universes that are close to our own within our surrounding multidimensional hyperspace when they remote view the future (as compared with many time lines in one universe). This would especially be true in cases in which the data are used to change the future. Remote viewing a future in a similar but nonetheless separate universe could cause one to establish a different sequence of future events in one's own universe.

But there is yet a different possibility, one which I sense is the correct one based on my own evaluation of the remote-viewing experience, and this possibility finds some correspondence with some of the current debates occurring in quantum physics. Let me state the "bottom line" of what I think is going on, and then let me back up to explain myself, knowing full well that many readers may think my so-called "bottom line" is preposterous at first glance. But if one considers the possibilities carefully, what I am about to explain really does seem to me to be the most likely explanation of what is going on within our own universe. [Now, remember to give me a chance to explain myself.] Here is the bottom line: Our universe is not really a solid physical universe. All that we experience in our reality is in fact the collapse of a probability wave that exists with respect to a certain frequency or set of frequencies. Moreover, with all likelihood, that frequency or set of frequencies is structured with respect to Planck's constant. In essence — and from the perspective of quantum physics, there is little or no fundamental difference between our macro universe and the quantum one. Indeed, I suggest that the remote-viewing phenomenon offers the first clear evidence of this.

Now let us back up to explain this. This all goes back to a famous experiment in quantum physics called the "two-slit experiment," and one can find accessible discussions of this experiment in a variety of sources, including Wolf (1988, pp. 34-9) and Hawking (1998, chapter 4). In this experiment, there is a monochromatic light source such as a laser or a more general bulb combined with a prism, plus two flat surfaces. The light source can be controlled to limit the amount of light that it allows into the system down to one photon at a time. This is done by a combination of limiting the brightness of the light and restricting the size of an aperture through which the light must travel in order to enter the system. One of the two flat surfaces has two parallel slits in it that can let light through. We will call the surface with the two slits "surface A." The slits are very small and closely spaced, typically only one wavelength apart with respect to the wavelength of the light being allowed to enter the system from the monochromatic light source mentioned above. The other flat surface has no openings in it, and we will call that surface B. The three objects are arranged as follows: first the light source, then the flat surface with the two parallel slits (surface A), and finally the flat surface without any openings (surface B). In the experiment, light emanates from the light source and passes through the two slits in surface A before it hits surface B (the one that has no openings in it). Surface B is normally a photographic plate or other type of sensitive detection device that can record the light that is emitted by the monochromatic light source and which passes through the two slits in surface A. The entire experimental setup is arranged as shown in figure 8.4. Note that this figure is conceptual only and not drawn to size.

A variety of strange things occur with the two-slit experiment. When a lot of light is allowed into the system (i.e., through the aperture for the monochromatic light), then a banded pattern of light and dark areas is formed on surface B, as is shown at the bottom of figure 8.4. Quantum theory argues that light acts as a wave, and that when there are two open slits, the light wave coming from the monochromatic light source has to break up into two separate. waves that travel through both slits before hitting surface B. But after the light passes through both slits, the light from one slit interferes with the light coming through the other slit. Effectively, some of the waves from the two slits cancel each other out when they mix on the other side of surface A, and it is this interference that causes the banded pattern on the photographic plate of surface B. If only one slit is open in surface A, then the entire wave coming from the light source would not be separated into two waves by the two open slits. Thus, the entire wave would hit surface B, and there would be no banded pattern visible on the photographic plate.

This above explanation of the banded pattern on surface B makes sense from a "common sense" perspective. The trouble is that this same phenomenon

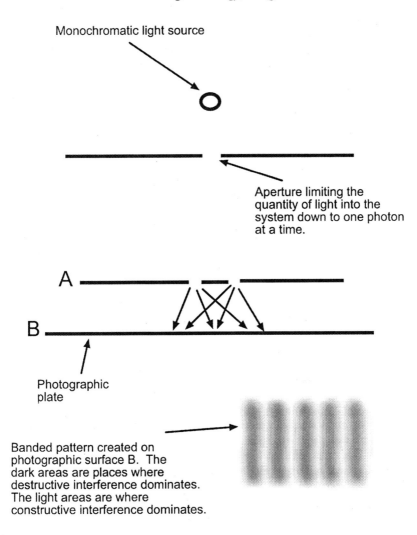

Figure 8.4. The two-slit experiment

of banded patterns of light and dark areas on surface B happens even if only one photon at a time is allowed to go through the slits of surface A! When a single particle hits surface B, it leaves an impression of a point, just as one would expect for a particle. But when one allows additional photos from the light source to enter the system one at a time and aims them at surface A, the particles hit surface B in patterns similar to when many photons are simultaneously aimed at surface A. (Note that since the photons are entering the system one at a time, the experimenter needs to wait a long time for a sufficient number of photons to hit the photographic plate on surface B before the banded pattern of light and dark areas becomes visible.)   This means that even when one particle is traveling through surface A to hit surface B, it is still running into an interference wave pattern on the other side of surface A (the side opposite the light source and facing surface B). But since there is only one photon in the system at a time, the photon must be interfering with itself, and the same single photon must be going through both slits at the same time! One can envisage a wave doing this, but a particle that hits surface B and registers only one spot on this surface is not so easy to imagine. How can the same particle that hits surface B in only one spot previously have passed through both slits of surface A at the same time? Moreover, this same experiment has been repeated more generally with electrons and other particles as well. The good news is that the above experiment is fully replicable and well-known. The bad news is that the experimental results are really all that is known with certainty.   After this, everything else is interpretation, which is where we turn next before connecting all of this back to the phenomenon of remote viewing.

This is not the place to go into a long discussion of the quantum physics issues related to the two-slit experiment. Rather, in the current context it is most crucial to focus again on the so-called "bottom line." One explanation of the above phenomenon is that the particle is actually a wave. But it is more than just a wave. The particle is actually a probability wave (sometimes called a "quantum wave function"). The particle entering the experimental system is "faced" with the probability of going through one or the other slits. Since the particle is actually a probability wave, then it can materialize in any one of a number of probable states when it is observed. Measuring the wave at a point by allowing the wave to interact with surface B in the above experiment acts to destroy the wave characteristics of the particle and transform it into a particle state. This is often referenced as a collapse of the probability wave by the so-called "Copenhagen interpretation" of the two-slit experiment.

The meaning of "collapsing a probability" is quite straightforward, and can be easily explained with an example. Let us say that someone is a guest on a television game show in which she is asked to locate the special prize (a round ball with money in it) behind door #1, door #2, or door #3. Let us also say that the prize was dropped behind one of the three doors by a truly random process that is kept secret from all witnesses. The guest does not know behind which door the prize is located. Thus, there is a one-third probability that she will pick the correct door. Let us say that the guest picks door #2, and that turns out to be the correct door. At the instant the door is opened and she (the observer) sees that she has chosen the correct door, the probability of her choosing the correct door is destroyed since she now knows the correct door with certainty, which means that the probability "collapses."

Returning to our discussion of quantum mechanics, there is a probability that a particle will be somewhere on a path along which a probability wave travels, and when someone makes an observation and locates the particle within this wave, the probability of the particle being somewhere along that path collapses, since the location of the particle is now certain. Thus, making the observation collapses the probability wave. With the Copenhagen interpretation of the two-slit experiment, until the observation is made, the particle exists only as a probability wave.

There is another prominent competing interpretation of the two-slit experiment, one that has been discussed in an accessible fashion by Wolf (1988), Davies (1992), and others. This other interpretation was originally discussed by Hugh Everett in 1956, and it involves the idea of other dimensional realities, or other universes (sometimes called "many worlds"). In a multiple universe reality, there could be various versions of the same particle, each of which would be facing the same probability of going through one or the other slits. The probabilistic view of physical matter is the same with both the Copenhagen and multiple universes interpretation. However, the multiple universes interpretation does not require that the observer of an event create a collapse of the probability wave. What happens is that a proportion of the particles from the other universes go through one slit, while the other particles go through the other slit. The particle/wave combination is effectively split along probabilistic lines due to the possibilities created by the two slits in surface A. This implies that these multiple universes essentially split along probabilistic lines due to the experiment's design. (For a more detailed discussion of this idea, see Wolf 1988.) What is most interesting from the perspective of this volume is that the quantum elements of one universe are able to affect the quantum elements of another universe if the universes are sufficiently close in some dimensional context. In the language of physics, the events in each of the universes become entangled. In the multiple universes perspective, the wave function of a particle never collapses due to observation. Rather, the act of observation and the wave of the particle are part of a single two-part probabilistic system, and the interaction of both parts of the system create the illusion of physical reality through a process known as "quantum decoherence." Quantum decoherence is essentially what happens when quantum processes interact with one another, producing what is known as an open system in a mixed rather than pure quantum state. The coherence of the quantum processes dissolves as the properties of a larger macro system (the physical reality we all know) takes shape.

There are two variations of the two-slit experiment that are worth mentioning here. The first has been discussed conceptually for many years, and it involves light which leaves a quasar and travels to Earth. But there is a galaxy between the quasar and the Earth. The galaxy has a huge gravitational field that acts as a lens that splits the light wave traveling from the quasar to the Earth much as a large post supporting a pier in the ocean would split a wave traveling to the beach. The basic scenario in this experiment is depicted in figure 8.5.

One photon leaves the quasar, hits the gravity lens of the galaxy, and then travels to earth following two paths on either side of the galaxy, producing two images of the quasar.

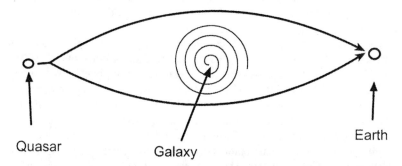

Quasar   Galaxy   Earth

The two images of the quasar are then merged together. An interference pattern results, indicating that both images are made from the same photons since different photons would leave the quasar at different times, and thus would not interfere with one another.

Figure 8.5. Galactic version of the two-slit experiment

When the light arrives at the Earth and is observed by an astronomer, there are two images of the quasar, one from each of the paths that the light traveled on either side of the galaxy while en route. The light that arrives at the Earth from the distant quasar is so little that it can be said that it is arriving one photon at a time. But when the two images of the quasar are delicately merged together, they form an interference pattern, the same type of interference pattern that occurs with the two-slit experiment. Yet if the two images of the quasar are being formed by different photons traveling one at a time, they would not produce an interference pattern since they would arrive on Earth at different times. The interference pattern indicates that the photons are the same! That is, each photon travels from the quasar to the Earth by passing around both sides of the galaxy simultaneously. Having a photon appear to travel through both slits in surface A at the same time in the two-slit experiment is troubling enough, but having a photon be on both sides of a galaxy at the same time is even more perplexing, even if it in principle involves the same process.

The final variation of the two-slit experiment that seems crucial to mention here is one in which the act of observation is directly challenged. This experiment was originally conceived in 1980 by John A. Wheeler, a physicist who once studied under Bohr and who worked at Princeton University. The idea is to conduct the two-slit experiment while deciding whether or not to observe a particular photon only after it passes the two slits in surface A. That is, if the decision to observe a photon is made *after* the photon has already been faced with the choice of traveling through one of the two slits, would the photon have previously gone through both slits, or only one? In the mid-1980s, the experiment was first conducted at two different universities independently. For the first part of the experiment, rather than using two-slits, a laser is split by a half-silvered mirror. Thus, half of the light goes through the mirror, and the other half is reflected in another direction. When the two beams are again merged onto a primary detector (which we shall label "detector #1"), an interference pattern is created, just as in the case of the two-slit experiment. The interpretation of this is that since the experimenters do not know which route a photon will take, it will take both routes, thereby interfering with itself upon arrival at the detector.

In the second part of this experiment, a Pockels cell crystal is placed in the path of one of the two routes after the light is split by the half-silvered mirror. When an electric current is applied to the crystal, it diffracts a photon to a different detector (not detector #1), and we shall label this new detector "detector #2." After each photon leaves the half-silvered mirror, a device using a truly random process sends an electric signal to the Pockels cell crystal, thereby deflecting the photon on one of the paths to detector #2. When the electric signal is absent, the photon passes through the crystal unhindered and hits detector #1, creating an interference pattern with its counterpart photon that took the other route at the mirror, indicating that the photon traveled both ways simultaneously. But when the electric signal is applied to the crystal (again, *after* each photon passes the mirror stage of the experiment), then knowledge of the photon's location is obtained, and the photon arrives only at either detector #1 or detector #2 (i.e., not both). Crucially, the photon under these circumstances does not travel through both routes simultaneously, since if it did it would be detected by both detectors at the same time. Thus, even if the decision to observe the photon is made *after* the photon has already left the mirror, the photon will still only travel one way or the other, not both. But if no effort is made to observe which way the photon is traveling, then it will take both routes. Clearly, observation or detection or measurement (however one wants to define the process of knowing something) affects the outcome of an event. Knowing something collapses its probability of occurring and transforms the probability into a "real thing."

The connection between knowing something and creating something as described above touches many aspects of the quantum world, including the specification of Heisenberg's Uncertainty Principle. The basic idea is that observing something on the quantum level (as compared with the macro level of planets and people) causes a change in the thing being observed. Again, there are controversies among various schools regarding how to interpret this quantum phenomenon, but we do not need to decide here which interpretation is correct. But from the perspective of the remote-viewing experience as described in this volume, we can clearly note that we have observed on the macro level a phenomenon that has a direct parallel to that observed on the quantum level, and indeed, the act of observation does seem to interact with the outcome of physical reality. That is, remote viewing can change the evolutionary course of history through the act of observation.

The cross-cutting psi channels problem described in chapter 3 is quite parallel to the two-slit experiment. With a remote-viewing experiment that is set-up such that there are multiple possible targets, only one of which is correct and the others are decoys, the correct target is chosen dynamically by some random event (such as flipping a coin, throwing a die, or using a random number generator). Thus each future (one associated with each potential target) has a probability, and thus a probability wave exists to carry the sequence of events from conducting the remote-viewing session to the analysis of the data by a panel of blind (to the dynamically chosen correct target) judges.

In a remote-viewing situation involving two possible targets, this probability wave will exhibit two events, one for each potential target. Moreover, the judges and the viewer are observing the events! This implies that the combined observing actions of the judges and the viewer are interacting with the target's probability wave such that an apparently "real" single event occurs. According to this theory, and supported by a great deal of experimental evidence, the outcome of such experiments can only be predicted probabilistically, and this is inherent in the nature of the experimental design. Real-life experience with the cross-cutting psi channels phenomenon argues strongly that the probability wave splits across various universes, and the results intermingle in each of the universes in a manner that is parallel to that which happens when a single particle passes through the slits on surface A to arrive at surface B, still producing (after repeated trials) the light and dark areas on surface B indicating that each particle passed through both slits in surface A simultaneously. What I have not yet done is to explain why remote viewing should behave like quantum phenomena in the first place. This will require me to introduce the subject of entanglement, which I do later in this chapter. I mention this now only so that readers will remain patient with me as I continue to explain each part of this truly interesting puzzle.

From the above reasoning I draw the following conclusion: When one remote views, one is observing a probabilistic future. One is actually perceiving one of various possibilities. Which one possibility is perceived depends on the act of observation. An observation that really matters is the act of comparing the remote-viewing data to the target or (in the multiple-target case) the target possibilities. It is this act of closing the session by the remote viewer, or judging the session data by a group of blind judges, that determines how the remote-viewing process will result. In the case of a remote-viewing experiment with multiple-target possibilities, the remote-viewing results will split along probabilistic lines as the probability wave collapses to one or another possibility. This is the ultimate explanation for the cross-cutting psi channels problem described in chapter 3 of this volume.

Cross-cutting psi channels are in fact probabilistic manifestations of a probability wave that is interacting with alternate futures across a set of universes. Moreover, these wave functions originate from the same starting point, which is determined by the existence of someone executing a remote-viewing session. Thus, the universes themselves are highly similar when they branch off at the beginning of the session, and they therefore influence each other in the manifestation of the remote-viewing results. (See also the section below involving the propagation of events across multiple universes.) It is because of this that the potential targets in a multiple-target experiment cannot be considered independent of one another. Obtaining remote-viewing results that correctly describe the wrong target (in the sense of one of the target possibilities that is not the target dynamically chosen) is explicitly (not analogously) a result of this cross-universe influence.

The cross-cutting psi channels experiment is the first directly observed evidence that probabilistic macro-level events which occur in our universe can result in varying outcomes divided along probabilistic lines among other universes. The only reason we do not recognize this immediately with respect to other types of common probabilistic events is that our memory is recorded in a manner such that we do not see (or at least remember) any more than one outcome to these events. The primary difference between cross-cutting psi channels experiments and other probabilistic non-psi experiments is that with remote-viewing we can witness the other-universe outcomes directly, something which is not possible to do using only the five physical senses in more traditional non-psi experiments. This, in fact, is the first direct evidence ever obtained suggesting that the multiple universe model of reality may apply equally to both the quantum and non-quantum realms.

One consequence of this line of thinking is that our experiences in our current universe are actually averages of experiences which "we" (i.e., the many versions of each individual person) are also having in other universes (i.e., on other hypersurfaces within our overall hyperspace). Thus, when we drink a cup of coffee, this is a probabilistic experience, not an isolated unique event. In other universes/hypersurfaces near our own, we are also drinking a cup of coffee. But in those other universes, perhaps the movement of our hand which is holding the cup is slightly different, or perhaps the color of the cup is different, and so on. In the language of our current chapter, there is apparently a mean (as in "an average") experience around which the normally distributed, probabilistically conditioned other universes hover. In order to avoid the problem of cross-cutting psi channels, one has to eliminate the possibility of splitting the probability wave function such that it collapses on (or entangles with, depending on one's point of view) multiple events other than the mean future event.

Again, this argument implies that there is a most probable future (the mean) for any point of existence on a hypersurface within the surrounding hyperspace. From my perspective, the value of Planck's constant for a given universe seems to affect the placement of this mean within the probability wave, thereby affecting the ways in which the probabilistic frequencies or the wave function interact with all other frequencies in our universe. The practical lesson to draw from all this with regard to public demonstrations of remote viewing is that such demonstrations need to be structured so that this mean future event has a high probability of manifesting, which is another way of saying that the remote viewer will tend on average to perceive the actual target chosen by the tasker in a tasking-post experimental design. The more carefully the experiment is set-up, the more regularly this will occur. Indeed, staying on this mean path along a collapsing (or entangled) wave function into the future is crucial for a public demonstration of remote viewing to succeed.

For each universe which is farther away from our own within our surrounding hyperspace, the mean probabilities of our behaviors would increasingly diverge. As the distance between universes gets sufficiently far away, universes should have few if any similarities left, which implies that their mean probabilities are surrounded by distributions that effectively no longer overlap with those of other more distant universes, except perhaps along the very unlikely tails of those distributions. Physicists often note that an electron (whose energy is known) only exists as a probabilistic "cloud" until one makes an observation that determines its precise location, at which point the electron's probabilistic wave function collapses to a point in three-dimensional space and we lose the ability to determine its energy. Sometimes physicists like to refer to the electron in its probabilistic cloud manifestation as a probabilistic "smear," and when they determine its location it becomes a particle (with the collapse of the probability wave). What I am arguing here is that when we remote view the future (as we routinely do with tasking-post experimental designs), we are looking into a probabilistic smear of the future and collapsing that smear down into a location in three-dimensional space by the fact of remote viewing it (i.e., observing it). These multiple universes to which I am referring throughout this chapter are actually separate possible manifestations of a collapsing/entangled quantum wave function applied to macro events.

Entanglement

Let us now directly ask why remote viewing seems to behave like a quantum phenomenon. If the two-slit experiment is one of the great mysteries of quantum mechanics, then quantum entanglement is the other. This is not the place to go into a detailed discussion of quantum entanglement, but I do need to make some brief observations here that may help shed light on the quantum processes which enable remote viewing to occur. One of the most intriguing results of quantum mechanics is that it is possible for certain particles to become entangled. In its most basic sense, this means that the state or condition of one particle will affect the state or condition of another particle. This can be true even if the particles are separated by very long distances. Also, if an experimenter makes an observation with respect to one of two entangled particles, that immediately affects the state of the other particle even if the experimenter has no direct access to that other particle. Quantum entanglement was initially rejected by Einstein and others who argued that there were essentially hidden variables that were affecting the seemingly entangled particles locally, and if one could discern these hidden variables (even stochastically), one could explain the apparent entanglement. However, many years later, John Bell, in a famous proof, demonstrated that this was not the case. It was only then that quantum entanglement began to be explored more seriously.

In the 1980s, quantum entanglement began to be viewed as something that could potentially be exploited for commercial purposes. Currently, many governments, universities, and companies are investing significant resources into harnessing quantum entanglement for the purpose of computing, as well as other things. The physics of entanglement may not be fully understood, but the phenomenon itself is reliably replicable in laboratory settings.

Although I cannot prove what I am now going to suggest, I do want to emphasize that the remote-viewing experience does seem to support the following idea. I suspect that the physical/subspace interface by which the human subspace aspect interacts with the physical brain involves quantum processes, and that these quantum processes include the possibility of entanglement. Essentially, I am saying that it appears that quantum processes working inside a conscious human mind can entangle a place, not just a particle, and I explain how the physics of this might occur below. But to begin, partial experiential evidence suggesting this (in my own view) includes many reports in which a remote viewer describes what appears to be an apparent "apparition" of another remote viewer at a target location. For example, let us say that remote viewer Tony perceives a target under totally double-blind conditions (i.e., neither he nor his monitor — if he has a monitor — knows the target when the session takes place). During the session, Tony reports that he perceives remote viewer Sue standing behind him with respect to his perspective at the target location. As it turns out, Sue was also tasked with the same target months or years previously, the fact of which Tony and his monitor are completely unaware. Yet what appears to have happened is that by remote viewing the target, Sue left some residual trace of herself which is later perceived by Tony. What is this residual trace?

If indeed remote viewing works because of some quantum process, then it is only logical to ask if entanglement may be involved. My suggestion is that

Sue's consciousness somehow entangles the place in the target that is occupied by her apparent apparition. However, there is more. It has long been a puzzle as to why remote viewing is normally unable to produce high-resolution perceptions on most occasions. The reason for this may have to do with the nature of the entanglement process itself. If entanglement is occurring, then it is possible that the perceptions are caused by quantum level inputs that are directly fed into the remote viewer's brain through the physical/subspace interface. Thus, entanglements between the target site and the viewer's brain may allow only limited amounts of information to pass using this process.

Interestingly, if entanglement is the underlying mechanism driving the remote-viewing phenomenon, then this would explain how remote viewing could occur with such low energy requirements. That is, remote viewing works without the need of, say, a black hole in the center of a galaxy to pierce a hole in the fabric of time and space. Entanglement does not require this either.

One should expect that some physicists would object to the idea that entanglement could explain remote viewing. There are two primary objections. The first is that in laboratory experiments entangled particles initially have to be together physically to set up the entanglement. An early procedure involved using a laser to excite the electrons in calcium atoms, and the electrons would shift to a lower energy level when the laser was discontinued. When shifting to this lower level, the electrons would release a pair of entangled photons. Once particles are entangled, they can then be separated by huge distances while still maintaining the state of entanglement. But with remote viewing, there is no evidence that entangled particles in the brain and at a target site have been together to get entangled in the first place. Yet consider these possibilities. (1) In the beginning of everything, there apparently was a "Big Bang" event. In such an event, all particles in our universe were essentially together. It may be that the universe is seeded with countless particles that have been entangled from that moment at the beginning of time. Particles do not come with labels declaring that they are entangled elsewhere, so it is natural that we would not be aware of even massive quantities of natural entanglement. It is also worth noting that the expansive distribution of matter following the Big Bang would have resulted in a large-scale and significant lowering of electron energy levels, an ingredient in the production of entanglement as mentioned above. [See, for example, Aczel's accessible discussion of this (Aczel 2003, pp. 170-1).] (2) It may also be that it is possible for distant particles to become entangled accidentally from time to time, perhaps in great numbers considering the essentially infinite number of particles that exist.

The second primary objection that a physicist might raise regarding the possibility of a connection between entanglement and the remote-viewing phenomenon is that even if entanglement could occur as suggested above, how would entangling a particle explain the ability to perceive a target on the macro level? From the remote-viewing perspective, it seems possible that entanglement can spread through some quantum process of contagion. This is not a new idea in quantum mechanics, and the essential concept is sometimes discussed in the context of "triple entanglement" (see Aczel 2003, Chapter 17, esp. pp. 222-223). Let us propose that a remote viewer may be able to entangle a place (that is, not just one particle) in the initial parts of a remote-viewing session. This would possibly require an entanglement process that could be initiated with a minimal threshold number of entangled particles. This would make sense experientially since only minimal information is usually perceptible in the beginning of a remote-viewing session. But as the session continues, the clarity of the perceptions of the target increases, which suggests that the process of entanglement is spreading as increasingly larger quantities of information are passed through the physical/subspace interface into the brain.

Indeed, the process of entanglement contagion may follow a two-way pattern orchestrated by the remote viewer's mind such that a ghostly "second body" would manifest at the target location as I mentioned earlier. Again, the phenomenon of having one remote viewer perceive such a manifestation of another remote viewer at a target location is not that uncommon. Accounts along this line are taken more seriously under conditions in which both remote viewers are tasked with the same target but are not informed of this at the time that the sessions take place. Moreover, this phenomenon has been recognized for many years. In one interesting case of this sort of which I am aware, two remote-viewing sessions of the same target were conducted by two different remote viewers, both of whom were pioneers in early U.S. government funded remote-viewing research. The second session was conducted years after the first, and the second remote viewer reported perceiving the presence of the first remote viewer (identified by name) "standing" behind him. At the time that the second remote-viewing session took place, the second remote viewer was not aware that the first remote viewer had ever been tasked with that target.

Probably the most significant physics experiment relating to the possible connection between entanglement and the remote-viewing phenomenon was conducted by Yanhua Shih, a physics professor at the University of Maryland. For those having an adequate background in physics and mathematics, his original article published in the *Annals of Physics* is truly an exciting read (Shih 2001). However, a very accessible short summary of Shih's experiment can be found in the book on the entanglement phenomenon by Amir Aczel (Aczel 2003, pp. 198-202). Briefly, Shih created a highly refined source of entangled photons. Mathematically, these entangled photons are not really separate, even though they are in different places at the same time. Thus, Shih refers to these entangled pairs of photons as single "biphotons." After separating the biphotons into what I shall call "side A" and "side B," Shih then sent the photons of side A through an aperture shaped by the initials UMBC, which stands for the University of Maryland, Baltimore County. Photons from side A that did not make it through the aperture were blocked, and thus were eliminated from the experiment. What remained was a stream of light that was shaped in terms of those initials. On the other side of the experiment, Shih sent the photons from side B into a sophisticated detector that was able to match photons from side B with entangled photons from side A. What happened then was most revealing. The photons from side B impressed what Shih calls a "ghost" image of the initials UMBC on the detector, which is why this experiment is called the "Ghost Image Experiment."

It is useful for the reader to remember that the photons from side B never went through the aperture shaped by the initials UMBC. But their entangled halves from side A did, and thus the photons on both sides responded in an entangled fashion even though the photons from each side were physically in different locations. What we have here is a clear experiment in which an image was conveyed from one location to another using the process of entanglement. It is also worth noting that the distance between sides A and B could theoretically have been of any length, and the experiment would still have worked.

The weakness in the above experiment as it relates to the possibility of linking entanglement with the remote-viewing phenomenon is that the experiment requires a classical connection between the detectors for sides A and B. Both of the detectors that are used to register the photons from sides A and B are connected to this classical connection. This classical connection includes a device called a "coincidence counter" that identifies the match between the photons from both sides. This is a form of observation that acts to register the quantum events. Without this classical connection, it is not possible to determine which of the photons on side A are entangled with which of the photons on side B. Using a telephone analogy, one can think of the two sets of photons on sides A and B as communicating with cell phones, while the classical connection is a land line. Two-particle entanglement requires this land line.

With remote viewing, there obviously is no land line. There is no classical connection that confirms and registers the images and other perceptions that are received by the remote viewer. But triple entanglement offers a mechanism by which other particles can become entangled through a contagion process with an initial pair of particles. If this contagion process can be extended to more than three particles, the possibility emerges that a feedback loop may form, and the entangled collection of photons (or other particles) can self-register as long as they are being observed on one end (that is, by one detector — the remote viewer). This is a classic result of self-organizing systems. We do not currently know how many entangled particles might be required to initiate a self-organizing feedback loop, but the number may be quite small. The existence of such self-organizing feedback loops with entangled particles can be approached experimentally by physicists who could test for self-organizing patterns among sets of potentially entangled particles. Computer algorithms that test for such patterns are now well known due in part to recent interest in mathematical topics such as fractals and chaos. But this issue may also be addressed theoretically in the form of a mathematical theorem. Ultimately, we will require both a theorem and experimental evidence of self-organizing entanglement patterns, but the remote-viewing phenomenon offers some hope that this may indeed be a worthwhile line of research.

Again, this speculation may be all wrong, and entanglement may not be at the root of the remote-viewing phenomenon. But the remote-viewing phenomenon acts as if entanglement is the underlying causal mechanism. Moreover, I am not the first person to suggest that quantum processes may be involved in the operation of consciousness. Scientists such as Fred Alan Wolf, Amit Goswami, Brian Josephson, Henry Stapp, and William Tiller have long theorized on this subject either directly or indirectly, as have others. Indeed, this is an active area of research currently. I suspect that progress will ultimately result from tracing the way nonphysical consciousness interacts with the human body, and thus the surrounding environment, and I eagerly look forward to continuing discussions by the scholars mentioned above as well as by others such as Penrose and Hameroff who are developing theories and models of quantum computing with respect to the human brain. (See especially, Penrose 1996, 2002; Hameroff 1994, 1998; Hameroff and Penrose 1996.)

Pulling Things Together with a Simplified Heuristic Model

I often find it helpful to create simplified mathematical models of complicated phenomena in order to understand the complexities involved with such phenomena more clearly. To understand my ideas presented below, it is necessary to put them into a proper modeling context. In general, there are three ways that are traditionally used to describe physical reality using mathematics, and each approach is very different from the other approaches in terms of philosophy and technique. By far the most common approach is called "statistical modeling," and this process uses a mathematical form that is normally developed by a statistician to look for correlations between variables. The goal of this approach is to explore how one or more variables (called "independent variables") in a data set appear to influence a particular variable of interest (the "dependent variable") that one wants to explain. The mathematical model used more often than not is a linear combination of the independent variables, with each variable having its own slope. Such models have an "off the shelf" flavor, in the sense that the same mathematical structure is used in many different settings where correlational evidence of causation is desired. This approach to modeling is sometimes also called "curve fitting."

A second approach to using mathematics to describe reality is called "mathematical modeling." With mathematical modeling, the modeler essentially constructs mathematical toys that caricature reality in desired ways. The models themselves are often significantly more complicated than the linear forms that are typical of statistical modeling. Fitting such models to collections of data can also be quite challenging, and sometimes the models are investigated using simulations or logical analyses to reveal their underlying characteristics across a broad range of parametric and environmental conditions. Using mathematical modeling, investigators often seek to understand various manifestations of regular, periodic, chaotic, and catastrophe processes of change.   Some mathematical modeling applications are quite famous, such as Lorenz's chaotic strange attractor, the Lotka and Volterra predator-prey models, Richardson's arms race models, all rational choice and game theory models, and all fractal models. As an academic, it is within this realm of mathematics where I do most of my own work.

The third approach to using mathematics to describe reality is sometimes called "exact mathematical specification modeling," or simply "EMS modeling." This is the approach to modeling that is predominantly used in physics, and to some extent chemistry, engineering, and occasionally some other fields. With this approach, the goal is to develop a mathematical equation (or set of equations) that exactly describes a given phenomenon. It is difficult to overstate the degree of precision that this type of modeling requires. Prediction errors are of enormous significance with this approach, even when the errors are extremely small. The idea is to make the math explicitly describe the exact truth of a given phenomenon, not an approximation of the phenomenon. For example, Einstein was led to develop his ideas regarding special relativity in large part due to small predictive errors encountered with Newton's mathematical formulations under conditions of great speed or significant gravitational forces. This is the realm of mathematics within which resides the theories of traditional cosmology. EMS modeling can become intractable when phenomena become too complex, which is why it is not used to model human behavior or social phenomena. Specifying the exact physical structure of the universe — which is the goal of traditional cosmology — may be near the upper limit in terms of EMS modeling's potential to describe anything. Beyond this limit — wherever that may eventually be — statistical modeling and mathematical modeling need to be used since these approaches allow for approximations to such greater levels of complexity.

The mathematical ideas presented below fall into the category of mathematical modeling as described above. The substantive ideas relating to remote viewing and physical reality presented in this chapter are sufficiently complex for me to naturally want to think about the basic ideas in a simplified context. This led me to search for a mathematical model that would parallel the cosmological ideas presented here without forcing me to deal prematurely with the complexities that would by necessity be required with EMS modeling. Essentially, I wanted a mathematical toy that would exhibit many of the traits of reality that I describe in this chapter and volume. The toy would then allow me the opportunity to explore these ideas within one integrated and simplified mathematical setting, thereby clarifying the arguments in ways that would be cumbersome or even impossible to accomplish with words alone.

Before I begin to describe my toy model of a universe with earnest, it is necessary to briefly outline a concept that is essential to quantum mechanics, and requisite here with regard to the interpretation of the model presented below. This concept is related to how probability waves can interact in such a manner as to create an event in space and time. Under some circumstances, many types of waves pass through one another without one wave influencing another. But under other circumstances, waves interact to produce new events or waves. These new events are called "wave packets," and they have their own characteristics that are often quite distinct from the characteristics of the waves upon which they are comprised.

An example best explains the idea of a wave packet. Figure 8.6 presents a number of sine waves, all with varying amplitudes and wavelengths. In this case, for heuristic reasons, the amplitudes of the sine waves are made approximately proportional to that of a chosen sine wave with a central wavelength, although this is not required to produce a wave packet. A wave packet can be created by adding such sine waves together. Note that the positive and negative regions for the value of sine differ with respect to different values of the variable X. Thus, when the positive and negative values are added together across the various waves, they cancel one another out. But for some values of the variable X, the values of sine are predominantly positive or negative, and in such regions, the different sine waves amplify one another if they are added together.

Figure 8.7 is an example of an isolated wave packet in which 20 sine waves similar to those presented in figure 8.6 are added together. The wave packet is the entire "blip" in the center of figure 8.7. Note that the sine waves cancel one another out to the right and left of the wave packet. This process of creating a wave packet from a collection of individual waves is called "superposition," and superpositions are crucial to quantum mechanical theory. Wave packets have their own characteristics, such as velocity. The velocity of a wave packet that is comprised of many other interacting waves is called "group velocity," and group velocity can differ greatly from the velocities of the component waves. Indeed, group velocity can be much greater than the velocity of the component waves, much slower, or somewhere in between. From a quantum mechanical perspective, a particle is a wave packet; it is a manifestation of the superposition of many interacting probability waves.

For the purposes of the current discussion, what is important to draw from the idea of superposition is how the various component waves that make up a wave packet interact by cancelling one another out or by amplifying one another. In areas along the horizontal axis of figure 8.7, the process by which the component sine waves cancel one another out is called "destructive interference." In other areas along the same axis, the process by which the component sine wave amplify one another when added together is called

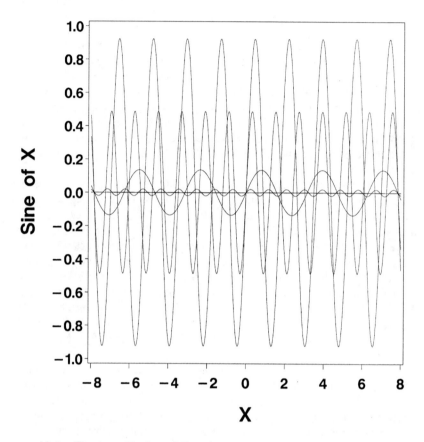

Note: The amplitudes of the sine waves are proportional to $\exp[-(k-k_0)^2/\Delta k^2]$, with $k_0=.4$ and $\Delta k=2$, and k are wave numbers.

Figure 8.6. Sine waves

"constructive interference." During periods dominated by destructive interference, it is said that the component sine waves are "out of phase." Similarly, during periods in which constructive interference dominates, the component sine waves are said to be "in phase." Constructive interference and destructive interference are fundamental concepts within quantum mechanics, and they are similarly crucial to my own interpretation of the universe from a remote-viewing perspective as I explain below.

At this point we can return to the matter of constructing my toy model of a universe. So far I have introduced the idea that our overall hyperspace is composed of both invisible and visible dimensions (subspace and physical). In the event that there may be a Planck's dimension, we can group that with the subspace dimensions since the primary concern with the definition of the subspace dimensions is that they be normally invisible from a perspective in the three physical dimensions. If our physical reality is a product of quantum wave functions, it must be assumed that these wave functions traverse or influence all dimensions, both subspace and physical. Yet these same wave functions leave identifiable patterns within the physical dimensions, which are a subset of the total dimensions (subspace plus physical) in our overall hyperspace. Thus, we have higher-dimensional wave functions creating what appear to be self-contained "things" in the lower-dimensional subset of physical dimensions. These "things" are self-contained in the sense that they have no superficially obvious connection to the other dimensions, and can be examined independently from the other invisible dimensions.

It is worth re-emphasizing at this point that the simple model presented

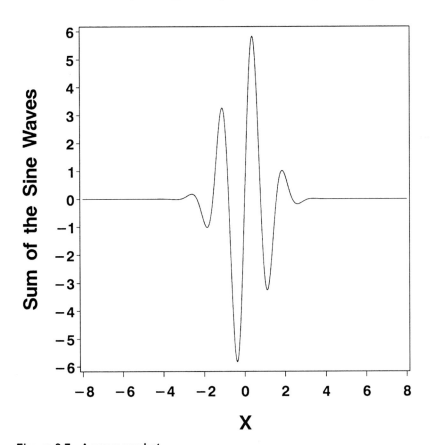

Figure 8.7. A wave packet

below is clearly not a model of our universe. The level of mathematics presented here is trivial when compared with that which is typical for any of the currently proposed traditional cosmological theories (such as string theory, etc.). Rather, the modeling efforts in this chapter are used to clarify the nature of the observations regarding our physical existence that seem obvious from a remote-viewing perspective. It is hoped that my presentation below is sufficiently clear such that all readers, regardless of mathematical background, will be able to unambiguously recognize the essential characteristics of this perspective that seem necessary to include in any ultimately successful traditional cosmological theory.

My search for a useful model was bounded by the following criteria. First, the model should be driven by wave functions, since wave functions are the dominant component in both the Copenhagen and multiple universes schools. Second, the wave functions should involve a minimum of four dimensions. This is necessary to parallel the idea that we have both visible and invisible dimensions (e.g., three physical dimensions, a possible Planck's dimension, and potentially multiple subspace dimensions). In the simplified model developed here, it is important to note that the three visible dimensions of the model should not be seen as an exact parallel to our three physical dimensions. The basic idea here is not to make an exact representation of our physical reality, but rather to construct a general wave-based model that occupies a larger set of dimensions with which we can isolate the lower-dimensional components. For example, in the multiple universe perspective, we do not see those other universes, but they exist as wave patterns in a lower-dimensional subset of the total collection of hyperspace dimensions. In our simple model, we want to include this basic idea.

Third, the model should be able to create identifiable patterns in three of the dimensions when one of the dimensions is suppressed (i.e., made invisible). This would parallel the situation in which wave functions in a higher dimensional quantum world (three physical dimensions plus however many subspace dimensions) produce patterns in a subset of fewer dimensions. These patterns would be comparable with probability waves that flow through our overall hyperspace and which ultimately seem to manifest into physical things *when observed.* The patterns created by the model as described in this paragraph would represent the probability waves themselves that could produce an infinite set of possible realities. The patterns would not represent only one given reality (i.e., our own particular universe). We now need to select one reality from this infinite set of possibilities, which is the next step.

Fourth, the model should have a lower-dimensional "catching function" that would act to select a universe from the set of all possibilities. By this I mean that the wave functions need to make an impression in some lower-dimensional hypersurface in a manner that parallels the act of observation in our own lower-dimensional "real world." This would be comparable with having a wave make an observed impression on something in our world, such as a spot on surface B in the two-slit experiment described earlier. To construct this catching function, the visible wave pattern described in the previous paragraph needs to be intersected by some other mathematical surface, in essence producing a visible universe comparable to our own visible universe by selecting these points of intersection. The simplest way to do this is to cut the visible wave pattern in the visible three dimensions with an "observing" plane. The points of intersection between this plane and the visible wave pattern would parallel our isolated three-dimensional physical reality in which wave functions produce impressions which we observe to be our universe. In general terms, this will enable us to watch what happens when four-dimensional waves create another wave pattern within a subset of those dimensions, that in turn intersects with a still lower-dimensional "observing" hypersurface. Finally, I must be able to graphically manipulate the three-dimensional representation of the model's patterns so as to be able to explore it.

Perhaps the simplest model to use here that fits the criteria established above is the well-known Lissajous figure that is created using a pair of harmonic oscillators. In this case, I use the following set of four first-order differential equations. The equations are printed here only for reference, and readers do not need to understand the mathematics behind them. The discussion that follows should be easy to follow regardless.

$$dX_1/dt = aX_3 \qquad\qquad (8.1)$$

$$dX_2/dt = bX_4 \qquad\qquad (8.2)$$

$$dX_3/dt = -aX_1 \qquad\qquad (8.3)$$

$$dX_4/dt = -bX_2 \qquad\qquad (8.4)$$

For this model, $a = 3.12121212$, and $b = 2.11111111$. The simulations of this model presented here were conducted using the program Phaser which was developed primarily by Hüseyin Koçak (www.phaser.com). This is a very accessible program which I have used for many years to teach dynamical systems at various universities, and some readers may enjoy conducting their own investigations using it. To assist readers who may want to replicate the construction of this model using Phaser, I have used parameter values suggested by Hüseyin Koçak.

Since this model is composed of four differential equations and four X_i variables, it has four dimensions. Each X_i variable oscillates in a sinusoidal wave-like manner as shown in figure 8.8. In this figure, the horizontal axis represents time, and the vertical axis represents the values of one of the X_i variables. Thus, we have four waves occupying a four-dimensional hyperspace, which is analogous to probability waves "flowing" through the overall hyperspace that houses our own universe and all other universes in the multiple universe model of reality.

In four dimensions, these harmonic oscillator waves produce a torus, which is a two-dimensional hypersurface shaped like the surface of a donut. When we suppress one of those dimensions (i.e., make it invisible), another hypersurface appears in the three remaining dimensions. This new hypersurface is in the shape of a cylinder and is shown in figure 8.9. This is the well-known Lissajous figure, and this shape resembles that produced on many oscilloscopes. The idea of this figure is to show how waves "flowing" in more dimensions can produce clear patterns when projected onto fewer dimensions. In this case, the surface of the cylinder is housed in three dimensions, although the surface itself has only two-dimensions, just as a balloon has only two dimensions but it is housed in three dimensions.

I am assuming here that the multiple universe model of reality would work in the same way, in the sense that the multiple universes would appear as patterns caused by probability waves "flowing" through a larger number of dimensions. For the moment, let us adopt this convention and call these multiple universes simply "patterns" that are produced by these probability waves. Thus, if the total number of dimensions in the hyperspace that houses everything that exists is N, then each of the universes in a multiple universe model would likely occupy a lower number of these dimensions, just as our own universe occupies only three dimensions out of the larger set of dimensions. The total number of dimensions used to house all other universes combined is not known, but we can call it N-m, where m is the number of unseen subspace dimensions. We do not know the value of m since we simply do not currently know how these extra dimensions (all of which are subspace from our perspective) are used with respect to all other universes. It may even be that some universes also occupy three dimensions, but those dimensions might be different from the three dimensions that house our universe. Nonetheless, the basic idea is that there are a total number of N dimensions, and the multiple universe model requires some of those dimensions to house these universes. One can think of the total Lissajous figure in figure 8.9 as analogous to the patterns produced by the probability waves creating all universes in the multiple universe model.

Just as our universe is but one of many universes, we need now to select a subset of the points in the Lissajous figure of figure 8.9. This is analogous to selecting our universe out of the total of all possible universes. In this case, I create a "catching function" that selects points from the Lissajous figure, and this catching function itself creates a new pattern. To do this I "slice" the Lissajous figure with a plane, and the intersection of this plane with the figure produces an ellipse. This ellipse is represented by the larger dots in figure 8.9, and it is called a "Poincare map." For all intents and purposes, the Poincare map is a one-dimensional self-contained pattern (since an ellipse is essentially a curved line) that is housed in two dimensions. An imaginary creature that lived on this

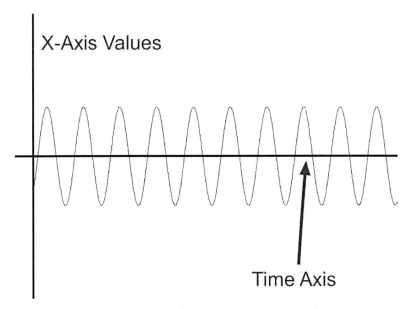

Figure 8.8. X-axis values plotted over time for the four-dimensional harmonic oscillator

Poincare map might not know that its own limited dimensional existence is not the total of all that exists. Indeed, unless one could step back and see how the two-dimensional ellipse is actually just a partial observation of more complex patterns created by waves "flowing through" a higher set of dimensions, one might never understand the true nature of one's own universe.

Again, the basic idea of creating this heuristic oscillator model is to show how waves in higher-dimensional spaces can leave clear and seemingly self-contained patterns in lower-dimensional realms. In the case of this model, we have moved from a torus housed in four dimensions, to a Lissajous cylinder housed in three dimensions, to a Poincare map housed in two dimensions. Yet all of these patterns are created by the exact same set of waves. To show how self-contained these patterns can appear in their lower-dimensional manifestations, we can easily manipulate the Lissajous figure. Figure 8.10 is a picture of the Lissajous figure from above, looking down and into the cylinder. Figure 8.11 moves the viewing perspective into the cylinder itself. Note that in figures 8.10 and 8.11, the Poincare ellipse is still visible as a string of larger dots.

Table 8.1 helps to summarize the correspondence between the various dimensional representations for the harmonic oscillator model and physical reality. Obviously the harmonic oscillator model is not a full model of reality. Again, it is used here merely to show how waves in higher-dimensional spaces

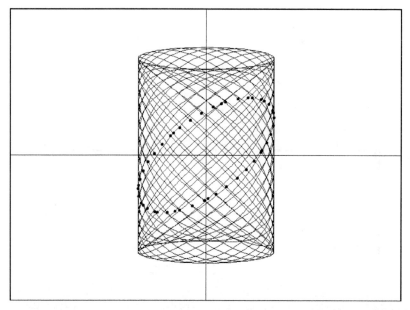

Figure 8.9. The harmonic oscillator as seen from the side (a Lissajous figure). The Poincare map is visible as the diagonal ring intersecting the cylinder shape.

can leave self-contained patterns in lower-dimensional spaces. The justification for using this model in the current context is because the remote-viewing experience suggests that physical reality behaves similarly. Probability waves that "flow through" higher-dimensional hyperspaces create patterns (i.e., hypersurfaces) in lower-dimensional realms. We view these realms as universes. Due to the dimensional context within which these hypersurface patterns are housed, a lower-dimensional pattern is essentially blind to the existence of a higher-dimensional pattern.

Planck's Wave

At this point I need to describe the wave characteristics of our universe in a way that makes sense with respect to the remote-viewing experience. What I describe below will seem very different from theories currently circulating in cosmological circles, and because of this some readers may initially want to dismiss these ideas. But the remote-viewing phenomenon cannot be explained within the context of contemporary theories of cosmology. Since I am fully convinced of the reality of the remote-viewing phenomenon, I am certain that the extant collection of contemporary cosmological ideas is incomplete at best. The

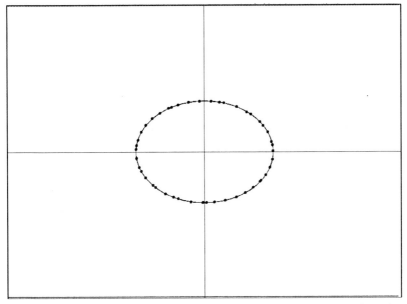

Figure 8.10. The harmonic oscillator as seen from above (rotated on the X axis 90°).

ideas that I present below do make sense with respect to remote viewing, and I posit their value as starting points in what I hope results in a more inclusive discussion about the fabric of our universe.

So far in this chapter, I have discussed the idea of a Planck dimension as a continuous axis along which Planck's constant may be any value. It is useful now to refine that idea with respect to the so-called "catching function" mentioned above. This view of the universe that I have described throughout this chapter suggests that Planck's constant for any particular universe would be determined by a wave function that is associated with Planck's dimension. I call this wave function "Planck's wave." It is this wave function that interacts with all other probability waves that exist in our universe to create what I call the "catching function."

I suspect that the process that is operating here involves at least one unseen geometric dimension (that is, a geometric subspace dimension). All waves that operate within our known universe would be linked with (and would thus operate within) this extra geometric dimension. What we see when we wake up in the morning or when we look up in the sky at night is actually the observation of superpositioned probability waves that are in momentary phase with respect to Planck's wave. The future and the past are no longer aligned in phase and probability (as I explain below), and thus are invisible to us, even though they

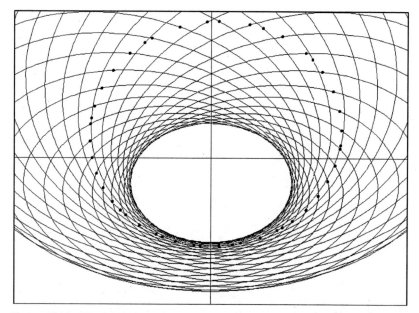

Figure 8.11.   The Lissajous figure as seen from a perspective of entering the cylinder shape from above

continue to exist. The key with this conceptualization is to allow for a wave function that operates along a subspace dimension, to which all material manifestations which occur in our universe must be linked. Seeing material things that oscillate with all known frequencies in our universe requires that all of those things also simultaneously oscillate in phase and with appropriate alignment with respect to Planck's wave. The issue of "appropriate alignment" is related to the matter of time and is more subtle than it at first appears. I discuss this further below.

How might we now connect the idea of Planck's wave with the Lissajous mathematical model/conceptual toy that was presented above? For this all to work, there needs to be a source from which such waves emanate. The physicist John Wheeler once noted, "No elementary phenomenon is a phenomenon until it is a registered (observed) phenomenon" (Aczel 2003, p. 93). Since observation is key to having quantum effects materialize in the physical universe, it seems reasonable to me to suggest that the act of observation is itself a complex form of superposition, and thus it is capable of acting in a manner characteristic of a wave to create further superpositions when combined with other waves. Remote viewing suggests that this observational characteristic of the quantum world can be extended to macro events. What I am calling "Planck's wave" seems to operate in many respects as a wave of consciousness

Table 8.1: Dimensional Correspondence Between the Harmonic Oscillator Model and Physical Reality

Simplified Harmonic Oscillator Model	Physical Reality
Four hyperspace dimensions house a torus (which is a two-dimensional hypersurface like the surface of a donut) created by the oscillator model. (The total number of possible dimensions is N, and $N=4$.)	N hyperspace dimensions house all that exists (a) three physical dimensions (b) N-3 subspace dimensions
Three dimensions house a Lissajous hypersurface (which is a two-dimensional surface of a cylinder). Here N-m = 4-1.	N-m dimensions house all hypersurfaces needed for the multiple universes model. The value of m is unknown.
Two dimensions house the Poincare Map.	Three dimensions house our physical universe.

that is sufficiently encompassing to register events on a macro scale. We obviously cannot currently identify the source of such waves, but their primary capability appears to allow for the manifestation of the material world as combinations of complex superpositions.

If the reader will allow me to extend my argument a bit further, let us posit for the moment that there is a source of such "Planck waves." The remote-viewing experience suggests (I think in this instance, incorrectly) that such Planck waves are discrete entities, like pulses, rather than continuous sinusoidal fluctuations. For example, perceived remote-viewing images quite often appear as frozen pictures rather than as moving scenes. I do not think that the Planck waves referenced here are in fact discrete; it is just that they often appear to create discrete frames from the remote-viewing experience. These Planck waves seem to exist in a 3+N dimensional universe that also houses apparently infinite probability waves which we describe with probability wave functions. The Planck waves themselves do not create our sense of time by themselves, but they contribute to this, as I describe below. I suggest that these waves vibrate in the form of "standing waves." Readers will note that a guitar string vibrates as a standing wave, in the sense that it vibrates but does not travel anywhere. I do not know if the Planck waves also travel as well as vibrate as standing waves, but for our current discussion we can say that they act simply as standing waves. Such a universe is depicted in figure 8.12 which shows an example of two such Planck waves.

In figure 8.12, a thread-like wavy line is used to represent a sequentially connected set of probabilities that exists in this universe, and they would exist as probability waves. For example, these probabilities can be associated with the flow of events associated with a war, or a person's life, and so on. Using the example of a person's life, at the beginning of the thread can be the probability of the person being born, followed at some later point by the respective probabilities of the person going to school, getting married, having a mid-life crisis, retiring, and finally dying. The Planck waves appear to be distributed throughout the universe as permanent and unchanging features. When the Planck waves intersect the event probabilities (such as those represented by the wavy line), superpositions result and the probabilities manifest as real events. The dotted lines on the Planck waves are the record of history (defined here as extending into both the past and future) as projected onto any given Planck wave.

Within any single Planck wave, there is only one current "now point." In figure 8.12, Planck wave A has an identified "now point" that exists at the intersection of the wave front with the sequentially connected event probability. If readers might imagine that the wave were to move upward in the figure, the

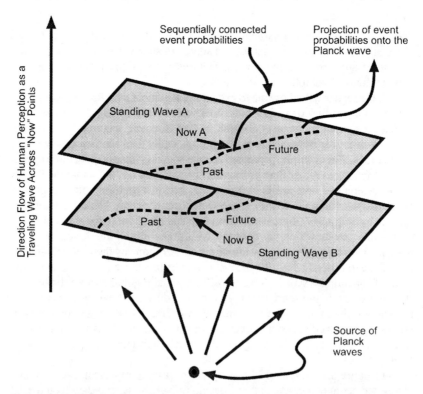

Figure 8.12. Planck standing waves in a probabilistic universe. Shifting perception across waves creates the appearance of movement and time.

intersection "now point" would change and follow the (dotted) history path that is traced along the moving intersection path. Other (and parallel) Planck waves (such as "wave front B") have their own dotted history paths. In most situations, the history paths are identical across waves, although the waves intersect the sequentially connected event probabilities in different places (that is, different "now points"). But with remote viewing, of course, it is possible to tune one's perceptions into a future "now point" (which means to perceive the future from a different Planck wave) and then to change the direction of history's path by altering one's current behavior. Nonetheless, for now let us consider a situation without such intervention, and the historical trajectories are traced identically across parallel Planck waves.

How does this compare with the Lissajous figure depicted in figure 8.9? The Lissajous figure is composed of lines that form the shape of a cylinder. The distribution of these lines (i.e., trajectories) are comparable to the distribution of the Planck waves in figure 8.12, with the primary exception being that the Planck waves in 8.12 are distributed throughout a probability space, and not with respect to time. Indeed, the Lissajous figure could have been constructed with respect to any variable, say W, and the time-based derivative was employed only for heuristic reasons given the introductory nature of the previous discussion. Also, note that the Planck waves shown in figure 8.12 appear as planes rather than lines.

More realistically, Planck waves must have at least three dimensions, and they help to create our reality as we perceive it from moment to moment. If one considers a sine wave, the crest of that wave is a point, and that point can be considered the point of maximum amplitude (or in this case, probability) for that wave. Increasing the dimensions by one, we have a rippled two-dimensional surface, and the crest of the wave becomes a line. This is how it is with ocean waves that one sees at the beach. That is, the crest of an ocean wave forms a line on the surface of the top of the wave, and one can think of that line as the position of maximum amplitude for the wave. Again increasing the dimensions by one, a wave becomes a "plane wave," and a sound wave traveling through air can be thought of as such a wave. The reader can imagine standing unhealthfully near the loudspeakers of a loud rock band at a concert, feeling the plane sound waves smash against your body. Light also travels as a plane wave. Increasing the dimensions by one yet again, and the waves are no longer planes but solid volumes, and it is within such waves that we live. Thus, the waves depicted as planes in figure 8.12 are presented as plane waves only to help the presentation of these ideas. The reality is that these waves have volume with at least three dimensions.

What then is time from this perspective? The intersection of the Planck waves in figure 8.12 with the sequentially connected event probabilities create the catching function discussed earlier with respect to the Lissajous figure. Time is the sequential experience of "now points" as they are perceived across parallel

Planck waves. That is, human time-based perception appears to move sequentially from wave B to wave A, and then on to an infinite series of other waves, one after another. The intersection of the Planck waves with the sequentially connected event probabilities creates the illusion of time for those who live within the volumes of the Planck waves when perception is structured sequentially from wave to wave. This means that we all experience a continuous stream of "now points" (that is, what we erroneously think of as our past and future) that seem invisible to one another. Each "now" point is located on a separate wave, and thus we can only remember the past with the help of our memory during normal wakeful consciousness. We experience time itself only instantaneously at any given "now point" associated with a superposition that results from an intersection of other probability waves with one and only one Planck wave.

But there is more to the idea of time, and I suspect strongly that the passage of time is connected directly to the value of Planck's constant. Planck's constant seems to be associated with the wavelength that separates the Planck waves, which may indeed be related to what some cosmologists call a "Planck length." (Note that we must use wavelength in this context, not period or frequency, since time is not yet an assumed quantity.) It is best to explain this from the perspective of a single photon. A photon exhibits qualities of both a wave and a particle because it is truly both. From the theory developed here, a photon is a static (i.e., non-moving) probability wave in a static probability universe. The photon's probability wave is intersected by Planck waves. As the amplitude of the Planck wave increases within the superposition, the probability of observing the photon as a particle increases, and the photon materializes as a discrete particle with a certain energy level, the energy level being dependent on the nature of the photon's probability wave at any given point. This is shown by example in figure 8.13.

Again, a Planck wave interacts with the probability wave of the photon to produce a superposition of both, thereby creating the manifestation of the physical photon. This superposition is, indeed, why observation registers any quantum event as a real event. If this theory outlined here turns out to be true, then this would resolve one of the mysteries of quantum mechanics, for it has never before been clear why observing a quantum event should cause the event to materialize. This also explains the "packet" quality of photons that Max Planck described, and it resolves why energy levels can only vary in discrete jumps that are multiples of Planck's constant. The photon can only manifest at intervals equivalent to the wavelength of a Planck wave. Outside of this, no superposition is possible regardless of energy level. Einstein later determined that these packets, or "quanta," not only materialize in discrete units, but they also travel as discrete quanta. But my analyses of these matters suggest that a photon appears to move as a wave not because it is actually moving, but because the Planck waves interact with the photon's probability wave in discrete steps (from crest to crest), much like frames in a movie. These discrete steps separated by the wavelength of Planck waves explain why time sometimes seems to have a discrete quality to it, an idea that finds some correspondence with the cosmological theory known as loop quantum gravity.

This, of course, leaves open the primary question of who or what is creating the Planck waves that flow through the probability universe. Indeed, many might say that this is the "million-dollar question." I have no immediate answer to this question. But from a cosmological perspective, this seems to suggest that the Big Bang was a focused and possibly instantaneous detonation of Planck waves within an otherwise static probability universe. Since remote viewing can perceive across time — and presumably back to the Big Bang — the Planck

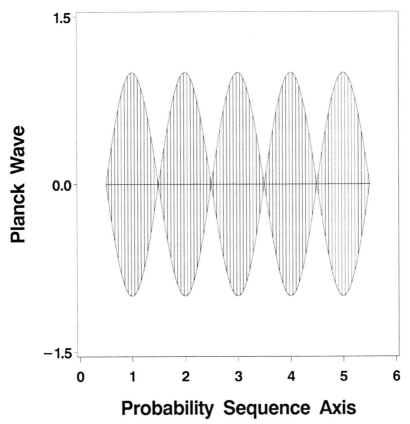

Probability Sequence Axis

Figure 8.13. A standing Planck wave over a photon's probability sequence axis. The photon materializes as a superposition at sequence states 1, 2, 3, 4, or 5 with increasing probability nearer the crests of the Planck wave.

waves may have immediately filled the entire universe. We perceive an evolving universe. But in fact, the evolution of the universe may already be complete; it is only our perception of this that is taking so very long.

There is no reason to assume that there exists only one wavelength for all Planck waves that permeate the universe. Indeed, a variety of such waves with different wavelengths could easily coexist, as seems the norm for nature with respect to waves in general. Indeed, if Planck waves do exist, I think we must assume that Planck waves of many wavelengths coexist until proven otherwise. If this is the case, then what we perceive as our universe would probably be limited to all those things within the larger probability universe that result from superpositions with Planck waves of a certain wavelength. If Planck's constant is directly related to the wavelength of such waves for our universe, then all other universes would be out of alignment with respect to us, superpositions would not occur due to destructive interference, and these universes would thus be invisible to us.

How might we refer to these universes that result from superpositions with Planck waves with wavelengths different from that of our own universe? Since wavelength is the key to the separation of universes, it might be best to describe universes that result from superpositions with Planck waves of shorter wavelength as having "higher density," whereas those universes resulting from longer wavelength superpositions as having "lower density." Here the term "density" corresponds to the closeness of spacing between the crests of the Planck waves. Yet it may turn out that the key here is not the wavelength spacing between individual Planck waves, but the vibrational frequency (or collection of frequencies) of each Planck wave, or perhaps a combination of these two things. The remote-viewing experience does not yet appear to shed light on such distinctions.

How might I summarize the discussion which I have made so far in this chapter? Perhaps there is a way to put all of this into a "nutshell," so to speak. The basic difference between my view of our universe and that of many other cosmologists is that they (the other cosmologists) tend to think of a person's perception as being fixed in one place while the universe is moving about the person. In my view, the remote-viewing evidence suggests that the reverse is true. Rather, the universe is fixed, and it is our perception of the universe that is moving. That is, our own consciousness acts as a moving or traveling wave that flows through an otherwise static universe (that is, one without physical movement). The universe appears to change and evolve as our perception shifts from frame to frame in discrete intervals separated by a length associated with Planck's constant. Our own waves of consciousness (one might call them waves of "awareness") do not travel through time, but rather establish a sense of time by the manner in which they manifest superpositions through their intermixing with other waves of apparent infinite variety. If any one of us were to cease to exist, the universe would not vanish. It would continue as a collection of superpositions, both vast and small. It is just that our own individual contribution to this would no longer be added to the mix. As odd as this may seem at first, it makes sense to me from the perspective of the remote-viewing experience.

I must here emphasize the obvious, that I do not know for certain whether these ideas are in fact true. But I can say without ambiguity that the remote-viewing experience seems to match these ideas more closely than it does any of the other extant cosmological theories. It should be possible for physicists eventually to devise laboratory experiments that directly test for the presence of Planck waves as I have described them here. It may be that these tests will require a combination of direct and indirect methods involving the elimination of alternative or competing hypotheses. I look forward to the day when such tests are devised and conducted.

The Meaning of Determinism

Let us now return to the two-slit experiment to help us define the meaning of "determinism." Einstein passionately felt that the universe was deterministic, that God did not play dice. If Einstein was correct, this would mean that there is an underlying cause that can explain every aspect of every phenomenon completely, with nothing being left to chance or probability. In such a universe, nothing would occur probabilistically. Stochasticity is simply the result of an observer not knowing what is really causing an event to occur. But quantum mechanics tells us that the universe really does behave probabilistically, and that there are no local hidden variables that would explain the manifestation of every event, if only one could know more about those variables. The cross-cutting psi channels remote-viewing experiment also suggests that at least some aspects of the macro universe are probabilistically structured. What then is determinism in the context of quantum events and remote viewing?

Determinism occurs when the probability of a single event collapses to unity. What causes this to happen from a probabilistic point of view? Consider a situation in which there is a line with three points equally spaced. Let us label these three points A, B, and C, and let us place point B in the middle of points A and C, as is done in figure 8.14. Any spot on the line given in this figure (or any line) is a point, and thus is infinitesimally small. But the space between any two points is entirely measurable. If one were trying to randomly choose a spot on the line between points A and C, there would be a 50 percent chance of

A   **B**   **C**

Figure 8.14. A line with three equally-spaced points

choosing a spot between points A and B, and another 50 percent chance of choosing a spot on the line between points B and C. But precisely choosing a particular point is a different matter from choosing any point from within a continuous range. If all points along a continuum on any line are given an equal probability of being chosen, the chance of choosing any given spot is infinitesimally small. Thus, from this point of view, the chance of randomly choosing exactly point B on the line in figure 8.14 is zero.

Now compare this with the situation encountered with the two-slit experiment. In that experiment, there is a 50 percent chance that a particle will travel through either of the two slits. Because a particle is actually a wave until it is observed, it travels through both of the slits simultaneously and subsequently records its encounter with measuring equipment probabilistically. But in other situations it is entirely possible to aim a particle at a particular spot and to hit it exactly. This is done with particle accelerators commonly, and it is the basis of many uses of radiation for medical purposes. The problem of not knowing where the particle will hit occurs when probability is inserted into its chosen path of travel. Similarly with remote viewing, it is relatively easy to remote view a single target accurately. But a probabilistic outcome occurs when competing targets are involved in the experiment. If we are to compare these situations with that presented in figure 8.14, we can analogously associate point B with our chosen target at which we aim our particle accelerator (without a two-slit barrier), or our single remote-viewing target. With such an analogy, it is easier for a particle accelerator or a remote viewer to precisely hit point B on the line in figure 8.14 than it is likely that a probabilistic process will yield a result that will hit any point either between A and B or between B and C. That is, with quantum events and remote viewing, it is easier to hit a point which occupies essentially a zero probability space along a continuum of possibilities than it is to manifest an event with a significant non-zero probability in the context of competing probabilistic outcomes! Moreover, with regard to probabilistically determined events, as long as the probabilities are significant, there will always be a probabilistic manifestation of all events given a sufficiently large number of repeated trials.

Recall that in an earlier chapter, we used the SAM computer program to choose targets that are assigned to a remote viewer. If SAM picks two targets and tries to determine if the remote-viewing data look like one or the other target, then a probabilistic event is created. Two attractors are formed which compete probabilistically. The discussion of the current chapter argues that it may be impossible to predict with deterministic certainty which target will be the correct target when it is subsequently chosen dynamically (that is, when the real target is chosen from among the two possibilities). Attempts to circumvent this phenomenon with SAM have focused on adding additional weight to one of the two targets by having SAM erase all evidence of one of the two targets (the one not chosen dynamically), and then having the remote viewer close the session on the chosen target. More work needs to be done with this to determine if this is a viable solution to this problem, thereby transforming what is essentially a probabilistic event into a deterministic one. While there is some reason to be hopeful in this regard, the final outcome is by no means certain at this point. It may not ever be possible to transform a probabilistic event into a deterministic event. But again, the book is not closed on this issue.

It is important to note here that when we have an experiment with only one remote-viewing target, we are still dealing with probability. It is just that the entire probability cloud is now focused on one target. Thus, the probability wave function collapses onto one event. From this we can draw a rule that is fundamental to the research presented in this volume.

BROWN'S RULE: The probability of being able to successfully remote view a target is inversely related to the size of this target's probability space relative to the combined probability space of all alternatives to this target under random choice conditions. For example, it is easier to remote view a target successfully that has a one in 500 chance of being chosen from a pool of 500 targets than it is to remote view a target that has a 0.5 probability of being chosen from a pool of two targets. This is due to the increased coherency of the interference caused by the probabilistic potential of the competing attractors that are associated with each of the possible targets when they are few in number. This coherency is produced by mental/observational activities which intentionally or unintentionally link the remote-viewing data collection process with the alternative targets. The most general conclusion to draw from this rule is that determinism results not from increasing the probability of a single outcome, but by eliminating the probabilistic coherency from the alternate attractors.

In remote-viewing experiments, when there are two competing targets, the interference pattern associated with the probability wave function becomes well established. As the number of targets increases, the interference pattern breaks down. To pick a target with deterministic accuracy requires one to randomize the interference pattern to the point where it essentially becomes white noise. Each remote-viewing target is a macro event, which means that by definition (at least my own) it is a superposition. Since each superposition is itself a wave, it can interfere constructively and destructively with another superposition. In the cross-cutting psi channels remote-viewing experiment, competing attractors are created as a by-product of this interference process. Drawing a remote-viewing target from a very large pool of possibilities breaks down the coherence of this interference process. Seen in this way, mathematicians will, of course, note that this is related to the probabilistic convergence of the Cauchy sequence $1/n$ as n approaches infinity, where n is the number of possible outcomes for an event. This is counter intuitive since the probability of choosing an outcome by chance decreases as the number of equally possible outcomes increases. With remote viewing it is the reverse due to the issue of attractor coherency across multiple targets. As *n* grows large, the probability wave function for remote viewing the correct target begins to collapse onto one point in the relevant probability space governing all possible outcomes, which means that the probability of remote-viewing the correct target under such circumstances moves in the direction of unity. Complete determinism is the total collapse of this probability wave function onto one point. At least, this is how it appears to me with respect to remote viewing.

World Lines, Relativity, and the Propagation of Events

This, of course, returns us to our universe. We observe only our own universe with our five physical senses. Due to speed of light limitations, there are severe limits even to our ability to observe this universe, and indeed there appear to be large realms of this universe that are simply off limits completely with respect to physical observation. (In particular, see Hawking and Penrose, 1996, pp. 97-8.) The other dimensions within which our physical reality is contained are also normally invisible to us. But then what do we really mean when we talk of "our universe?" Although I have made some suggestions regarding this above, I suspect that we do not yet truly know what defines a universe. More concretely, what separates one universe from another is not clear at all. Minimally, we can perhaps approach this question from the negative side and say that what is not in our universe is at least all that is not accessible to our five physical senses. In a more positive approach, we can say that a universe is most likely to consist of all those things (however distantly separated in time and space) which sit coherently in a setting of sequentially linked events.

Remote viewing apparently by-passes many of the limitations that are imposed on our physical ability to interact within our universe or across alternative universes. This means that physicists and cosmologists can now conduct experiments using remote viewing to further understand our overall dimensional context. But this also means that rules which we have applied to our own seemingly self-contained universe may not apply to these larger-dimensional settings, and we will likely have to modify our rules to account for what we discover using remote-viewing in our laboratories. For example, relativity theory does allow for breakdowns in the fabric of time and space. But such breakdowns (called "singularities") require huge amounts of energy, such as what one finds with black holes that seem to reside commonly in the center of galaxies. But physicist John Russell has noted to me in a private communication that such large quantities of energy are obviously missing from the remote-viewing experience, and if remote viewing is a real phenomenon, then there is something profoundly missing from the relativistic view of the universe.

One of the most important issues relating to the implications of remote viewing to cosmology is the ability to determine a set of possible future trajectories from any one point in space and time. That is, any given setting in our three-dimensional universe will evolve in time, at least as we perceive it. In practical terms, this will mean that things will move and change over time. Let us take the simple idea of something moving from point A to point B. Cosmologists often look at such changes in terms of something called a "world line." Using world lines, things can move about in our three-dimensional universe, but they cannot move faster than the speed of light. This means that there are certain future histories (and past histories) which are prohibited, in the sense that they cannot be "timelike." Such an impossibility would be if something moved from point A to point B with a velocity faster than the speed of light. Broadly interpreted, this means that some futures are impossible from the perspective of any given starting point since the evolution to that future could not occur without violating the laws of space and time.

Remote viewing adds a new perspective to this debate regarding what futures may be possible from a given starting point. This is because it appears possible to transfer at least information from a point A to a point B at a speed faster than light. I state that it only "appears" possible because we truthfully have not tested this exact proposition. We have used remote viewing to perceive into the past and the future, but it remains unclear exactly how this information is being transferred, and physicists will certainly want to know how this is done with respect to relativistic limitations of the speed of light. In a private communication with physicist John Russell, he discussed a possible test that many physicists might feel would be appropriate to evaluate this issue, and we also discussed the problems inherent in conducting such a test from a remote-viewing perspective. The idea is to have a remote viewer perceive when something is happening at a distance, and to report this information before the information could be reported via normal channels of communication. For example, if a robotic vehicle on Mars were to send a signal, and if the transmission of this signal could be perceived by a remote viewer before the signal could reach Earth via normal radio communications, this would be a significant experiment. The trouble from a remote-viewing perspective is that remote viewing tends to penetrate the future with ease, and the remote viewer would likely not be able to discern the difference between a perception of a future in which the signal will be sent and a perception of viewing and signal transmission in which both occur simultaneously. That is, the viewer might not be able to tell when the signal is sent, even if he or she can perceive the signal being sent. This is because it is not easy for a viewer to distinguish between the future, present, or past when remote viewing.

After working intensively with the remote-viewing phenomenon for a number of years, time clearly does not seem to be as concrete as it does in normal daily life. Bluntly, the remote-viewing experience suggests that there is no such thing as a universe whose evolution is truly structured by time. Rather, there is only a universe across space at an instant in time. What we perceive as time is actually a smooth and continuing transition from one point in a static universe that has no time to another point in a static universe that has no time. Using our simple model presented in figure 8.9, this would be accomplished by smoothly manipulating the catching function, which in terms of the model means gradually moving the cutting plane that dissects the Lissajous figure, thereby creating the elliptical Poincare map. As one moves this plane, the elliptical Poincare map would evolve in a continual fashion as it moves through different regions of the cylindrical Lissajous figure. This cutting plane that produces the Poincare map is analogous to our selecting and observing a set of points in a probabilistic universe. Moving the map creates the illusion of time. This simplified heuristic process outlined with this model helps explain how a remote viewer can perceive one future (that is, a possible future Poincare map) and then create another future in which the originally perceived events do not occur. Indeed, in my own way of thinking, I like to think of myself as living a "Poincare life." We are all living Poincare lives in the sense described here.

All this implies that there is little essential difference between alternate universes and the future or past of one universe. The future of one universe is in reality only the selection of a perception path across a diverse collection of probability waves such that a sequential history seems to manifest. A different selection of alternative points produces the appearance of an alternate universe, with each universe having suggestive coherence like separate pages in a large book. But this may be a false sense of reality. The universes may not really be separate and distinct. What seems to really matter is that which defines the catching function such that it intersects the existent probability waves in a manner that gives the appearance of universal coherence at an instant in time. It is my bet that this catching function is crucially determined by the spacing between Planck waves, and that our ostensible universe is created by the alignment of observable wavelengths as limited and structured by the value of Planck's constant. This is why we cannot sense the past or the future with our five physical senses any more than we can perceive the realities of other universes.

Our physical perceptions are strictly limited by that which is defined by the catching function. It is the nature of how Planck waves create a multiplicity of discrete (and thus separate) observing hypersurfaces that create the illusion that all that is past ceases to exist, and all that is in the future does not yet exist. In a single universe that is composed of superpositions with Planck waves of one wavelength, we cannot see the past or the future with our physical senses because our "now point" is not aligned with a past or future superposition. In the alternative case of perceiving a universe composed of superpositions with Planck waves of one wavelength from the perspective of a different universe composed of superpositions with Planck waves of a different wavelength, the result is the same. We cannot perceive the other universe with our normal senses because the superpositions of both universes are out of alignment.

It is useful for us to simplify our discussion of many universes. We can loosely use the words "alternate universes" in many contexts to include both alternate time paths in one universe and truly alternate universes with Planck waves of varying wavelengths. This simplification of our language is useful as long as we understand that these various universes differ primarily in terms of the selections of points of intersection between the catching function and the extant probability waves that in total define the possibilities of all that may exist across all universes. Moreover, it does no harm also to describe these various universes as separate collections of perception points that resemble leaves in a large book, as long as we recognize that this is a simplification of what is actually a much more complex phenomenon of multiple realities. Further simplifying our language, we can also talk of universes that evolve in time, since this is how we perceive them.

Employing this looser definition of the term "universe," how then does an event in "spacetime" evolve? The remote-viewing experience suggests that there exists a Poincare set in the collection of all such possible sets as described above for which the conditions are such that a particular event will have the highest probability of occurrence. That is, there is a unique universe for which one particular event will most likely happen. I call this the universe of origin for this event. There are, however, many other universes (that is, Poincare sets) that are very similar to this universe of origin. What appears to happen is that the event which begins in the universe of origin propagates through the other universes in a probabilistic fashion. That is, the probability of an event happening in any given universe depends on how similar that universe is to the universe of origin with respect to that particular event. As universes increasingly diverge in character, the probability of that event occurring in such universes decreases.

In my own view, this reduction in probability for an event to occur in universes which differ significantly is due to the way probability waves which create all events interfere with one another. That is, in universes which are highly similar, the probability waves which create events amplify one another via the process of constructive interference. When universes differ significantly, the waves conflict with one another and the process of destructive interference dominates. In an overly simplistic sense, an event manifests in one universe as a consequence of the interaction of many quantum-originating probability waves. Certain interactions among these probability waves result in the creation of particular events. In similar universes, the waves are similarly in alignment with regard to their potential to closely reproduce these events. When the various and interacting probability waves which result in the manifestation of an event in one universe are no longer in approximate wavelength alignment with the probability waves in a different universe with respect to this event, the process of destructive interference dominates and the event does not replicate in the second universe. This means that other events happen in such universes as the probability waves for those universes interact in different ways.

The propagation of events across universes is just one of many problems that physicists and cosmologists will want to consider with respect to remote viewing. Such problems may seem minor to some people when compared with some of the other issues raised in this chapter and volume. Nonetheless, they are all part of the same puzzle, one which we will have to deal with in new and innovative ways as we learn more about our own existence.

Perhaps the greatest puzzle upon which I ponder regularly is the role of observation. Of course, I do not think that we ourselves are the creators of the universe because we look up into the sky. Nor do I think (as Einstein once mocked this aspect of the quantum view) that the Moon would disappear if we did not look at it. But the remote-viewing experience nonetheless seems to suggest that all which we see around us is an interactive consequence involving observation, which is another way of saying "measurement," "awareness," or "consciousness."

All of this put together implies that all of physical reality may actually be an artifact of observation in some fashion, and that our true nature as beings in this universe is in the form of interacting probability waves which encompass the many-universe collection of ourselves. If this is true, then the real question becomes not so much what is physical reality, but rather what is consciousness such that it can interact with these probability wave functions with such a high degree of structure? In this chapter I have spoken of consciousness as a wave capable of producing a superposition with other waves. But if this is true, then how do multiple consciousnesses of many humans interact probabilistically to produce through superposition a collective reality that we recognize as a society? Finally, if our relatively small consciousnesses can interact with quantum realities to materialize elementary events, whose consciousness is materializing the remainder of our universe, and all other universes? We return, of course, to the ultimate cosmological question.

Some critics will certainly argue that the primary problem with my theories outlined here is that quantum phenomena work only on the quantum level, and there is a big difference between that level and the macro level which is better understood relativistically. But this is not a fair argument. For example, physics experiments often investigate complex wave phenomena in which there are essentially an infinite number of ways in which frequencies (and thus waves) interact. To understand some of this complexity, physicists conduct a simplified experiment involving a light source and two flat surfaces (the two-slit experiment) to demonstrate that a photon or electron can be in two places at the same time. This simplified experiment does not explain all of the other complexities in which waves behave bizarrely in the macro universe. It does however point to an underlying reality of physical existence that in turn reveals a more complex underpinning to "all that is."

Similarly, I have pointed to a simplified remote-viewing experiment that also demonstrates an underlying reality to our physical existence. All of my research presented in this volume began with the observation that under certain circumstances (i.e., the cross-cutting psi channels experiment of chapter 3) a remote-viewing outcome depends probabilistically in a manner consistent with the two-slit light experiment in physics. This observation does not allow me to explain every other macro behavior. But remote viewing is at least one phenomenon that can be demonstrated on the macro level that appears to mirror a phenomenon that has previously been identified only on the quantum level, thereby establishing a link between the macro and quantum levels that has heretofore not been known to exist. Simply noting that remote viewing is a real phenomenon that breaks many of the previously understood laws of Einstein-defined relativistic reality that govern the relationships of time and space surely argues the case that what I write in this chapter is at least plausible. Even if some of my arguments are incorrect, recognizing their plausibility at least moves us forward in terms of understanding both who we are and the realm within which we exist.

That there is at least one dimension that connects all of these probabilistic universes should now be clear, and in this discussion I have chosen to call this Planck's dimension. Cosmologists will certainly want to think about whether or not this particular dimension is in fact at the root of variations in our probabilistic existence. But the fact that one or more non-physical dimensions must exist should now be beyond doubt, at least from my perspective. Perhaps we can at least agree on that much.

As interesting as I find the idea of nonphysical dimensions, there will nonetheless be people for whom there will be a different "bottom line" for the research that I have presented here. For some this may very well be the understanding that (from a remote-viewing experiential perspective) there is nothing truly unique about ourselves or any particular thing that we do. Nothing is "set in stone," so to speak. No person nor any history is totally unique. We can remote view into the future or the past as if all events are simultaneous, and in so doing we collapse or entangle a probability wave so that this point which we observe changes from a probabilistic smear into what we would like to think of as a "real thing." If we remote view the future, and if we want to arrive at that future, we set a mental path to that future that effectively collapses a probability wave to produce a sure-footed trajectory in phase space. On the other hand, just because we distill a probabilistic future from a "future smear," we may not want to go there. Thus, it is possible to remote view ourselves doing things that we eventually may or may not do, depending on whether or not we consciously choose to follow a perceived "future history," or to create another. This latter case seems truly to be a consequence of free will, and if our existence is in fact defined in terms of probability waves, free will is a real possibility.

I am fully aware that all of this sounds strange from the perspective of normal everyday experience. But this is the way the universe seems to work from at least my own subjective remote-viewing perspective. Again, I am assuming and expecting that cosmologists who specialize in such theories will look at these ideas through their own intellectual lenses. But given the conflicting nature of many cosmological theories and the sparse degree of physical evidence that exists for some of their theoretical components, it certainly would not hurt — and indeed it may well be worthwhile — for cosmologists to consider remote-viewing derived ideas such as those presented in this volume as a means of assisting the development of their own theories.

CHAPTER 9

A Theory of Mind

These investigations bring us to a new precipice in our understanding of the human mind. In my view, it now seems certain that humans have a nonlocal and nonphysical mind in addition to their physical brains. The research presented in this volume clearly points to what I suggest we should now call "the fact" that the human mind perceptually extends beyond the five physical senses due to the existence of a nonphysical component of consciousness that is not bound — at least in part — by the laws of Newtonian and relativistic physics that govern the behavior of traditionally understood physical systems. Remote viewers directly experience realities to which they are not physically connected and to which they have no physical source of information. It is simply not possible to continue to claim that human consciousness is a total by-product of only the activity of the brain since nonphysical mechanisms of perception that transcend the range of the five physical senses are logically required to explain the remote-viewing phenomenon. If we can accept this reality that should by now be transparent to those capable of objectively evaluating the facts of this case, we can proceed to interesting questions which address the nature and psychology of the nonphysical (subspace) mind, which are relatively unexplored areas of research in this field.

Yet we still need to deal with the subject of the dimensional residence for the nonphysical mind. As is consistent with the vocabulary used throughout this volume, we refer to the nonphysical mind as the "subspace mind." The use of the term "subspace" is tied to the idea that the nonphysical mind — while indeed nonphysical — is nonetheless totally real and that it must exist within some dimensional space that encompasses and simultaneously extends beyond the physical realm. This nonphysical realm we define as "subspace," and up to this point I have posited that the term refers to all dimensions not included in our normally perceived three dimensional space. But some may wish to argue that the subspace realm can include the physical realm, since the subspace mind clearly has easy access to the physical realm. In general, I see no need to quarrel with the idea that subspace is the more encompassing category. But the reverse is not true; the physical realm appears to stop at its own borders.

The idea that the physical realm should be contained within the subspace realm may be seen as a logical requirement of the fact that remote viewing is a phenomenon that is performed by physical human beings who exist in physical reality. It is the interface between our physical and subspace minds that allows the subspace mediated perceptions to be known to physical consciousness. Our subspace minds have access to all of physical reality, and these same subspace minds feed information into our physical brains. But our brains do not have reciprocal capabilities. For example, our physical brains cannot perceive physical realities that are separated by long distances without technological assistance, and it is impossible for our physical brains to simultaneously perceive through any known technological means physical realities that are separated in time. Thus, subspace may indeed be considered the broader dimensional category of existence, and physical reality is at best a subset of subspace.

Let us now cut to the chase. Since the subspace mind must exist (at least from my perspective) in order to explain the remote-viewing experience, and since a dimensionally compatible subspace realm must exist as a residence for all that exists in subspace, then we may have identified what appears to be the human soul and its realm of existence. Also, since the word "mind" carries with it the connotation of a computational device that works on the level of ideas — a process that is most likely physiologically dependent — it makes sense to refer to the subspace mind not as a "mind" but as an "aspect," to which the brain is its physical counterpart. For this reason we refer to the nonphysical component of the self as the "subspace aspect." Are we then ready to state that the human subspace aspect is the human soul?

Readers should be aware that a lively debate "quietly rages" in academia as to whether or not a human soul actually exists. Some people think that a physiological basis for consciousness is all there is. For example, the late Dr. Francis Crick, who discovered with Dr. James D. Watson DNA's structure as a double helix, had recently been investigating with Dr. Christof Koch the nature of consciousness as a by-product of brain physiology. He extended his interpretation of his findings on the brain to suggest that there is no human soul. For example, Dr. Crick was quoted in *The New York Times* to say, "I'm not convinced that people want to know how consciousness works. They feel cast out of the world of meaning." He then concludes that an understanding of how the brain organizes consciousness "will lead to the death of the soul.... In the fullness of time, educated people will believe there is no soul independent of the body, and hence no life after death" ("After the Double Helix: Unraveling the Mysteries of the State of Being," by Margaret Wertheim, *The New York Times*, Tuesday, 13 April 2004, p. D3[N]).

In my view, the findings presented in this volume contrast starkly with Dr. Crick's interpretation of consciousness. From the perspective of remote viewing, it seems clear that consciousness is not limited to the physical brain. I can state this unambiguously even though we do not yet fully understand the physics of the human soul. Something that we like to call "consciousness" extends beyond the physical boundaries brain, and this same "something" is able to pierce the cloak of time with ease. If a remote viewer can perceive a target that existed before he or she was born, or a target that exists in the future after he or she is physically dead, it seems premature (at least to me) for anyone to claim that there is "no life after death."

Subspace Psychology

Let us deal with this most pregnant topic from the perspective of what we have already observed. We have already begun a new field of science, subspace psychology. Traditional psychology has deep roots in the physiological underpinnings of consciousness. Indeed, psychiatry is nearly totally based on the understanding of the human mind from a physical perspective, and the treatments of mental diseases are nearly entirely restricted to chemical palliatives and physical interventions. Even traditional psychotherapy attempts to cure mental dysfunctionality by allowing patients the ability to work through thoughts or ideas that have physiological representations in the storage machinery of the brain. But the idea that our mental functioning may transcend the physical brain to a nonphysical realm is generally a new element to the study of the human mind. Only rarely have mainstream outlets for traditional psychological analysis dared to extend their reach beyond the physical domain, such as was done in the January 1994 issue of the *Psychological Bulletin* in its report of research by psychologists Daryl J. Bem and Charles Honorton on the subject of telepathic communication between human subjects.

If we are to initiate this new field of subspace psychology, let us begin by organizing what we now know about the behavior of the human subspace aspect. From the basic remote-viewing experience we first note that the subspace aspect does appear to work on the level of awareness and not on the level of ideas. That is, when a remote viewer receives a subspace mediated perception, the perception is not a word or phrase but rather a collection of impressions that directly appeal to the five senses. For example, if a remote viewer is to perceive a beach on the ocean, the viewer will likely perceive the gritty texture of the sand (without knowing for sure if it is sand), the wetness of the water (without knowing for sure that it is water), the smell of perfume (without knowing for sure if this is suntan oil), the sound of the pounding waves (without knowing for sure that waves are making the sounds), and so on. That is, the perceptions are direct from the target, and these perceptions arrive raw without being translated (that is, "decoded") into words that identify and label the source of the perceptions. Words and their associated ideas are the currency of the physiological brain. The human subspace aspect bypasses words and ideas, and thus it is necessary for remote viewers to re-introduce these things into the remote-viewing process by associating words and ideas with these direct perceptions. Scientific Remote Viewing as well as some other remote-viewing methodologies work by establishing a method by which these associations can be made in a relatively reliable fashion.

Remote viewing is a reductionist process. It takes the perceptions mediated through the subspace aspect and describes them using words that have the lowest levels of abstract meaning. The process has interesting parallels with dream interpretation, an extensively developed area in psychology. A heuristically useful approach to dream interpretation was once explained to me by the gifted theologian, Dr. John Rossner, Director of the Montreal based International Institute of Integral Human Sciences. Dr. Rossner bases his dream interpretation method on the answers to the three properties (1) do, (2) look, (3) feel. Using one of his own examples, if a person has a dream with, say, a lion, the person would then be asked, "What does a lion do that is unique to the lion?" The person may say that a lion roars. Then the person with the dream would be asked, "What does the lion look like?" The answer may be that the lion looks big, strong, bold, and admirable. Finally the person is asked how the lion makes him or her feel, to which the person may respond that the lion frightens. From the answers to these questions a therapist can begin to discern the nature of the things that may be affecting the person by seeing parallels between the given answers and the physical, social, and economic realities of the person's life. That is, the lion is a word that represents a high-level idea or set of ideas. The trick to interpreting the meaning of the lion is to break the high-level idea down into parts that have the lowest level of intellectual abstraction, thereby arriving at the true meaning of the dream experience.

The remote-viewing decoding process works in reverse by trying to avoid the really high-level ideas in the first place. With remote viewing, one begins with direct perceptions and then learns to decode these perceptions into low-level ideas and their associated words. These words are accumulated and a higher-level picture is gradually developed. In the dream example given above, if we are to frame it in the manner in which remote viewing works, we would begin with the sounds of a roar, the concepts of big, strong, bold, and admiration, and the feelings of fear. From there we begin to develop the idea of a lion, which in SRV would probably be recorded as a "deduction" (see glossary). Now in the dream, the idea of a lion comes first, and it means something entirely else. This is to say that the lion does not mean a lion in the dream, and thus we are not really interested in the lion per se. We decode the dream into its low-level components in order to arrive at the original meaning of the dream. With remote viewing we work directly with the original perceptions and attempt to maintain our process of decoding the original perceptions on a low-level of description, thereby producing a collection of words that do not over-interpret the original perceptions.

Dr. Rossner works with drama in dreams in a similar fashion, again using a process that is somewhat the reverse of the SRV process. First he sketches the story in the dream using high-level words, such as describing someone driving a car. Next he has the person who has the dream repeat the story using only synonyms, which forces a re-phrasing of the process in the dream into more universal terms that are inherently low-level. In the car example, the person may then say that he was moving from point A to point B in a vehicle. Again, with remote viewing we would proceed in the opposite fashion, first noting that a person is moving from point A to point B in some sort of moving structure. Only later — after we are given the target specific — would we know for certain that the person was driving a car, the ideas of "driving" and a "car" being relatively high-level. The goals for both remote viewing and the dream interpretation process are the same, however. To understand the true meaning behind both dreams and subspace originating perceptions one needs to reduce their content down into descriptions of their most basic components.

The bottom-line message relevant to the process of remote viewing that we are to draw from this is that the physical/subspace interface must transmit direct perceptions, while the brain must process these perceptions into ideas and their associated words. If we jump into interpreting the perceptions too quickly at a high-level of abstraction, we are likely to lose the real meaning of the perceptions.

This, of course, reminds us of Edmund Husserl's pregnant statement, "Generally speaking, perception is original consciousness" (Husserl, 1999, p. 222). Indeed, Husserl was profoundly concerned with the matter of original consciousness, and his method of phenomenological reduction is designed to identify original consciousness as it can be re-understood from the confused interpretations of direct perceptions. For Husserl, the world as it is interpreted by the individual in the aftermath of original perceptions is what he calls the "world in brackets." (See Husserl, 1999, p. 325).

There are, in fact, strong parallels between the SRV process and phenomenological reduction. From Husserl, "The method of phenomenological reduction (to the pure 'phenomenon,' the purely psychical) accordingly consists (1) in the methodical and rigorously consistent epoché of every objective positing in the psychic sphere, both of the individual phenomenon and of the whole psychic field in general; and (2) in the methodically practiced seizing and describing of the multiple 'appearances' as appearances of their objective units and these units as units of component meanings accruing to them each time in their appearances" (Husserl, 1999, p. 325). The process of phenomenological reduction acts to return the experiences of an individual back to their original state as manifestations of original consciousness. This is analogous to putting a baby back into the womb. One then has to re-understand the experience while avoiding the pitfalls of automatically associating high-level ideas to that experience that are reflexively tied to a process of categorization.

To re-understand the original meaning of an experience, one follows phenomenological reduction with eidetic reduction. With eidetic reduction, intuition is used to perceive what Husserl calls the "essence" of all things and experiences. From a practical point of view, this is done by varying the perception of an object or experience. This is analogous to changing one's perspective, say, of a table, looking at it from above, then below, and so on. One then notes that which does not change during this process. The unchanging element Husserl calls the "invariant," and this is the essence of the object of perception.

Once one locates the essence of an object of perception, it is then necessary to place this pure essence of awareness within the structure of time or process. This is done in a third step that Husserl calls "transcendental reduction," following (with modification) Kant's understanding of transcendental consciousness. Husserl's methods of phenomenological investigation (further developed by Martin Heidegger and others) through the three-step process of reduction is fundamentally designed to discover the manner in which knowledge of the world manifests. Although SRV as well as some other remote-viewing methodologies were developed without a conscious a priori connection to Husserl's reduction process, it is striking to note the parallels in approach.

Subspace psychology is then the psychology of the pure self as it exists prior to the redefinition of being that occurs when original perceptions are channeled through the physical/subspace interface into physiologically based consciousness. The reinterpretation of direct experience within the framework of a biological computational device such as the brain produces an artificial form of intelligence that humans tend to mistake for their essential selves. Again, the low-bandwidth perceptual connection of the physical/subspace interface makes this situation of mistaken identity nearly impossible to avoid without the use of extraordinary means that are specifically designed to circumvent the limitations of the interface. The remote-viewing process is one such means that works by training remote viewers to recognize direct perceptions while simultaneously utilizing a reductionist process that accumulates a written record of observed elements (data) which associates as little interpretive meaning as possible to the elements and their organization. Remote viewing is possible because it is also possible to train people to restrain their normal thought-categorizing processes of physiological consciousness. It is necessary to do this because the processes of thought as we commonly understand them are apparently alien to the psychology of the human subspace aspect. Thus, by knowing what it is not, we understand a bit more about what the subspace aspect actually is.

All of these matters really address only attributes of the human subspace aspect. We really do not yet understand its overall psychology, even though these attributes are part of its overall psychological superstructure. But does the human subspace aspect have a personality that is independent of the personality exhibited by physiological consciousness? I do not know the answer to this. I suspect that my own personality is probably one component of a larger personality held by my larger self as defined by my subspace aspect. But I have no proof of this. Indeed, the need to answer questions such as this one is one of the driving motivations to continue research in this area of subspace psychology.

But let us now pull back a bit. This is not the first volume of research that has been motivated by a desire to understand the nature of the human soul, as is evidenced (to cite just one notable example) by F. W. H. Myers seminal and wide ranging report of psychic functioning and the human personality originally published in 1903 (Myers, 2001). While it is not possible here to review all of the various attempts to offer a theoretical framework of the soul together with empirical support for such frameworks, a few pointed examples from a particularly interesting approach seems likely to bear great fruit.

Alternative Perspectives of the Human Subspace Aspect

Doctors Raymond A. Moody, Melvin Morse, and Gary E. R. Schwartz have been pioneers (among others) in studying the phenomenon known as the near-death experience. Some individuals such as Betty J. Eadie, Dannion Brinkley, and Joseph McMoneagle have had such experiences and have become well known to the general public. (For example, see Moody 1975; Brinkley and Perry 1994; Schwartz, et al. 2002; McMoneagle 1993, pp. 27-34.) These are situations in which a person experiences either a sudden or gradual deterioration in their health leading to near death. Typically they are then resuscitated, and they explain to those who are willing to listen that they saw wonders beyond imagination while in that state of near death. The stories told usually include the perception of their physical bodies from an outside perspective, usually from above. These people then tend to report that they witnessed the events surrounding the attempts to resuscitate their bodies, often including details of these experiences that should have been unknown to their physical consciousness at that time. The stories often also include descriptions of other nonphysical beings, "light beings" so to speak, who counsel them and show them seemingly miraculous places while they await a return to their physical bodies. These death-induced out-of-body experiences also typically involve a visual perspective that originates from an other-dimensional reflection of their physical bodies, one which is in full health and which does not feel the pain associated with their physical bodies.

Critics of the out-of-body experience, especially those induced by a near-death experience, have argued — among other things — that these experiences are the product of physiological consciousness under conditions of extreme stress. That is, the brain is firing neurons in a dream-like state to produce stories of seemingly wondrous conditions as a means of mentally escaping the reality of near-death trauma.

I once returned from a conference in Montreal in which I heard both Dr. Moody and Dr. Morse explain in detail the nature of the experiences that their patients have experienced. The experiences seem to have too much conformity to be a product of individual imagination. Particularly telling are the incidents described by Dr. Morse in which his patients are young children who would be less susceptible to correlating their stories with a culturally established pattern. The question remains as to what we can make of these experiences given what we know of subspace psychology from our studies in remote viewing.

There are two primary issues here. The first is the nature of the pseudo body that houses the perspective of the near-death experiencers during the time when they seem to be out-of-body. Is this reflection of the human physical body the person's soul? The second issue that we need to deal with here is the nature of the nonphysical realm that is reported by the near-death experiencers.

With regard to the first issue, the remote-viewing experience suggests that the human subspace aspect is not localized in any sense. It can focus its perceptions through the physical body, but it is not the physical body. It acts almost like an ever-present and omnipresent energy field. On the other hand, the near-death out-of-body "body" seems very real to those who experience it, even though it cannot be seen by other physical beings. What then is this out-of-body "body?" (See also the interesting description of this phenomenon from the perspective of hypnagogia by Mavromatis 1987, pp. 131-59).

In this volume I have dealt solely with remote-viewing experiences using totally verifiable physical targets, such as a monumental structure, Mt. Everest, and so on. What I have not reported is an entirely different set of remote-viewing experiences that nearly everyone who practices remote viewing extensively eventually has, and that is the experience of perceiving beings that are more subspace than physical. Remote-viewing experiences of this kind need to be examined with a grain of salt. First, the remote viewer needs to have a record of accurately perceiving physical targets. Second, the perception of nonphysical or subspace beings (complete with subspace "bodies") needs to occur under conditions of total blind controls in which the viewer does not know or even suspect that the target can have nonphysical components. Nonetheless, under situations that are as well controlled as those reported in this volume, experienced remote viewers have reported perceiving persons, places, and events in the nonphysical realm that I describe here as subspace. Importantly, the shape of subspace persons seems to parallel closely their physical counterparts. Assuming this to be true (if only for the purpose of continuing this line of thought), do these subspace beings that seem localized in some sense also have access to a more encompassing subspace aspect that is not localized?

At the current time we do not know the answers to these questions. However, speculation is probably worthwhile in the current setting. Since the reports of near-death induced out-of-body experiences seem to correspond with remote-viewing data that suggest that localized subspace entities do exist, I suspect it likely that both are true. Let me make the following suggestions, and I offer these suggestions not as things proven but rather as possibilities worth thinking about. First, I suspect that the human subspace aspect has an ability to produce "localized manifestations." (Note that I do not add "of itself.") These localized manifestations are probably analogous to a form of concentrated energy, and they can take a form, such as the form of a human body. These localized manifestations are subspace things in their entirety, and we can think of them as subspace entities. But in reality they are more like extensions of a much larger thing, which is the entirety of the subspace aspect itself. From this depiction, I suspect that the out-of-body "bodies" that are reported by the near-death experiencers are actually localized manifestations of the subspace aspect.

Is it possible for the subspace aspect to create more than one localized manifestation? I see no reason why this could not be so. If a subspace aspect is everywhere at all times, I see no reason why we should enforce an artificial limit on this aspect of one localized manifestation. It indeed may be possible (perhaps probable) that a subspace aspect could focus its perceptions through more than one localized manifestation. This touches the subject of re-incarnation, of course, which goes well beyond the purpose or extent of this volume. Also, in the absence of time as per the results for the Alpha Project, it would seem that the idea of reincarnation is a misnomer itself, since multiple localized manifestations would occur following the rule of sequential simultaneity rather than as separate events truly removed from one another in time.

These speculations necessarily address the experiences not just of people who came breathtakingly close to death, but also those of spiritual leaders who have claimed equally profound experiences that they insist extend beyond the physical realm. For example, St. Augustine wrote elegantly about the nature and form of the human soul. In his *Confessions* (Book XII) he writes, "And my mind stopped questioning my spirit — (filled as it was) with the images of formed bodies, changing and varying them as it would. And I devoted myself to the bodies themselves, and looked more deeply into their changeable character, by which they ceased to be what they had been, and began to be what they were not. This same shifting from form to form I suspected to be through some formless condition, not through a mere nothing.... But what is this changeableness? Is it soul? Is it body? Is it the outward appearance of soul or body?" (Helms 1986, p. 261). Truly St. Augustine was as perplexed as we are about this very question of the definition of the soul, and he too questioned the relationship between what I would call the overall subspace aspect (his "formless condition") and the local manifestations described above.

The Apostle John in the book of Revelations similarly reports profound perceptions that extend beyond the physical realm. The Apostle John and St. Augustine are examples of individuals who spent years attempting to perceive the greater realm that their intuitions told them *must be*. Given what we know about the value of training in obtaining successful perceptions through the physical/subspace interface, it makes sense that such deeply spiritual people would at least occasionally have authentic and profound "visions" that were not a product of their imagination. When John writes in Revelations 1:12-3, "Then I turned to see whose voice it was that spoke to me, and on turning I saw seven golden lampstands, and in the midst of the lampstands I saw one like the Son of Man, clothed with a long robe and with a golden sash across his chest," it is not hard for me to suspect that he probably witnessed an authentic localized manifestation of a subspace entity. And of the dual nature — both physical and subspace — of the bodily form, this seems directly correspondent with what St. Paul refers to when he declares in 1st Corinthians 15:42-4, "So it is with the resurrection of the dead.... It is sown a physical body, it is raised a spiritual body. If there is a physical body, there is also a spiritual body."

One spiritual tradition that has interesting parallels with the physical/subspace interpretations drawn in this volume concerns the Hekaloth mystical experience of Cabalistic Judaism. Roughly translated, "Hekaloth" means mansions, or realms, and its use probably parallels Jesus's meaning when he states, "In my Father's house are many mansions" (John 14:2). In the earliest forms of Cabalism, Merkabah mystics practiced various techniques in order to produce trance states in which they attempted to pierce the veil of higher dimensional realities that they believed to exist. The point that is relevant in this setting is that these early mystics clearly understood that there was another realm greater than the physical, and that it was not easy to perceive this realm. They eventually concluded that there were various levels to this greater reality (all of which we would call subspace in the current context), and that these various levels were populated by entities in great variation.

Islam also has its own approaches to mystical spirituality, and Sufism is one such tradition. Within Sufism are orders such as the Whirling Dervishes, Howling Dervishes, Shaven Dervishes, Silent Dervishes, and others. The common bond between these orders is the belief that it is possible to do things (mostly in trance-like states) that enable a person to have true experiences that are of a nonphysical nature. Again, the idea is that special techniques are needed in order to perceive beyond the physical barrier to subspace. In this respect, Sufism correlates with aspects of Hinduism, Buddhism, and other approaches to spirituality that maintain their own lists of methods for piercing this barrier.

While it is easy for those from a more Western "scientific" tradition to dismiss these historically rooted practices and beliefs, given our current understanding of subspace it seems more productive to assume that the intense efforts of these early mystics across a variety of traditions probably produced occasional results that helped them obtain perceptions through the physical/subspace interface. Their interpretations of these perceptions undoubtedly were mixed with many of the ideas and beliefs that were current in their day. But the more one understands the nature of the human subspace aspect, the more one understands the historical drive of humans to be spiritual. Indeed, the inner need to understand our spirituality is not an artifact of confused thinking linked to an inadequate understanding of physical reality. Rather, the need of humans to understand their inner spiritual nature is a natural consequence of the fact that we are indeed spirits in the true sense of the word. Perhaps we can now claim this as a scientific fact.

Remote viewing works as a reduction method to systematically record and organize subspace derived perceptions. This is not the out-of-body experience. When people hover near death, they are apparently thrown into a powerfully transformative experience that re-positions a localized and partial manifestation (or perhaps "concentration" might be a better word) of their subspace aspect. Remote viewing works without this powerful re-positioning of this localized manifestation of the subspace personality. Others who have attempted to use different methods are likely to have had a mixture of good and bad results, depending on various thematic and idiosyncratic conditions. But the bottom line is that such experiences can be real, not imaginary. That some of these experiences may have become a historical basis for belief systems in various spiritual traditions should not surprise anyone. There will always be a need for humans to put into context experiences that seem so alien to the "normal" perceptual processes that depend only on the five senses. We may now be at a stage in our own intellectual development to be able to understand the underlying true nature of these experiences from a scientific perspective, and this also should not surprise most reasonable people. It is only natural to assume that we will eventually understand all phenomena which initially perplex us. Patience is more valuable than intellectual rejection in this context.

Of Time and Free Will

We cannot close this volume without returning to the issue of time. Interestingly, St. Augustine came to conclusions similar to my own with respect to time. He felt that the past, present, and future could not really be as distinct as our physical perceptions made them appear to be. In Book XI of his *Confessions*, he writes, "For what is time? Who can readily and briefly explain this? .... Those two times, then, past and future — how are they, when the past is no longer and the future is not yet? But should the present always be present and never pass into time past, truly it would not be time, but eternity. If, then, the very condition of the present's being 'time' is that it passes away into the past, how can we assert the existence of that whose only cause of *being* is that it shall *not be* — so that in truth we assert the present to be time only because it tends toward *not-being*?" (Helms 1986, pp. 241-2.) Similarly, St. Augustine writes, "O my God, rule and guide me. Who will tell me that there are not three times, as we learned when we were boys, and as we taught boys, the past, present and future, but only present, because past and future do not exist? Or do they also exist and when from the future it becomes present, does it come out of some secret place, and the same when from the present it becomes past, does it retire to something secret? For where have they, who foretold things to come, seen them if they do not yet exist? For what is not cannot be seen. And they who relate things past could not relate them if they did not perceive them in their mind, and if they were not, they could not be discerned in any way. Therefore, future and past times *are*" (Helms 1986, p. 244).

St. Augustine's words on the nature of time and the human soul so closely parallel my own interpretation of many of the remote-viewing data described in this volume that I suspect his deeply spiritual views are truly tied to profound perceptions of existence beyond the physical realm. Could it be that he obtained these insights from merely a physically based consciousness? Must it not be that he perceived a greater reality to his existence as it was transmitted through his own physical/subspace interface?

But what of this thing called "time?" If time truly is an illusion of perception, and the past, present, and future all simultaneously exist, can it be said that human beings have free will? That is, if the future already exists, can we determine our own fate? The basis of this question rests with the assumption that free will is possible only if the future does not exist, and free will is needed to create the future out of whole cloth, so to speak. But this view is too closely tied to an intellectually circular dead end that is most certainly a result of the fact that we have long believed that the future is yet to happen, and that it does not exist until we make it happen. Thus, we have created a definition of free will that is dependent on the nonexistence of the future. But what if we now learn that the future does exist? How can we still have free will under this newly understood condition?

For humans to have free will does not require the nonexistence of the future from the perspective of the present. We still have free will to choose our future, even if that future is already known to someone — even if not us. In fact, its existence is essentially irrelevant to our choice of creating a historical path. The theory of how the future can exist simultaneously with the present is an issue that will concern cosmologists for years to come.

What does all this have to do with the future? While my comments in this matter must remain on the level of speculation, I suspect that the future exists, as does the present, as a manifestation of a potential existence that is associated with a probability. This means that there is a most likely future, and when we conduct experiments using the future we need to be careful to do nothing that could alter the probabilities of that future occurring if we want to see the remote-viewing data confirmed. Besides the issue of credibility, this is the main reason why the remote-viewing session transcripts in the public demonstration project of remote viewing presented in a previous chapter had to be encrypted. If the tasker was to receive any indication from any source of the content of the remote-viewing sessions, he could alter his thinking about his choice of a target, even subconsciously, such that the target chosen would differ from that which was remote viewed. Thus, time lines are like endangered species; you need to protect them if you want them to continue to be yours.

What about free will? Clearly remote viewing adds a new dimension to the issue of free will. If the future already exists in some probabilistically manifested way, then we can remote view it. What if we like what we see? The rule here would be to tell no one what you find lest they do something that changes the probabilities of the future manifesting as it was perceived by the remote viewers. On the other hand, what if you do not like what is found? Here the matter changes to clearly encompass the issue of free will. There are no experimental results of which I am aware that would suggest it possible to prohibit someone from changing his or her current behavior in order to "prevent" the future from manifesting in a way that is perceived by remote viewing. Indeed, at The Farsight Institute we have conducted what appear to be successful experiments (not presented here) that do precisely this, and others have suggested that subjects may psychically survey the future when making decisions in order to pick optimal future time lines (see May, Utts, and Spottiswoode 1995a and 1995b; May, Utts, Spottiswoode, and James 1995; see also Radin 1997, chapter 7 for related material). That is, it is possible to remote view one time line, and to use this information to manifest another. By all definitions, this would truly be an exercise of free will.

But if we change the future, does this mean that the first future time line no longer exists? That is a good question, and I do not know the answer to this. However, as one can surmise from my discussion in the previous chapter, I suspect that the first future time line probably does exist even if we create another. The skeptic will of course say, "If it exists, where is it?" But this is a spurious question since we currently do not yet know where even one future exists, even though we can remote view it and thus demonstrate that it exists in at least some measurable way. This forces the question of whether or not we manifest (create) the first time line by remote viewing (detecting) it. I know this sounds odd to most people, but these are real questions related to issues that quantum physicists deal with regularly, and the empirical laboratory evidence seems to be slowly but surely supporting many of these ideas as real possibilities, however illogical they may at first appear.

The Human Condition

By now the reader must understand that I view the study of human society much differently than most of my contemporary social scientific colleagues. Indeed, as one can see from the previous chapter alone, I do not really see how one can study human social evolution without a substantial understanding of quantum mechanics, and this perspective alone is certainly not typical among social scientists. In many respects, the remote-viewing experience appears more similar to phenomena that manifest on the quantum level than those that are structured by macro-level relativistic effects. By studying quantum mechanics and remote viewing together, I suspect that we will gain potent insight into the true nature of our own individual and collective existence.

If this is true, then when we study society, is it not also appropriate to ask which society we are really studying? Within which universe? When we predict the future using statistical and mathematical models, whose future is it? What is unique about revolutions, stock-market fluctuations, terror events, democratic elections, and all other social phenomena that demands that these events become irrevocably associated with what we perceive to be our own collective existence and no one else's? When change happens in our perceived universe, is this a result of a contagion process of event propagation that has its origin in a different but sufficiently similar universe? Can we really study ourselves without simultaneously studying the other variations or manifestations of ourselves that populate these other universes? These are profound questions that must no longer be relegated to the realm of science fiction. While I know of few other social scientists who take these questions seriously, I can nonetheless see the logic in asking the questions. Once one accepts the proposition that remote viewing is a real phenomenon, then such questions seem an obvious next and unavoidable step.

Where then do we place the research presented in these pages within the academic world? The social sciences span a variety of disciplines, including political science, sociology, economics, anthropology, and psychology. Social scientists typically study the behaviors of humans. Normally, social scientists never need to connect human behavior with the laws that describe physical reality, such as Newton's laws of motion or Einstein's understanding of relativity. On the other hand, physical scientists (such as physicists and chemists), study the nature of our physical reality. For example, physicists conduct research on particles, waves, crystal formation, all forms of electromagnetic radiation, and so on. Physicists normally never have to connect human behavior with their investigations of this physical reality. Thus, social scientists study people, and physical scientists study physical reality, but neither normally connect the study of people with the study of physical reality.

The results presented in this volume clearly bridge the realms of the social sciences and the physical sciences in ways that are not typical for the academy. Here I have examined human perception and behavior from the perspective of many of the theoretical constructs found in the physical sciences. In particular, I employ an experimental method involving human perception to engage relativistic and quantum theories of time and space to explain the nature of our existence. As such, this volume is really a work of "sociophysics," if the reader will acknowledge the need to coin a new term describing the type of research presented in these pages. It would be interesting to consider the idea that one day universities may hire sociophysicists to work in their social science departments, and that these scientists would work in an interdisciplinary fashion with their colleagues in the physical sciences. But perhaps our human society will first need to accept more broadly the reality of the remote-viewing phenomenon itself before our universities follow this social acceptance by grappling with the serious academic implications of this new and increasingly sophisticated understanding of physical reality.

Perhaps the best way to view the current human condition is parallel to

Plato's allegory of the Cave as he describes in Book VII of the *Republic*. In this story he tells of people (like prisoners) who have been bound in a cave since childhood, with their heads forcefully positioned such that their eyes gaze only at a raised wall. Behind them is a fire that produces great light, and there is only one opening to the cave. The people see shadows on the wall of the cave, and eventually have difficulty discerning that which is real from that which is shadow. The shadows that they see would be named as things. But if the prisoners are taken into direct sunlight, they would avert their eyes to look back to the more familiar shadows, and they might initially think the real objects that caused the shadows to be imaginary. And if they hear a voice, they would be certain that it comes from a shadow. Efforts to "free" the prisoners from their own mentality would likely cause great concern, pain, and initial refusal.

This is our current state of affairs as Hannah Arendt so pointedly noted when she wrote of the Cave allegory, that "the soul is not the shadow of the body, but the body the shadow of the soul," and her condemnation of "the senseless doings of men who do not leave the cave of human existence to behold the eternal ideas visible in the sky" is as appropriate today as in the days of Plato (Arendt 1958, p. 292). But the difference between our current situation and that of the past is that our science has now matured sufficiently to be able to pierce — finally — the physical/subspace divide. Our modern scientific demands of repeatability and replicability can now be met, albeit with considerable effort and delicacy of method. But we are truly at a new era in our human intellectual evolution.

We are now at the point at which true liberation from our bondage as spiritual prisoners is a real possibility. This will ultimately be the legacy of human research into consciousness. Our research into the nature of the soul is our gift to the future, a future that already exists, and at least one version of which we will someday perceive in its full glory.

How to Construct a Target for a Public Demonstration of Remote Viewing

Nothing is more important to the successful completion of a remote-viewing experiment than the creation of a proper remote-viewing target. I have met many people — from experienced remote viewers to skeptics — who think that target construction is relatively unimportant. They place the abilities of the remote viewer first, assuming that a remote viewer should be able to perceive anything. Skeptics especially seem to trivialize the importance of target construction. Often remote-viewers take up challenges from such skeptics, each side daring the other in an "I told you so!" match, only to be disappointed when the results come in because the target was of a sort that simply will not work with remote viewing. Remote viewing is a nontrivial and complex phenomenon, and a remote viewer cannot simply see "anything" based on whatever a tasker may throw at him or her. Improperly chosen or constructed targets will not work. Properly constructed targets have a decent chance of working, depending on how well the other elements of the experiment are set-up, and on how well the remote viewers do their jobs.

This appendix is included in this volume to sketch out the basic parameters of target construction as it should be used in a public demonstration of remote viewing. It is assumed here that the tasker is someone who is not a remote viewer, but rather someone of significant reputation who has volunteered to designate targets to be viewed by remote viewers who are operating in a properly constructed public experiment which utilizes all necessary security and scientific controls. The tasker's job is to choose targets that correspond to previously established criteria concerning target construction. If the experimental situation is such that the remote viewers conduct, encrypt, and distribute their sessions prior to a target being selected by the tasker (a "tasking-post" condition), then it would be acceptable in most cases for the essential target to be chosen by the tasker, and then for an experienced target-writer either to approve the target or to suggest minor modifications (i.e., repairs) to the formal language and syntax of the target as long as the tasker has the last say as to the target's meaning.

In determining what would constitute an acceptable target for remote viewing, one has to begin with an understanding of the purpose of the remote-viewing demonstration. The purpose is to convince not just the tasker — but also the public at large — that remote viewing is a real phenomenon. For this reason, all targets chosen for a public demonstration must have notable characteristics which can be unambiguously described by remote viewing. Many people begin by thinking that interesting people make good targets for public demonstrations. But this is not correct. Interesting people are interesting because they have interesting stories to tell, or because there are interesting stories to be told about them. Remote viewing cannot tell stories. People can interpret remote-viewing data to tell a story, but this remains an interpretation. The data themselves rarely yield stories without heavy interpretation of a sort that is not desirable or even possible in a demonstration setting that is focusing on basic descriptive accuracy.

For example, once a person tasked some remote viewers at the Institute the target "Richard Nixon," and he wanted us to discern the correct target from a collection of five targets that included four decoys, all names of people. This was a near-impossible test of remote viewing. In that situation, any data for Nixon at any time — before, during, or after he was alive as a human being — would have been acceptable since no further specifications were offered. I am sure that in the tasker's mind, Richard Nixon was an interesting person, and the tasker was probably thinking of all the interesting things that happened around the former U.S. president, including the Vietnam War, the Watergate scandal, the resignation, his famous trip to China ... the works. He might even have wanted the remote viewers to identify Mr. Nixon by name. But this is simply not how remote viewing works. Remote viewers produce lots of low-level descriptive data of a target, and the target needs to have characteristics that lend themselves well to this type of description. The name "Richard Nixon" is as high-level as one can get. Add to this the fact that the target does not specify a context or time or event associated with this person and the target is simply not possible to do in any type of effective manner.

Similarly, a different tasker once briefly considered tasking Institute remote viewers with the target of Tiger Woods playing a particular golf championship. This was better than the Richard Nixon target, since at least a time and place were specified. In this instance perhaps the tasker was influenced in this choice of a target because of a personal interest in the story of Tiger Woods, the magnitude of his personality, his uniqueness to the field of golfing, and so on. Again, these are not criteria that work well with public demonstration targets. Moreover, in plain descriptive terms, Tiger Woods is simply a human subject walking or standing on generally flat, grass-covered land. Even if the remote viewers described a human subject walking on flat land, there is not much unique in that setting to convince the public that the data were obtained through remote viewing. The setting is boring, and boring is not believable in a remote-viewing demonstration.

Good remote-viewing targets must have unique, physical characteristics that unambiguously identify a target. This absolutely means that all good remote-viewing targets must be real and verifiable. Thus, no esoteric or nonverifiable targets should ever be permitted in a public demonstration of remote viewing. The public must be able to easily verify with total certainty the physical characteristics of any given target. If there are mountains at the target site, the public must be able to know this. If there was a nuclear explosion at a target site, the explosion must be a matter of obvious public record. If there is a flying structure (such as an orbiting space station) in the target, the public must be able to know that this structure is real, and so on.

Good remote-viewing targets should have prominent topological features that will attract the attention of a proficient remote viewer. Someone's backyard lawn is a bad remote-viewing target. It is flat land with nothing topologically unique about it. Similarly, a stretch of desert with nothing on it is a terrible remote-viewing target. With such a target, the tasker is asking a viewer to perceive nothing but a flat surface. Remember that the remote viewer will undoubtedly spend approximately an hour in a session thinking that the target must be more complicated than empty flat land. This could even cause the viewer to doubt his or her own data, thereby tempting the conscious mind to invent data. Thus, good remote-viewing targets must have enough in them to interest both the remote viewer and the public that wants to see truly descriptive results. Thus, a better target would be a mountain, a mountain range, a large cliff, a city with interesting building topologies, a rocket launch, a landing or expedition on the Moon in a location of significant topological variety, and so on. People want to see remote-viewing data that unambiguously describe a target with significant uniqueness in a public demonstration of remote viewing. It is the tasker's job to supply a target that satisfies this requirement.

Avoid targets that are relatively insignificant when compared with their surrounding context. A small object in a backyard lawn (or, similarly, a flower in a house) is such a target. With such a target, the viewer will likely end up describing the yard and house rather than the small object. Such targets are called "embedded targets," since they are typically small components of a larger scene, and this larger scene is often called the "macro-target." In general, and especially with respect to remote-viewing sessions conducted solo (i.e., without a monitor), a tasker should always avoid embedded targets. The viewer will inevitably observe elements of the surrounding macro-target, and unless there is a monitor to help focus the viewer on a particular point within the macro-target, the viewer will likely miss describing the embedded target.

Good targets can also have significant levels of activity. Activity is interesting and often helpful in a public demonstration of remote viewing, although it is not required. Thus, large battle scenes are good targets, both on water and on land. Riots, the burning of cities, parades, wartime events (including major destruction events) are also good targets. Such targets offer lots of interesting activity that is physical in nature, and remote-viewing data can normally describe such activity well.

All remote-viewing targets must include exact time and location descriptions. It is not sufficient to task a landing on the Moon. Rather, a properly written remote-viewing target must explicitly identify a particular landing on the Moon, the time of the landing, and the location of the landing (and/or walking expedition after landing). The tasker does not have to be specific as to the second, or even the minute. But the day and general time should be stated. The time can also be further identified by specifying a specific and well-known event, such as when the words were first spoken on the Moon, "A small step for man, a giant leap for mankind."

If a picture is used to identify a target (always a good idea whenever possible), then one can specify that the target time is the moment that the photograph was taken. If a photograph of a target is used, be sure that it is a photograph that is in the public domain, since the public demonstration will require that the photograph be available for others to see. Many public-domain photographs of well-known historic places and events that would serve well as remote-viewing targets can be obtained as web-art collections that are sold inexpensively in computer software stores. Be sure to avoid pictures that are used for secondary purposes such as advertisements. Such pictures are often highly stylized and processed using filtering techniques available with graphics software. More damaging, such photographs typically have advertising lettering written on them, and the use of such photos blends the idea of the product being advertised (and all of its commercial uses) into the meaning of the target. Also, such advertising photos are not normally in the public domain.

In general, taskers need to remember that public demonstrations are conducted in order to show people that remote viewing is a real phenomenon. Thus, targets need to have significant physical and event characteristics such that people who examine the data can say that the remote-viewing data described those special characteristics well. This points to the need for most public demonstrations of remote viewing to be designed to have a series of experiments. Just one target and one viewing will normally not convince many people that anything special really happened. People can always say it was just a fluke. Rather, a series of, say, five or ten targets — each viewed sequentially — are normally needed to conduct an effective demonstration of remote viewing. Remember also that not every remote-viewing session works. You need to give the remote viewers enough chances to demonstrate that on average they can do their jobs well. Moreover, the targets in the series need to be chosen such that they are significantly different from each other. Thus, the targets should not all be mountain targets, or all battle targets, or all space targets, and so on. A tasker needs to vary the mix of targets so that the remote viewers really cannot predict what type of target will be next in the series.

To assist in providing the greatest possible variety of target content within any given set of demonstration targets, the following list of target categories is suggested. Taskers may wish to consult this list from time to time to see if a different type of target from a different category may add more variety to their own target ideas. Taskers may supplement this list of target categories with ideas of their own as long as these ideas correspond to the above content parameters.

1. Train, aviation, and maritime events (of all types)
2. Monumental stone structures, with or without activities
3. Manned space flight events of all types
4. Mountains, waterfalls, and other large and significant natural formations, with or without human activities
5. Major wartime battles, riots, terrorist incidents
6. Natural disasters of all types involving significant topological features and activities
7. Notable and topologically distinct structures of all types
8. Governmental leaders and other significant persons at historic moments within significant and topologically distinct settings (such as within or near major structures)
9. Adventurist events, successes, and disasters of all types

Numbered Aspects

Often public demonstration targets are required to have "numbered aspects." Such aspects are typically used to move a viewer's perspective around one physical central target location. It is analogous to moving a camera around while taking pictures from a variety of perspectives. This allows the target construction to offer alternative viewing perspectives for one primary target. Numbered aspects can also be used to shift the viewer's perspective in time. When used, there should be a limit of at most three numbered aspects, and the first numbered aspect should be simply a repetition of the primary target cue. For example, if the target is the Titanic, then one numbered aspect may be when the ship first encounters the iceberg with which it fatally collided, yet another aspect can be when it is half-way submerged, and yet a final numbered aspect can be when it first rests on the surface of the ocean bottom after it sank. Similarly, if the target is the destruction of the World Trade Center buildings in New York on 11 September 2001, then the first numbered aspect can be when the first jet collides with the first building, and a second numbered aspect can be immediately after the second building has collapsed. With all numbered aspects, the tasker should specify the perspective that the viewer should assume when describing the target. Thus, if the viewer should be describing the World Trade Center attack from the perspective of the New Jersey shore in Liberty Square Park in Jersey City, then this should be specified in the appropriate numbered aspect. The second numbered aspect may specify that the viewer shift the viewing perspective to Ground Zero itself where all the rubble is piled up.

Note that the data for each aspect can overlap with the expected content for other aspects. After moving one's perception to a new numbered aspect, in many cases a viewer may continue to perceive data that are clearly related to another target aspect. That is, the movement exercises conducted by the viewers to the various numbered aspects usually move the perspective of the viewers to those aspects. But sometimes a viewer's perception remains with the prior or another aspect for reasons that are not entirely understood. It is known that the problem is exacerbated when the target aspects are substantively distinct (see below). Thus, the remote-viewing data for each aspect are normally evaluated broadly with respect to their correspondence with known characteristics of the target, even if those characteristics are applicable to one or more numbered target aspects.

There is a common temptation for taskers to use numbered aspects to answer complex plot or story questions by shifting the perception of the viewers across a set of substantively distinct separate targets. This must be avoided. For example, one may want to know who shot John F. Kennedy, and a tasker may write an initial numbered aspect to focus on Kennedy being hit by a bullet while riding in a car in Dallas, and a later numbered aspect to focus on the assassin trying to escape. These are two separate targets, and it is normally not wise to combine them into one target using numbered aspects. In such cases in which the foci of the numbered aspects are substantively distinct, the perceptions of viewers may "lock-on" to one of the two aspects while ignoring the other. This can increase confusion when interpreting the data across the numbered aspects.

When writing numbered aspects, it is most important to remind oneself repeatedly that a viewer's perspective is like a camera. If the camera is well placed, the viewer's perspective will be well placed, and a great deal of useful data may be perceived. If the camera is poorly located, then the viewer's perspective may not produce as high a yield of useful data. Many examples of targets with numbered aspects have been included in this volume. Note that some of the example numbered aspects also specify a visual perspective at the end. (Note also the format of how this is done.) In such cases, the perspective is not demanding that the viewer notice any particular part of the target. Rather, the perspective simply states the location of the viewing perspective relative to the rest of the overall target location. The viewer may or may not notice all of the target components that are listed in the description of the perspective.

One final point. The publicity promoting all public demonstrations of remote viewing should point out that the tasker is volunteering his or her time in a personally generous manner. Any involvement with remote-viewing demonstrations should not be minimalized. Lots of people still scoff at the idea of remote viewing as a real phenomenon. When a person of significant reputation volunteers to choose targets for a public demonstration, the person is giving the demonstration a significant degree of visibility and legitimacy. The public wants to watch public demonstrations when they involve people (especially taskers) whom they trust. The publicity surrounding the public demonstration of remote viewing should amply describe the tasker's credentials, as well as note the appreciable nature of the person's offer to contribute to the project.

Glossary of Remote-Viewing Vocabulary and Abbreviations

Advanced SRV - Of the three current forms of SRV (Basic, Enhanced, and Advanced) that are used to describe physical targets, this is the most sophisticated. It involves the use of complex pre-printed templates, highly-structured spacial and temporal moving exercises, and significant detail in sketching, probing, and analysis. The intent of the Advanced SRV procedures is to assist the viewer in assembling a more coherent picture of the target by "gluing" various partial perceptions together. This is often used to produce a map of the target and its surrounding environment.

Basic SRV - This is a version of SRV that is used by all beginning viewers. It incorporates all of the essential components of Enhanced SRV, but it does not utilize some of the more advanced sketching and movement procedures.

Bilocation - At some point during the SRV session, the viewer's attention is so strongly directed toward the target that the viewer's awareness is split between his or her physical location and the target site.

Concepts - these are intangible attributes of something that is perceived using SRV. For example, the ideas of "good" or "important" are concepts.

Cue - one or more words used at various points during an SRV session in order to direct a remote viewer's perception to focus on a target, or perhaps to perceive specialized information for a target. The first cues used in a remote-viewing session are the target coordinate numbers. Subsequent cues are entered into the Phase 4 matrix.

Data types - When remote-viewing sessions are conducted under certain conditions, the data obtained from those sessions are classified as being of a certain "type." There are six types of remote-viewing data.

   Type 1: Solo, viewer front loaded (rarely done, data are usually of poor quality)

   Type 2: Solo, viewer blind, target selected from a pre-determined list of targets by a computer or some other tasking device (commonly done)

   Type 3: Solo, viewer blind, target assigned by a human tasker (commonly done)

   Type 4: Monitored session with monitor front-loaded and viewer blind (very common during training)

   Type 5: Monitored session, monitor and viewer blind (commonly done)

   Type 6: Monitor and viewer front-loaded (rarely done, data are usually of poor quality)

Decoding - The process of trying to figure out how to describe an intuitive feeling about a target or target component using words.

Deduction - A deduction has two aspects. First, it is a mental conclusion (as in "to deduce") reached during a remote-viewing session. It represents logical mental analysis that may or may not be correct. Second, a deduction is a subtraction from the flow of data. The procedures of Scientific Remote Viewing require that a viewer declare (and thus rid the mind of) all deductions. This is necessary so that the viewer does not carry the impression of the deduction into the remainder of the session, thereby compromising the data.

Emotionals - refers to the emotions that are associated with a site. These emotions can originate from beings actually present at the site. However, a site may resonate with emotionals due to previous or even future events. Emotionals do not refer to emotions experienced by the viewer, which are VFs.

Energetics - a sense while remote viewing that a significant amount of energy is being expended at the target location. This energy can be of any type, such as kinetic or radiant.

Enhanced SRV - a version of SRV that is used by more advanced viewers. It includes expanded sketching procedures as compared with Basic SRV, as well as more specialized movement exercises. (See also *Advanced SRV.*)

Event - a cue that is used to direct a viewer's perception to a target location during the time of some significant activity.

Gestalt - From *Webster's Third New International Dictionary*, a gestalt is a "configuration of physical, biological, or psychological phenomena so integrated as to constitute a functional unit with properties not derivable from its parts in summation." With remote viewing, gestalts are normally represented with ideograms (see below).

Guided deduction - a particular type of deduction that occurs at regular intervals in the procedures of Scientific Remote Viewing. In general, such deductions are allowed to occur at specified times so as to release (and thus rid the mind of) analysis that may be developing in the mind during the session but is as yet undetected.

Ideograms - These are marks that are drawn very quickly by a remote viewer, normally in the beginning of a remote viewing session. Ideograms often resemble squiggles, sometimes curvy, sometimes straight, and sometimes with angles. The various characteristics of the ideograms tend to reflect aspects of the target for the remote-viewing session. Thus, there are ideograms for gestalts associated with mountains, structures, land, air, movement, subjects, water, and so on. Ideograms that reflect more than one gestalt are called "complex ideograms."

Magnitudes - the magnitudes of the various dimensions that are perceived in Phase 2 and Phase 4 of Basic and Enhanced SRV.

Matrix - a collection of labeled columns written on a piece of paper while remote viewing. Data are entered into the appropriate columns during the remote-viewing session.

Monitoring levels - When the viewer has a monitor who is listening to and guiding the remote-viewing session, then the level to which the monitor is involved with the data collection process needs to be stated before the session begins. These levels are defined below.

Level 1 (Type 5 data): The monitor does very little guiding at this level. The monitor's primary role is to suggest movement exercises when the data flow slows or stops. The monitor also corrects any deviations from authorized procedures. The monitor can also guide the viewer with respect to a script that specifies movement exercises at certain points during the session.

Level 2 (Type 5 data): The monitor is actively engaged in directing the remote viewer by suggesting numerous movement exercises whenever they may seem appropriate. The data flow does not have to slow for the monitor to suggest a movement exercise. The monitor also corrects any deviations from authorized procedures. The monitor can also guide the viewer with respect to a script that specifies movement exercises at certain points during the session.

Level 3 (Type 4 data): The monitor's primary role is to suggest movement exercises when the data flow slows or when the viewer no longer seems focused on the target. Using occasional movement exercises only, the monitor should ensure that the viewer achieves the maximum degree of target description possible by the end of the remote-viewing session. The monitor also corrects any deviations from authorized procedures. The monitor can also guide the viewer with respect to a script that specifies movement exercises at certain points during the session.

Level 4 (Type 4 data): The monitor is actively engaged in the data collection process by offering numerous movement exercises that assist the viewer in focusing on the most important target attributes. The data flow does not have to slow for the monitor to suggest a movement exercise. The monitor also corrects any deviations from authorized procedures. The monitor can also guide the viewer with respect to a script that specifies movement exercises at certain points during the session.

Level 5 (Type 4 data): The monitor is actively engaged in all aspects of the data collection process. This includes an evaluation of all or most data entries. This type of monitoring level is appropriate for occasional use only, or in certain instructional situations. The monitor can state the word "check" after each datum that is appropriate for the target, or the monitor can remain silent if it is unclear whether or not a datum is appropriate. The monitor can state the word "reject" if a datum is inappropriate for the target. The viewer records all data, but puts a line through all rejected data entries.

Movement exercise - an SRV procedure that relocates a viewer at a new location relative to the previous target perspective.

Numbered target aspects - (See ***target aspects***)

Outbounder - A person who physically travels to — and witnesses — a target location as a means of guiding the perceptual focus of a remote viewer. The remote viewer is usually tasked with describing the target as seen by the outbounder.

Phases 1 through 5 - separate phases of Basic and Enhanced Scientific Remote Viewing. The specific phases are structured as follows:

> **Phase 1**: This phase allows the viewer to make initial target contact based on the target coordinates only.
>
> **Phase 2**: This phase increases the contact with the target. Information obtained in this phase includes sounds, textures, temperatures, visuals (such as colors, luminescence, and contrasts), tastes, and smells.
>
> **Phase 3**: This phase involves an initial sketch of the target.
>
> **Phase 4**: Target contact in this phase can be profound. Phase 4 involves the use of a matrix within which to enter the data.
>
> **Phase 5**: In this phase, the remote viewer can engage some limited conscious intellectual activity to do certain specified tasks. This is where time lines and geographical locational diagrams are performed.

Physicals - physical items that are perceived and identified in SRV.

Senses - sounds, textures, temperatures, visuals (such as colors, luminescence, and contrasts), tastes, and smells.

Session time - the date and time that a remote-viewing session takes place.

Signal/signal line - the data stream that is perceived during the SRV session.

SRV - Scientific Remote Viewing.

Structure - the formal procedures of SRV. "Remaining in structure" refers to a viewer closely adhering to these procedures during a remote-viewing session.

Subspace - anything that is on the other side of the physical divide. Such things include subspace beings (for example, spirits), but can also include subspace planets, vehicles, and virtually anything else that may or may not have a parallel in the physical realm.

Target - something that is described by remote viewing. Typical remote-viewing are places, events, or people. Targets normally are specified with respect to time and date.

Target aspects - Often it is useful to place two or more numbered target aspects in a target cue. These are normally locations from which the viewer is to perceive the target. The remote viewer is only told how many target aspects exist for a given target, and the viewer then executes movement exercises at precise moments during a session to place his or her perspective at that location before continuing the session. Target aspects are more effective than target qualifiers (see ***Target qualifiers***) in shifting the location of a remote viewer's perspective.

Target directional - In experimental research, the first page of an SRV session often uses a form called a "target directional." This form contains perspective instructions for perceiving the target. The target directional contains no content information regarding the identity or characteristics of the target. Content information (the identity or description of the target) is restricted to the target specific (see below).

Target qualifiers - This is a list of two or more items that the tasker wants the remote viewer to observe during the remote-viewing session. Qualifiers help define a given target, especially when the target is not accompanied by a picture. Target qualifiers are not as effective as target aspects (see *target aspects*) in shifting the viewing perspective of the remote viewer.

Target specific - the actual content of the target, such as a place, subject, event, etc. The viewer sees the target specific only after the remote-viewing session is completed.

Target time - the date and time of the target event.

Tasking time - the time and date that a person assigns (i.e., determines) a target for a remote-viewing session.

Viewer feeling - an emotional response by the remote viewer to something that is perceived during the remote-viewing session. SRV requires viewers to declare (and thus to rid the mind of) all VFs to prevent contamination of the data with internalized emotions.

Viewing time - same as session time (see above)

References

Aczel, Amir D. 2003(2001). *Entanglement: The Unlikely Story of How Scientists, Mathematicians, and Philosophers Proved Einstein's Spookiest Theory.* New York: Plume.

Arendt, Hannah. 1958. *The Human Condition.* Chicago: The University of Chicago Press.

Barrow, John D. 2002. *The Constants of Nature: From Alpha to Omega — The Numbers that Encode the Deepest Secrets of the Universe.* New York: Pantheon.

Bem, Daryl J., and Charles Honorton. 1994. Does Psi Exist?: Replicable Evidence for an Anomalous Process of Information Transfer. *Psychological Bulletin,* 115(1), 4-18.

Bierman, Dick J., and Dean I. Radin. 1997. Anomalous Anticipatory Response On Randomized Future Conditions. *Perceptual & Motor Skills* 84: 689-90.

Born, Max. 1962. *Einstein's Theory of Relativity.* New York: Dover Press.

Braud, William. 2003. *Distant Mental Influence: Its Contributions to Science, Healing, and Human Interactions.* Charlottesville, Virginia: Hampton Roads Publishing Company.

Brinkley, Dannion and Paul Perry. 1994. *Saved by the Light.* New York: HarperCollins Publishers.

Brown, Courtney. 1991. *Ballots of Tumult: A Portrait of Volatility in American Voting.* Ann Arbor: University of Michigan Press.

Brown, Courtney. 1995a. *Serpents in the Sand: Essays on the Nonlinear Nature of Politics and Human Destiny.* Ann Arbor: University of Michigan Press.

Brown, Courtney. 1995b. *Chaos and Catastrophe Theories.* Thousand Oaks, CA: Sage.

Brown, Courtney. 1996. *Cosmic Voyage.* New York: Dutton.

Brown, Courtney. 1999. *Cosmic Explorers*. New York: Dutton.

Chalmers, David. 1996. *The Conscious Mind: In Search of a Fundamental Theory*. Oxford: Oxford University Press.

Danby, J.M.A. 1985. *Computing Applications to Differential Equations*. Reston, Virginia: Reston Publishing Company.

Davies, Paul. 1992. *The Matter Myth: Dramatic Discoveries that Challenge Our Understanding of Physical Reality*. New York: Simon & Schuster.

Dunne, J.W. 2001 . *An Experiment with Time*. Charlottesville, Virginia: Hampton Roads Publishing Company.

Feller, William. 1968. *An Introduction to Probability Theory and Its Applications*, 3rd edition. New York: John Wiley & Sons.

Goswami, Amit, with Richard E. Reed and Maggie Goswami. 1993. *The Self-Aware Universe: How Consciousness Creates the Material World*. New York: Penguin Putnam Inc.

Greville, T.N.E. 1944. On Multiple Matching with One Variable Deck. *Annals of Mathematical Statistics*, 15, 432-434.

Grof, Stanislav. 1983. East and West: Ancient Wisdom and Modern Science. *Journal of Transpersonal Psychology*, 15(1).

Hameroff, Stuart R. 1994. Quantum coherence in microtubules: A Neural basis for emergent consciousness. *Journal of Consciousness Studies* 1 (1): 91-118.

Hameroff, Stuart R. 1998. Funda-Mentality: Is the conscious mind subtly linked to a basic level of the universe?. *Trends in Cognitive Sciences* 2 (4):119-127.

Hameroff Stuart and Penrose Roger. 1996. Orchestrated reduction of quantum coherence in brain microtubules: a model for consciousness. In: *Toward a Science of Consciousness - The First Tucson Discussions and Debates*. Eds. S. Hameroff, A. Kaszniak, A. Scott, MIT Press, Cambridge MA.

Hansen, George P., Jessica Utts, and Betty Markwick. 1992. Critique of the PEAR Remote-Viewing Experiments. *Journal of Parapsychology*, 56(2), 97-113.

Hawking, Stephen. 1998 (10ᵗʰ Edition). *A Brief History of Time*. New York: Bantam.

Hawking, Stephen, and Roger Penrose. 1996. *The Nature of Space and Time*. Princeton, New Jersey: Princeton University Press.

Helms, Hal M. (translator). 1986. *The Confessions of St. Augustine*. Orleans, Massachusetts: Paraclete Press.

Hirsch, Morris W. and Stephen Smale. 1974. *Differential Equations, Dynamical Systems, and Linear Algebra*. New York: Academic Press.

Honorton, Charles. and Diane C. Ferrari. 1989. Future Telling: A Meta-analysis of Forced Choice Precognition Experiments, 1935-1987. *Journal of Parapsychology* 53: 281-308.

Houtkooper, Joop M., Dieter Vaitl, and Ulrich Timm. 2000. A Further Note on Walach and Schmidt's Empirical Evidence for a Non-Classical Experimenter Effect. *Journal of Scientific Exploration*, 14(4), 643-4.

Husserl, Edmund. 1999. *The Essential Husserl: Basic Writings in Transcendental Phenomenology*. Edited by Donn Welton. Bloomington, Indiana: Indiana University Press.

Hyman, Ray. 1996. Evaluation of a Program on Anomalous Mental Phenomena. *Journal of Scientific Exploration*, 103, 31-58.

Jahn, Robert. G. 1982. The Persistent Paradox of Psychic Phenomena: an Engineering Perspective. *Proc. IEEE*, 70, 136.

Jung, Carl G. 1960. *The Structure and Dynamics of the Psyche*. New York: Pantheon.

Kaku, Michio. 1994. *Hyperspace : A Scientific Odyssey Through Parallel Universes, Time Warps, and the Tenth Dimension*. Oxford: Oxford University Press.

Koçak, Hüseyin. 1988. *Differential and Difference Equation s through Computer Experiments*. New York: Springer-Verlag.

Kress, Kenneth A. 1999. Parapsychology In Intelligence: A Personal Review and Conclusions. *Journal of Scientific Exploration*, 13, 69-87.

•

Lantz, Nevin D., Wanda L. W. Luke, and Edwin C. May. 1994. Target and Sender Dependencies in Anomalous Cognition Experiments. *The Journal of Parapsychology*, 58(3), 285-302.

Mavromatis, Andreas. 1987. *Hypnagogia: The Unique State of Consciousness Between Wakefulness and Sleep*. New York: Routledge.

May, Edwin C. 1996. The American Institutes for Research Review of the Department of Defense's STAR GATE Program: A Commentary. *Journal of Scientific Exploration*, 10, 89-108.

May, Edwin C., S. James P. Spottiswoode, and Christine L. James. 1994a. Managing the Target-Pool Bandwidth: Possible Noise Reduction for Anomalous Cognition. *The Journal of Parapsychology*, 58(3), 303-13.

May, Edwin C., S. James P. Spottiswoode, and Christine L. James. 1994b. Shannon Entropy: A Possible Intrinsic Target Property. *The Journal of Parapsychology*, 58(4), 384-401.

May, Edwin C., S. James P. Spottiswoode, and Laura V. Faith. 2000. The Correlation of the Gradient of Shannon Entropy and Anomalous Cognition: Toward an AC Sensory System. *Journal of Scientific Exploration*, 14(1), 53-72.

May, Edwin C., Jessica M. Utts, and James P. Spottiswoode. 1995a. Decision Augmentation Theory: Toward a Model of Anomalous Mental Phenomena. *Journal of Parapsychology*, 59(3), 195-220.

May, Edwin C., Jessica M. Utts, and James P. Spottiswoode. 1995b. Decision Augmentation Theory: Applications to the Random Number Generator Database. *Journal of Scientific Exploration*, 9(4), 453-88.

May, Edwin C., Jessica M. Utts, James P. Spottiswoode, and C. J. James. 1995. Applications of Decision Augmentation Theory. *Journal of Parapsychology*, 59(3), 221-50.

May, Edwin C., Jessica Utts, Beverly S. Humphrey, Wanda L. W. Luke, Thane J. Frivold, and Virginia V. Trask. 1990. Advances in Remote-Viewing Analysis. *Journal of Parapsychology*, 54(3), 193-228.

May, Robert M. 1974. *Stability and Complexity in Model Ecosystems*. Princeton, N.J.: Princeton University Press.

McMoneagle, Joseph. 2000. *Remote Viewing Secrets: A Handbook.*

Charlottesville, Virginia: Hampton Roads Publishing Company.

McMoneagle, Joeseph. 1998. *The Ultimate Time Machine: A Remote Viewer's Perception of Time, and Predictions for the New Millennium.* Charlottesville, Virginia: Hampton Roads Publishing Company.

McMoneagle, Joseph. 1993. *Mind Trek: Exploring Consciousness, Time, and Space Through Remote Viewing.* Norfolk, Virginia: Hampton Roads Publishing Company.

Moody, Raymond A., Jr. 1975. *Life After Life.* New York: Bantam Books.

Myers, F.W.H. 2001. *Human Personality and Its Survival of Bodily Death.* Charlottesville, Virginia: Hampton Roads Publishing Company.

Nelson, R. D., B. J. Dunne, Y. H. Dobyns, and R. G. Jahn. 1996. Precognitive Remote Perception: Replication of Remote Viewing. *Journal of Scientific Exploration*, 10(1), 109-10.

Paramahansa Yoganada. 1947(1974). *Autobiography of a Yogi.* Los Angeles, California: Self-Realization Fellowship.

Penrose, Roger. 1996. *Shadows of the Mind: A Search for the Missing Science of Consciousness.* Oxford: Oxford University Press.

Penrose, Roger, with Martin Gardner. 2002. *The Emperor's New Mind: Concerning Computers, Minds, and the Laws of Physics.* Oxford: Oxford University Press.

Puthoff, Harold E. 1996. CIA-Initiated Remote Viewing Program at Stanford Research Institute. *Journal of Scientific Exploration*, 10(1), 63-76.

Puthoff, Harold E. 1984. ARV (Associational Remote Viewing) Applications. *Research in Parapsychology 1984*, edited by Rhea White and J. Solfvin. Metuchen, NJ: Scarecross Press.

Puthoff, Harold E. and Russell Targ. 1979. Direct Perception of Remote Geographical Locations. In *The Iceland Papers: Select Papers on Experimental and Theoretical Research on the Physics of Consciousness*, edited by Andrija Puharich, pp. 17-48.

Radin, Dean I. 1997. *The Conscious Universe: The Scientific Truth of Psychic Phenomena.* New York: HarperCollins Publishers.

Ramana Maharshi. 1972. *The Spiritual Teachings of Ramana Maharshi.* Berkeley: Shambhala.

Russell, John. 2004. A Century of Brachytherapy. *Nuclear News*, December, 44-6.

Schnabel, James. 1997. *Remote Viewers: The Secret History of America's Psychic Spies.* New York: Dell.

Schrödinger, Erwin. 1969. *What is Life? And Mind and Matter.* London: Cambridge University Press.

Schmidt, Stefan and Harald Walach. 2000. Reply to "A Further Note on Walach and Schmidt's 'Empirical Evidence for a Non-Classical Experimenter Effect.'" *Journal of Scientific Exploration* 14(4), 644-6.

Schwartz, Gary E. R., William L. Simon (contributor), and Deepak Chopra (contributor). 2002. *The Afterlife Experiments: Breakthrough Scientific Evidence of Life After Death.* New York: Atria Books.

Shih, Yanhua. 2001. Quantum entanglement and quantum teleportation. *Annals of Physics* 10(1-2), 45-61.

Sinclair, Upton. 2001(1930). *Mental Radio.* Charlottesville, Virginia: Hampton Roads Publishing Company.

Smolin, Lee. 2004 (January). Atoms of Space and Time. *Scientific American* 290(1), 66-75.

Stanford, Rex G., and Adam G. Stein. 1994. A Meta-analysis of ESP Studies Constrasting Hypnosis and a Comparison Condition. *Journal of Parapsychology* 58(3), 235-269.

Swami Sri Yukteswar. 1949. *The Holy Science.* California: Self-Realization Fellowship.

Swann, Ingo. 1998. *Penetration: The Question of Extraterrestrial and Human Telepathy.* Rapid City, South Dakota: Ingo Swann Books.

Targ, Russell. 1996. Remote Viewing at Stanford Research Institute in the 1970s: A Memoir. *Journal of Scientific Exploration*, 10, 77-88.

Targ, Russell. 1999. Comments on 'Parapsychology In Intelligence: A Personal

Review and Conclusions.' *Journal of Scientific Exploration*, 13, 87-90.

Targ, Russell. and Keith Harary. 1984. *Mind Race: Understanding and Using Psychic Abilities*. New York: Villard Books.

Targ, Russell, Harold. E. Puthoff. 1977. *Mind Reach*. New York: Delacorte Press.

Tart, Charles T., Harold E. Puthoff, and Russell Targ. 2002. *Mind At Large: Institute of Electrical and Electronics Engineers Symposia on the Nature of Extrasensory Perception*. Charlottesville, Virginia: Hampton Roads Publishing Company.

Thom, Rene. 1975. *Structural Stability and Morphogenesis*. Reading, MA: W. A. Benjamin.

Ullman, Montague, Stanley Krippner, and Alan Vaughan. 2002. *Dream Telepathy: Experiments in Nocturnal Extrasensory Perception*. Charlottesville, Virginia: Hampton Roads Publishing Company.

Utts, Jessica M. 1996. An Assessment of the Evidence for Psychic Functioning. *Journal of Scientific Exploration*, 10(1), 3-30.

Utts, Jessica M. 1991. Replication and meta-analysis in parapsychology (with discussion). *Statistical Science*, 6(4), 363-403.

Utts, Jessica M. 1999. The Significance of Statistics in Mind-Matter Research. *Journal of Scientific Exploration*, 13(4), 615-638.

Vasiliev, L.L. 2002. *Experiments in Mental Suggestion*. Charlottesville, Virginia: Hampton Roads Publishing Company.

Vaughan, Frances. 1991. Spiritual Issues in Psychotherapy. *Journal of Transpersonal Psychology*. 23(2).

Walsh, Roger. 1993. On Transpersonal Definitions. *Journal of Transpersonal Psychology*, 25(2).

Walsh, Roger. 2000. *Essential Spirituality: The 7 Central Practices to Awaken Heart and Mind*. New York: John Wiley and Sons.

Warcollier, René. 2001. *Mind to Mind*. Charlottesville, Virginia: Hampton Roads Publishing Company.

Watt, C.   1988.   Characteristics of Successful Free-Response Targets: Theoretical Considerations. *Proceedings of the 31ˢᵗ Annual Parapsychological Association Convention*, pp. 247-263. Montreal, Canada.

Wilber, Ken.   1977.   *The Spectrum of Consciousness*. Wheaton, Ill.: The Theosophical Publishing House / Quest.

Wilkins, Sir Hubert, and Harold M. Sherman. 2004. *Thoughts Through Space: A Remarkable Adventure in the Realm of the Mind*. Charlottesville, Virginia: Hampton Roads Publishing Company.

Wolf, Fred Alan. 1988. *Parallel Universes: The Search for Other Worlds*. New York: Simon and Schuster.

Wolf, Fred Alan. 1998. *The Spiritual Universe : One Physicists Vision of Spirit, Soul, Matter, and Self*. Portsmouth, NH: Moment Point Press.

Zeeman, E. C. 1972. Differential Equations for the Heartbeat and New Impulse. In C. H. Waddington (Ed.), *Towards a Theoretical Biology* (Vol. 4, pp. 8-67). Chicago: Edinburgh University Press.

Index

CPSIA information can be obtained at www.ICGtesting.com
Printed in the USA
LVOW08*1227180713

343504LV00002B/8/A